The Criminal Court in Action

The Criminal Court in Action

Third Edition

David Barnard, BA
of Gray's Inn and of the South-Eastern Circuit, Barrister
Sometime Reader in Civil and Criminal Procedure at the
Council of Legal Education

assisted by
Peter L Gray, LLB
of the Inner Temple and of the South-Eastern Circuit, Barrister

Paul S Bogan
of Gray's Inn and of the South-Eastern Circuit, Barrister

London
Butterworths
1988

United Kingdom	Butterworth & Co (Publishers) Ltd, 88 Kingsway, LONDON WC2B 6AB and 61A North Castle Street, EDINBURGH EH2 3LJ
Australia	Butterworths Pty Ltd, SYDNEY, MELBOURNE, BRISBANE, ADELAIDE, PERTH, CANBERRA and HOBART
Canada	Butterworths, A division of Reed Inc., TORONTO and VANCOUVER
New Zealand	Butterworths of New Zealand Ltd, WELLINGTON and AUCKLAND
Singapore	Butterworth & Co (Asia) Pte Ltd, SINGAPORE
South Africa	Butterworth Publishers (Pty) Ltd, DURBAN and PRETORIA
USA	Butterworths Legal Publishers, ST PAUL, Minnesota, SEATTLE, Washington, BOSTON, Massachusetts, AUSTIN, Texas and D & S Publishers, CLEARWATER, Florida

British Library Cataloguing in Publication Data
Barnard, David
    The criminal court in action.—3rd ed.
    1. Criminal procedure—England
    I. Title
    344.205′1   KD8329

    ISBN Hardcover 0 406 55614 8
    ISBN Softcover 0 406 55615 6

Typeset by Phoenix Photosetting, Chatham, Kent
Printed in Great Britain by Mackays of Chatham Ltd, Chatham, Kent

Preface to the Third Edition

It is difficult to learn criminal procedure from a textbook; the rules (which are sometimes very complex) only begin to make sense when one sees their application in practice. For this reason we have tried in this book to bring the experience of criminal trials to life by using as many realistic examples as we can to illustrate the rules of procedure. In particular, since this book is intended to be of use to the advocate in his first years in practice, we have placed the greatest emphasis on the rules which are most frequently encountered in the course of a criminal trial. This book therefore does not attempt to deal with the more abstruse complexities of criminal procedure (which can be explored in *Archbold* and *Stone's Justices' Manual*.

The method of work which we adopted in preparing this edition was that we each were responsible for research in particular areas but in order to achieve uniformity of style the final text was written by the original author. Nonetheless, the book very much represents the pooling of our joint experience in practice.

We wish to thank the editorial staff of Butterworths for their great assistance in preparing this book. We are grateful to the Crown Prosecution Service, the Commissioner of Metropolitan Police, and the Kent Constabulary for permission to reproduce forms which are used in the text. We are particularly grateful for help from our colleagues at the Bar, in the Criminal Appeal Office and in the Magistrates' Court Service who have contributed ideas based on their experience of the law in practice.

In the text, for the sake of realism, we have sometimes used examples which refer to actual localities and courts. All the examples, however, are purely fictional and no reference is intended to any persons living or dead.

While this book was in preparation, the Criminal Justice Bill was going through Parliament. Quite apart from the more controversial proposals in the Bill (such as restrictions on the right of silence), it contains important changes in the law of evidence and these have been referred to in the text, because it seems certain they will be enacted.

Gray's Inn
OCTOBER 1987

David Barnard
Peter L Gray
Paul S Bogan

Table of Contents

Preface   v
Table of statutes   ix
List of cases   xv

PART ONE – THE CASE OF OLIVER TWIST   1
 CPS v Oliver Twist: Arrest and remand   3
        Committal proceedings   8

 The Queen v Oliver Twist: Brief to counsel   11
        Transcript of the trial   26

PART TWO – THE RULES OF CRIMINAL PROCEDURE   49
 1 The investigation of crime   51
 2 At the police station   65
 3 Magistrates' courts jurisdiction   85
 4 Committal proceedings   99
 5 Trial at the Crown Court   111
 6 Trial before magistrates   153
 7 Appeals from magistrates' courts   163
 8 Appeal from the Crown Court   175
 9 Bail   187
 10 Costs and legal aid   205

PART THREE – SENTENCING   219
 11 The process of sentencing   221
 12 Imprisonment   231
 13 Non-custodial sentences upon adults   245
 14 Young people in trouble   261
 15 Mentally ill offenders   267

APPENDIX 1 STATUTES   271
 Magistrates' Courts Act 1980   273
 Bail Act 1976   283
 Powers of Criminal Courts Act 1973   288
 Police and Criminal Evidence Act 1984   305
 Criminal Justice Bill 1987   312
 Codes of Practice   314

APPENDIX 2 ROAD TRAFFIC PENALTIES   347

Index   357

Table of statutes

References in this Table to *Statutes* are to Halsbury's Statutes of England (Fourth Edition) showing the volume and page at which the annotated text of the Act may be found.

Page references printed in **bold** type indicate where the Act is set out in part or in full.

	PAGE
Accessories and Abettors Act 1861	
s 8	115
Administration of Justice Act 1960 (12 *Statutes* 332)	
s 1	171
(1),(2)	170
Administration of Justice (Miscellaneous Provisions) Act 1933 (12 *Statutes* 225)	
s 2	110
Air Force Act 1955 (3 *Statutes* 247)	309
Army Act 1955 (3 *Statutes* 49)	309
Attachment of Earnings Act 1971	
s 1(3)	251
Aviation Security Act 1982	
s 27(2)	314
Bail Act 1976 (12 *Statutes* 709)	273
s 3	192, **283**
(4)	287
(5)	285, 287
(6)	287, 288
(6A),(7)	287
4	189, 273, **284,** 285
5	**284**
(6A)	195
6	92
(1)	187
(5)	113
(6)	187
8	**286**
(2)	192
(3)	193, 273
(4)	273
(5)	193, 273
(6)	273
Sch 1	189, 193, 195, 197, 284, **287**
Pt I	191
Pt II	189

	PAGE
Child Care Act 1980	
s 64(1)	306
Children and Young Persons Act 1933	
s 31	162
34	162
(2)	306
35(2)	226
46	159, 160
47(2)	162
49	162
53	236
(1)	261
(2)	261, 280
55	265
56(1)	160
Children and Young Persons Act 1969 (6 *Statutes* 227)	160, 263
s 1(2)	161
(3)	263
4	281
5	162
(8)	162
7(7)	263, 264
(8)	160
7A	263
11	306
12(1),(2)	264
(3c),(4),(5)	264
15(4)	264
16	264
20A	263
21(2)	263
28(2)	84
Civil Aviation Act 1982	
s 92	111
Contempt of Court Act 1981	
s 1	103
2	150
4(2)	135

PAGE

Contempt of Court Act 1981 – *contd*
s 8(1) 150
11 150
Costs in Criminal Cases Act 1973 (27
Statutes 60)
s 1(2) 103
2(4) 103
Courts Act 1971 111
s 4(8) 150
10(2),(3) 174
Criminal Appeal Act 1964
s 5 110
Sch 2 110
Criminal Appeal Act 1968
s 1 175
(2) 198
2(1) 175, 176
3(1) 176
7(1) 176
9, 10 177
11(1) 177
(1A) 198
(3) 177, 178
13(4) 177
15, 16 177
17 179
18 178
19 198
23 .... 176, 177
29 179
31 178
33 179
50(1) 178
Criminal Attempts Act 1981
s 4 233
9 93
Criminal Damage Act 1971
s 1 96
Criminal Evidence Act 1898
s 1 .... 144, 145, 146, 181
Criminal Justice Act 1925
s 33(3) 124
Criminal Justice Act 1967 (12 *Statutes*
389; 27 *Statutes* 45; 34 *Statutes* 694): 103,
300
s 9 .... 134, 138
(2) 138
10(1) 142
(2),(4) 143
11 102
(1),(4),(8) 146
13 149
22 196
56 .... 223, 282
60, 61 236
62(1) 236
67 190
Criminal Justice Act 1972 (12 *Statutes*
567; 27 *Statutes* 56; 34 *Statutes* 714)
s 35 236
36(1) 180
49 251

PAGE

Criminal Justice Act 1982 (12 *Statutes*
868; 27 *Statutes* 321; 34 *Statutes*
721)
s 1(1) 231, 281
(4) 262
2 262
(2) 226
3 .... 208, 262
4 262
(5) 262
5(2),(5) 262
6(1) 261
7(5) 282
13 261
14 282
15(11) 262
16 264
17 291
30 241
37(1) 250
60 195
Sch 14 .... 242, 262
Criminal Justice Act 1987
s 1(3),(5) 109
2(2),(3) 109
(5),(13) 109
4 .... 109, 123
(1),(2) 109
6 312
(1),(2) 109
(8),(9) 109
7 109
8 124
9 124
(3) 109
10 124
Criminal Law Act 1967 (12 *Statutes* 358)
s 6(1) 125
(3) 125, 149
Criminal Law Act 1977 (12 *Statutes*
742)
s 3 233
43 131
44 175
46 223
47 .... 241, 242
(3) 241
57 245
Sch 9 .... 241, 243
12 .... 125, 149, 252
Criminal Procedure (Attendance of
Witnesses) Act 1965 (12 *Statutes*
352) 106
s 3 150
94 106
Criminal Procedure (Insanity) Act 1964
s 1 150
4(2) 129
5(1) 268
Sch 4 129
Criminal Procedure (Right of Reply)
Act 1964 (17 *Statutes* 153) 147

PAGE

Criminal Procedure (Scotland) Act 1975
  s 182, 183, 392 310
Customs and Excise Management Act
  1979
  s 49 255
    170 112
      (2) 128
Drug Trafficking Offences Act 1986 . . . 255
Explosives Act 1875
  s 73 60
Firearms Act 1968
  s 16 210
    46 60
    47 56
    52 255
Immigration Act 1971 (31 *Statutes* 47) . . 256
  s 3(6) 255
    7 255
  Sch 2 340
Indictments Act 1915
  s 4 116
    5 . . . . 27, 122
Insolvency Act 1985
  s 119 256
Juries Act 1974
  s 1 130
    5(2) 130
    6(1) 132
    8(1) 130
    9(2) 130
    12(1),(6) 131
    20(1) 130
  Sch 1
    Pt III 130
Justices of the Peace Act 1361 (27
  Statutes 10) 247
Justices of the Peace Act 1979
  s 6 85
Justices Protection Act 1848
  s 1, 2 52
Legal Aid Act 1974
  s 28(2) 207, 210
    (3) 207
    (5) 207, 210
    (6)–(8) 207
    29(1) 193
    (6) 208
    30(1A) 207, 210
    31 210
  Sch 1 207
Legal Aid Act 1982
  s 1 207
    (1) 210
    2 . . . . 207, 210
    8(5) 206, 209, 210
Licensing Act 1872
  s 12 93
Magistrates' Courts Act 1980 (27
  Statutes 157) 94
  s 1 . . . . 52, 89
    (2) 89
    2(6) 89

PAGE

Magistrates' Courts Act 1980 – *contd*
  s 3 89
    4(1) 86, 99
    5 188
    6 . . . . **273**
    (1) 99, 107
    (2) 100, 104, 105, 107,
                                       280
    (3) 196
    8 . . . . 103, **274**
    (2A) 104
    10(1) 289
    (2) 276, 277
    (3) 189, 276, 277
    11 . . . . **275**
    (1) 155, 277, 289
    (2) 155
    (4) 155, 166
    12 . . . . 154, **276**
    13(1) 155, 289
    (2),(5) 289
    14 155
    17 . . . . **277**
    18 . . . . **277**
    (4) 188
    19 . . . . 277, **278**, 279
    (1) 94, 280
    (4) 94
    20 . . . . 95, 277, **278**, 279, 280
    (2) 281
    21 . . . . 277, **278**, 280
    22 . . . . 96, 277, 278, **279**
    (1) 280
    (2) 280, 281
    (3)–(6) 280
    (7),(11) 96
    23 . . . . 277, 278, **279**
    (3),(5) 277
    24 . . . . 159, **280**
    (1) 160
    25 . . . . **281**
    (2) 275
    (3) 274
    (6) 275
    (7) 274
    29 160
    30(1) 283
    (2) 284, 288
    31 261
    (1) 232
    32 94
    (1) 250
    33 . . . . 279, 282
    35 250
    36 265
    37 . . . . 166, 177, 222, **282**, 289
    38 . . . . 94, 166, 177, 221, 222,
                   223, 278, **282**, 289,
                                       304
    39 . . . . **282**
    40 . . . . 253, 303
    41 . . . . 273, 284

PAGE

Magistrates' Courts Act 1980 – *contd*
s 76, 77, 85 251
88 250
102 .... 101, 104, 108,
                                273
    (2),(4),(5) 101
103 .... 101, 108
105 101
108 .... 163, 166
111 170
117 .... 92, 188
    (3) 92
121 86
123(1) 88
126(3) 54
127 88
128 282
    (1) 189
    (3A) 189, 278
    (3B)–(3E),(6) 189
131 189
132 232
133(2) 232
134, 135 232
144 153
Sch 1 .... 93, 277
Sch 2 279
**Magistrates' Courts (Appeal from
Binding Over Orders) Act 1956 (27
Statutes 43)** 248
Mental Health Act 1959
s 28 268
60(2) 154
**Mental Health Act 1983 (28 Statutes
632)** 290
s 12 .... 284, 290
37 267
    (2) 291
    (3) 267
38, 41 267
43 222
47 268
54(2),(3) 291
**Misuse of Drugs Act 1971 (28 Statutes
500)** 329
s 5 93
    (2) 180, 185
23 .... 56, 58
    (3) 59
27 255
**Murder (Abolition of Death Penalty)
Act 1965 (12 Statutes 357)** 232
**National Health Service Act 1977 (30
Statutes 805)** 290
**Naval Discipline Act 1957 (3 Statutes
442)** 309
s 50 309
Nursing Homes Act 1975 290
Obscene Publications Act 1959
s 3 .... 60, 255
Offences Against the Person Act 1861
s 9 112

PAGE

Offences Against the Person Act 1861
  – *contd*
s 18 .... 93, 113, 119, 224
20 .... 93, 113, 224
47 93
Official Secrets Act 1911
s 1 106
**Oil and Gas (Enterprise) Act 1982 (29
Statutes 672)** 111
Pakistan Act 1973
Sch 3 255
Perjury Act 1911
s 9 110
Police Act 1964
s 51 .... 58, 93
64 311
**Police and Criminal Evidence Act 1984
(12 Statutes 941; 17 Statutes 207; 33
Statutes 676)** 76, 92, 100
s 1(2) 55
    (3) 56
    (7) 55, 56
    (8) 55
2 54
    (2) 56, 58
    (3),(9) 56
3 54
    (6)–(9) 56
4 58
    (1),(12) 58
5 56
6(1) 314
8 60
    (1) 62
9 .... 57, 62, 322
    (2),(10) 62
10 320
11 62
    (1) 62
14 62
15 317
    (2) 63
16(3)–(6) 63
    (9),(10) 63
17 .... 317, 318
    (1) 54
18 .... 59, 317, 318
    (7) 318
24(1)–(5) 52
    (6),(7) 53
25 54
    (1),(3) 53
26(2) 53
27 .... 342, 343
    (4) 342
28 76
    (1) 54
30(1) 54
31 76
    (1) 84
32 .... 59, 317, 318
    (1)–(5) 58

PAGE

Police and Criminal Evidence Act 1984
– contd

s 34, 36	65
37(1)	65
(2)	66, 67, 187
(4)–(6)	66
38	188
(1)	81, 82
(6)	335
40	334, 335
41	141, 334, 337
(1)	80
(2)	305, 307
(3),(8)	82
42	82, 334
(1)	82
43	82
(4),(14)	83
44	82
46	89, 188
(1),(5)–(8)	81
47	89
(3)	188
54	59
56	67, 71, **305**, 337
(1),(2)	67
(5),(6)	67
57	**306**
58	207, **306**, 337
(1)–(5)	70
(6)	70, 84
(7)–(9)	70
60	308
61	342
(3),(4)	79
62	344
(1)	79
63	79, 344
65	306, 344
66	**308**, 314, 317, 322, 340
67	**308**, 314, 317, 322, 340
(11)	75, 141
69	140, 312
73	225, **309**
74	134, **309**
(1),(2)	134
75	**310**
76	75, 141, 157, 184, **310**, 312
(2),(8)	74
77	**311**
78	63, 75, 134, **311**
104	308
116	58, 60
(6)	58
118(2)	337
Sch 1	62, 317, 318, 320
Sch 2	53
Sch 5	56

Police (Property) Act 1897 (33 *Statutes* 567) ... 304, 321

s 1(1)	304

PAGE

Police (Property) Act 1897 – *contd*

s 2(1)	304

Police (Scotland) Act 1967 (33 *Statutes* 651) ... 287

Powers of Criminal Courts Act 1973 (12 *Statutes* 597) ... 245

s 1	251, **288**
(1)	251
(4A)	254
2	245, **289**
(3)	245
3	246, 268, 289, **290**
(5)	246
4	246, 252, 289
4A, 4B	289
6	284, **291**
(3)	247
(4)	222
(6)	247
7	252, **292**
(1)	247
8	247, 292, **293**
(6)	222
10	291
(3)	291
13	240, 310
14	248, **294**
(2)	292
15	**295**, 296
(2)	296
16	249, 284, 295, **296**
17	249, 295, **296**
(1),(5)	295
17A, 17B	294
19(1)	261
20	**298**
(1)	231
20A	226, **298**
(1)	231
(3)	232
21	208, **299**
(1)	232
22	**299**
(1),(2)	238
(3)	239
23	276, 298, 299, **300**, 302
(1)	240
24	300, **301**
(2)	223
25	243, **301**
26	240, **301**
(4)	303
(10)	240
27	**302**
28(2),(3)	243
31(2),(3)	250
(3A)	251
32(4)	251
35	245, 252, 289, 295, **303**
(1A)	253
(4)	254
39	256, 295

PAGE

Powers of Criminal Courts Act 1973 –
  contd
s 42 282
  43 .... 254, 255, 295, **303**
  44 .... 295, **304**
  57(2) 242
  Sch 1 .... 289, 290
Prevention of Crime Act 1953
  s 1 115
  (2) 254
Prevention of Terrorism (Temporary
  Provisions) Act 1984 (12 *Statutes*
  908) 329, 337
  Sch 3 .... 56, 340
Prison Act 1952 (34 *Statutes* 643) 234
  s 6(3) 234
Probation Act (Northern Ireland) 1950
  s 8 310
Prosecution of Offences Act 1985
  s 16 205
  (6) 205
  (8) 206
  17, 18 .... 205, 206
  19–21 205
  22, 23 97
Public Order Act 1986 93
Rehabilitation of Offenders Act 1974
  (12 *Statutes* 680) 225
Road Traffic Act 1972 .... 93, 304
  s 1, 2 93
  3 257
  5 .... 63, 170, 340
  6, 7 .... 63, 340
  8 .... 63, 327, 340
  9–11 .... 63, 340
  12 340
  93 283
  94(1) 259
  94A 259
  95 259
  (4) 304
  101 257
  (2) 257
  (4) 304
  105(5) 304
  159 58
  161 54

PAGE

Sexual Offences Act 1956
  s 12 .... 223, 224
  13 93
  14 52
  30, 32 93
Sexual Offences (Amendment) Act 1976
  s 4 .... 104, 274
  6 274
Solicitors Act 1974 327
Summary Jurisdiction (Process) Act
  1881 (27 *Statutes* 19) 277
Sunday Entertainments Act 1932 168
Supreme Court Act 1981 (11 *Statutes*
  756)
  s 28 178
  (1) 180
  29(3) 166, 180
  43 166
  48(4) 163
  75 105
  76 111
  81 195
  (1B) 198
Territorial Waters Jurisidiction Act
  1878
  s 2 111
Theft Act 1968 (12 *Statutes* 514) 93, 303
  s 1 102
  8 93
  9 8
  (1) 26, 28
  12 .... 8, 26, 28, 43, 52, 159,
                                223
  21(1) 112
  22 .... 180, 185, 254
  25 52
  26 .... 59, 65, 115
  28 .... 254, 283, 295
Transport Act 1981
  s 19 258
  (1) 257
  (2), (6) 258
Treatment of Offenders Act (Northern
  Ireland) 1968
  s 19 .... 298, 299
Trial of Lunatics Act 1883
  s 2 150

List of cases

PAGE

A

Advocate (HM) v Cairns (1968) . . 127
Ajodha v The State (1982) . . . 75, 142
Alderson v Booth (1969) 49
Anderton v Cooper (1980) 88
Associated Provincial Picture Houses
   Ltd v Wednesbury Corpn (1948) . 84, 169
A-G v Leveller Magazines Ltd (1979) . 150
A-G v Times Newspapers Ltd (1974) . 150
A-G's Reference (No 3 of 1979) (1979) . 135

B

Baksh v R (1958) 133
Balogh v Crown Court at St Albans
   (1975) 151
Baynes v Brewster (1841) 52
Bentley v Brudzinski (1982) . . . 49
Boardman v DPP (1974) 118
Brangwynne v Evans (1962) . . . 155
Buchanan v Motor Insurers' Bureau
   (1955) 173

C

Christie v Leachinsky (1947) . . . 52
Collins v Wilcock (1984) 49
Connelly v DPP (1964) 127

D

Dallison v Caffery (1965) . . . 54, 132
Daniel v Morrison (1979) 57
DPP v Humphrys (1977) 128
DPP v Kilbourne (1973) 118
DPP v Merriman (1973) 119, 122
DPP v Ottewell (1970) 243
DPP v Shah (1984) 88
DPP v Stonehouse (1978) 112
DPP for Northern Ireland v Maxwell
   (1978) 115

G

Gelberg v Miller (1961) 171

PAGE

Ghani v Jones (1970) 59, 60

H

Hargreaves v Alderson (1964) . . . 88
Harrison v Hill (1932) 173
Hart v Chief Constable of Kent (1983) . 49
Horrix v Malam (1984) 88
Hutchinson (Cinemas) Ltd v Tyson
   (1969) 88

I

IRC v National Federation of
   Self-Employed and Small Businesses
   Ltd (1982) 169

J

Jeffrey v Black (1978) 59, 63
Jemmison v Priddle (1972) . . . 88, 122
John Lewis & Co Ltd v Tims. See Lewis
   (John) & Co Ltd v Tims

K

Kenlin v Gardiner (1967) 49

L

Lau Pak Ngam v R (1966) 135
Lewis (John) & Co Ltd v Tims (1952) . 54
Ludlow v Burgess (1971) 49
Ludlow v Metropolitan Police Comr
   (1971) 117, 118, 180, 184

M

McCarthy v Grant (1959) 170
Meredith, ex p (1973) 178
Metropolitan Properties Co (FGC) Ltd v
   Lannon (1969) 166
Moles, Re (1981) 192
Money v Leach (1765) 52
Moore v Clerk of Assize, Bristol (1970) . 150
Murdoch v Taylor (1965) 145

PAGE

O

Owen v Edwards (1983) 136

P

Piggott v Sims (1973) 158
Police Prosecutor v Humphreys (1970) . 257
Practice Direction [1966] 2 All ER
929 225
Practice Direction [1967] 3 All ER
137 . . . . 148, 149
Practice Direction [1970] 1 WLR 916 . 149
Practice Direction [1978] 2 All ER
912 . . . . 105, 111
Practice Direction [1979] 1 WLR 497 . 179
Practice Direction [1981] 2 All ER
831 158
Practice Direction [1983] 1 All ER 64 . 135
Practice Note [1962] 1 All ER 448 . 101, 157
Practice Note [1971] 3 All ER 829 . 105, 111
Practice Note [1974] 2 All ER 794 . . 197
Practice Note [1975] 2 All ER 1072 . 225
Practice Note [1980] 1 All ER 555 . . 179
Practice Note [1982] 3 All ER 1152 . 133,
153, 206
Practice Note [1983] 3 All ER 608 . . 198
Prasad v R (1981) 142

R

R v Alberta Law Society, ex p Demco
(1967) 170
R v Allamby (1974) 115
R v Anderson (1868) 111
R v Anderson (1929) 142
R v Ashmore (1974) 250
R v Assim (1966) 120
R v Ball (1951) 177
R v Balls (1871) 123
R v Ballysingh (1953) 88, 122
R v Banes, ex p Lord Vernon (1910) . 170
R v Barker (1977) 143
R v Barnsley Licensing Justices, ex p
Barnsley and District Licensed
Victuallers' Association (1960) . . 166
R v Barrell and Wilson (1979) . . . 117
R v Barry (Glamorgan) Justices, ex p
Kashim (1953) 158
R v Bass (1953) 137
R v Bell (1984) 117
R v Bibi (1980) 237
R v Birmingham Justices, ex p Hodgson
(1985) 95
R v Blackstock (1979) 118
R v Board of Visitors of Hull Prison, ex
p St Germain (1979) 234
R v Brentford Justices, ex p Wong
(1981) 88
R v Brigg Justices, ex p Lynch (1984) . 209
R v Britton (1987) 137
R v Britzman (1983) 146
R v Brown (1983) 144
R v Browning (1974) 115

PAGE

R v Bryant (1946) 132, 153
R v Bullock (1964) 166
R v Burles (1970) 129
R v Bushell (1670) 148
R v Callum (1975) 137
R v Cambridge Justices, ex p Fraser
(1985) 102
R v Canterbury and St Augustine
Justices, ex p Klisiak (1982) . . . 96
R v Casement (1917) 112
R v Chandler (No 2) (1964) 131
R v Charles (1976) 147
R v Clark (1955) 184
R v Clarke (1982) 241
R v Cockley (1984) 179
R v Cocks (1976) 148
R v Colchester Stipendiary Magistrate,
ex p Beck (1979) 100
R v Collinson (1931) 173
R v Collister (1955) 133, 154
R v Considine (1979) 96
R v Courtie (1984) 224
R v Crown Court at Cambridge, ex p
Hagi (1979) 209
R v Crown Court at Cardiff, ex p Jones
(1974) 178
R v Crown Court at Chichester, ex p
Kayode Shola Abodunrin and Tunji
Taofee Sogbanmu (1984) 208
R v Crown Court at Croydon, ex p
Bernard (1980) 168
R v Crown Court at Huntingdon, ex p
Jordan (1981) 165
R v Crown Court at Reading, ex p
Malik (1981) 196
R v Crown Court at Snaresbrook, ex p
Gavi Burjore (1979) 165
R v Crush (1978) 70
R v Daly (1974) 254
R v Davies (1980) 226
R v Deputy Governor of Camphill
Prison, ex p King (1985) 234
R v Derby and South Derbyshire
Magistrates, ex p McCarthy (1980) . 221
R v Dickson (1946) 153
R v Doot (1973) 112
R v Dossi (1918) 115
R v Dudley and Stephens (1884) . . 149
R v Durham Quarter Sessions, ex p
Virgo (1952) 154, 165
R v East Kerrier Justices, ex p Mundy
(1952) 158
R v Electricity Comrs, ex p London
Electricity Joint Committee Co (1920)
Ltd (1924) 168
R v Epping and Harlow Justices, ex p
Massaro (1973) 100
R v Falconer-Atlee (1973) 144
R v Ferguson (1970) 254
R v Forde (1923) 175
R v Fulling (1987) 74, 141
R v Fuschillo (1940) 116

PAGE

R v Galbraith (1981) 143
R v George (1984) 252
R v Gilby (1975) 252
R v Gormley (1966) 225
R v Gravesend Justices, ex p Sheldon
(1968) 157
R v Gray's Justices, ex p Tetley (1979) . 100
R v Greenfield (1973) 122
R v Gregory (1972) 116
R v Guildford Justices, ex p Harding
(1981) 158
R v Hall (1983) 145, 146
R v Harbax Singh (1979) 187
R v Hardman (1982) 94
R v Harris (1927) 158
R v Harward (1981) 118
R v Hassan (1970) 146
R v Hatfield Justices, ex p Castle
(1980) 96
R v Hayden (1975) 178, 207
R v Hazeltine (1967) 125
R v Highbury Corner Metropolitan
Stipendiary Magistrate, ex p Weekes
(1985) 96
R v Horsham Justices, ex p Bukhari
(1982) 100
R v Horsham Justices, ex p Farquharson
(1982) 104, 135
R v Howell (1982) 52, 53
R v Hudson (1980) 75
R v Inwood (1973) 55, 253
R v Islington North Juvenile Court, ex
p Daley (1983) 159, 168
R v Ithell (1969) 240
R v Jones (1974) 121
R v King (1970) 239
R v Kneeshaw (1975) 253
R v Knight (1980) 250
R v Kray (1970) 117, 131
R v Lake (1976) 121
R v Lambeth Metropolitan Stipendiary
Magistrate, ex p McComb (1983) . 107
R v Lawrence (1982) 248
R v Laws (1973) 175
R v Lawson (1952) 123
R v Leeds Justices, ex p Sykes (1983) . 104
R v Lemsatef (1977) 54
R v Lewis (1984) 160
R v Leyland Justices, ex p Hawthorn
(1979) 153
R v Lidster (1976) 254
R v Liverpool Juvenile Court, ex p R
(1987) 157
R v Llandrindod Wells Justices, ex p
Gibson (1968) 166
R v Lymm Justices, ex p Brown
(1973) 221
R v McCarthy (1983) 242
R v McKenna (1960) 148
R v Mason (1981) 130, 131
R v Mason (1987) 63, 75
R v Medford (1974) 115

PAGE

R v Metropolitan Stipendiary
Magistrate, ex p Zardin (1971) . . 95
R v Miles (1890) 127
R v Milligan (1982) 224
R v Millwood (1982) 248
R v Moylan (1970) 240
R v Mutford and Lothingland Justices,
ex p Harber (1971) 165
R v Nazari (1980) 256
R v Newton (1982) 224
R v No 14 (London West) Legal Aid
Area Committee, ex p Bunting
(1974) 208
R v Nottingham Justices, ex p Davies
(1981) 193, 195, 196
R v Novac (1976) 118
R v Oddy (1974) 254
R v O'Keefe (1969) 238
R v Oliva (1965) 133
R v Paraskeva (1982) . . . 133, 154
R v Parish Dighton (1835) . . . 146
R v Parker (1960) 176
R v Pattinson (1973) 175
R v Peace (1976) 124
R v Phillips (1947) 192
R v Pilcher (1974) 157
R v Plain (1967) 144
R v Podola (1960) 129
R v Prager (1972) 75
R v Prater (1960) 147
R v Priestley (1965) 75
R v Raymond (1981) 110
R v Reeves (1972) 250
R v Richardson (1971) 135
R v Roads (1967) 150
R v Roberts (1953) 54
R v Robertson (1987) 134
R v Robinson (1969) 225
R v Rochdale Justices, ex p Allwork
(1981) 165
R v Rogers and Tarran (1971) . . . 121
R v Rose (1982) 177
R v Ryan (1976) 252
R v St Helens Justices, ex p McClorie
(1983) 96
R v Sang (1980) 63
R v Sapiano (1968) 239
R v Saunders (1970) 240
R v Savundranayagan and Walker
(1968) 103
R v Scarrott (1978) 118
R v Secretary of State for Home Affairs,
ex p Santillo (1981) 256
R v Secretary of State for the Home
Department, ex p Tarrant (1985) . 234
R v Seisdon Justices, ex p Dougan
(1983) 155
R v Shaw (1972) 134
R v Shipton, ex p DPP (1957) . . 127
R v Slough Justices, ex p Duncan and
Embling (1983) 197

List of cases

PAGE

R v Socialist Worker Printers and
Publishers Ltd, ex p A-G (1975) . . 150
R v Starie (1979) 239, 248
R v Sullivan (1971) 146
R v Sussex Justices, ex p McCarthy
(1924) 168
R v Tanner (1977) 145
R v Tarry (1970) 240
R v Thibeault (1983) 254
R v Thomas (1950) 127
R v Tomlin (1954) 123
R v Turnbull (1977) 147
R v Turner (1970) 124, 126
R v Varley (1982) 145
R v Wakefield Justices, ex p
Butterworth (1970) 154
R v Warrington Justices, ex p Mooney
(1980) 221
R v Waters (1963) 173
R v Webb (1969) 129, 177
R v Wells Street Stipendiary Magistrate,
ex p Seillon (1978) 100
R v Wilkinson (1970) 239
R v Wilson (1979) 88, 123
R v Wright (1979) 255

PAGE

Roberts, Re (1967) 103
Rookes v Barnard (1964) 49

S

S (infant) v Manchester City Recorder
(1971) 165
Sambasivam v Malaya Federation
Public Prosecutor (1950) 128
Selvey v DPP (1968) (1970) 145
Shaaban Bin Hussien v Chong Fook
Kam (1970) 52
Stapylton v O'Callaghan (1973) . . . 144

T

Treacy v DPP (1971) 112
Tsang Ping-Nam v R (1981) . . . 144

W

Walters v W H Smith & Son Ltd
(1914) 53
Ware v Fox (1967) 88
Wong Kam-Ming v R (1980) . . . 142
Worley v Bentley (1976) 135
Wright v Nicholson (1970) 88

Part one

The Case of Oliver Twist

The Case of Oliver Twist

CPS v OLIVER TWIST: ARREST AND REMAND

One evening in April 1986 a young solicitor's clerk called Anthony Jobling decided to take his girlfriend to see a film at the Regal Cinema in Barking in East London. They drove to the cinema in his motor car – a Ford Escort – which they left in the cinema car park. When they came out of the cinema they discovered to their dismay that the Escort was no longer in the car park. Anthony telephoned the police straight away and within a very short space of time the central information office at New Scotland Yard had circulated the number of the car and its description to police stations all over the London area.

The same night at about one o'clock two plain clothes police officers, Detective Sergeant Dixon and Detective Constable Bucket, were driving in a patrol car along the main London-to-Southend road. They had been investigating a disturbance in Romford involving some youths who had had too much to drink and something one of the boys had let slip led them to the conclusion that it would be worth looking out for a young man called Oliver Twist. They thought Oliver might well be found with his friends at a transport cafe on the Southend road.

Now Oliver, who was aged 22, and lived on a large housing estate near Romford, was very well known to the police. He had been in trouble on a number of occasions and was at that time subject to a suspended sentence for a drugs offence committed a couple of months earlier.

When the police arrived at the transport cafe they saw parked in the forecourt a Ford Escort with the registration number which had been circulated that evening over the radio; and they were not at all surprised when they went into the cafe to see Oliver trying his luck at a fruit machine beside the counter. The police told Oliver that they wanted to ask him some questions about the Escort parked outside. Oliver denied any knowledge of the car and asked what they thought it had got to do with him. Since Oliver appeared to be alone, the police asked him how he had got to the cafe. Oliver said that a friend of his had brought him there. 'Well', said one of the police officers, 'in that case, where is your friend now?' Oliver paused for a moment and then said he didn't know. The next question the policeman asked was where Oliver was living at the moment. Oliver said he was living at home with his parents at Colletts Row. The officer pointed out that that was a very long way away – how was Oliver proposing to get home? 'Well', said Oliver, 'perhaps you'd like to give me a lift?' Both the police officers were quite satisfied in their own minds that Oliver's story about being brought to the cafe by somebody who had apparently disappeared was untrue and it seemed obvious to them that Oliver had arrived at the cafe in the Escort and was going to use it for getting home. They then and there told Oliver they were arresting him for taking the car without the owner's consent and 'cautioned' him – that is, told Oliver that he was not obliged to say anything unless he wanted to do so, but that if he did say anything, what he said would be put in writing and might be given in evidence. What Oliver in fact said when he was told he was being arrested for taking the car was 'You think you are so clever – you prove it'.

It is worth noting at this stage that *whenever* the police arrest a suspect they *must*:

(1) tell him precisely for what offence he is being arrested;
(2) remind him of his right not to answer police questions;
(3) warn him that anything he does say will be recorded and may later be repeated in court.

Oliver was taken by the police to Romford Police Station. When they arrived at the station, the officer who had arrested Oliver took him to the uniformed station sergeant and told him in outline why Oliver had been arrested. At every police station one senior officer (usually a sergeant) will be carrying out the functions of Custody Officer. He has by law the responsibility of deciding whether a person who has been arrested should be kept in custody. If he decides to authorise such detention then he is responsible for opening a Custody Record which will set out everything that happens to the detained person while he remains at the police station.

In Oliver's case the following steps were taken:

(1) the Custody Officer told Oliver that he was going to be detained for questioning on suspicion of taking the Ford Escort without the owner's consent;
(2) he told Oliver that he had the right to have someone informed of his arrest. Oliver asked for his father to be told;
(3) he told Oliver that he had the right to consult a solicitor;
(4) he also told him that he was going to be searched and a list of his property would be compiled on the Custody Record.

You can see from the Custody Record at pp 20–21 how these matters are recorded.

While Oliver was waiting to be searched he noticed a lady sitting on the other side of the station office. She seemed to be in a very distressed condition and kept looking at Oliver. After a while she went over to the station sergeant and started speaking to him – they both looked across at Oliver – but, before anything more could happen, Oliver was taken to the detention room to be searched. When Oliver was searched no car keys were found on him but when the police searched the car (which was unlocked) a set of car keys were found in the glove compartment: these were eventually sent away for forensic analysis but no fingerprints were found.

After Oliver had been searched, and while the charge sheet was being filled in, Dixon, the police officer who had arrested Oliver, was called away for a few minutes. When he came back he told Oliver that he had been speaking to the lady Oliver had noticed earlier, and had received some very interesting information. It seemed she had arrived at the police station because earlier on that evening her shop had been broken into and she had surprised the burglar in the very act. She had just told the officer that, although she had only caught a glimpse of the man, that had been enough for her to recognise Oliver as the intruder. She said that after the burglar had run out of the shop she had seen a Ford Escort drive away quickly from outside the shop. Oliver was adamant that he had nothing to do with this burglary. 'Alright', said Dixon, 'where were you before you went to the cafe?' Oliver began to say he'd been at a discotheque in Market Street in Romford. Dixon cut him short: that was nonsense, he said, the discotheque had been closed for the last week for redecoration. Oliver started to say there had been a mistake but Dixon wasn't interested. He told Oliver that a glove had been found at the shop and asked Oliver to try it on. It fitted. He then said to Oliver that it was obvious that he had taken the car and used it to commit the burglary. Oliver certainly made a reply to this remark. We shall see later that there is going to be a considerable dispute about what he said. According to the police, Oliver said 'Alright I nicked the car but I didn't do the old girl's shop'. According to Oliver he said nothing of the kind: he just said 'Alright you think what you like'.

At this stage Dixon told Oliver that he proposed to begin a formal interview with the questions and answers written down; Oliver at once made it clear that he was not taking part in any interview.

The police decided that, on the basis of what Mrs Snagsby had told them, he should be charged with burglary as well as with taking the Escort car. And so Oliver found himself facing two charges when the charge sheet had been compiled. When Oliver was formally charged, he was cautioned again by the officers and (perhaps very sensibly) made no reply to the caution.

Once Oliver had been charged, the police were bound to consider the question of bail. Decisions on bail are the responsibility of the Custody Officer although, of course, he will normally follow the view of the officers who are actually conducting the investigation. In Oliver's case bail was refused because the police thought there was a risk that Oliver (who was under a suspended sentence) would not attend court. This meant that Oliver would remain in custody until his appearance at Havering Magistrates' Court on the following Monday.

Over the weekend, Oliver had ample opportunity to consider his predicament and decided that he was going to plead 'not guilty' to the charges. He also rang up his father and asked him to be at court on the next Monday. He was also aware from past experience that he could apply to the magistrates for his case to be adjourned while he was granted legal aid. Indeed, even if Oliver had wanted the case to be heard by the magistrates on the Monday, the likelihood would be that the police would have asked for the matter to be adjourned in order for them to prepare their case and for Oliver to be in the meantime *remanded*.

On Monday morning, Oliver was taken from the police station to the cells below Havering Magistrates' Court. All criminal cases begin in the magistrates' court. Many cases, probably about 90 per cent, are disposed of before the magistrates. The remainder are committed by the magistrates to the Crown Court for the offenders to be tried by a judge and jury. Oliver would be taken to the magistrates' court for the area, called a petty sessional division, in which one or more of the alleged offences had been committed or in which he lived. When he was brought into the court, he said he wanted legal aid, and his case was put back for a few minutes so that he could consult the 'duty solicitor'. The Law Society runs a statutory scheme whereby local solicitors make themselves available on a rota to give advice and represent people at court who have no solicitor to act for them. (A similar scheme operates to provide advice for people detained at police stations and it may be that Oliver was foolish not to have taken advantage of it.)

When Oliver met the duty solicitor, Mr Fogg, at court he gave him a brief account of what had happened. Mr Fogg discussed the case with the Crown Prosecution Service representative and everyone agreed that the case would be adjourned. The only issue that day would therefore be whether Oliver should be granted bail. In due course the case was called on and the CPS advocate told the magistrates that the prosecution objected to bail because Oliver was under a suspended sentence and so he had a real incentive not to turn up for his trial. He handed in a list of Oliver's convictions. DS Dixon was then called to give evidence and told the court that Oliver had admitted taking the car and had been identified by an eye witness to the burglary. At this stage Mr Fogg had a difficult task. He told the magistrates that Oliver intended to dispute both charges – that the alleged confession was challenged and that the identification was no more than a glimpse by a witness. He pointed out to the court that Oliver had always been granted bail in the past and had never failed to attend. He told the magistrates that Oliver's father, who was present and willing to stand as a surety, had confirmed that Oliver had been offered a job to start that week. The magistrates decided to retire to their private room to discuss the question. The problem facing them can be summarised as follows:

(1) the law presumes that an accused person is innocent until proven guilty;
(2) therefore, the Bail Act expressly provides that generally bail should only be refused if there is a real likelihood that he will fail to attend at his trial;
(3) a person who is already under a suspended sentence will normally go to prison if he is convicted of a further offence, so there is a much greater temptation upon such a person to abscond;
(4) on the other hand, in the instant case, Oliver would lose the chance of getting a job if he was kept in custody and he had already indicated that he intended to contest the charges.

In the end, the magistrates came back into court, and the Chairman announced that they would grant Oliver bail but only on certain conditions. The terms of Oliver's bail were:

(1) that a surety acceptable to the police should be prepared to ensure his attendance at court or to forfeit £5000;
(2) that Oliver should report every evening at Romford Police Station.

At this stage Oliver's father stepped forward and agreed to enter into a surety to guarantee Oliver's attendance. If he had not been available, Oliver would have been kept in custody while the police contacted his father and arranged for him to sign the surety forms at a convenient police station.

Later that week, Mr Fogg received a copy of the legal aid order made by the court assigning his firm to conduct Oliver's defence. Oliver then came round to the office for an interview. He told the solicitor that he intended to plead 'not guilty' to the charges and that on the evening in question he had been out with some friends in Romford and later had driven out with them to the cafe on the Southend road where the police had arrested him. He said that at the cafe his friends had decided to continue on to Southend but he did not want to go with them and so had stayed behind intending to hitch a lift home. He also told the solicitor that he was under a suspended sentence so that, if he was convicted, he would probably go to prison. The solicitor then explained to him that there were three main types of criminal cases:

(1) those which, like robbery, were so serious that they could only be tried by a judge and jury at the Crown Court;
(2) those which, like driving without due care and attention, were comparatively trivial and could only be tried by the magistrates' court;
(3) those which, like most types of burglary and taking cars, could be tried in either court depending on the accused's choice.

Since Oliver was charged with burglary and taking a motor car, he could decide either to be tried before the magistrates' court or at the Crown Court. Before he decided, he should consider the merits and demerits of the alternative courses. In summary, what the solicitor told Oliver was:

(1) the real advantage to an accused person in agreeing to be tried before a magistrates' court is that the whole case can be dealt with in a short time, while cases often take months to come on before the Crown Court;
(2) however, most lawyers think that a jury is a more sympathetic tribunal towards an accused person (or possibly just more naïve) than a bench of magistrates. Whatever the reason, it is generally believed that there is a higher chance of acquittal before a jury.

Not surprisingly, Oliver told his solicitor that he would prefer to be tried before a judge and jury at the Crown Court. In that event, said Mr Fogg, the magistrates at the next hearing would merely decide whether to commit him for trial or not. Indeed it would be possible for Oliver to *agree* to be committed for trial on the basis of written statements supplied to him in advance by the prosecution without the magistrates considering this evidence at all. This might well be the sensible course in his case because, on what Oliver had already told him about the circumstances of the arrest, there appeared to be a clear *case to answer* so that a *preliminary enquiry* before the magistrates' court would not assist him and would merely provide a dress-rehearsal of the trial for the prosecution witnesses.

It should perhaps be noted at this stage, that whenever an accused person elects trial by jury, or has to be committed to the Crown Court because the magistrates have no jurisdiction over the offence, the accused can choose between:

(1) a full *preliminary enquiry* at which the magistrates consider the evidence (either oral or written), and decide whether the prosecution have disclosed a *case to answer*; or
(2) a *formal committal* at which the accused, through his lawyer, agrees that there is a case to answer, so that the magistrates do not have to look at the evidence.

In practice magistrates normally now only hold preliminary enquiries (in the sense of *considering* the prosecution evidence) when the defendant wishes to contest the evidence or submit there is no case fit to be committed or where he is not legally represented (in which case he is not allowed to agree to a formal committal) or where the prosecution wish to test the evidence of their own witnesses (as sometimes happens in an identification case).

In Oliver's case, we can assume his solicitor was served by the police with copies of the prosecution statements, and these confirmed his opinion that there was obviously a case for Oliver to answer. He therefore agreed to a formal committal to the Crown Court. The actual mechanics of this procedure can best be understood by reading a transcript of the committal.

CPS v OLIVER TWIST: COMMITTAL PROCEEDINGS

Transcript of proceedings before Justices of the Peace for the North Eastern Commission Area of Greater London sitting at Havering Magistrates' Court, Romford, on 18 May 1986.

Clerk: Is your name Oliver Twist?

Defendant: Yes.

CPS Solicitor: Sir, I would respectfully ask for summary trial on both charges.

Chairman: What is the nature of the charges?

CPS Solicitor: The first charge is taking a car (which has been recovered) and the second charge relates to a non-domestic burglary.

Chairman: Was any property stolen?

CPS Solicitor: Yes sir – £15.

Chairman: Has it been recovered?

CPS Solicitor: Yes sir.

Chairman: Very well, we agree this is a proper case for summary trial if the accused consents.

Clerk (reading from the charge sheet prepared at the police station when Oliver was formally charged): Oliver Twist you are charged that on 19 April 1986 you took a Ford Escort motor car without the owner's consent from the car park at the Regal Cinema Barking contrary to section 12 of the Theft Act 1968 and you are further charged that on 19 April 1986 you entered a shop at 136 Lindum Road, Romford as a trespasser and stole the sum of £15 therein contrary to section 9 of the Theft Act 1968.

Now on these charges you can be tried either by the magistrates at this court or you can choose to be tried by a judge and jury at the Crown Court.

But before you choose I must warn you that, if you decide to be tried at this court and are convicted, the magistrates can still send you to the Crown Court for sentence if they decide, having heard about your character and antecedents, that they do not have adequate powers of punishment. Do you understand this?

Defendant: Yes.

Clerk: Do you wish to be tried by this court or by the Crown Court?

Defendant: By the Crown Court.

Solicitor: May it please your Worships I appear on behalf of Mr Twist and it might assist if I say now that we are prepared to agree to a formal committal to the Crown Court under section 6(2).

Clerk: Thank you. In that case I must ask if all the prosecution evidence is in the form of written statements?

CPS Solicitor: Yes *(hands bundle of original statements to Clerk)*. I produce the statements of Anthony Jobling, Elsie Snagsby, Detective Constable Bucket and Detective Sergeant Dixon.

Clerk (to the solicitor): Have you received copies of all these statements?

Solicitor: Yes.

Clerk: Do you wish to object to any of them at this stage?

Solicitor: No.

CPS Solicitor: I also produce two exhibits, a glove and a pair of keys.

Clerk (to the solicitor): Do you wish to submit that the defendant should not be committed for trial?

Solicitor: No.

Clerk: Then I have to ask whether the defendant wishes to give evidence before the magistrates or call witnesses.

Solicitor: No.

Clerk: Is this a case where the defendant should be told about the rules requiring him to serve notice of any alibi defence?

Solicitor: Yes.

Clerk: Very well. Now Mr Twist you must understand that at your trial at the Crown Court you will not be allowed to give evidence in support of an alibi (that is saying you were somewhere else when the offence was committed) unless you have given notice to the prosecution setting out particulars of the alibi. You can give those particulars now or your solicitor can send them within the next seven days to the prosecution. Do you want to give particulars of alibi now?

Solicitor: No.

Clerk (to Chairman of the Justices): In that case, sir, all the formalities have been complied with and the papers are in order.

Chairman: Very well. Mr Twist, you are committed to stand your trial on this charge before a judge and jury at Snaresbrook Crown Court.

Clerk (to the CPS Solicitor): Are full witnesses orders to be made?

CPS Solicitor: Yes, except in the case of the witness Anthony Jobling who only gives formal evidence.

Solicitor: Yes, I agree to a conditional witness order being made in respect of his evidence since it will not be contested.

Chairman: Then we make the orders as you have indicated.

Clerk: Are the police retaining the exhibits until the trial?

CPS Solicitor: Yes.

Solicitor: Your Worships, this defendant has been on bail and I ask that bail should be renewed to cover the committal.

Chairman; Are there any conditions of bail?

Solicitor: A surety in the sum of £5000 and there is a condition of reporting once daily at Romford Police Station between six and seven o'clock each evening.

Chairman: Have the police any objections to bail being renewed on those terms?

CPS Solicitor: No, your Worship, we have received no instructions to that effect.

Chairman: Very well.

Clerk: Is the surety here now?

Solicitor: Yes he is. It's the defendant's father.

Clerk: Mr Twist, will you go into the witness box.

Usher: What religion, sir?

Mr Twist: Church of England. *(He is handed the New Testament and reads from a card.)* I swear that I will truthfully answer all such questions as the Court shall demand of me.

Clerk: Mr Twist, do you have property or savings to the value of £5000 after all your debts (if you have any) are paid?

Mr Twist: Yes sir.

Clerk: What sort of property have you got?

Mr Twist: Well, I own my house – the mortgage has been paid off now.

Clerk: That's fine. Now do you understand that you are promising to make sure your son does turn up at the Crown Court and that if he doesn't you are liable to pay £5000?

Mr Twist: Yes, sir.

Chairman: Then we renew bail on the same terms as before.

Solicitor: There is just one other matter, your Worship. The defendant was granted legal aid by this court for the purpose of the present proceedings. His means have not changed and I ask that he be granted a certificate to cover the trial at the Crown Court.

Chairman: We will make the order. Mr Twist, you understand you are committed to the Crown Court on bail and a legal aid order will be made to cover your trial there.

The Queen v Oliver Twist:
Brief to Counsel

The next stage is for Mr Twist's solicitor to instruct counsel for the defence.
He prepares a brief to counsel containing the statements tendered at the
committal and the defendant's evidence. In the brief are included reports
on Oliver from the police and the probation service. In fact these reports are
normally only supplied to the defence after the jury retire but, for the sake of
convenience, they have been included here.

Read through the brief carefully and jot down on a piece of paper what
you think would be the main points for counsel for the defence to remember
in dealing with the prosecution witnesses. Are there any questions he ought
to ask Oliver? For instance, would it be worth finding out why Oliver
changed his mind about travelling with his friends to Southend? It is
suggested that you also note down the points (if any) which you think could
be used in mitigation if he is convicted.

When you have done this go on to read the transcript of the trial and note
as you do so the various procedural steps.

In the Snaresbrook Crown Court   Legal Aid

                                                  86/1246

THE QUEEN

V

OLIVER TWIST

Brief to Counsel
for the Defendant

Counsel has herewith:

1. Copy Indictment
2. Prosecution Statements tendered at
          Committal Proceedings
3. Proofs of Evidence of Defendant and
          Witness
4. Copy custody record
5. Antecedents of Defendant
6. Social Enquiry Report.

Counsel is instructed on behalf of Mr. Oliver Twist
who has been committed to the Crown Court to stand
trial on charges of burglary and taking a conveyance.
The facts of the case appear from the statements;
points of challenge have been indicated in the margins.
Counsel is asked to consider whether objection could
be taken to the admissibility of the passages under-
lined in the statement of D/S Dixon. It will be
noted that the Defendant is subject to a suspended
sentence and Counsel is particularly requested to
consider whether in the event of his being convicted,
any argument could be put forward to prevent the
suspended sentence being brought into effect.

                         Counsel is instructed
                         to represent the Defendant
                         and endeavour to secure
                         his acquittal and, if he
                         be convicted, to enter a
                         plea in mitigation.

No. 861246

INDICTMENT

The Crown Court at SNARESBROOK

THE QUEEN -v- OLIVER TWIST

OLIVER TWIST

is **charged as follows:-**

COUNT 1   STATEMENT OF OFFENCE
Taking a conveyance without authority, contrary to Section 12(1) of the Theft Act 1968.

PARTICULARS OF OFFENCE
OLIVER TWIST, on the 19th day of April 1986 without the consent of the owner or other
lawful authority, took a conveyance namely a Ford Escort motor car registration
number PRX 124V for his own use.

COUNT 2   STATEMENT OF OFFENCE
Burglary, contrary to Section 9(1)(b) of the Theft Act 1968.

PARTICULARS OF OFFENCE
OLIVER TWIST, on the 19th day of April 1986, having entered as a trespasser a
building known as 136 Lindum Road, Romford in the London Borough of Havering
stole therein £15 in cash

Signed *Q. Burgess*
Officer of the Court

Form 5668

S6226 (27610) Dd.8982710 38m 5/86 G.W.8.Ltd.Gp.870

No. 991

STATEMENT OF WITNESS
(C.J. Act, 1967, S. 9; M.C. Act, 1980, S. 102; M.C. Rules, 1981, r.70)

Statement of ...Anthony JOBLING

Age of Witness (Date of Birth) ...20

Occupation of Witness ...Solicitors Articled Clerk

Address and Telephone Number ...28 Acacia Gardens

Ilford

This statement,* consisting of   1   pages each signed by me, is true to the best of my knowledge and belief and I make it knowing that, if it is tendered in evidence, I shall be liable to prosecution if I have wilfully stated in it anything which I know to be false or do not believe to be true.

Dated the   20th   day of   April   , 1986 .

Signed ...*Anthony Jobling*
A. JOBLING
Signature witnessed by ...*George Dixon*
GEORGE DIXON, D.S. 156X

On Saturday 19th April 1986 at about 7.30 pm I left my Ford Escort motor car registration number PRX 124V at the Regal Cinema car park in Barking. When I left the cinema at 10.35 pm I found my car was missing. I have today identified my car at Romford Police Station. No one had my permission to remove the car from the car park.

Signed ...*Anthony Jobling*   Signature witnessed by ...*George Dixon*
A. JOBLING   GEORGE DIXON, D.S. 156X
                                        (Print name.................................)

M.P.84(E)

No. 991

STATEMENT OF WITNESS
(C.J. Act, 1967, S. 9; M.C. Act, 1980, S. 102; M.C. Rules, 1981, r.70)

Statement of ...... Elsie SNAGSBY

Age of Witness (Date of Birth) ...... Over 21

Occupation of Witness ...... Newsagent

Address and Telephone Number ...... 36 Jordans Road

Romford

Essex

This statement,* consisting of   1   pages each signed by me, is true to the best of my knowledge and belief and I make it knowing that, if it is tendered in evidence, I shall be liable to prosecution if I have wilfully stated in it anything which I know to be false or do not believe to be true.

Dated the   20th   day of   April   , 19 86.

Signed   *Elsie Snagsby*
E. SNAGSBY (Mrs.)
Signature witnessed by ...... *Alan Black*
ALAN BLACK, P.C. 129X

On 19th April 1986 I closed my newsagent shop at 136 Lindum Road Romford, at 6.15 pm. I went back to the shop just before 11.00 pm to fetch certain account books. I went round by the back door and found that a pane of glass in the door had been broken and that the door was unlocked. I went into the back room (which we use as an office) and then heard a noise coming from the shop front. As I looked into the shop front I saw a youth aged about 20, wearing a leather jacket, trying to open the front door. On hearing me, he turned round, pushed past me and ran out through the back door. I was too shaken to follow. A minute later I heard a car door slam outside and saw a Ford Escort car driving off down the road at high speed. When I recovered I telephoned the police. The bureau in the office had been disturbed and £15 (3 five pound notes) had been taken from the petty cash box. No other property had been taken. In the front shop beside the door, I found a black leather glove (exhibit ES1) which I handed to the police when they arrived. On Sunday 20th April, today I was at Romford Police Station when I saw a man I know to be OLIVER TWIST. He looks like the man I saw in my shop.

Signed ...... *Elsie Snagsby* ......   Signature witnessed by ...... *Alan Black* ......
ELSIE SNAGSBY(Mrs.)   (Print name ...... ALAN BLACK, P.C. 129X ......)

M.P.84(E)

No. 991

STATEMENT OF WITNESS
(C.J. Act, 1967, S. 9; M.C. Act, 1980, S. 102; M.C. Rules, 1981, r.70)

Statement of ..... George DIXON, D.S. 156X Division

Age of Witness (Date of Birth) .. Over 21

Occupation of Witness .. Detective Sergeant

Address and Telephone Number .. Romford Police Station

This statement,* consisting of   2   pages each signed by me, is true to the best of my knowledge and belief and I make it knowing that, if it is tendered in evidence, I shall be liable to prosecution if I have wilfully stated in it anything which I know to be false or do not believe to be true.

Dated the   20th   day of   April   , 1986

Signed   *George Dixon*
GEORGE DIXON, D.S. 156X

Signature witnessed by   *Alan Black*
ALAN BLACK, P.C. 129X

On 20th April 1986 at 0055 hours, acting on information received, I went together with D.C. BUCKET to Meg's Cafe, Romford roundabout on the A13 London-Southend road. Parked outside the cafe I saw a Ford Escort motor car registration number PRX 124V. I went into the cafe and saw a man I know to be OLIVER TWIST (aged 22) of 36 Colletts Row, Romford. I went over to him, introduced myself and said 'We would like to have a word with you about the Escort outside'. TWIST said 'What Escort?'. D.C. BUCKET said 'The car that was nicked outside the Regal in Barking'. TWIST said 'What's it got to do with me?' I said 'How did you get here?' TWIST said 'I got a lift with my mate Ginger'. I said 'Where is he now?' TWIST 'I've no idea'. D.C. BUCKET said 'Where do you live?' TWIST said 'In Colletts Row'. I said 'But that is over six miles away. How are you going to get home?' TWIST said 'Would you be going my way?' I then told him I was arresting him for taking the Escort, cautioned him and he said 'You think you are so clever – you prove it'. TWIST was then taken to Romford Police Station. At the police station TWIST was taken

I told him Ginger had gone down to Rayleigh and I was going to hitch a lift home.

Signed ....   Signature witnessed by ....

(Print name..)

M.P.84(E)

No. 991B

STATEMENT OF WITNESS
(C.J. Act, 1967, S. 9; M.C. Act, 1980, S. 102; M.C. Rules, 1981, r.70)

Continuation of statement of ....

through the main reception area to the Custody Officer. I then took him to an interview room to be searched prior to being charged. After TWIST had been placed in the interview room a lady, I now know to be ELSIE SNAGSBY of 136 Lindum Road, Romford, was introduced to me and she said 'That is the man that did my shop'. I subsequently saw TWIST and said to him 'What can you tell me about a burglary at Lindum Road earlier tonight?' TWIST said 'Leave off, Mr. Dixon. I haven't done no burglary'. I said, 'But the lady outside has recognised you as the man who broke into her shop'. He said 'She must be some kind of nut'. I then told TWIST he would be charged with burglary in due course and I said to him 'Where had you been before you went to the cafe?' He said 'I'd been down the disco in Market Street'. I said 'But it was closed last week for redecoration'. He said 'Oh, I must have made a mistake'. I said 'It's obvious to me you stole the car and used it for the burglary at Lindum Road'. He said 'Alright I nicked the car but I didn't do the old girl's shop'. I then told TWIST that I proposed to conduct a formal interview in which questions and answers would be written down. He said 'You know me, Mr. Dixon I'm not making no statement. When do I get bail?' I told him the question of bail would be considered after our other enquiries were complete. At 03.00 hours TWIST was charged with taking a conveyance and burglary and was cautioned and made no reply.

M.P.82(E)

Signed *George Dixon*   Signature witnessed by *Alan Black*
GEORGE DIXON, D.S. 156X   ALAN BLACK, P.C. 129X

PROOF OF EVIDENCE OF DEFENDANT

<u>Oliver Twist</u> of 36 Colletts Row, Romford,
                              will say:-

I am a single man living with my parents at the above
address. I have been in trouble on a number of occasions
before, the details of which I cannot now remember. I am
under a suspended sentence for a drugs offence. I am at
present unemployed although until recently I was working
as a messenger boy in Fleet Street. About 4 years ago I
had a bad accident to my hand when I was working in Ealing
and I am expecting to receive compensation.

Last Saturday I met up with my friend Ginger Peterson
and we decided to go to the disco in Market Street.
Unfortunately when we arrived we found it was closed so
we sent instead to "The Ilford Arms" a public house in
Victoria Road. We left the pub at closing time and went
for a meal. At the Wimpy Bar we met Ginger's girlfriend,
Judy Smallweed. We all decided to go to see Judy's sister
in Rayleigh. On the way we stopped at Meg's cafe on the
Southend road and I decided to leave them and go home as
it was getting late. I was just finishing my coffee when
D.S. Dixon and another officer came in. Dixon accused me
of nicking an Escort that had been parked outside and I
told him that I'd been drinking at the Ilford Arms. I
told him my mate Ginger had dropped me off and was going
on to Rayleigh and I was going to hitch a lift home.
I didn't take his questions seriously and was surprised
when he told me that he was arresting me. When we arrived
at the police station I was taken into the reception room
and an old lady came up and stared at me and then went off
and spoke to the station sergeant. Dixon then came in
and told me I'd been pointed out as the man that had broken
into her shop and that I was going to be charged with
burglary. He asked me to explain my movements that night
up to before I arrived at the cafe. I started to tell
him we'd gone to the disco but he interrupted to say it
was closed and before I could explain told me it was
obvious to him I had nicked the car and done the burglary.
I was fed up with his attitude so I said "Alright, you
think what you like". He asked me if I was going to make
a statement and I said "No not till I see my lawyer."
I then asked about bail. The version of the conversation
given in his statement is wrong. I think my friend Ginger
would be willing to make a statement and come to court to
give evidence. I do not think Judy would be prepared to
help.

PROOF OF EVIDENCE

Ginger Peterson, 27 Paradise Gardens, Harold Hill,
   unemployed fitter, will say:-

On Saturday, 19th April I met Oliver Twist at Romford bus
station and we went down to the disco in the market but it was
closed. We then went to the "Ilford Arms" and stayed there
until closing time. When we came out we met my ex-girlfriend,
Judy Smallweed, and we all went to have a hamburger. We
decided to go down to Rayleigh but on the way Oliver changed
his mind, so we dropped him off at Meg's cafe.

I have been in trouble with the police in the past.
Last year I was given a suspended sentence on a burglary
charge. I have also been convicted of taking a conveyance
and driving whilst disqualified and I was sent to Send
Detention Centre for that offence.

I do not think Judy will give evidence since we have
now broken up and she has gone to work at Clacton with her
aunt.

FORM 57

Custody Record

Custody No:	651

Police station:	Station code:	Charge No:
Romford	30	60

Reasons for arrest:

Suspicion of taking motor vehicle
Ford Escort PRX 124V without
owner's consent

Other references:

computer in block capitals

Surname: (Mr. Mrs Miss) TWIST

First Names: OLIVER

A notice setting out my rights has been read to me and I have been provided with a copy.

Signature of
person detained: *O. Twist*

Time: 0130   Date: 20/4/86

Address: 36 COLLETS ROAD
ROMFORD

~~I want a Solicitor as soon as practicable*~~
I do not want a Solicitor at this time*

Signature of
person detained: *O. Twist*

Time: 0135   Date: 20/4/86

Occupation:	UNEMPLOYED			
Age:	22	D.O.B:	15 / 3 / 64	
Place of Birth:	EALING			
Ident. code:		Height: 5'8"	Sex: M/~~F~~*	

At the time of service of notice - notification of detention to named person requested/~~not requested~~*

Named person: Albert Twist
36 Colletts Road,
Romford

Time: 0135   Date: 20/4/86

Arrested by:			
Name:	DIXON (block capitals)		
Rank: D/S	No.: 210	Station or Branch: ROMFORD	
	Time	Date	
Arrested at	0055	20/4/86	
Arrived at station	0115	20/4/86	

Officer opening Custody Record:

Signature: *Charles Soap*

Name: C. SOAP
(block capitals)

Rank: P/S   No: 266

Officer in the case:

Name: DIXON, GEORGE
(block capitals)

Rank: D/S   No.: 210   Station or Branch: ROMFORD

* delete as appropriate
* record action overleaf

	PROPERTY CLEAR
	SUPERVISING OFFICERS INITIALS

Property

Kept by Person Detained	Kept by police
Total Personal Cash £5 x 2 : £1 x 3 56 pence One (1) wallet One (1) keyring One (1) lighter Two (2) boxes of matches One (1) packet of n3/os Refused to sign *J. Coombs* 705 P/C	1 set car keys (found elsewhere) *J. Coombs* 705 P/C

1

Last review of detention conducted at:

Custody No:

Name:

Date	Time	Full details of any action/occurrence involving the detained person (Include full particulars of all visitors/officers) Individual entries need not be restricted to one line All entries to be signed by the writer
20/4/86	1.45 am	Relevant time started at 1.25 am I authorise detention pending investigation of involvement in taking motor vehicle and in burglary at Linden Road. P. Small / Insp.
	1.50	Taken for interview by D/S Dixon. Refused to be interviewed. ✓ 265
	2.00	Returned to cell. ✓ 265
	2.15	Out of cell. CHARGED. 2.19 am. fingerprint and photograph procedure explained Given into custody of DS Dixon for this purpose J. Thomas D/S.
	2.30	REVIEW NO BAIL I believe that if bail were granted it would interfere with inquiries. Prisoner informed. No representations made. P. Small / Insp.
	2.35	To cells. ✓ 265
	3.00.	I spoke to TWIST in his cell. He stated that he did not wish to make any complaint about his treatment by police since his arrest. The bruise on his face had been caused in an incident before his arrest J. Thomas. D/S.
	4.30	Visit OK. ✓ 265
	7.15	Light meal accepted. ✓ 265
	8.00	Wash. ✓ 265
	10.00	REVIEW NO BAIL I believe he would interfere with witness and impede inquiries if granted bail. A. Wade supdt.
	12.15	Visit by father. S. Coombs PC 705

2

N.I.B. 74C
To enable this Form to be microfilmed it MUST be typed.

ANTECEDENTS

*No known previous convictions.
*List of previous convictions attached.

C.R.O. No.

1 **FULL NAME**   OLIVER TWIST   97544/81

2 **Address**   36 COLLETT'S ROW ROMFORD

3 **Age** 22   4 **Date of birth** 15.3.64   5 **Place of birth** EALING   6 **Nationality** BRITISH

7 **Date of 1st entry into U.K.**   N/A   8 **Occupation**   UNEMPLOYED

9 **Education**

He attended St Joseph's School, Ealing and
Dotheboys Hall Community Home.

10 **Home conditions, Domestic circumstances and Financial commitments.**

He lives at 36 Collett's Row, Romford with his parents. He contributes
£10 pw for his board. He was unable to give details of his other
commitments.

11 **MAIN EMPLOYMENTS** during last 5 years *(show dates, places and positions held, reasons for leaving and in the case of present employment—WAGES).*

He has had several jobs since leaving school. He has worked as a trainee
machine operator and as a messenger.

12 Outstanding matters *(e.g., breach of suspended sentence, probation order, conditional discharge, on licence from prison, on bail for other offences, 'totting up', driving disqualification).*

Twist is in breach of a suspended sentence passed 5.1.86.

13 Any other useful antecedent information. (**IMPORTANT:** *please see Instruction on Form N.I.B. 74F* **BEFORE** *completion).*
(show brief summary of convictions when used as a Court antecedent form).

Committed for *trial/sentence at

                    Havering Magistrates   Court
for offence(s) of (briefly) Burglery and Taking
                    Conveyance

Date of Arrest 20.4.86   *IN CUSTODY/ON BAIL
*delete as appropriate
M.P.83(E)

Officer in Case D S 247 DIXON

Station ROMFORD

Tele. No. 201010   Date 29.4.86

Supervising Officer

N.I.B. 74C

DATE	COURT	OFFENCE(S) (With details of any offence taken into consideration)	SENTENCE	DATE OF RELEASE	Show if 'spent'
1.3.80	Ealing Juvenile	Burglary	Supervision Order		
11.5.80	Acton Juvenile	Theft (5 cases taken into consideration)	Care Order (London Borough of Ealing)		
23.2.85	Middlesex Crown	Burglary	3 months Detention Centre	22.4.85	
12.8.85	Southend Magistrates	Assault	Fined £5		
5.1.86	Snaresbrook Crown	Unlawful Possession of Dangerous Drugs (Class A)	6 months Imprisonment Suspended 2 years		

M.P.76-92973

NORTH EAST LONDON PROBATION SERVICE

SOCIAL ENQUIRY REPORT

Subject: Oliver Twist – Age 22 years

Occupation: Unemployed (Unemployment Benefit £26.40
              per week)

Offence: (i) Taking conveyance and
              (ii) Burglary

Family: Father Patrick Twist   (42) unemployed
              Mother Nancy Twist   (40)
              Subject Oliver Twist   (22)
              Brother Paul   (18)
              Brother Gary   (15) Care Order
              Sister Sharon   (12) Care of L/A
              Sister Tracey   (6) Care of L/A
              Brother Sean   (18 months)

Home: 4 bedroomed house

Health: Good

Education: Attended local schools to 13 years. Thereafter
              attended Dotheboys Hall Community Home, S. Yorks.

Employment: Twist was unfortunate in that shortly after
              commencing work he sustained a serious injury
              to his right hand which has left him
              permanently disabled. He found work in
              1984 as a newspaper messenger boy in Fleet
              Street but left that employment after six
              months because of the anti-social hours.
              He is now unemployed and registered as
              disabled.

Present
Offence: Since he intends to plead "not guilty" I have
              not discussed the circumstances of the present
              case with him.

General
Report: I have interviewed Oliver Twist twice at my
              office and attempted to contact his parents
              at their home address by prior appointment
              on three occasions but unfortunately they have
              not been at home or contacted me. I have
              studied reports from the London Borough of

Ealing Social Services Department and Dotheboys Hall Community Home which Twist attended after he was placed in the Authority's care in 1980. These reports indicate that there were initially serious behavioural problems but that after a few months at the school he settled well and the staff were optimistic about his future. Upon his return home his Social Workers found him employment at a factory in Hayes but due to the unfortunate accident referred to above he lost this employment. In 1985 he was sent to Send Detention Centre after being convicted for burglary. Reports from the centre indicated that he was "sullen" and "unresponsive to discipline" and appeared to have a "chip on his shoulder". After his parent moved to Essex in 1983 the local Social Services Dept. were notified by the Care Authority and agreed to undertake supervision as the care order was still running. The social workers concerned made several visits to the home address but it proved difficult to establish meaningful contact with the family or with Twist. Twist contacted the office and suggested appointments at different times but unfortunately failed to keep to these arrangements.

In January this year he was given a suspended sentence for possession of cocaine. He tells me that since that date he has been spending a great deal of his time in coffee bars and public houses in the Romford area and has not managed to settle to any regular way of life. He assures me he is no longer taking drugs and claims that he is seriously looking for work. I find it doubtful however whether he has a genuine motivation to work. Twist does not appear unduly concerned at the possibility of receiving a custodial sentence. I feel at this stage that there is a substantial risk of his drifting into further anti-social behaviour unless fairly definite steps are taken at this point in time.

Peter Mawson

2nd June 1986

Peter Mawson
Senior Probation Officer.

THE QUEEN v OLIVER TWIST: TRANSCRIPT OF THE TRIAL

(The Crown Court, Snaresbrook, 5 January 1987. It is just before half past ten. In the courtroom the dock is at the moment empty except for a prison officer. In front of the dock are the seats for the solicitors and counsel. To the left sits Mr Stryver, the prosecuting counsel. To the right of counsel's row is Mr Carton, the defence counsel. He is sitting nearest to the jury box which, at the moment, is empty. Facing the dock is the Bench and below, the table at which the Clerk of the Court is sitting. As the clock strikes the half-hour, the usher calls for silence and the judge enters.)

Usher: Silence.
Clerk: Put up Oliver Twist. *(Oliver is brought into the dock.)* Is your name Oliver Twist?
Oliver: Yes, sir.
Clerk: Oliver Twist, you stand charged in an indictment which contains two counts; in the first count you are charged with taking a conveyance contrary to section 12 of the Theft Act 1968, the particulars of the offence being that you, on the 19th day of April 1986 without the consent of the owner or other lawful authority, took a conveyance, namely a Ford Escort motor car, registration number PRX 124V, the property of Anthony Jobling for your own use. To that count do you plead guilty or not guilty?
Oliver: Not guilty.
Clerk: In the second count you are charged with burglary contrary to section 9(1)(b) of the Theft Act 1968 and the particulars of that offence are that you, on the 19th day of April 1986 having entered as a trespasser, a building namely a shop at 136 Lindum Road, Romford, stole therein £15 the property of Elsie Snagsby. To that count do you plead guilty or not guilty?
Oliver: Not guilty.

(Normally at this stage, the clerk calls the jurors-in-waiting into court and proceeds at once to empanel a jury. In our case, however, defence counsel has decided to apply to the judge for a ruling that Oliver should be tried separately on each count, i e that the charges should be tried by different juries neither knowing of the charge it is not considering. Such a course is obviously to Oliver's advantage because there is always the risk that a jury hearing together the evidence on two separate charges (each weak in itself) will convict on both although they would not have convicted on either charge if they had heard the evidence on that charge alone.)

Counsel for the Defence: Your Honour, before the jury is empanelled I have an application to sever the indictment. I don't know whether your Honour has had a chance of seeing the depositions?
Judge: I've been able to glance through the statements Mr Carton, so I have a rough idea of what it is all about.
Counsel for the Defence: I'm much obliged. Your Honour will have noted that, although by coincidence the police discovered the matters relating to the second count – the burglary charge – whilst Mr Twist was at the police station in connection with the first charge – the taking the car charge – the two matters are really separate. If I could refer your Honour to paragraph 1-75 of *Archbold* where the principles are set out.
Judge: Just one moment while I find that . . . Yes, I see. It's Rule 9 of the

Indictment Rules isn't it? [*reads*] 'Charges for any offences may be joined in the same indictment if those charges are founded on the same facts, or form or are a part of a series of offences of the same or a similar character.'

Counsel for the Defence: Your Honour, yes. I would respectfully submit that the charges in the indictment are quite separate and there is no connection between them at all and if they are tried together, however carefully the jury is directed to consider the evidence on each count separately, there is an obvious and real risk that the defence will be prejudiced.

Judge: What do you say, Mr Stryver?

Counsel for the Prosecution: I say, your Honour, that this application is quite misconceived. The cases are directly connected; for instance, part of the evidence that Twist took the car is in the statement of Mrs Snagsby who saw a Ford Escort driving away from outside her shop. And the defendant has served notice of alibi so that the defence in each case raises the same issue.

Judge: Do you wish to say anything else Mr Carton?

Counsel for the Defence: Only this, your Honour, that the mere fact that there is *some* evidence common to both charges in my submission doesn't affect the proposition that this jury is being asked to consider two quite different offences.

Judge: In this case, counsel for the defence applies that the indictment may be severed and separate trials ordered on each count. The first question I have to decide is whether the charges can be properly joined in the same indictment under Rule 9 of the Indictment Rules as 'a series of offences of . . . similar character'. I have to consider whether both as regards law and fact there is sufficient similarity between the offences charged. These are both offences of dishonesty and with regard to the facts there is a clear link – if the prosecution evidence is believed, it would appear that the defendant used the car he is alleged in the first count to have taken for the purpose of effecting the burglary charged in the second count. I am quite satisfied that this indictment complies with Rule 9. I have still to consider whether, nevertheless, I should exercise my discretion under section 5 of the Indictments Act and direct separate trials. I see that in the case of *Ludlow* which is referred to at paragraph 1-77 in *Archbold* Lord Pearson said 'The judge has no duty to direct separate trials . . . unless in his opinion there is some special feature of the case which would make a joint trial of the several counts prejudicial or embarrassing to the accused.' I can find no such special feature in this case and accordingly the application is rejected. Very well, let a jury be sworn.

Clerk: Usher, will you bring in the jury-in-waiting. . . . Ladies and Gentlemen, as I call your names will you answer and go into the jury box. James Edwards, Peter Pratt, Vivian Mosses, Julian Feather, George Duncan, Charles Lamb, Sidney Turner, George Meadows, Sylvia Wentworth, Frank Cammack, Richard Hartzig, Garth Dales.

(As the Clerk calls out the jurors' names they go and sit in the jury box. When twelve have entered the box):

Clerk: Twist, the names I am about to call are the persons who will form a jury to try you; if you object to them or any of them you must make your objection as they come to the Book to be sworn and before they are sworn and you shall be heard. James Edwards!

Usher: Take the Book in your right hand and read the words on the card.

Juror: I swear by Almighty God that I will faithfully try the defendant and give a true verdict according to the evidence.

Clerk: Peter Pratt!

Counsel for the Defence: Challenge!

Clerk: Mr Pratt, will you leave the jury box and will John Stevens take his place in the box and take the oath.

(Note: the defence counsel has the right to make three peremptory challenges in this manner, i e objecting to individual jurors without being required to give reasons. Another member of the panel will be called to replace the juror and the process of swearing-in continues.)

Juror 12: . . . true verdict according to the evidence.

Judge: The jurors who have not been called can be released.

Clerk: Members of the jury, you are all sworn. The defendant Oliver Twist stands charged in an indictment which contains two counts. In the first count he is charged with taking a conveyance contrary to section 12 of the Theft Act 1968 the particulars of the offence being that he, on the 19th day of April 1986, without the consent of the owner or other lawful authority, took a conveyance, namely a Ford Escort motor car registration number PRX 124V, for his own use. In the second count he is charged with burglary contrary to section 9(1)(b) of the Theft Act 1968 the particulars being that he, on the 19th day of April 1986, having entered as a trespasser a building known as 136 Lindum Road, Romford in the London Borough of Havering, stole therein £15 in cash and it is your charge, members of the jury, having heard the evidence to say on each count whether he be guilty or not guilty.

Judge: Very well, let the defendant sit down. Yes, Mr Stryver.

Counsel for the Prosecution: May it please you, your Honour, members of the jury, I appear in this case for the prosecution and my learned friend, Mr Sydney Carton represents the defendant. You have just heard, members of the jury, that this young man, Oliver Twist, faces two charges. The first count or charge accuses him of taking a car that didn't belong to him. The second count charges him with burglary. It is now my task to explain to you what the prosecution seek to prove against Mr Twist but, before I do so, let me tell you straight away – because it's of the greatest importance that you remember this – that in this case, as in every criminal trial in this country, it is for the prosecution to prove the case against the defendant and prove the case so that you are satisfied that you feel sure of guilt. If at the end of the day you are left in doubt, then you acquit the defendant. And one other thing, the defendant faces an indictment charging two counts: it is only fair and right that you should consider the evidence on each count quite separately . . . *(Counsel then goes on to outline the evidence on each charge to the jury and to explain how such evidence if accepted is proof of guilt.)* . . . Well, members of the jury, those are the facts of the case and I've explained to you why if you find those facts proved the prosecution say the defendant is guilty on both counts. And now, with his Honour's permission, I shall call the evidence before you. Call Elsie Snagsby.

Usher: Mrs Snagsby, will you take the Book in your right hand and read the words on the card.

E Snagsby: I swear by Almighty God that the evidence I shall give shall be the truth, the whole truth and nothing but the truth.

Counsel for the Prosecution: Is your full name Elsie Snagsby and do you live at 36 Jordans Road, Romford?

E Snagsby: Yes, that's right.

Counsel for the Prosecution: And do you run a newsagents shop in Romford?

E Snagsby: Yes sir, in Lindum Road.

Counsel for the Prosecution: Now Mrs Snagsby, I want you to take your mind back to April this year. Do you remember Saturday, 19 April?

E Snagsby: The nineteenth?

Counsel for the Prosecution: Yes.

E Snagsby: No.

Counsel for the Prosecution: Let me put it another way, do you remember a night something happened at the shop?

E Snagsby: Oh, was that the nineteenth?

Counsel for the Defence: As far as the defence are concerned there is no dispute that somebody broke into Mrs Snagsby's shop on 19 April – the issue is going to be identity – so I have no objections if my learned friend leads Mrs Snagsby on these preliminary matters.

Judge: Well that's very helpful. Then you can take it fairly shortly Mr Stryver.

Counsel for the Prosecution: I'm much obliged. Mrs Snagsby, I think you locked up your shop at about quarter past six on that Saturday but went back just before eleven o'clock to get your account books.

E Snagsby: That's right.

Counsel for the Prosecution: And when you got back did you find that a pane of glass had been broken in the door?

E Snagsby: Yes.

Judge: Was that the front or back door?

E Snagsby: The back door, your Honour.

Counsel for the Prosecution: Did you go inside?

E Snagsby: Yes, I went into the back room.

Counsel for the Prosecution: Did you hear anything?

E Snagsby: There was someone in the shop front.

Counsel for the Prosecution: What did you do?

E Snagsby: I opened the door and saw a man trying to unlock the front door.

Counsel for the Prosecution: And I think he turned round when he heard you.

Counsel for the Defence: Well really. I do hope my concession that my friend can lead on matters not in dispute isn't going to be abused.

Judge: Yes. Mr Stryver I think you had better be careful not to lead on anything which could relate to identification.

Counsel for the Prosecution: If your Honour pleases. Tell us what happened, Mrs Snagsby, when you opened the door.

E Snagsby: He turned round and rushed past me – he pushed me out of the way – I came over all funny – I just had to sit down.

Judge: It must have been a very frightening experience madam?

E Snagsby: It was, my Lord – I wake up thinking about it at night.

Counsel for the Prosecution: What was the next thing that happened?

E Snagsby: I heard a car outside and went to the window.

Counsel for the Prosecution: What did you see?

E Snagsby: I saw a car.

Counsel for the Prosecution: Were you able to see the car distinctly?

E Snagsby: Yes it was parked opposite – I saw a man jump in and the car drive off.

Counsel for the Prosecution: Could you tell us what sort of car it was, Mrs Snagsby?

E Snagsby: Oh yes, it was like my son's.

Counsel for the Prosecution: What sort of car has he got?

E Snagsby: It's a Ford.

Counsel for the Prosecution: Do you know what type?

E Snagsby: Oh yes – it's a Cortina.

Counsel for the Prosecution: Are you sure?

Counsel for the Defence: Really, your Honour, my friend seems to be proposing to cross-examine this witness.

Judge: Well of course it's very easy to make mistakes about car types.

Counsel for the Defence: In my submission that is neither here nor there. I want to make it quite clear that I object on behalf of the defendant to any attempt by the prosecution to cross-examine their own witnesses.

Judge: Yes thank you Mr Carton, I am familiar with the basic rules of questioning. Mr Stryver, I think you had better leave this point.

(What has happened is that prosecuting counsel has received an answer from Elsie Snagsby on a crucial point – the type of car outside – which contradicts her original statement to the police. In such a case counsel calling the witness is not allowed to refer his own witness to her original statement – he simply must accept the answer he has received. Counsel for the defence quite rightly objected to prosecuting counsel's attempt to put the question a second time to Elsie and the judge should have upheld the objection at once – without himself making the gratuitous comment suggesting Elsie might have made a mistake.)

Counsel for the Prosecution: What happened to the car?

E Snagsby: It drove off down the road.

Counsel for the Prosecution: What did you do then?

E Snagsby: I went and phoned the police and they came ever so quickly. I was most impressed.

Counsel for the Prosecution: Was anything missing?

E Snagsby: Yes, the bureau had been opened and three five pound notes had been taken from the cash box.

Counsel for the Prosecution: Now while you were looking around, did you happen to find something?

E Snagsby: You mean the glove?

Counsel for the Prosecution: Did you find a glove?

E Snagsby: I just said I did.

Counsel for the Prosecution: Your Honour, could the witness be shown the exhibit?

E Snagsby (shown a glove): That's it – that's the one.

Counsel for the Prosecution: You recognise it?

E Snagsby: Yes.

Judge: Let that be marked 'exhibit one'.

Counsel for the Prosecution: Did you go down with the police to Romford Police Station?

E Snagsby: Yes.

Counsel for the Prosecution: Do you remember seeing anybody at the police station?

E Snagsby: Oh yes, I saw the burglar – the accused.

Counsel for the Prosecution: For the sake of the transcript I should indicate that Mrs Snagsby has pointed to the defendant.

E Snagsby: Yes, that's right, it was him – there couldn't be any doubt about it.

(Now it is the turn of defence counsel to cross-examine the witness. The whole point of this exercise is to show that Mrs Snagsby could be mistaken in the very positive identification she has now made of the defendant as being the intruder in her shop. Notice that whilst prosecuting counsel was not allowed to correct the witness by reference to her earlier statement, the rule is reversed in cross-examination. Indeed one of the standard techniques of cross-examining is to discredit the witness by showing how the evidence given in court conflicts with what the witness has said earlier. We return to the trial as counsel begins to deal with the identification point.)

Counsel for the Defence: Mrs Snagsby, did you put the light on in the back room?

E Snagsby: No sir.

Counsel for the Defence: Was the light on in the front room?

E Snagsby: No sir.

Counsel for the Defence: Of course the whole incident in your shop was over in a very short time wasn't it?

E Snagsby: Yes sir.

Counsel for the Defence: A matter of seconds would you say?

E Snagsby: I don't know sir.

Counsel for the Defence: It was dark in the shop front wasn't it?

E Snagsby: No, there was a street lamp outside.

Counsel for the Defence: When you opened the door he turned round?

E Snagsby: Yes.

Counsel for the Defence: So the light would have been behind him?

E Snagsby: I don't remember.

Counsel for the Defence: But it's obvious isn't it?

E Snagsby: I suppose so.

Counsel for the Defence: And the moment he saw you he rushed past you?

E Snagsby: Yes, and pushed me out of the way.

Counsel for the Defence: And all this took a matter of seconds?

E Snagsby: I shall never forget it.

Counsel for the Defence: Of course not. And it was a very frightening and upsetting experience.

E Snagsby: Yes, it was.

Counsel for the Defence: The young man you saw at the police station – had you ever seen him before that evening?

E Snagsby: No.

Counsel for the Defence: And of course when you were at the police station all you said was that the defendant looked *like* the man you'd glimpsed in the shop front.

E Snagsby: Oh no, there was no doubt about it – I was quite certain that he *was* the man.

Counsel for the Defence: Do you remember making a written statement to the police, Mrs Snagsby, a couple of days after the incident?

E Snagsby: Yes I think I did.

Counsel for the Defence: Your Honour, perhaps the witness could be shown the statement.

(At this stage the Clerk of the Court takes the original statement signed by Mrs Snagsby from the bundle of committal papers sent up to the Crown Court from the magistrates' court.)

Counsel for the Defence: Would you look at the statement Mrs Snagsby. Is it signed by you?

E Snagsby: Yes.

Counsel for the Defence: And is there a declaration at the top stating that it is true?

E Snagsby: Yes.

Counsel for the Defence: Would you read out loud the last two sentences.

E Snagsby (reading): 'On Sunday, 20 April, I was at Romford Police Station when I saw a man I now know to be Oliver Twist. He looks' – oh yes, I see.

Counsel for the Defence: Will you carry on please Mrs Snagsby.

E Snagsby: '. . . he looks like the man I saw in my shop'.

Counsel for the Defence: You see Mrs Snagsby what you said at the time was that the defendant was *like* the man you'd seen, not *was* the man.

E Snagsby: It is him. I'm sure of it. The statement is wrong. . . .

(Counsel for the Defence concludes his cross-examination. Counsel for the Prosecution may then re-examine his witness, i e question the witness upon any matters arising out of the cross-examination.)

Counsel for the Prosecution: When you were at the police station you saw the defendant?

E Snagsby: Yes.

Counsel for the Prosecution: What were you doing when you saw him?

E Snagsby: I was waiting for the CID officer who was taking particulars about my case.

Counsel for the Prosecution: What did you do?

E Snagsby: I went straight over to the desk sergeant and I said . . .

Counsel for the Defence: I really must object.

Judge: Would the defendant have heard what you said to the sergeant, madam?

E Snagsby: Oh no – he was on the other side of the room.

Judge: Then, Mr Stryver, we can't have what the lady told the sergeant – or what the sergeant said – it's obviously hearsay.

Counsel for the Prosecution: If your Honour pleases.

Judge: I take it that concludes your re-examination?

Counsel for the Prosecution: Your Honour, yes.

Judge: Then unless either counsel has any objection I propose to release Mrs Snagsby. Thank you for coming, madam.

Counsel for the Prosecution: Your Honour, perhaps at this stage the statement of Mr Anthony Jobling could be read to the jury.

Judge: Yes. Members of the jury, the Clerk is going to read to you now the evidence of Mr Jobling. Now his evidence is not disputed, and so to save time and the nuisance of making Mr Jobling come here to tell us something that is accepted by both sides, the Defence allow this evidence to be read to you in the form of a written statement. But I must tell you that you pay just as much attention to it as if he had come here and given the evidence orally. Very well.

Clerk: The statement of Anthony Jobling, aged 20 who lives at 28 Acacia Gardens, Ilford, and who says after the usual declaration: 'On Saturday, 19 April . . .' (*The Clerk now reads aloud to the jury the evidence of Mr Jobling that his car was taken from the Regal Cinema in Barking on the evening of 19 April.*)

Clerk: Your Honour, that is the statement of Mr Jobling.

Judge: Thank you, Mr Clerk.

Counsel for the Prosecution: Your Honour, the next witness will be Detective Sergeant Dixon, but before he gives evidence there are certain legal matters upon which we would wish to seek your ruling.

Judge: Yes, and no doubt this wouldn't really concern the jury.

Counsel for the Prosecution: Your Honour, no.

Judge: Very well, members of the jury, I am going to ask you to go to your private room while I discuss certain legal questions with counsel.

(*Now the jury are escorted out of court. What has happened is that the Defence have already told the Prosecution that they are going to object to part of the police evidence on the grounds that it is inadmissible. This is a legal matter which the Judge must decide alone. It would be a pointless exercise if, although the judge was to exclude the evidence, the jury had already heard the evidence in question in the course of the argument.*)

Judge: Yes, Mr Carton. You are going to object to something in the officer's evidence?

Counsel for the Defence: Your Honour, I object to the whole of the evidence of the conversation between this officer and the defendant at the police station.

Judge: Now let me see. Just where does that appear in the statement?

Counsel for the Defence: It's on the second page your honour, about two lines down. It's the passage beginning 'At the police station . . .'

Judge: Ah yes, and it deals with the interview after Mrs Snagsby has identified the defendant.

Counsel for the Defence: Yes.

Judge: I see. Well what is the nature of the objection?

Counsel for the Defence: My objection is quite simply that there has been a complete failure to comply with the Code of Practice.

Judge: You mean the defendant wasn't cautioned?

Counsel for the Defence: Yes, certainly that is my first objection but it goes further than that because, so far as the charge relating to the car is concerned, the defendant shouldn't have been asked any questions in any event. By the time he was in the interview room the police had decided to charge him – the statement specifically says that he was going to be charged – and I would submit that it's a general principle that once the police have decided to prefer a charge they must stop the process of interrogation so far as *that* charge is concerned.

Judge: What is your authority for that?

Counsel for the Defence: If your Honour would look at paragraph 11.2 of the Code [*reads*]: 'As soon as a police officer who is making enquiries of any person about an offence believes that a prosecution should be brought against him and that there is sufficient evidence for it to succeed, he shall without delay cease to question him. And your Honour will see paragraph 17.5 provides that questions relating to an offence may not be put to a person after he has been charged.

Judge: I suppose you would say that a police officer can't get out of paragraph 17 by simply delaying the process of charging the defendant.

Counsel for the Defence: If I may say so, your Honour has put the point exactly. And your Honour there is authority under the Judges' Rules (which were to the same effect as the new Code) in the case of *Conway v Hotten* which is reported in the second volume of the All England Reports for 1976 at page 216.

Judge: Do I have a copy?

Counsel for the Defence: I took the precaution of asking the clerk to have it sent down from the library. *(The report is handed up to the judge.)*

Judge: Yes, of course the facts of that case are very different.

Counsel for the Defence: I respectfully agree but I wish to refer to the judgment of Mr Justice Watkins at page 219 as authority for the general proposition that questioning after the accused has been told that it has been decided to charge him is a breach of the Rules.

Judge: Even if that was so, the learned judge makes it quite clear that a mere breach of the Rules (and the same must apply to the Code) doesn't render the statement inadmissible – the issue at the end of the day is still whether there was anything oppressive in the conduct of the police or anything which might have stopped this being a voluntary statement.

Counsel for the Defence: That is correct but I would submit that where, as here, one has two quite clear breaches of the Code – questioning in breach of paragraph 17 and the complete absence of any caution, the conduct of the questioning has departed so far from the practice required by the Code that this evidence should be excluded.

Judge: I needn't trouble you Mr Stryver. If, and I make no specific finding, the questioning here was in breach of the Code, I am quite satisfied that the breaches were technical. The defendant had been cautioned earlier and the questioning relating to the car arose quite naturally out of the new matter that has arisen – the burglary investigation. I can see no grounds for excluding this evidence. Very well, let the jury be brought back into court.

(The jury return to their places in the jury box.)

Counsel for the Prosecution: Detective Sergeant George Dixon.

Dixon: I swear by Almighty God that the evidence I shall give shall be the truth, the whole truth and nothing but the truth. George Dixon, Detective Sergeant, Romford CID your Honour.

Counsel for the Prosecution: Sergeant, on 20 April this year did you have occasion to go to a cafe at the Romford roundabout on the A13 Southend road?

Dixon: Yes, your Honour.

Counsel for the Prosecution: Were you alone?

Dixon: No sir, I was accompanied by Detective Constable Bucket.

Counsel for the Prosecution: What happened when you arrived at the cafe?

Dixon (producing a note book and reading directly from it): Parked outside the cafe
I saw a Ford Escort motor car registration number PRX 124V . . .

Counsel for the Prosecution: Just one moment sergeant. I see you are referring
to some notes. When were those notes made up?

Dixon: As soon as possible after the event, sir.

Judge: Yes, but when was that?

Dixon: That would have been within half an hour of the defendant being
charged, your Honour.

Counsel for the Prosecution: So were the events recorded when fresh in your
memory?

Dixon: Yes sir.

Counsel for the Prosecution: Then I would ask that the officer be allowed to use
his notes.

Judge: Yes, very well. Sergeant you may refer to your note book to refresh
your memory.

*(This exchange almost always occurs when a police officer is called as a witness since he
will invariably give evidence by reading directly to the jury the notes he wrote out after the
events recorded had occurred. The general rule is, of course, that a witness is not allowed
to read a prepared statement to the jury. In practice an exception to this rule is made in the
case of the police by the fiction that the officer is not reading a prepared statement but
simply referring to notes to 'refresh his memory'. Normally the officer proceeds to read his
notes more or less directly to the jury at this stage. However, since Dixon's note if
unexpurgated would make it clear that he knew Oliver very well (and hence the jury could
infer that Oliver had been in previous trouble) counsel for the prosecution has agreed with
the defence to intervene whenever a passage occurs which would show that Dixon knew
Oliver.)*

Counsel for the Prosecution: I think, Sergeant, you went into the cafe.

Dixon: Yes sir.

Counsel for the Prosecution: And I think the defendant was in the cafe.

Dixon: Yes sir.

Counsel for the Prosecution: What did you do?

Dixon: I went over to him, introduced myself and said 'We would like to
have a word with you about the Escort outside'. The defendant said
'What Escort?' Detective Constable Bucket said to him 'The car that
was nicked outside the Regal in Barking'. The defendant said 'What's it
got to do with me?' I said 'How did you get here?' The defendant said 'I
got a lift from my mate Ginger'. I said 'Where is he now?' Twist said 'I've
no idea'. DC Bucket then said to the defendant 'Where do you live?'
Twist said 'In Colletts Row'. I said to him 'But that is over six miles
away'.

Counsel for the Prosecution: Can you just help us on that point, sergeant? Is
there a bus service at that time of night?

Dixon: No sir.

Counsel for the Prosecution: Thank you, go on officer.

Dixon (continuing to read from his note): I said to him 'How are you going to get
home?' He said 'Would you be going my way?'

Counsel for the Prosecution: I think you then told him that you were arresting
him for stealing the Escort, and cautioned him.

Dixon: Yes sir.

Judge: Just one moment. When you cautioned him, what exactly did you say?

Dixon: I said 'You do not have to say anything unless you wish to do so but what you say may be given in evidence'.

Judge: So you let him know what his rights were?

Dixon: Yes, your Honour.

Judge: Yes, thank you very much, sergeant.

Counsel for the Prosecution: Did he make any reply to the caution?

Dixon: He said 'You think you are so clever – you prove it'.

Judge: Oh, that was his answer was it, sergeant?

Dixon: Yes, your Honour.

Judge: I see.

Counsel for the Prosecution: I think the defendant was then taken to Romford Police Station.

Dixon: Yes sir.

Counsel for the Prosecution: Shortly after you arrived at the police station did you have a conversation with a lady called Mrs Snagsby?

Dixon: Yes sir.

Counsel for the Prosecution: And as a result of what she told you, did you speak to the defendant?

Dixon: Yes sir.

Counsel for the Prosecution: What did you say to him?

Dixon (reading from his note book): I said 'What can you tell me about a burglary at Lindum Road, earlier tonight?' He said 'Leave off, Mr Dixon, I haven't done no burglary'. I said 'But the lady outside has recognised you as the man who broke into her shop'. He said 'She must be some kind of nut'. I then said to him: 'Where had you been before you went to the cafe?' He said 'I'd been down the disco in Market Street'.

Judge: Would that be in Romford?

Dixon: Yes, your Honour.

Counsel for the Prosecution: What did you say then?

Dixon: I said 'But it was closed last week for redecoration'. He said 'Oh I must have made a mistake'. I said 'It's obvious to me you stole the car and used it for the burglary at Lindum Road'. He said 'Alright I nicked the car but I didn't do the old girl's shop'.

Counsel for the Prosecution: I think you then told the defendant you proposed to conduct a formal interview but, as was his right, he declined to answer further questions.

Dixon: Yes sir.

Counsel for the Prosecution: Did you show the defendant this glove (*holds up exhibit*)?

Dixon: Yes sir. He agreed to try it on and it fitted.

Counsel for the Prosecution: Was any glove found in the Escort?

Dixon: No sir.

(It is now the turn of defence counsel to cross-examine the officer. He must challenge the evidence Dixon has given that, at the police station, Oliver admitted taking the motor car. Of course, what Oliver is really saying is that Dixon has made up this admission. Counsel however cannot put this allegation of fabrication directly to the police witness because if he does so the judge will rule this to be an attack on the character of the witness and may then allow the prosecution to cross-examine Oliver about previous convictions. (See Criminal Evidence Act 1898 discussed at p 144 below.) In order to challenge the police evidence without losing the advantage that the jury do not know Oliver has been in trouble before, counsel adopts the technique of putting to the officer that he is wrong in his

evidence without alleging fabrication. This device may prevent the accused losing the protection of the Act although it adds a certain air of unreality to the proceedings. Note that before reaching this point in the cross-examination, counsel has also to challenge the police record of what was said by Oliver at the cafe because he has instructions that the evidence of his conversation has been wrongly recorded and it is his duty to put to the witness every point of substance which will be challenged in the defendant's evidence.)

Counsel for the Defence: At what time did you arrive at the cafe, sergeant?

Dixon: Five to one, sir.

Counsel for the Defence: And at what time did you get back to the police station?

Dixon: About one fifteen, sir.

Counsel for the Defence: And when was the defendant charged?

Dixon: At three o'clock sir *(consulting his note book).*

Counsel for the Defence: So the notes you've been reading out were made at about three o'clock in the morning.

Dixon: Yes, that would be about right.

Counsel for the Defence: If we deal with the conversation in the cafe first, the notes would have been made up two hours after the conversation had occurred.

Dixon: Yes.

Counsel for the Defence: Because you didn't make up any notes at the time, did you sergeant?

Dixon: You mean at the cafe, sir?

Counsel for the Defence: Yes.

Dixon: No, I didn't.

Counsel for the Defence: Now you are not saying that the note made at the police station is a *verbatim* record of what occurred at the cafe?

Dixon: I don't understand you sir. *(He does.)*

Counsel for the Defence: Well I'm suggesting you may have left things out – you couldn't reproduce word for word two hours later what was said in the cafe.

Dixon: What was said in the cafe is written down in my note book, sir.

Counsel for the Defence: Yes, but when you came to write out your notes I suggest you forgot some of the things that were said. You see I'm instructed the defendant told you whilst you were at the cafe that he had been drinking with his friends at a public house in Romford called 'The Ilford Arms'.

Dixon: That's not in my note, sir.

Counsel for the Defence: Exactly, I suggest you forgot that when you were making up your note book.

Dixon: No sir, if he had said that it would be in the note book.

Counsel for the Defence: You don't make mistakes sergeant?

Dixon: If it had been said it would have been in my note.

(Counsel goes on to put other points of difference between Oliver's recollection of what was said and the police evidence. He then turns to the alleged admission in the police station.)

Counsel for the Defence: Now whilst you were at the police station there came a time when you started questioning the defendant about the burglary at Lindum Road?

Dixon: Yes.

Counsel for the Defence: And he emphatically denied that he had anything to do with the burglary?

Dixon: He denied it, yes.

Counsel for the Defence: And you asked him to explain his movements that evening?

Dixon: Yes.

Counsel for the Defence: He said he went to the discotheque in Market Street.

Dixon: I told him that was rubbish – it had been closed down because of the decorators.

Counsel for the Defence: Exactly – and without giving him any proper chance to explain you told him he was a liar and that it was obvious to you that he had stolen the car.

Dixon (reading from his note): He said 'Oh I must have made a mistake'.

Counsel for the Defence: I suggest what he started to say was that he and his friends had made a mistake because they'd forgotten the disco was closed and you then interrupted him without giving him a chance to tell you what they then did.

Dixon: No sir.

Counsel for the Defence: And you said to the defendant 'You nicked the car and did the burglary' and he said 'Alright you think what you like'.

Dixon: No sir, he said 'I nicked the car but I didn't do the old girl's shop'.

Counsel for the Defence: I suggest you made a mistake when sometime later you came to write out your note. You may think he was admitting taking the car but all he was actually saying was that you could think what you liked.

Dixon: No sir.

Counsel for the Defence: You are saying this defendant suddenly confessed his guilt to you officer?

Dixon: Yes.

Counsel for the Defence: And yet you asked him no further questions about the matter?

Dixon: I don't understand.

Counsel for the Defence: Well weren't you interested to know whether he had taken the car by himself or with other people?

Dixon: I would have been.

Counsel for the Defence: Well why didn't you ask him that?

Dixon: I don't know.

Counsel for the Defence: And didn't you ask him how he managed to get into the car?

Dixon: No sir.

Counsel for the Defence: But surely if this man had admitted his guilt to you you'd want to know this sort of thing?

Dixon: I had a fair idea already, sir.

(After Dixon has concluded his evidence his colleague, Detective Constable Bucket, is called by the prosecution and gives identical evidence to Dixon. In cross-examination the same challenges are put to him. He freely admits his notes are identical with Dixon's because they wrote them out together. This is in fact common police practice although of course it may have the effect of perpetuating any mistake that has been made. After Bucket's evidence, counsel for the prosecution formally closes his case.)

Counsel for the Prosecution: Your Honour, that is the case for the prosecution.

Counsel for the Defence: Your Honour, at this stage I have certain legal submissions to put to your Honour relating to the second count on the indictment – the charge of burglary.

Judge: Yes, and since this of course is a matter of law it doesn't really concern the jury, so, members of the jury, I am going to ask you once again to retire to your private room while I discuss these legal questions with counsel.

(The jury retire.)

Counsel for the Defence: I would respectfully submit that your Honour should direct the jury to acquit the defendant on the second count on the indictment because the evidence which has been adduced is so unsatisfactory that no reasonable jury could convict.

Judge: The issue is entirely one of identification isn't it?

Counsel for the Defence: Yes. And the evidence is of a momentary sighting of a person the witness had never seen before. Your Honour will of course be familiar with the recent guidelines laid down by the Court of Appeal in the case of *Turnbull*?

Judge: Yes of course – let me just see. What paragraph in *Archbold*?

Counsel for the Defence: Your Honour will see at para 14-2 it says 'When . . . the quality of the identifying evidence was poor, as for example, when it depended solely on a fleeting glance . . . the judge should then withdraw the case from the jury and direct an acquittal unless there was other evidence which went to support the correctness of identification'.

Judge: So the question here is whether there is other evidence which backs up Mrs Snagsby's identification of the defendant? And you of course say there isn't Mr Carton?

Counsel for the Defence: Yes, your Honour.

Judge: What do you say about this Mr Stryver?

Counsel for the Prosecution: Your Honour, the prosecution take the view that it's open to the jury, in the absence at the moment of any satisfactory explanation by the defendant as to where he was at the material time, to accept Mrs Snagsby's evidence. In my submission it's of considerable significance that the identification in this case took place only a very short time after the commission of the offence. There is, of course, in addition, for what it's worth, the fact that the burglar left a glove behind which fitted the defendant.

Judge: I see the force of what you are saying, Mr Stryver, but I think following as best I can the guidelines laid down by the Court of Appeal in *Turnbull* this is the sort of case where the identification is suspect and there simply isn't sufficient corroborative evidence to justify leaving the matter to the jury. Very well, we had better have the jury back.

(The jury return to court.)

Judge: Members of the jury; in your absence I have discussed with counsel the state of the evidence on the second count – that is the burglary charge. I have come to the conclusion that as a matter of law the evidence of identification given by Mrs Snagsby – which is substantially all the evidence comes to on that charge – just isn't satisfactory. So I intend to direct you at the end of the trial to return a formal verdict of not guilty on that charge. That means that from now on in this case we are only going to be concerned with the first count – the charge of taking the motor car. Yes, very well Mr Carton.

Counsel for the Defence: Your Honour, I will call the defendant straight away.

(Oliver is sworn and proceeds to give evidence of his name and address and then counsel starts to ask him about his account of the evening of 19 April.)

Counsel for the Defence: What time did you go out that evening?
Oliver: About half past seven.
Counsel for the Defence: Where did you go?
Oliver: I went down Romford.
Counsel for the Defence: Did you meet anyone when you got to Romford?
Oliver: Yes, I met Ginger Peterson.
Counsel for the Defence: Is he a friend of yours?
Oliver: Yes.
Counsel for the Defence: What did you do?
Oliver: We decided to go to the disco in Market Street.
Counsel for the Defence: Did you go there?
Oliver: Yes, but it was closed.
Counsel for the Defence: What did you do then?
Oliver: We went over to the pub on the corner of Market Street.
Counsel for the Defence: Is that 'The Ilford Arms'?
Oliver: Yes.
Counsel for the Defence: How long did you stay there?
Oliver: Until eleven o'clock – we left at closing time.
Counsel for the Defence: Where did you go then?
Oliver: To the Wimpy in Station Road.
Counsel for the Defence: Did you meet anyone there?
Oliver: Ginger's girlfriend, Judy Smallweed.
Counsel for the Defence: What happened then?
Oliver: We had a milkshake . . .
Counsel for the Defence: Let me put it another way . . . did there come a time when you left the Wimpy Bar?
Oliver: Yes.
Counsel for the Defence: Where did you go?
Oliver: We went back to Ginger's car.
Counsel for the Defence: And where did you go?
Oliver: Well, we were going to go down to Rayleigh.
Counsel for the Defence: That is near Southend?
Oliver: Yes – we were going to see Judy's sister.
Counsel for the Defence: Did you stop on the way?
Oliver: Yes, we stopped at Meg's Cafe.
Counsel for the Defence: Was there a conversation in the cafe?
Oliver: Yes – Ginger and Judy were going to spend the night at Rayleigh but I decided I wanted to go home.
Counsel for the Defence: How were you going to get home?
Oliver: I would have hitched a lift.
Counsel for the Defence: Did the other two leave?
Oliver: Yes, I stayed and had another coffee.
Counsel for the Defence: And were you still in the cafe when the police arrived?

Oliver: Yes. Mr Dixon and another officer.
Counsel for the Defence: What did they say to you?
Oliver: Dixon said I had nicked an Escort that had been left outside the cafe.
Counsel for the Defence: What did you say?
Oliver: I told him I didn't know nothing about any Escort.
Counsel for the Defence: Did he ask you where you'd been?
Oliver: Yes and I said I'd been drinking down Romford and I told him that Ginger had dropped me off at the cafe.
Counsel for the Defence: Did he ask you how you were going to get home?
Oliver: Yes.
Counsel for the Defence: And did you say 'Are you going my way'?
Oliver: Yes – you see I knew I hadn't done anything so I was a bit cheeky.
Counsel for the Defence: And at that stage the officer arrested you?
Oliver: Yes.

(Counsel then goes on to deal with the interview between Dixon and Oliver at the police station.)

Counsel for the Defence: Did he ask you to explain where you'd been that evening?
Oliver: Yes.
Counsel for the Defence: What did you say?
Oliver: I started to tell him how we went down to the disco but he shut me up. He said, 'Don't give me that, I know the disco has been closed down'. He said he knew I'd nicked the car. So I said – because he wasn't going to listen to me – 'Alright clever, you think what you like'.
Counsel for the Defence: Did the sergeant at any time invite you to take part in a formal interview with the questions and answers written down?
Oliver: Yes – but I said I wasn't going to make any statement until I had seen my lawyer.

(Counsel for the prosecution now cross-examines Oliver. He has to try to break down Oliver's alibi – ie his assertion that he was in Romford when the car was stolen in Barking. He will have had advance warning of where Oliver says he was because of the 'notice of alibi' served by Oliver's solicitors after the committal but he will have no idea of the detail of Oliver's case. We rejoin the case at one of the key points in his attack.)

Counsel for the Prosecution: When did you decide to go to Rayleigh?
Oliver: When we were in the Wimpy Bar.
Counsel for the Prosecution: To see Judy's sister?
Oliver: Yes.
Counsel for the Prosecution: Did you know Judy well?
Oliver: She was Ginger's girlfriend.
Counsel for the Prosecution: Did you know her well?
Oliver: Not very well.
Counsel for the Prosecution: Is she coming here today?
Oliver: No.
Counsel for the Prosecution: What time did you plan on arriving in Rayleigh?
Oliver: I don't know.
Counsel for the Prosecution: But think Mr Twist – it would take about forty-five minutes from Romford wouldn't it?
Oliver: I dare say.

Counsel for the Prosecution: And of course you stopped at Meg's Cafe at half past twelve?

Oliver: Yes.

Counsel for the Prosecution: So you would have arrived at Rayleigh at about half past one?

Oliver: Yes.

Counsel for the Prosecution: Did Judy's sister know you were coming?

Oliver: No.

Counsel for the Prosecution: How well did you know Judy's sister?

Oliver: I'd met her.

Counsel for the Prosecution: How often?

Oliver: Once or twice.

Counsel for the Prosecution: Did it occur to you she might not be very happy to see you on her doorstep in the middle of the night?

Oliver: I don't know.

Counsel for the Prosecution: Were you going to stay at Rayleigh?

Oliver: We hadn't decided.

Counsel for the Prosecution: You were going to turn up in the middle of the night and expect this lady to put you up?

Oliver: Something like that.

Counsel for the Prosecution: This is just nonsense isn't it? You went to the cafe in the Escort?

Oliver: No.

Counsel for the Prosecution: Why didn't you tell Detective Sergeant Dixon you and Ginger were going down to Rayleigh?

Oliver: I did.

(After Oliver has finished giving evidence, counsel for the defence calls Ginger Peterson to confirm Oliver's story. Notice that while counsel for the prosecution could not question Oliver so as to disclose his previous convictions, the prohibition does not apply to defence witnesses. We resume at the point where prosecuting counsel is cross-examining Ginger.)

Counsel for the Prosecution: You remember fairly clearly the events of 19 April?

Ginger: Yeah.

Counsel for the Prosecution: Going to the public house and then to the Wimpy Bar and then down to Rayleigh.

Ginger: That's right.

Counsel for the Prosecution: What day of the week was it?

Ginger: Wednesday.

Counsel for the Prosecution: You're sure of that?

Ginger: Yeah.

Counsel for the Prosecution: How are you so sure?

Ginger: Because I signed on on Thursday – so I had to be back from Rayleigh next morning.

Counsel for the Prosecution: Would it surprise you Mr Peterson, if I told you that the incident we are concerned with in this court took place in the evening of Saturday, 19 April and the early hours of Sunday, 20 April?

Ginger: Oh, yes.

Counsel for the Prosecution: But the night you met Oliver was a Wednesday night wasn't it?

Ginger: No, I must have got it wrong. I remember now – it was the weekend.

Counsel for the Prosecution: When were you first asked to make a statement, Mr Peterson?

Ginger: About a month ago.

Counsel for the Prosecution: Did you discuss the case with Mr Twist after he was arrested?

Ginger: No.

Counsel for the Prosecution: So it came as a complete surprise to you when you were asked to give a statement?

Ginger: You could say that.

Counsel for the Prosecution: And of course you were prepared to say anything that would help your friend?

Ginger: No.

Counsel for the Prosecution: I suggest that you didn't spend Saturday evening in Romford with Mr Twist at all, did you?

Ginger: I did.

Counsel for the Prosecution: You've been in trouble with the police yourself for taking cars haven't you?

Ginger: What do you mean by that?

Counsel for the Prosecution: Only last year you were sent to a detention centre for taking somebody else's car, weren't you?

Ginger: That's got nothing to do with this case . . .

(After Ginger's evidence, the defence case is closed. The next stage is for counsel to address the jury. The prosecution go first – they say that the evidence points to Oliver's guilt beyond a doubt and that his explanation of his presence in the cafe where the car was parked is really beyond belief. Then the defence – who always have the last word – say that the case is not proven beyond all reasonable doubt – there remains the very real possibility that Oliver and Ginger have been telling the truth and that Dixon simply got it wrong what Oliver was saying at the police station. We return to the trial as the Judge begins to sum up to the jury.)

Judge: Members of the jury, you have had the advantage of hearing counsel on both sides. Now it's my turn to sum up to you. Let me begin by explaining our different functions. You alone are the sole judges of fact. It may be that I shall express some view to you about the facts: if I do, you are entirely free to disregard it if you disagree with it – because you are the only people who decide the facts.

On the other hand, it is my job to rule on all the legal questions which have arisen in this case and you must accept the law as I tell it to you. If I am wrong, I can be put right by the Court of Appeal. So let me say just once more – questions of fact are for you, but on questions of law you accept my ruling.

We are only concerned now with one charge against the defendant. You will recall that I have withdrawn the charge of burglary from you – so you put out of your minds entirely in considering the case the evidence which went to that charge. The charge you have to consider is the count which charges Mr Twist with taking a conveyance. Now this is an offence under section 12 of the Theft Act – the offence is committed where a person – and I now read to you from the statute – 'without having the consent of the owner or other lawful authority, takes a conveyance for his own or another's use . . .'. In this case there is no dispute that someone took Mr Jobling's Ford Escort from the Regal Cinema car park in Barking on the evening of Saturday, 19 April last year. And there is no dispute whatever that the Escort was found in the early hours of Sunday morning at the cafe on the roundabout on the Southend road – or for that matter, that the accused was in the cafe drinking a cup of coffee. The issue in the case is whether this accused was the person who took that car from the cinema car park. That is the question you have to decide.

And I must tell you now – as counsel have already told you – that the onus is on the prosecution to prove that the defendant took the car and to prove it beyond all reasonable doubt – or, to put it another way, to satisfy you so that you feel sure this is the man who took the car. Now it's my task to remind you of the evidence. . .

(The learned Judge then proceeds to summarise the evidence given on both sides reading from the longhand notes he has taken as the witnesses were giving evidence.)

. . . The defendant gave evidence. He didn't have to give evidence – an accused man is entitled to remain silent and in effect say to the prosecution – 'you have brought this charge against me: now you prove it'. But since Mr Twist chose to give evidence on oath, the prosecution were entitled to cross-examine him. You must pay most careful attention to what he said. He explains his presence at the cafe after midnight miles away from home without transport by saying that he had arrived there en route for Rayleigh (which, as I think you know is near Southend). He says he originally intended to call in the middle of the night with his friend Peterson and a young woman called Judy on an unannounced visit to Judy's sister – who he had met, he says, once or twice before. Well, members of the jury, it's a matter for you whether you agree with counsel for the prosecution when he says the defendant's explanation is an obvious lie . . .

(The judge then goes on to deal with the evidence of Ginger Peterson.)

Well there you are members of the jury, that is the evidence. The defendant's defence in a nutshell is that he didn't take the car from the car park in Barking – he was never in Barking that evening – he was at all relevant times in Romford or on the road to Southend. That is of course what a lawyer would call an alibi defence. Although the alibi is put forward by the defendant, it is not for him to prove that what he says is true. It is, members of the jury, for the prosecution to prove the alibi is false and to prove that so that you are sure. If you feel Mr Twist's account is true – or even that it might be true – then of course you acquit. On the other hand, if you find the case has been proved beyond reasonable doubt then it is your public duty to convict. One last thing. As you may know, the law permits me in certain circumstances to accept a verdict which is not the verdict of you all. Those circumstances have not as yet arisen so that when you retire I must ask you to reach a verdict upon which each one of you is agreed. Should, however, the time come when it is possible for me to accept a majority verdict, I will give you a further direction. Members of the jury, will you now retire and consider your verdict and first you may find it helpful, before you do anything else, to choose one of your number to act as foreman and he can act as chairman in your discussions.

(The jury retire 1.00 pm.)
(2.30 pm the jury return.)

Clerk: Your Honour, this jury retired at one o'clock. It is now half past two o'clock so that the jury have retired for one and a half hours.

Judge: Yes.

Clerk: Mr Foreman, I want you to answer the question I am about to ask you by just saying 'yes' or 'no'. Members of the jury, on the first count of this indictment which charges the defendant with taking a conveyance, have you reached a verdict upon which you are all agreed?

Foreman: Your Honour, yes.

Clerk: Do you find this defendant guilty or not guilty of theft?

Foreman: Guilty.

Clerk: And is that the verdict of you all?

Foreman: Yes.

Judge: Yes, thank you. Then I shall ask you to return now a formal verdict of 'Not Guilty' on the second count – the burglary charge which I withdrew from your consideration.

Clerk: Members of the jury, on the second count do you find on his Honour's direction the defendant 'Not Guilty'?

Foreman: Yes.

Clerk: And that is the verdict of you all?

Foreman: Yes.

Counsel for the Prosecution: Your Honour, I will call the officer to tell you what is known about him.

Dixon: I swear by Almighty God that I will truthfully answer all such questions as the Court shall demand of me.

(He now proceeds to read over the antecedent form – see pp 22–23.)

Counsel for the Prosecution: Officer, I think this defendant is aged 22 having been born in Ealing in 1966.

Dixon: Yes, your Honour.

Counsel for the Prosecution: And I think there are three convictions and two findings of guilt recorded against him. Would your Honour wish to hear only the last three?

Judge: Perhaps I can shorten this – he was taken into care in 1980, then no trouble until 1985 when he was sent to a detention centre for burglary. There is an assault charge in August 1985 for which he was fined and then in January last year at this court he was given a suspended sentence for drugs. What were the drugs?

Counsel for the Prosecution: Cocaine your Honour.

Judge: And now I suppose this conviction puts him in breach of the suspended sentence.

Counsel for the Prosecution: Your Honour, yes.

Judge: Very well, let it be put to him.

Clerk: Twist, stand up. Do you admit that on 5 January 1986 at this court you were sentenced to six months' imprisonment suspended for two years for unlawful possession of drugs?

Twist: Yes.

Clerk: And do you further admit that by reason of your present conviction you are liable to have that sentence brought into effect?

Twist: Yes.
Judge: Very well.
Counsel for the Prosecution: I think the defendant was educated . . .

(Prosecuting counsel continues through the antecedent form with the police officer. The next person called by the court is the court liaison probation officer who formally produces the Social Enquiry Report. The defence counsel can ask him any question he wishes about the report or the recommendations in it but since it has been prepared by a local probation officer who, as is usually the case, is not present there is little point in questioning him. Finally the defence counsel addresses the court in mitigation.)

Counsel for the Defence: Your Honour, I of course have to face the fact that, in view of the suspended sentence, I would imagine that your Honour has in mind now to make some form of custodial order. I am going to ask your Honour to consider the possibility of taking another course because of some rather important developments which have occurred since the committal proceedings and which I would venture to suggest indicate that at last this defendant has decided to make an effort to settle down and behave himself. Your Honour will see that in the Social Enquiry Report (which is dated June 1986) the defendant is described as unemployed and the probation officer who compiled the report in his conclusion doubts whether the defendant has the motivation to obtain regular employment. I am able to tell your Honour that in July 1986 the defendant obtained work as a van driver for a small second-hand goods business in Clerkenwell and has held down that job for the last six months. I have a letter from his employer, a Mr Fagin, from which your Honour can see that Twist has obviously been working satisfactorily (*letter put in*). The other matter which I should mention to bring, as it were, the report up to date is that the defendant has become engaged to a young lady whom he has known for the last 18 months and who is indeed here today. I hope your Honour will take it from me that she has told me that despite the trouble he is in now and despite whatever sentence he may receive she intends to stand by him. Your Honour will have seen that this young man has had the misfortune of sustaining a very serious injury just after leaving the community home to start work. It may be fairly said against him that he has taken a long time to get back on his feet but what I would urge is important and significant is that the evidence shows a real effort over the last six months. Of course it might be said that the knowledge of his appearance at this court may have had something to do with this change in his behaviour – but what I would ask your Honour to consider is whether he could not obtain more benefit now from a period of supervision under the probation service than some form of custodial order.
Judge: But only last year we passed a suspended sentence on him and he was told then what would happen if he got into trouble – any sort of trouble – again.
Counsel for the Defence: Your Honour, yes, but that was for an offence of a very different nature. What I respectfully submit is that an order now which gives the court the chance to see if he is capable of keeping up this improvement may be the right way of dealing with him at this stage.
Judge: Thank you very much, Mr Carton. Twist, stand up. You have been convicted of an offence of taking other people's property and you have a

lamentable record of other offences of dishonesty. At no stage have you shown the slightest contrition. You have compounded the dishonesty of your offence by the lies you have told in this court. I take into account everything that has been said so well on your behalf by your counsel but I should be failing in my duty to the public if I did not make a custodial order. In the circumstances the sentence of the court is twelve months' prison. So far as the suspended sentence is concerned, that will be brought into force to run consecutively. That means you will serve eighteen months in total. This offence involves taking a motor vehicle so that I would normally order you to be disqualified but, since your new job involves driving, I am not going to make any order lest it interferes with your chances of getting work when you leave prison. There will therefore be simply an endorsement on your licence. Very well, that is the sentence of the court.

The rules of criminal procedure

Chapter 1

The investigation of crime

ARREST

An arrest occurs where a person is forcibly detained; this may involve his physical restraint (for example, by the use of handcuffs) or a symbolic restraint (for example, by touching him and indicating that he is not free to go) or merely telling him that he is under legal compulsion to remain where he is or to accompany the person purporting to arrest him[1]. The law places such importance on the liberty of the subject that any such detention by whatever method achieved is both criminal and tortious unless it can be justified by lawful authority made known to the person arrested at the time of his detention. Where a person is unlawfully detained the High Court will order his release on a motion for *habeas corpus,* and he is then free to prosecute or sue the persons responsible for his detention. Where the executive (including the police) are responsible, he may obtain exemplary damages against them[2]. The law relating to arrest must be seen against this background, ie that any person wrongfully arresting another can be brought before the courts to account for his actions. Perhaps as important in practice is the principle that a person unlawfully detained is entitled to resist and use reasonable force to secure his release; issues as to the validity of an arrest will frequently arise where a person is charged with assault on the police; it is a valid defence on such a charge for the defendant to show that he was using reasonable force to resist an unlawful arrest[3].

In the last resort, the criminal law can only be enforced by the compulsory attendance of accused persons at court. To this end magistrates are

1 *Alderson v Booth* [1969] 2 QB 216, [1969] 2 All ER 271, DC (on a breathalyser case the prosecution had to prove the defendant had been arrested; the only evidence was that a police officer had said 'I shall have to ask you to come to the police station'; the Divisional Court held the magistrates were entitled to hold that these words did not constitute an arrest because they would not have brought home to the accused unequivocally that he was under compulsion). If mere words are used the defendant must have submitted before he is in law arrested – see *Hart v Chief Constable of Kent* [1983] RTR 484.
2 *Rookes v Barnard* [1964] AC 1129, [1964] 1 All ER 367.
3 *Kenlin v Gardiner* [1967] 2 QB 510, [1966] 3 All ER 931 (plain clothes police officers seized hold of two schoolboys in order to detain and question them – the boys then struck the officers; held; there is no right to detain for questioning and the defendants were entitled to resist with force). See also *Ludlow v Burgess* (1971) 75 Cr App Rep 227; *Bentley v Brudzinski* (1982) Cr App Rep and *Collins v Wilcock* [1984] 3 All ER 374, [1984] 1 WLR 1172.

empowered to issue warrants[4] for the arrest and production before them of such persons. Any police officer who is authorised to arrest a person under a magistrates' warrant is protected from civil and criminal liability[5]. In practice, arrests under warrant occur in only a small proportion of cases; most arrests occur where the police exercise their common law or statutory powers of *arrest without warrant*. Where no warrant has been issued by a magistrate, then the police officer who effects the arrest and all who assist him must show a lawful justification for their actions, and are personally liable to an action for damages if they are unable to do so.

The law also permits a private person to carry out an arrest, but his powers are more limited than those granted to the police. A private person may arrest without warrant anyone he sees actually in the process of committing a *breach of the peace*[6] or who is in the act of committing an *arrestable offence*[7]. An arrestable offence is defined as an offence for which the sentence is fixed by law or for which the maximum term is five years' imprisonment or more. Thus the law ensures that every[8] citizen should have the right to detain persons caught *in flagrante delicto* committing serious offences or disturbing the peace.

Where, however, the offence has already been *committed*, the powers of private persons to effect an arrest are more restricted. Thus a private citizen may only arrest for a *breach of the peace* which has already occurred, if there are reasonable grounds for apprehending its immediate renewal[9]. So far as past *arrestable offences* are concerned, a private person may arrest anyone whom he has reasonable grounds for suspecting committed the offence[10]. The arrest however is only lawful if it transpires that such an offence has in fact been committed; if it eventually turns out that no offence has been committed, the person who made the arrest will be liable for false imprisonment.

4   The power to issue a warrant is set out in Magistrates' Courts Act 1980 s 1. A warrant is an order which is signed by a magistrate on the basis of a formal information that an offence has been committed directing the police to arrest the person or persons named therein and stating specifically the offence alleged. A warrant issued in general terms (eg, to arrest all persons concerned in the publication of a seditious newspaper) is illegal and void: see *Money v Leach* (1765) 3 Burr 1742.
5   The magistrate who issued it is however accountable although he can only be sued by the person arrested if that person is eventually acquitted and if either the magistrate's action was inspired by malice *and* was without reasonable or probable cause; or the magistrate had no jurisdiction to issue the warrant (and no earlier summons served on the person named had been ignored); see Justices Protection Act 1848 ss 1 and 2.
6   See *R v Howell* [1982] QB 416 where Watkins LJ defined a 'breach of the peace' in the following terms: 'there is a breach of the peace whenever harm is actually done or is likely to be done to a person or in his presence to his property or a person is in fear of being so harmed through an assault, an affray, a riot, unlawful assembly or other disturbance'.
7   Police and Criminal Evidence Act 1984 s 24(4).
8   Ibid s 24(1)–(3). Note by sub-s (2) certain offences though not punishable by five years' imprisonment are made arrestable offences (eg, indecent assault on a woman (Sexual Offences Act 1956 s 14), taking a motor vehicle without authority and going equipped for theft (Theft Act 1968 ss 12 and 25). Note also that by sub-s (3) there is power to arrest for conspiracy, attempt, incitement and aiding and abetting the commission of arrestable offences.
9   *Baynes v Brewster* (1841) 2 QB 375, 114 ER 149.
10 Police and Criminal Evidence Act 1984 s 24(5). As to the meaning of reasonable suspicion in this context, see *Shaabon Bir Hussain v Chong Fook Kam* [1969] 3 All ER 1626 at 1630: per Lord Devlin 'Suspicion in its ordinary meaning is a state of conjecture or surmise where proof is lacking: I suspect but I cannot prove'.

Example. A, a store detective, stops B who is leaving a department store and asks whether he has paid for a certain item in his bag. B is wholly unable to give an explanation. A arrests him. B, who is absent-minded, subsequently remembers that he purchased the item in question in another store and is able to produce a receipt as proof of purchase. Although A had reasonable cause to suspect B of having committed the arrestable offence of theft, he will still be liable to B in tort for false imprisonment because the offence had not in fact been committed[11].

A police officer has all the powers of a private person to effect arrests but in addition he has certain other rights. Where he has reasonable grounds for suspecting that an arrestable offence has been committed then, whether or not his suspicion is correct, he may arrest without warrant anyone whom he has reasonable grounds for suspecting to be guilty of the offence[12]. Thus, in the example above, a policeman would have been safe in arresting the suspected thief although the store detective was not. A police officer also has power to arrest any person who is, or whom on reasonable grounds he suspects to be, *about* to *commit an arrestable offence.*[13] A police officer also has the additional power to arrest, for offences which are not serious enough to constitute 'arrestable offences' (eg driving while disqualified and breach of bail[13a]). In addition the police have very wide powers of arrest by statute where certain conditions (called *general arrest conditions*) are satisfied. These powers arise where it appears to the police that it is necessary to detain a person straight away or where there are grounds for believing he would not answer a summons to attend court[14]. The *general arrest conditions* are as follows:

'(a) that the name of the relevant person is unknown to, and cannot be readily ascertained by, the constable;
(b) that the constable has reasonable grounds for doubting whether a name furnished by the relevant person as his name is his real name;
(c) that –
   (i) the relevant person has failed to furnish a satisfactory address for service; or
   (ii) the constable has reasonable grounds for doubting whether an address furnished by the relevant person is a satisfactory address for service;
(d) that the constable has reasonable grounds for believing that arrest is necessary to prevent the relevant person –
   (i)   causing physical harm to himself or any other person;
   (ii) suffering physical injury;
   (iii) causing loss of or damage to property;
   (iv) committing an offence against public decency; or
   (v) causing an unlawful obstruction of the highway;
(e) that the constable has reasonable grounds for believing that arrest is necessary to protect a child or other vulnerable person from the relevant person[15].'

It should be noted that a police officer has the right to enter private

---

11 See *Walters v W H Smith & Son Ltd* [1914] 1 KB 595.
12 Police and Criminal Evidence Act 1984 s 24(6).
13 Ibid s 24(7). Note: a private person and the police may arrest for an *anticipated breach of the peace* where they can show that they reasonably and honestly believed that such a breach would be committed in the immediate future: *R v Howell* (above).
13a Ibid s 26(2) and Sch 2.
14 Ibid s 25(1).
15 Ibid s 25(3). Note: an arrest because of an offence against public decency can only be made where members of the public going about their normal business cannot reasonably be expected to avoid the person arrested.

premises without a warrant and against the wishes of the occupier to effect an arrest for an arrestable offence[16].

Although an arrest may be justified in the sense described above (ie under a specific statutory power), it will still be unlawful unless the arrested person is informed of the reason for his detention. Thus, every warrant for arrest must state the offence charged against the person named or described in the warrant[17]. Again, although a police officer need not have the warrant in his possession when he effects an arrest, he must, on demand, show it to the arrested person as soon as practicable[18]. Whenever a private person, or a police officer, makes an arrest without a warrant, he must at once inform the person arrested of the grounds upon which he seeks to justify his detention[19]. In any subsequent proceedings, the arrest can only be supported by the reason given at the time. Whenever a private person arrests another, he must take him to the police or before a justice of the peace within a reasonable time[20]. Where a police officer arrests a person he must take him to a police station as soon as practicable[1]. The only exception to this is where the presence of the arrested person elsewhere is necessary in order to carry out immediate investigation (eg, to check an alibi or other matter which would show he had a valid defence[2]).

Generally, a person cannot be detained except in the circumstances outlined above. Before we leave this topic it is worth emphasising that no policeman has any power at common law to:

(1) require a citizen to give his name and address[3];
(2) stop a citizen in order to question him[4];
(3) require him to attend at a police station[5].

The basic principle of the law is that the police can only interfere with the freedom of the citizen if they have decided to arrest; if the police are not prepared to take the step of arresting, the citizen is free to walk away from them. The position has been summarised by Devlin J[6] as follows:

'You may sometimes read in novels and detective stories perhaps written by people not familiar with police procedure, that persons are sometimes taken into

---

16 Ibid s 17(1).
17 Magistrates' Courts Rules 1981 r 96(2).
18 Magistrates' Courts Act 1980 s 126(3).
19 Police and Criminal Evidence Act 1984 s 28(1), and see *Christie v Leachinsky* [1947] AC 573, [1947] 1 All ER 567.
20 *John Lewis & Co Ltd v Tims* [1952] AC 676, [1952] 1 All ER 1203.
 1 Police and Criminal Evidence Act 1984 s 30(1). Note that if he is to be detained for more than six hours he must be taken to a *designated* police station (see below).
 2 Ibid s 30(1). See *Dallison v Caffery* [1965] 1 QB 348, [1964] 2 All ER 610 where it was held that an officer was entitled to take an arrested person to a house to check his alibi.
 3 See Williams (1950) 66 LQR 465. Note that if the officer suspects an offence has been committed and the person in question refuses to give his name and address he may arrest under the Police and Criminal Evidence Act 1984 s 25 but *not* otherwise.
 4 But see the *statutory* powers of stop and search discussed below.
 5 There are certain statutory exceptions to this – eg, Road Traffic Act 1972 s 161, which enables a police officer to require a driver to produce his licence at a police station.
 6 *R v Roberts* (1953) unreported, and see per Lawton LJ in *R v Lemsatef* [1977] 2 All ER 835 at 839: 'it must be clearly understood that neither customs officers nor police officers have any right to detain somebody for the purposes of getting them to help with their enquiries. . . . If the idea is getting around amongst either customs and excise officers or police officers that they can arrest or detain people as the case may be for this particular purpose the sooner they disabuse themselves of that idea the better.'

custody for questioning. There is no such power in this country. A man cannot be detained unless he is arrested.'

In practice however the police do often 'invite' suspected persons to go with them to the police station to assist in their enquiries. In theory such persons are free to leave the police station at any time and can resist any forcible attempt to stop them leaving (unless the police there and then arrest them)[7]. The Code of Practice[8] provides that:

'Any person attending a police station voluntarily for the purpose of assisting with an investigation may leave at will unless placed under arrest. . . . If he is not placed under arrest but is cautioned [ie warned of his right not to answer questions] the officer who gives the caution must, at the same time, inform him that he is not under arrest, that he is not obliged to remain at the police station but that if he remains at the police station he may obtain legal advice if he wishes.'

THE POWER TO STOP AND SEARCH

We have seen above that the general rule is that the police are not entitled to stop and detain people unless they have decided to arrest them. One important exception to this rule is that the police have certain statutory powers to stop and search suspected persons to see if they have stolen or prohibited articles on them. Such searches undoubtedly provide a major means by which the police detect crime[9]. However, every such stop and search violates the ordinary citizen's perception that he is entitled to go about his affairs without interference from anyone – including the police. Where such searches (as in the majority of cases) lead to no evidence being found, they breed resentment against the police. This seems particularly to be the case among young people belonging to minority groups who feel they have been unfairly selected. The aim of the law is to provide a framework under which these powers will be exercised responsibly and with proper accountability; whether this aim is achieved depends in the ultimate on the desire of the police to operate the system properly.

A police officer has the right to stop and search a person (or a motor vehicle) in a public place or any place (such as a private car park) to which people have ready access if he has reasonable grounds for suspecting he will find:

(i)   stolen articles[10];
(ii) articles intended to be used for burglary, theft, taking motor vehicles or obtaining property by deception[11];

---

7 See *R v Inwood* [1973] 2 All ER 645, [1973] 1 WLR 647.
8 Code on Detention, Treatment and Questioning para 3.9.
9 The statistics compiled for the Royal Commission on Criminal Procedure amply bear this out. For example, in London in the month of January 1979 the police stopped persons suspected of being in possession of stolen goods on 35,298 occasions; the stops resulted in 4,189 arrests (12% success rate). In 1978 the police stopped 6,412 persons on suspicion of possession of controlled drugs and made 2,483 arrests. See Royal Commission on Criminal Procedure, Law and Procedure Vol App 2 and 3.
10 Police and Criminal Evidence Act 1984 s 1(2).
11 Ibid s 1(7) and (8).

(iii) offensive weapons[12];

(iv) controlled drugs[13].

The vast majority of cases fall into one of these categories but it should be noted that there are certain other statutory powers to stop and search[14].

It should be noted that although the powers of stop and search are found in a number of statutes, the conduct of all such searches is regulated by ss 2–3 of the Police and Criminal Evidence Act 1984 and the Code on Powers of Stop and Search. These provisions require the following conditions to be satisfied:

(a) the officer must have *reasonable grounds for suspecting* he will find stolen goods or prohibited articles[15]. Annex B of the Code on Powers of Stop and Search (which is set out at p 314 below) contain important guidance to the police as to how they are to exercise this power. In particular it draws the distinction between 'reasonable suspicion' founded on fact and 'a hunch or instinct'. The fact that the suspect belongs to a group within which offenders of a certain kind are relatively common cannot be sufficient grounds for stopping him: 'a person's colour of itself can never be a reasonable ground for suspicion. The mere fact alone that a person is carrying a particular kind of property or is dressed in a certain way or has a certain hairstyle is likewise not of itself sufficient. Nor is the fact that a person is known to have a previous conviction for unlawful possession of an article';

(b) the officer must either be in uniform or produce documentary evidence that he is a constable before commencing any search[16] and in all cases he must tell the suspect (i) his name, (ii) the police station to which he is attached, (iii) the object of the proposed search, (iv) his grounds for making it and inform the suspect of his right to have a copy of the record of the search (see below);

(c) the officer is bound to make a record of the search setting out (i) the object of the search, (ii) the grounds for making it, (iii) the date and time when it was made, (iv) the place where it was made, (v) whether anything, and if so what, was found, (vi) whether any, and if so what, injury to a person or damage to property appears to the constable to have resulted from the search. The record must identify the constable making the search[17];

(d) the person searched is entitled to a copy of the record if he asks for one in the 12 months beginning with the date on which the search was made[18].

The origin of the complex provisions is to be found in the Report of the Royal Commission on Criminal Procedure:

12 Ibid s 1(7)(a). Note: offensive weapons and articles for the use of theft etc, are termed 'prohibited articles' in the Act.

13 Misuse of Drugs Act 1971 s 23.

14 Eg Firearms Act 1968 s 47; Prevention of Terrorism (Temporary Provisions) Act 1984, Sch 3.

15 Police and Criminal Evidence Act 1984 s 1(3).

16 Ibid s 2(2).

17 Ibid s 3(6).

18 Ibid s 3(7)–(9). Note: identical provisions apply in respect of the owner of a vehicle which is searched. Note also that provision is made in s 5 for the chief constable to monitor and report on searches recorded.

'We have proposed putting police powers to stop and search in a public place in connection with crime on a uniform footing and a limited extension of these powers (ie in the case of offensive weapons) to enable the police to perform their proper functions of detecting crime and protecting the public. We recognise that even the limited extension proposed may give rise to concern that the powers will be improperly used, and we acknowledge that, without stringent controls, such abuse is possible. There must be safeguards to protect members of the public from random, arbitrary or discriminating searches. Clarification of powers will help but the principal safeguard must be found in the requirement for and strict application of the criterion of reasonable suspicion. Some have complained that the police interpret this too loosely at present and that the courts are not as a matter of course required to test it; this increases the risk of random stops. We acknowledge the risk that the criterion could be loosely interpreted, and have considered the possibility of trying to find some agreed standards which could form the grounds of reasonable suspicion and could be set out in a statute or in a code of practice . . . we have concluded that the variety of circumstances that would have to be covered makes this impracticable. We have therefore looked for other means of ensuring that the criterion of reasonable suspicion is not devalued. We consider that the notification of the reason for the search to the person who has been stopped, the recording of searches by officers, and the monitoring of the records by supervising officers would be the most effective and practical way of reducing the risk[19].'

It should be noted that:

(a) a police officer conducting such a search has the right to ask the suspect questions although the suspect need not answer[20];
(b) searches in public places must be restricted to superficial examination of the outer clothing. There is no power to require a person to remove any clothing in public other than an outer coat, jacket or gloves. If the officer wishes to go further he must either take the suspect to a non-public place (e g, inside a police van) or arrest for a specific offence, and take him to the police station[1].

The sanctions against the police for abuse of the power to stop and search are to be found in the civil law remedies and in the police complaints machinery. In very rare cases it may be possible to put forward an argument that evidence obtained should be excluded (see p 75 below). In practice however the courts are likely to find themselves considering these powers in the context of charges of assault on the police; because the defendant who has used reasonable force to prevent a search will have a good defence to such a charge if the police are unable to prove they were acting within the precise terms of their statutory powers[2].

Example. On 2 January 1987 at 2.30 am Twist was observed by police officers in plain clothes leaving a discotheque in North London and shouting abuse at a group of young people. The police stopped Twist and told him they proposed to search him; he says they did not give any reasons for the search. He says that he was told to stand still and take his jacket and pullover off. One of the officers started to run his hands over Twist's clothing at which point Twist lost his temper and pushed the officer away. The officer then grabbed hold of Twist and Twist punched him. Twist was then arrested and charged with assaulting a police

19 Report of the Royal Commission on Criminal Procedure (Cmnd 8092-1 (1981)) paras 3.24–3.25.
20 *Daniel v Morrison* (1979) 70 Cr App Rep 142, [1980] Crim LR 181.
1 Police and Criminal Evidence Act 1984 s 9.
2 See p 63 below.

officer contrary to s 51 of the Police Act 1964. At his trial the issues will be (a) whether Twist's detention was lawful and (b) if not, whether he used more force than was reasonable to secure his release. On both issues the burden of proof is on the prosecution. The defence advocate (who will have obtained a copy of the search record from the police prior to the hearing) will have to consider the following points:

(i)   whether the officers produced their warrant cards to Twist to show they were police officers (Police and Criminal Evidence Act 1984 s 2(2));
(ii) whether they had reasonable grounds to suspect that he was in possession of stolen goods or prohibited articles or drugs (Misuse of Drugs Act 1971 s 23 and s 23 and Code on Powers of Stop and Search Annex B);
(iii) whether they gave him the information as to the object of the search (s 2(3));
(iv) whether they required him to remove clothing in public (s 2(9)).

ROAD BLOCKS

The police are given a limited power to stop all vehicles in a particular locality[3]; where such a 'road check' is in progress the police may stop *any* driver: they are not confined to stopping drivers whom they suspect have committed offences. There are few circumstances in which the police are justified in setting up a road block:

(i)   if there are reasonable grounds for believing a person who has committed a 'serious arrestable offence'[4] is in the locality;
(ii) if the police are looking for a witness to such a 'serious arrestable offence';
(iii) if they believe that a person who intends to commit a 'serious arrestable offence' is in the area;
(iv) if there are reasonable grounds for believing that an escaped prisoner is in the area[5].

A road block must normally be authorised in advance in writing by an officer of the rank of superintendent or above: the written authority must state the reason for setting up the road block; the authority will remain in force in the first instance no more than seven days[6].

SEARCH AFTER ARREST

Once a person has been arrested, the police have very extensive powers of search (*without* warrant):

(i)   the arrested person may be searched *at once* for evidence relating to the offence (or for any object he might use to escape from custody)[7];
(ii) the arrested person will also be searched on arrival at the police station; the articles found on him are to be entered on the custody

---

3 Police and Criminal Evidence Act 1984 s 4. This section extends the existing power of the police under the Road Traffic Act 1972 s 159 to stop motorists.
4 Police and Criminal Evidence Act 1984 s 116. A 'serious arrestable offence' is an offence listed in Sch 5 (eg, murder, rape, possession of a firearm with intent) or an arrestable offence which is likely to result in serious harm or loss: see s 116(6).
5 Ibid s 4(1).
6 Ibid s 4(12).
7 Ibid s 32(1)–(5).

record (see p 68 below). At this stage intimate body searches may be carried out (see p 79 below)[8];

(iii) the police may search the premises where the arrest in question took place for evidence relating to the offence[9];

(iv) the police may enter premises occupied or controlled by the arrested person and search for evidence that relates to the offence[10]. The limit on this power should be noted – the police do *not* have the right to enter and search a detained person's home simply to see whether they can find evidence to show that he has committed some *other* crime[11].

It should be noted that in practice the police place great reliance on this last power, i e the right to search the premises of arrested persons, and regularly exercise this power: it accounts for possibly half of all police searches[12].

SEARCH WARRANTS

The powers of stop and search discussed above and the searching of arrested persons and their homes are carried out *without* warrant. The police act on their own responsibility and they do not need to obtain permission from any judicial authority. By contrast, where the police wish to search other premises (for example occupied by a suspect who they have insufficient evidence to arrest) they must first obtain a *search warrant*. Without the warrant they have no right to enter private property:

'The poorest man may in his cottage bid defiance to all the Forces of the Crown. It may be frail – its roof may shake – the wind may blow through it – the storm may enter – the rain may enter – but the King of England cannot enter – all his forces dare not cross the threshold of the ruined tenement[13].'

The police are entitled to obtain warrants to enter and search premises for evidence under certain statutory provisions[14]; of these the most important are:

(1) to enter and search for *stolen goods*[15];
(2) to enter premises and search them and any persons found therein and to seize controlled *drugs*[16];

---

8 Police and Criminal Evidence Act 1984 s 54.
9 Ibid s 32. This also applies to 'any premises in which he was . . . immediately before he was arrested'.
10 Ibid s 18. They may also search for evidence of some other arrestable offence which is connected with or similar to that offence.
11 See *Jeffrey v Black* [1978] QB 490, [1978] 1 All ER 555 where, after arresting the defendant for stealing a sandwich in a public house, the police searched his home and discovered cannabis. The Divisional Court held the search was unlawful. Per Lord Widgery CJ: 'I do not accept that the common law has yet developed to the point, if it ever does, in which police officers who arrest a suspect for one offence at one point can as a result thereby authorise themselves as it were to go and inspect his home at another place when the contents of his home, on the face of them, bear no relation whatever to the offence with which he is charged or the evidence required in support of that charge'.
12 Royal Commission on Criminal Procedure, Law and Procedure Vol App 7. In the sample, 43 per cent of searches took place after arrest without warrant.
13 William Pitt cited in *Ghani v Jones* [1970] 1 QB 693, [1969] 3 All ER 1700.
14 A complete list is set out in App 5 of the Royal Commission's Law and Procedure Volume.
15 Theft Act 1968 s 26. Note this can be issued by a superintendent as well as by a justice of the peace.
16 Misuse of Drugs Act 1971 s 23(3).

(3) to enter and search for *firearms* and *ammunition*[17];
(4) to enter and search for *explosives*[18];
(5) to enter and search premises and to seize and remove any articles which there is reason to believe are *obscene* and kept for publication or gain[19].

In addition to these specific powers to search for stolen or prohibited articles there is a general power to obtain a search warrant where a serious arrestable offence[20] has been committed (such as murder, kidnapping, or theft of substantial sums of money). A magistrate may issue a warrant in such a case if he is satisfied there are reasonable grounds for believing that:

(i)   a serious arrestable offence has been committed;
(ii)   there is material on the premises specified in the application which is likely to be of substantial value in the investigation;
(iii) such material is likely to be relevant evidence;
(iv)   it does not consist of items subject to legal privilege or excluded or special procedure material (as to which see p 62 below);
(v)   one or more of the following conditions is satisfied:
   (a) that it is not practicable to communicate with any person entitled to grant entry to the premises;
   (b) that it is practicable to communicate with a person entitled to grant entry to the premises but it is not practicable to communicate with any person entitled to grant access to the evidence;
   (c) that entry to the premises will not be granted unless a warrant is produced;
   (d) that the purpose of a search may be frustrated or seriously prejudiced unless a constable arriving at the premises can secure immediate entry to them[1].

There will also be more cases where the police will need to act with great urgency and will not have the time to resort to a magistrate for a warrant; in such cases, provided they have *entered* the premises with the consent of the occupier they may seize property if they have reasonable grounds for believing that:

(i)   a serious offence has been committed; and
(ii)   the article in question is either:
   (a) the fruit of the crime (eg stolen goods); or
   (b) the instrument by which the crime has been committed (eg a murder weapon); or
   (c) material evidence to prove the commission of the crime (eg a letter setting out the plan for a robbery); and
(iii) the person in possession of it has committed the crime, or is implicated in it, or is accessory to it, or at any rate his refusal to give it to them is quite unreasonable[2].

17 Firearms Act 1968 s 46. This power includes the right to search persons found therein.
18 Explosives Act 1875 s 73.
19 Obscene Publications Act 1959 s 3.
20 Police and Criminal Evidence Act 1984 s 116 defines what amounts to a serious arrestable offence.
 1 Ibid s 8.
 2 *Ghani v Jones* [1970] 1 QB 693, [1969] 3 All ER 1700.

Police and Criminal Evidence Act 1984, s. 15

WARRANT TO ENTER AND SEARCH PREMISES

HATTON GARDEN   Magistrates' Court

(Code) 1873

Specify name of applicant

On this day an application was made by: JAMES TRUSCOTT (D/S)

State enactment under which warrant to be issued

for the issue of a warrant under S 26 Theft Act 1968

Specify premises

to enter and search the premises situated at:

21A SAFFRON HILL, LONDON EC.

and search for:

Identify, so far as possible, the articles or persons to be sought

Television sets, video equipment and computers

AUTHORITY IS HEREBY GIVEN for any constable, accompanied by such person or persons as are necessary for the purposes of the search, TO ENTER THE SAID PREMISES on one occasion only, within one month from the date of issue of this warrant and TO SEARCH for the articles or persons in respect of which the above application is made.

A copy of this warrant should be left with the occupier of the premises or, in his/her absence, a person who appears to be in charge of the premises, or if no such person is present, in a prominent place on the premises.

DATED the   1st March   1987   Time ..10.15.am..........

Lionel Fang   ~~Justice of the Peace~~ Metropolitan Stipendiary Magistrate

ENDORSEMENT – to be made by constable executing the warrant.

1. The following articles or persons sought were found: *(continue overleaf or attach separate sheet if necessary)*

One (1) Amstrad computer

One (1) Phillips videocamera

2. The following articles other than articles which were sought were seized: *(continue overleaf or attach separate sheet if necessary)*

Quantity of herbal substance

3. This warrant was executed on   1st March   1987, at 11⁰⁰ am/~~pm~~.

4. The name(s) of the officer(s) executing this warrant are:

James Truscott DIS

Andrew Bucket DIC

5. A copy of this warrant was [handed to the occupier] [left on the premises *(specify where)*]

Date 1st March   1987.   Signature of constable *James Truscott* DIS

Cat. No. MF 156   Printed by SHAW & SONS LTD., Shaway House, London SE26 5AE   MLY 2162

There are certain categories of documents to which special rules apply:

(a) *Documents subject to legal privilege.* Documents made in connection with giving legal advice or in contemplation of or during the conduct of legal proceedings cannot be seized by the police[3];

(b) *Excluded material.* Personal records and other articles (such as blood samples) cannot be seized by the police from priests, doctors, psychiatrists and other members of the caring professions. Journalistic material held in confidence is also immune from search and seizure[4]. Warrants cannot be issued to search for such articles (except in the very unusual case where the article in question has been stolen or forged)[5].

(c) *Special Procedure material.* The law recognises that police powers of search and seizure should be subject to restrictions where, although the material in question does not fall within either of the above categories, it is nevertheless in a very real sense 'confidential' (eg the records held on behalf of a client by his accountant or bankers). Again it is undesirable that the police should be allowed to search the offices of newspapers or the broadcasting stations for material whether confidential or not. For this reason, it is provided that a warrant to search for and seize such material (eg photographs or videotapes of people taking part in an affray) can only be issued by a circuit judge[6]. It must generally be shown that it is in the public interest that such search and seizure should occur.

The issue of a search warrant involves the serious infringement of the citizen's right to maintain the privacy and security of his own home. The theory of our law has been that such a search should only be permitted after an independent tribunal in the form of a magistrate has concluded the police have proper grounds. In practice, the safeguard has become illusory because magistrates have not been prepared to exercise independent judgment in determining whether or not to accede to requests for warrants:

> 'the judicial hurdle of the warrant application is no more than a stepping stone. Magistrates see the "information from a reliable source" formula as an impenetrable barrier beyond which they cannot or will not go. This, together with an almost unquestioning trust in the police, the clerk or both, allied to a lack of knowledge of how the police actually operate and an over-glamourised view of specialist squads, combine to impair the proper exercise of the independent judicial function[7].'

The law in fact attempts to provide machinery to check the possibilities of abuse. An officer applying for a warrant is bound to deliver a written statement (information) containing the following information:

3 Police and Criminal Evidence Act 1984 ss 8(1)(d), 9(2), and (10).
4 Ibid s 11(1). This subsection defines excluded material as: '(a) personal records which a person has acquired or created in the course of any trade, business, profession, or other occupation or for the purposes of any paid or unpaid office and which he holds in confidence; (b) human tissue or tissue fluid which has been taken for the purposes of diagnosis or medical treatment and which a person holds in confidence; (c) journalistic material which a person holds in confidence and which consists (i) of documents; or (ii) of records other than documents'.
5 Ibid ss 8(1)(d), 9(2) and 11.
6 Ibid ss 8(1)(d), 9 and 14 and Sch 1.
7 See Lidstone [1984] Crim LR 449.

(i)   the ground on which he makes the application;
(ii) the enactment under which the warrant would be issued;
(iii) the premises it is desired to enter and search;
(iv) the articles or persons to be sought[8].

Entry and search under a warrant must take place within one month of its issue[9] and should be carried out at a 'reasonable hour'[10]; the occupier of the premises must be shown the original warrant and given a copy[11]; if he is not present, the warrant must be left in a prominent place on the premises. The warrant must be endorsed with the date of execution and a list of property seized and returned to the magistrates' court[12].

The law attempts to provide a legal framework within which powers of search are to be carried out but in practice there are few effective sanctions for breach: in particular, although the law provides a remedy against unlawful seizure by way of an action for trespass to land or chattels, the evidence so obtained may still be used against the owner in criminal proceedings:

> 'It is not part of a judge's function to exercise disciplinary powers over the police or prosecution as respects the way in which evidence to be used at the trial is obtained by them. If it was obtained illegally there will be a remedy in civil law; if it was obtained legally but in breach of the rules of conduct for the police, this is a matter for the appropriate disciplinary authority to deal with. What the judge at the trial is concerned with is not how the evidence sought to be adduced by the prosecution has been obtained but with how it is used by the prosecution at the trial[13].'

It is however possible that if the conduct of the police in seizing property or documents was outrageously unfair, the court might exclude such evidence under s 78 of the Police and Criminal Evidence Act 1984 which provides that:

> 'In any proceedings the court may refuse to allow evidence on which the prosecution proposes to rely to be given if it appears to the court that, having regard to all the circumstances, including the circumstances in which the evidence was obtained, the admission of the evidence would have such an adverse effect on the fairness of the proceedings that the court ought not to admit it.'

Thus the court might exclude evidence obtained by a trick[14] (ie where the principle that no suspect can be required to be his own betrayer was infringed). The only other exception to the general rule is where a statute itself lays down as a condition precedent to conviction that evidence should be obtained in a specific way (eg intoximeter tests)[15].

---

8 Police and Criminal Evidence Act 1984 s 15(2) and Code of Practice for Searching of Premises para 2.
9 Ibid s 16(3).
10 Ibid s 16(4).
11 Ibid s 16(5) and (6).
12 Ibid s 16(9) and (10).
13 Per Lord Diplock in *R v Sang* [1979] 2 All ER 1222 at 1230; and see *R v Mason* (1987) 131 Sol Jo 973, CA.
14 See *Jeffrey v Black* [1978] QB 490, [1978] 1 All ER 555.
15 Road Traffic Act 1972 ss 5–11.

Chapter 2

At the police station

Once the police have arrested a person they are entitled to keep him in detention for a limited period while they decide, by questioning him and by making other enquiries, whether or not to institute criminal proceedings against him. For the purpose of this chapter we shall consider an example based on an arrest for a serious office

Example. On Friday, 3 January 1986 police officers arrive at Sunnyfields Farm, an isolated farmhouse about ten miles from Barchester. The police search the farm with a warrant issued under s 26 of the Theft Act 1968 (see p 59 above). Substantial quantities of property (including valuable antiques and paintings) are seized from the house and adjoining outhouses. The police estimate the value of the property seized as in excess of £500,000 and believe much of it is referable to burglaries committed over the last three years all over the south of England. The owner of the farmhouse, Sikes, is arrested on suspicion of receiving stolen property and taken to Barchester Police Station.

ARRIVAL AT THE POLICE STATION

When an arrested person is brought to a police station the responsibility for his continued detention rests in the *custody officer*[1]. The custody officer will be a member of the uniformed branch of at least the rank of sergeant. The theory is that there should be a senior police officer, independent of the investigating officers, who should have the overall responsibility for deciding what is to happen to detained suspects. Thus, when the arrested person first arrives at the police station, the custody officer must make a decision whether he should be charged with an offence straight away[2]: this would be appropriate where there was already clear evidence that he had committed the offence (eg caught red-handed causing criminal damage). However, it seldom happens in real life that an arrested person is immediately charged because once he has been charged the investigating officer is not allowed to ask any further questions about the offence. This is because para 17.5 of the Code on Detention, Treatment and Questioning provides:

1 Police and Criminal Evidence Act 1984 ss 34 and 36.
2 Ibid s 37(1).

'Questions relating to an offence may not be put to a person after he has been charged with that offence . . .'[3].

Normally therefore what will happen is that the custody officer will authorise the continued detention of the suspect for questioning:

'If the custody officer determines that he does not have . . . evidence [sufficient to charge] before him, the person arrested shall be released either on bail or without bail, unless the custody officer has reasonable grounds for believing that his detention without being charged is necessary to secure or preserve evidence relating to an offence for which he is under arrest or to obtain such evidence by questioning him[4].'

Once the decision is made to detain the suspect, a *custody record* will be started on which the grounds for his detention must be recorded[5]. This form of custody record varies from force to force; at pp 68–69 is an example of the form used by the Metropolitan Police; we have used for the purpose of this chapter the shorter form used by the Kent Police. Note that whatever form is used, the custody record essentially comprises two parts: (i) a record of the arrested person's initial detention; and (ii) a log showing precisely what happened to him thereafter (eg times in cells, times interviewed, meals, visits, etc). It is important to note that the arrested person is entitled to have a copy of the custody record: thus the Code provides:

'2.4 When a person leaves police detention he or his legal representative shall be supplied on request with a copy of the custody record as soon as practicable. This entitlement lasts for 12 months after his release.'

In any contested case it should be standard practice to obtain a copy of the custody record; it will be of the greatest importance, for example, when the defendant intends to raise questions of the conduct of the investigating officers at the police station.

At the initial stage the custody officer will arrange for the arrested person to be *searched* and for a list of the property found on him (or brought with him to the police station) to be set out on the custody record. The Code of Practice provides:

'4.1 The custody officer is responsible for:
(a) ascertaining:
   (i) what property a detained person has with him when he comes to the police station;
   (ii) what property he might have acquired for an unlawful purpose while in custody;
(b) the safekeeping of any property which is taken from him and which remains at the police station.

To these ends the custody officer may search him or authorise his being searched to the extent that he considers necessary (provided that a search of intimate parts of the body or involving the removal of more than outer clothing may only be made in accordance with Annex A to this Code). A search may only be carried out by an officer of the same sex as the person searched.

3 Code on Detention, Treatment and Questioning para 17.5. There are limited exceptions to this rule where questioning is 'necessary for the purpose of preventing or minimising harm or loss to some other person or to the public or for clearing up an ambiguity in a previous answer or statement, or where it is in the interests of justice that the person should have put to him and have an opportunity to comment on information concerning the offence which has come to light since he was charged. See also para 11.2.
4 Police and Criminal Evidence Act 1984 s 37(2).
5 Ibid s 37(4)–(6).

4.2 A detained person may retain clothing and personal effects at his own risk unless the custody officer considers that he may use them to cause harm to himself or others, interfere with evidence, damage property or effect an escape, or they are needed as evidence. In this event the custody officer can withhold such articles as he considers necessary. If he does so he must tell the person why.

4.3 Personal effects are those items which a person may need to use or refer to while in detention but do not include cash.

4.4 The custody officer is responsible for recording all property brought to a police station that a detained person had with him or had taken from him on arrest. The detained person shall be allowed to check and sign the record of property as correct.

4.5 If a detained person is not allowed to keep any article taken from him either on arrest or on detention, the reason must be recorded.'

Also at this preliminary stage, the suspect should be informed of his right to have someone informed of his detention and his right to consult a solicitor (see below). He will also be given a copy of a notice explaining his rights in custody. He should be asked to sign the custody record to signify whether or not he wants legal advice[6].

Example. In Sikes' case it can be seen that the custody officer authorised his continued detention for questioning (s 37(2)). A record of the property found on him was made and he was then notified of his right to legal advice and to have a named person notified of his detention. He asked for a Mr Fagin to be contacted but this request was refused. We discuss this below.

THE SUSPECT'S RIGHTS WHILE IN CUSTODY

When a person has been arrested s 56 of the Police and Criminal Evidence Act 1984 provides that he has the right to have the news of his arrest and the address of the police station where he is being detained given as soon as practicable to a friend, relative, or some other person who is known to him or who is likely to take an interest in his welfare[7]. This right is exercisable at the initial stage of detention (and at any time thereafter). If the investigating officers wish to prevent the suspect exercising this right they must obtain authorisation from an officer of at least the rank of superintendent[8]. The superintendent can only authorise refusal if the detained person has been arrested for a *serious arrestable offence* and there are reasonable grounds for believing that telling the named person of the arrest:

(a) will lead to interference with or harm to evidence connected with a serious arrestable offence or interference with or physical injury to other persons; or

(b) will lead to the alerting of other persons suspected of having committed such an offence but not yet arrested for it: or

(c) will hinder the recovery of any property obtained as a result of such an offence, (Police and Criminal Evidence Act s 56(5)).

If the police decide to refuse such a request they must tell the suspect the reason and a note to that effect must be entered on the custody record[9].

6 Code paras 3.1–3.4.
7 Police and Criminal Evidence Act s 56(1); Code para 5.
8 Police and Criminal Evidence Act s 56(2).
9 Ibid s 56(6).

BARSET COUNTY CONSTABULARY   FORM 57

Custody Record

	Custody No:

Police station:	Station code: 30	Charge No:

Reasons for arrest:

Suspicion of receiving stolen property

A notice setting out my rights has been read to me and I have been provided with a copy.

Signature of person detained: W Sykes

Time: 12.40   Date: 4.1.86

I want a Solicitor as soon as practicable*
I do not want a Solicitor at this time*

Signature of person detained: W Sykes.

Time: 12.41   Date: 4.1.86

At the time of service of notice - notification of detention to named person requested/not requested*

Named person: J. FAGIN

REFUSED TO SIGN

Time: 12.30   Date: 4.1.86

Officer opening Custody Record:

Signature: D Lanchester

Name: LANCHESTER
(block capitals)

Rank: DIS   No: 64

* delete as appropriate
* record action overleaf

Other references:

(complete in block capitals)

Surname: SYKES
(Mr. Mrs. Miss)*

First Names: WILLIAM

Address: SUNNYFIELDS FARM
NEAR HADLOW
BARSET

Occupation: DEALER

Age: 41   D.O.B: 15 / 7 / 44

Place of Birth: PADDINGTON

Ident. code: Height: 5'8" Sex: M/F*

Arrested by:

Name: CHARLES TRUSCOTT
(block capitals)

Rank: DIS No.: 206   Station or Branch: BARCHESTER

	Time	Date
Arrested at	10.35	4.1.86
Arrived at station	12.00	4.1.86

Officer in the case:

Name: AS ABOVE
(block capitals)

Rank: No.:   Station or Branch:

	PROPERTY CLEAR
Property	SUPERVISING OFFICERS INITIALS

Kept by Person Detained				
Total Personal Cash £ 110 : 00				
WALLET				
£5 — X2 NOTES				
£50 — X2 NOTES				
BARCLAY CARD				
BUSINESS CARDS				
CHEQUE BOOK				

1

Last review of detention conducted at:

Custody No:

Name:

Date	Time	Full details of any action/occurrence involving the detained person (Include full particulars of all visitors/officers) Individual entries need not be restricted to one line All entries to be signed by the writer
4.1.86	12.30	Search completed I authorise detention I authorise Refused notification for questioning DL refusal of reason : person named likely to be notification suspect / witness, would alert other suspects
	12.45	Solicitor (Mr. Dodson) Dodson + Fogg 01-242-1873 telephoned - private conversation Custody Officer speaks to Mr. Dodson - unable to attend until 9.00 am 6/1/86
	12.55	To cells DL
	4.00	Supt Smith authorises interview DL
	4.05	To interview room DS Truscott + Brown DL
	5.16	To cells DL
	5.35	I authorise continued detention
	6.00	Supper provided. Refused. DL
	11.55	I authorise continued detention for questioning
5/1/86	7.30	Breakfast provided DL
	8.30	Detained for questioning
	10.15	To interview room DS Truscott DC Rugg DL
	11.30	To cells " " DL
	11.50	Continued detention authorised for twelve hours. S. Walker (Chief Superintendent)

2

Section 58(1) of the Police and Criminal Evidence Act also provides that a person held at a police station also has the right to access to legal advice:

'A person who is in police detention shall be entitled, if he so requests, to consult a solicitor privately at any time[10].'

The police are only entitled to delay access to legal advice where an officer of at least the rank of superintendent is prepared to authorise such delay; he is only entitled to do so in the case of a serious arrestable offence where one of the grounds set out above (the same grounds as for refusing notification) applies[11]. The position has been summarised as follows:

'The only reason . . . for delaying access to a legal adviser relates to the risk that he would either intentionally or inadvertently convey information to confederates still at large that would undermine an investigation in progress[12].'

In the past the police sometimes refused access to solicitors in serious cases, because they believed their chance of obtaining evidence by questioning the suspect would be diminished if he was advised by a solicitor not to answer questions. Sometimes, the police would refuse access because the solicitor who had attended at the police station had been instructed by friends or relatives as opposed to the suspect himself[13]. It is now clear from the Notes for Guidance annexed to the Code that neither of these reasons is sufficient to justify delaying access:

'Access to a solicitor may not be delayed on the grounds that he might advise the person not to answer any questions or that the solicitor was initially asked to attend at the police station by someone else, provided that the person himself wishes to see the solicitor[14].'

The police cannot take advantage of the period which must necessarily elapse between the time the solicitor is contacted and his arrival at the police station:

'A person who asks for legal advice may not be interviewed or continue to be interviewed until he has received it[15].'

To this general rule there are two exceptions: (a) terrorist cases; and (b) where a senior officer authorises interviewing to continue on the grounds that: (i) delay would involve an immediate risk of harm to persons or serious loss or damage to property; or that (ii) awaiting the arrival of a solicitor would cause unreasonable delay to the process of investigation; or (iii) the person has given his agreement in writing or on tape that the interview may be commenced at once[16]. Any request for legal advice and refusal or delay must be recorded on the custody sheet[17].

Once the solicitor arrives at the police station facilities must be provided for him to interview his client *in private*[18]. The police must permit the solicitor to be present while his client is interviewed and he is entitled to

10 Ibid s 58(1).
11 Ibid s 58(6)–(8). The maximum period of delay is 36 hours (48 hours in terrorist cases).
12 Home Office minister, Mr Douglas Hurd, HC Official Report, SCE, 2 February 1984, col 1417.
13 See *R v Crush* [1978] Crim LR 357.
14 Code Annex A para 2.
15 Code para 6.3.
16 Ibid.
17 Police and Criminal Evidence Act s 58(2)–(9).
18 Police and Criminal Evidence Act s 58(1).

object to improper questioning and to insist on giving his client further advice. The Code provides that the solicitor may only be required to leave the interview if 'his conduct is such that the investigating officer is unable properly to put questions to the suspect'[19]. The Notes for Guidance (para 6D) amplify this:

> 'a solicitor is not guilty of misconduct if he seeks to challenge an improper question to his client or the manner in which it is put or he wishes to give his client further legal advice, and should not be required to leave an interview unless his interference with its conduct clearly goes beyond this'.

Although the Police and Criminal Evidence Act only provides for access by a solicitor, para 6.9 of the Code makes it clear that a clerk or legal executive should normally be offered the same facilities as a solicitor.

Many suspects, when they arrive at a police station, have no idea of how to contact a solicitor even though their right of access to legal advice may be pointed out to them. The Code provides that the police must tell the detained person of the availability of free advice from the duty solicitor and provide him with a list of local solicitors who have indicated they are available for the purpose of providing legal advice[20]. There are limited exceptions to this rule where questioning is necessary for the purpose of preventing or minimising harm or loss to some other person or to the public or for clearing up an ambiguity in a previous answer or statement, or where it is in the interests of justice that the person should have put to him and have an opportunity to comment on information concerning the offence which has come to light since he was charged.

We must now consider how these provisions would be likely to operate in the serious type of case taken as our example:

> *Example (contd)*. The superintendent was satisfied on the basis of the investigating officer's information that notification of Sikes' arrest to Fagin would lead to interference with evidence and the alerting of other persons not yet arrested; notification was therefore refused (s 56). Contact with Sikes' legal adviser, Mr Dodson, could hardly be refused on such grounds and so Sikes was permitted to make a telephone call to London. Mr Dodson stated that he would not be available at Barchester Police Station until the next morning. The superintendent therefore authorised questioning in the meantime under para 6.3.b of the Code because awaiting the arrival of the solicitor 'would cause unreasonable delay to the processes of investigation'. Note Sikes was told that Mr Dodson would not be available until the following morning and that he had the right to have legal advice provided by someone else (para 6A). In fact, Sikes declined the offer of another solicitor because he had already decided (on the basis of Mr Dodson's advice) to say nothing until his solicitor arrived.

INTERROGATION

In many cases the principal evidence against the accused is the answers he has given to questioning at the police station. A suspect is under no obligation to answer police questions, and indeed he is expressly told of his

19 Code para 6.6.
20 Notes for Guidance to Code para 6B.

right to silence when he is cautioned before interviewing begins, but in practice very few suspects exercise their right to remain silent.[1]

The practitioner has to understand two quite different problems which arise in respect of interrogation evidence. The first is how to challenge the *accuracy* of the record – in real life this is the most common problem. The second is how to *exclude* such evidence *as inadmissible* where it has been improperly obtained; the law recognises that there is a risk that persons in custody may confess to things that they have not done and so a legal framework has to be developed to protect the suspect during interrogation. In order to understand both these problems it is necessary to describe the various different methods which the police use to question suspects and record their answers:

(i) Notes made after interview concluded

Until about ten years ago the standard police practice was for the investigating officers not to record questions and answers while the interview was taking place. Instead, after the interview was concluded, the officers present pooled their recollections of what was said in an agreed note of the interview. This method of recording interviews was open to criticism firstly, because there was always a possibility of genuine error in recording a detailed conversation some time after it had occurred and, secondly, because of the opportunity given to the officers to misrepresent the defendant's answers to suit the prosecution case. From the police point of view, this method had the disadvantage that, although the court would hear the interview read over from the officers' note books, it would not (except in very rare cases) be given a copy of the interview record because the note book itself could not be exhibited. As we shall see below the Code of Practice provides that this method of recording answers is not normally to be used.

(ii) Contemporaneous notes

The practice which is usually adopted today involves one of the officers present at an interview acting as a 'scribe' and making a contemporaneous note in the form of 'questions and answers'. This will be read over to the suspect who will be asked to sign it to acknowledge that it is an accurate record of what has been said; provided it is signed the notes of the interview will become an exhibit at the trial.

(iii) Tape recording

Over the last three years various police forces and the Customs and Excise have carried out experimental schemes whereby interviews have been tape recorded. The interview is recorded on two cassettes, one of which is sealed immediately upon conclusion of the interview; the second cassette is copied and the copies are made available to the prosecuting authorities and the defence. The investigating officer in due course provides a witness statement summarising the interview; if this is not accepted the passages in dispute can be played over at court or in the last resort a transcript can be made.

---

1 See Baldwin and McConville 'Confessions in Crown Court Trials' (Royal Commission on Criminal Procedure Research Study No 5) (HMSO, 1980).

(iv) Voluntary statement under caution

When during the course of an oral interview it becomes clear that a suspect is admitting his guilt, the police will want to get a written confession signed by him. This will of course be extremely important evidence if he changes his story and pleads not guilty when he appears in court. Moreover, since it will be signed by the suspect it will be exhibited at his trial: in other words, the document itself will be given to the court and not merely read aloud. In theory, such statements are supposed to be either written by the suspect or at least dictated by him and recorded in his own words; in practice they are almost inevitably written by the investigating officer at the request of the suspect; the suspect only writes out the words of the caution and signs the completed statement.

The Code of Practice makes detailed provisions for the way interviews should be recorded; the most important points can be summarised as follows:

(a) The practice of writing up notes of interviews after they have been concluded should not normally be followed. Paragraph 11.3 of the Code requires that the interview record 'must be made during the course of the interview unless in the investigating officer's view this would not be practicable or would interfere with the conduct of the interview, and must constitute either a *verbatim* record of what has been said or, failing this, an account of the interview which adequately and accurately summarises it'[2]. If the interview record is not completed in the course of the interview the reason must be recorded in the officer's pocket book[3].

(b) Voluntary statements under caution are to be made on forms specifically provided for this purpose[4]. Where (as is the usual case) the suspect asks for the statement to be written by the interviewing officer, 'he must take down the exact words spoken by the person making the statment; he must not edit or paraphrase it. Any questions that are necessary (eg to make it more intelligible) and the answers given must be recorded contemporaneously on the statement form[5].'

(c) A detailed code has been prepared by the Home Office for the method to be employed in tape recording interviews.

Where an interview is tape recorded, or a contemporaneous note has been made and signed by the defendant, there will often be little ground for challenging the record. However, where no contemporaneous note is taken or it is suggested that important passages of the interview have not been recorded, it is worth noting that the Code provides that the interview record must state 'the place of the interview, the time it begins and ends, the time the record is made (if different), any breaks in the interview and the names of all those present'[6].

A quite different point from the accuracy of the record is whether the police have acted properly in conducting the interrogation. Where a solicitor is present at an interview (under para 6.5 of the Code) there is unlikely to be any suggestion of impropriety. However, there will be cases where a

2 Code para 11.3.
3 Ibid para 11.6.
4 Ibid para 12.13.
5 Ibid Annex D.
6 Ibid para 11.3

suspect declines the offer of legal assistance or where the police refuse access to a legal adviser or where questioning begins before a solicitor can arrive at the police station. In all these cases, the question of improper questioning is liable to arise. The basis of the present law is to be found in s 76(2) of the Police and Criminal Evidence Act 1984 which provides:

> 'If in any proceedings where the prosecution proposes to give in evidence a confession made by an accused person, it is represented to the court that the confession was or may have been obtained –
> (a) by oppression of the person who made it; or
> (b) in consequence of anything said or done which was likely, in the circumstances existing at the time, to render unreliable any confession which might be made by him in consequence thereof,
> the court shall not allow the confession to be given in evidence against him except in so far as the prosecution proves to the court beyond reasonable doubt that the confession (notwithstanding that it may be true) was not obtained as aforesaid.'

It will be appreciated that this section in effect makes the evidence of a confession inadmissible in two different (but possibly overlapping) circumstances:

(i)   where the police have behaved oppressively;
(ii) where the conduct of the interview is such as to render the answers given unreliable.

It is necessary to consider both circumstances. 'Oppression' is defined so as to include 'torture, inhumane or degrading treatment and the use of threat of violence'[7] but this definition is not exhaustive. It would seem that conduct is oppressive wherever it destroys the suspect's freedom of will – in other words, renders negatory the protection the law gives him against self-incrimination. Thus Lord MacDermott has described such questioning as that:

> 'which by its nature, duration or other attendant circumstances (including the fact of custody) excites hope (such as the hope of release) or fears, or so affects the mind of the suspect that his will crumbles and he speaks when otherwise he would have stayed silent'[8].

In considering whether there has been oppressive conduct reference should be made to the detailed provisions in the Code of Practice which regulate the way in which the suspect should be treated while in custody; it is suggested that the following provisions are particularly relevant:

(i)   the right not to be held incommunicado (para 5 of the Code);
(ii)   the right to legal advice (para 6);
(iii) the right to retain personal clothing and watches (para 4.2);
(iv)   access to washing facilities (para 8.4);
(v)   provision of meals (para 8.6);
(vi)   medical treatment and medication (para 9);
(vii) adequate rest (para 12.2).

Where there have been deliberate breaches of the above provisions of the Code of Practice it may be that the court will hold that the cumulative effect has been 'oppressive'. It is important to note that the court is specifically directed to take into account breaches of the Code:

7 Police and Criminal Evidence Act 1984 s 76(8). See *R v Fulling* [1987] QB 426, [1987] 2 All ER 65.
8 Address to Bentham Club (1968) 21 Current Legal Problems 10.

'In all criminal . . . proceedings any such code shall be admissible in evidence, and if any provision of such a code appears to the court . . . to be relevant to any questions taken into account in determining that question[9].'

It should be noted that where the issue of oppression arises:

(a) it is for the prosecution to prove beyond reasonable doubt that the confession was not obtained by oppression;
(b) the court is entitled to determine this question by reference to the character and personality of the accused[10].

The second ground for excluding evidence of a confession is that the conduct of the interviewing officer may have induced the accused to confess to what he has not done and so is unreliable. It is submitted that the sort of conduct which is relevant would be, for example:

(i) a promise to grant bail if a statement was made;
(ii) a promise not to proceed against the accused's wife or children.

The Code of Practice deals specifically with such inducements:

'No police officer . . . shall indicate, except in answer to a direct question, what action will be taken on the part of the police if the person being interviewed answers questions, makes a statement or refuses to do either. If the person directly asks the officer what action will be taken in the event of his answering questions, making a statement or refusing to do either, then the officer may inform the person what action he proposes to take in that event provided that the action is itself proper and warranted[11].'

Once again it will be appreciated that if the issue is raised it is for the prosecution to prove beyond reasonable doubt that the confession was not obtained in circumstances which might render it unreliable.

The advocate should bear in mind the provisions of s 78 of the Police and Criminal Evidence Act 1984, which enable the court to exclude unfairly obtained evidence. It is arguable that an application could be made under this section where the provisions of s 76 did not apply; eg deliberate breaches of the Code (such as refusal of access to a solicitor) so that the overall impression of the interview was that it had been conducted in a grossly unfair manner.[12]

It may be convenient at this stage to set out how these matters are dealt with at a trial;

(i) the issue of admissibility of a confession is determined by the judge in the absence of a jury. Frequently this involves taking evidence from the police officers concerned and the accused: this process is known as the 'voire dire'[13];

9 Police and Criminal Evidence Act 1984 s 67(11).
10 Per Sachs J in *R v Priestley* (1965) 50 Cr App Rep 183: 'What is oppressive as regards a child, an invalid or an old man or somebody inexperienced in the ways of the world may turn out not to be oppressive when one finds that the accused person is of a tough character and an experienced man of the world'. See also *R v Prager* [1972] 1 All ER 1114, [1972] 1 WLR 260 and *R v Hudson* (1980) 72 Cr App Rep 163.
11 Code para 11(1).
12 See *R v Mason* [1987] 3 All ER 481, CA where a confession was excluded where the police had tricked a defendant and his solicitor by falsely telling them that his fingerprints had been found on a bottle used as a petrol bomb.
13 See per Lord Bridge in *Ajodha v The State* [1981] 2 All ER 193 at 201. Note also that the defence counsel is not obliged to take the point of admissibility: he may decide for tactical reasons to abandon the point and thus avoid a cross-examination on the voire dire which

(ii) if the judge excludes the evidence, the jury will never hear of the confession;

(iii) if the judge is not prepared to exclude the evidence, the defence are still entitled to submit to the jury that no reliance should be placed upon it because of the circumstances in which it was obtained. In legal theory the judge is determining the question of admissibility and the jury is determining the issue of probative weight; in reality the defence are getting a second chance to attack the statement.

THE ROLE OF THE SOLICITOR

The Police and Criminal Evidence Act 1984 and the Code of Practice are designed to ensure that arrested persons should not be without legal advice and assistance while they are in custody. Until recently, only a minority of solicitors had regular experience of attendance at police stations; after January 1986 however such attendance has become one of the standard (and most important) duties of the solicitor engaged in a criminal practice. It seems, therefore, worth setting out the various different tasks which the solicitor may have to undertake at the police station. Detailed and authoritative guidance on this topic has been provided by the Law Society's Criminal Law Committee *Guidelines on Advising a Suspect in the Police Station.*

At the police station the solicitor should endeavour to see (a) the custody officer and (b) the investigating officer before interviewing his client. Although he is under no obligation to do so, the custody officer may be prepared to show the custody record; if so, the solicitor should note especially (i) the time of the initial detention, (ii) the time and duration of any interviews and (iii) whether there has been any refusal to provide notification of arrest or earlier access to a solicitor. In rare cases a solicitor consulted by a wife or relative may be faced with a custody officer who insists that the suspect has not asked for a lawyer. In this event, the solicitor should write a note to the suspect informing him of his instructions and asking whether he confirms them. The note should be delivered unsealed to the custody officer (with a copy for him) and he should be asked to deliver it at once.

It is also of great importance to speak with the investigating officer; the Law Society advise:

'Unless the suspect has been charged, seek to find out from the investigating officer: the suspected offence; the evidence in support; what further evidence is to be sought on questioning; has an admission been made: oral, written, on tape. When previous questioning has been recorded, seek to read or listen. When a written statement has been made, seek to read. The suspect has a right to be informed of the grounds of his arrest (s 28); but there may be other offences in contemplation in respect of which he has not yet been rearrested under s 31. There is no requirement on the officer to supply the further information indicated; he does so at his discretion. However, if details of alleged admissions are refused, and the suspect denied the opportunity of commenting on them, you may wish to make a note of this as it may have evidential implications. Consider, if appro-

would subsequently have to be repealed (possibly with much less effect) before the jury. Per Lord Bridge: 'though the case for the defence raises an issue as to the voluntariness of a statement in accordance with the principles indicated earlier in this judgment, defending counsel may for tactical reasons prefer that the evidence bearing on that issue be heard before the jury, with a single cross-examination of the witness on both sides, even though this means that the jury hear the impugned statement whether admissible or not'.

priate, whether to advise the suspect that he should exercise his right of silence in respect of further questions and/or make a statement[14].'

When interviewing the suspect it is very important to remember that he has the right to see his legal adviser in private[15].

'Seek the suspect's instructions *in private* and, whatever the circumstances, insist on a private interview; that is, one that is at least out of earshot of any third person, and preferably in a closed room, and be aware of the possible need to converse quietly. If obstructed, make representations to the senior officer available; explain the situation to the suspect and do *not* proceed with the interview but give appropriate advice[16].'

At the beginning of the interview it is important to reassure the suspect that anything said is totally confidential. The solicitor should then:

(a) explain what he has learnt from the police;
(b) ask the suspect for his account of the matters under investigation;
(c) check with him whether he has already been questioned and, if so, whether he has made any admissions;
(d) check whether he asserts that the questioning has been oppressive; (if so, he may well be advised to refer to this in any subsequent statement).

At this stage the most important question may be whether the suspect should be advised not to answer further questions. The Law Society point out that a suspect:

'may wish to remain silent in interview with the police for a number of reasons, apart from fear of confessing guilt, e g because the matter is complex and he needs time for thought, or he is not satisfied as to the sufficiency of the disclosure of the prosecution case, or he wishes to speak, if at all, within the context of a trial and the safeguards there provided or because of the need for more extensive legal advice than is then available'[17].

Although the advice to be given at this stage depends on all the circumstances, the following suggestions may be helpful:

(i) if the client tells his solicitor that he is guilty, then it may be in his interest from the point of subsequent mitigation in court to make a statement under caution. Before this is done the solicitor should check that the police have sufficient evidence to charge; if they have not, it may be better for him to remain silent. The suspect is entitled to have his solicitor present and the solicitor should certainly discuss in advance with him what he proposes to say; the solicitor may even privately assist the suspect to prepare his statement in draft which the suspect may then copy or dictate[18];
(ii) where the client tells his solicitor that he is not guilty, the question of what advice to give is more complex. If the suspect is anxious to give his account of events, it would be very seldom right for the solicitor to attempt to dissuade him; the role of the solicitor is then to check before interview what the defendant wants to say and to try to ensure that he gets an opportunity to put this across at the interview. Similarly, if the

14 Law Society Guidelines para 6.2d.
15 Code, para 6.1.
16 Law Society Guidelines para 8.1a.
17 Ibid para 8.3.f.
18 Ibid para 9.4.b.

suspect does not wish to answer further questions, it would almost always be wrong to seek to persuade him to the contrary. The problem area is where the suspect does not know what to do. In such a case the defence solicitor has to bear in mind that sometimes there may be a real advantage in agreeing to an interview so that a written record of the defendant's version of events should be in front of the jury (or magistrates). This would, for example, be particularly true where the defence was an alibi or self-defence. On the other hand if the defendant's version of events seems unlikely or if the solicitor feels the police have held back on relevant information in their possession, the best advice to the suspect may be that he should exercise his right of silence.

Once it is decided that the suspect should answer further questions, then the solicitor should be present at the questioning. He should bear in mind:

(a) that it is important for him to keep an accurate note of the interview – this may prove critical at the trial if the police version is to be challenged. The Law Society advise: 'Good police practice requires the officer to keep contemporaneous notes. You do likewise and where practicable check as the interview proceeds that your record corresponds'[19];

(b) that the role of the solicitor is *not* as a passive observer. The Law Society make the point:

'Your role is to assist the suspect: you are not there merely as an observer. The purpose of your presence is: to advise the suspect; to satisfy yourself and the suspect that the interview is being and will be conducted fairly; to assist communications between the suspect and his questioner'[20];

(c) that the solicitor may advise the suspect at any stage not to answer further questions or that he should receive further legal advice in private before the interview continues[1]. Of course great discretion is required on such matters particularly because it may embarrass the client if it subsequently emerges at the trial that at a key point in the questioning he was advised not to answer.

IDENTIFICATION

In many cases there is no issue that an offence has been committed; the issue is whether the person arrested by the police is in fact the person who committed the offence. In such a case, if the suspect does not admit his complicity under questioning, the police must obtain evidence which proves he was the person responsible.

FINGERPRINTING

The police have power to take fingerprints or palmprints from a suspect detained at a police station by force; they do *not* need a magistrate's authority to take such prints; the fingerprinting of a suspect can be authorised by a police officer of the rank of superintendent or above if he has reasonable grounds:

19 Ibid para 9.2.b.
20 Ibid para 9.2.a–b.
 1 Ibid para 9.3.h–i.

(a) for suspecting the involvement of the person from whom fingerprints are to be taken in a criminal offence; *and*

(b) for believing that his fingerprints will tend to confirm or disprove his involvement[2].

Where the police have charged a suspect they will as a matter of routine practice take his fingerprints; at that stage the authority of a senior officer is not necessary[3]. The reason why the police are given such a power after charge is so that they may check the identity of the person charged with the Criminal Records Office.

INTIMATE AND OTHER SAMPLES

There will be cases such as murder and serious wounding and sexual assaults where the police will wish to identify the suspect by forensic evidence of blood, saliva or other body fluids or pubic hair. The police do *not* have the right to take such samples unless the suspect gives his consent[4]. Where the police wish to obtain such a sample the investigating officer must first obtain the authority of an officer of at least the rank of superintendent. The suspect must be informed why the police require the sample and the suspect should be cautioned in the following terms:

> 'You do not have to provide this sample/allow this swab to be taken, but I must warn you that if you do not do so, a court may treat such a refusal as supporting any relevant evidence against you[5].'

Other samples (e g of hair or from under a nail) can be taken by force with a superintendent's authority on the grounds that such samples will tend to confirm or disprove the suspect's involvement in a serious arrestable offence[6].

IDENTIFICATION BY WITNESSES

(a) By photographs
Where a crime has been committed and the police are trying to identify the culprit they may wish to show eye witnesses photographs of likely suspects who have not yet been arrested. The correct procedure is laid down in Annex C to the Code on Identification of Suspects:

(a) Only one witness is to be shown the photographs at any one time. He must be shown not less than 12 photographs at a time. If the photographs include that of a person suspected by the police, the other photographs must resemble the suspect as closely as possible. When the witness is shown the photographs he shall be told that the photograph of the person whom he has said that he has seen previously may or may not be among them.

---

2 Police and Criminal Evidence Act 1984 s 61(3)–(4). The fingerprints must be destroyed if the suspect is subsequently acquitted or not prosecuted.
3 Ibid s 61(3)(b) – this power only arises in the case of a 'recordable offence' but that expression covers all offences punishable with imprisonment.
4 Ibid s 62(1)(b).
5 Code on Identification of Suspects para 5.2 and Note 5A.
6 Police and Criminal Evidence Act 1984 s 63.

(b) If he makes a positive identification from photographs the other eye witnesses are *not* to be shown photographs.

(c) The witness (and any other eye witnesses) should be asked to attend an identification parade.

(d) The suspect and his solicitor must be told at the parade that the witness in question has made a photograph identification[7].

This procedure must *not* be followed when there is a suspect already available to be asked to stand on an identification parade[8].

(b) By identification parade

Where a suspect has been arrested and has denied committing the offence (possibly on the grounds that he was not present or that, although present, he did not take part in the commission of the offence) an identification parade *must* be held if he asks for one[9]. If the suspect does *not* ask for a parade, the investigating officer can request that he attends a parade but he cannot be compelled to take part. (If he refuses to participate then the police can arrange for a confrontation with one or more eye witnesses[10].) Detailed rules are laid down for the conduct of identification parades; the parade must be conducted by a senior police officer not directly concerned with the enquiry[11] and the suspect must be told of his right to have a solicitor or friend present[12]. A detailed record is made of the parade (including wrong identifications by the eye witnesses and anything they may have said) and this must be made available to the defence. If a parade is held without a solicitor or friend of the suspect being present a colour photograph of the parade must be taken[13].

LIMITS ON POLICE DETENTION

Where the custody officer has authorised the initial detention of a suspect (see p 66) above he may then be kept at the police station for a period of 24 hours for the purpose of questioning him or while other investigations are carried out[14]. During this 24-hour period the question of the suspect's continued detention must be considered on at least two occasions by an inspector (the 'review officer'). The first review must take place not later than six hours after his detention was first authorised and the second review not less than nine hours thereafter. At these reviews both the suspect and his solicitor have the right to make representations to the review officer (Code para 16.1). A solicitor should consider making written representations, which must be retained and annexed to the custody record and may even be referred to subsequently in court if issues arise as to oppressive conduct. (The custody sheet in the example of Sikes (pp 68–69 above)

---

7 See Code on Identification of Suspects Annex C paras 2–9
8 Code on Identification of Suspects para 2.6.
9 Ibid para 2.1 (unless the police can show it is not practicable to hold one).
10 Ibid paras 2.4, 2.5. Confrontation must *not* take place unless the suspect has withheld his consent to a parade or a group identification or for some reason such identification is not practicable.
11 Ibid para 2.2.
12 Ibid Annex A para 1.
13 Ibid Annex A para 20. It is difficult to see why such a photograph should not be taken in all cases.
14 Police and Criminal Evidence Act 1984 s 41(1).

illustrates how this record is made.) If at any stage during this 24-hour period it becomes clear that there is sufficient evidence to charge the suspect then the investigating officers must stop questioning him and prefer a charge:

'As soon as a police officer who is making inquiries of any person about an offence believes that a prosecution should be brought against him and that there is sufficient evidence for it to succeed, he shall without delay cease to question him[15].'

'Where an officer considers that there is sufficient evidence to prosecute a detained person he should without delay bring him before the custody officer who shall then be responsible for considering whether or not he should be charged[16].'

Once the defendant has been charged then the custody officer has to determine how the police are to secure his attendance at court. There are three possibilities:

(i)   he may be released on the basis that the police will in due course issue and serve a summons for him to attend court (see p 89 below). This would be appropriate, for example, in an intoximeter case;

(ii) he may be released on bail to attend the magistrates' court. The custody officer may require sureties to secure his attendance at court[17];

(iii) he may be detained in police custody until his appearance before the magistrates' court[18]. In such a case he must be brought before a magistrates' court as soon as practicable and not later than the first sitting after he is charged[19]. Where such a sitting will not occur on the day of the charge or the following day, then the clerk to the justices must be notified and a special court will be arranged[20].

The third option described above (ie detention pending appearance at court) is only permitted where:

(i)   the suspect's name and address cannot be ascertained or the custody officer has reasonable grounds for doubting whether a name and a home address furnished by him are his real name and address;

(ii) the custody officer has reasonable grounds for believing that the detention of the person arrested is necessary for his own protection or to prevent him from causing physical injury to any other person or from causing loss or damage to property; or

(iii) the custody officer has reasonable grounds for believing that the person arrested will fail to appear in court to answer his bail or that his

15 Code on Investigation of Suspects para 11.2.
16 Code on Investigation of Suspects para 17.1. Note: para 17.5 provides that questions relating to an offence may not be put to a person after he has been charged 'unless they are necessary for the purpose of preventing or minimising harm or loss to some other person or to the public or for clearing up an ambiguity in a previous answer or statement, or where it is in the interest of justice that the person should have put to him and have an opportunity to comment on information concerning the offence which has come to light since he was charged or informed that he might be prosecuted'.
17 Police and Criminal Evidence Act 1984 s 38(1). As to bail and sureties see p 187 below.
18 Ibid.
19 Ibid s 46(1). Where he is not appearing at the local court and so is transferred to another police station, he must appear at the first sitting after his arrival at the police station.
20 Ibid s 46(5)–(8). For this purpose Sundays do not count.

detention is necessary to prevent him from interfering with the administration of justice or with the investigation of an offence or of a
particular offence[1].

Once the 24-hour period has expired without a charge being preferred
the police must release the suspect (although they are entitled to require
him to attend on a subsequent occasion at the police station by which time
their enquiries may have provided them with sufficient evidence to charge):

> 'a person who at the expiry of 24 hours after the relevant time is in police detention
> and has not been charged shall be released at that time either on bail or without
> bail'[2].

In most cases the police will not wish to detain the suspect for anything
like 24 hours. There will however be rare but serious cases where the police
require further detention before they can decide whether or not to charge.
The scheme set out in ss 42–44 of the Police and Criminal Evidence Act
1984 is to permit further periods of detention in exceptional cases:

*(i) Authorisation of continued detention for a period ending not more than 36 hours after
initial detention (s 42).* A superintendent may authorise detention for a period
ending not later than 36 hours from the time when detention began[3]. He is
bound to consider any representations by the suspect or his solicitor. At this
stage the solicitor should certainly record his representations in writing.
The superintendent must record the reasons for authorising such detention
and must be satisfied of each of the three conditions discussed below for
continued detention under a magistrate's warrant. (During the authorised
period of further detention, a review officer must consider the case every
nine hours.)

*(ii) Warrants of further detention for periods of 36 hours up to a maximum of four days
(96 hours) from initial detention (s 43).* A magistrates' court (of at least two
justices or a stipendiary magistrate) can authorise detention for further
periods (each of up to 36 hours) in very exceptional cases. The suspect must
be present when the application for a warrant of further detention is made
and he is entitled to be legally represented free of charge. The police must
satisfy the court that:

(a) the suspect's detention without charge is *necessary* to *secure* or *preserve
evidence* relating to an offence for which he is under arrest or to *obtain such
evidence by questioning* him;

(b) at least one of the offences for which he is under arrest is a *serious
arrestable offence*;

(c) the investigation is being conducted diligently and expeditiously[4].

1 Ibid s 38(1).
2 Ibid s 41(8).
3 Report of the Royal Commission on Criminal Procedure para 3.96: 'Overall, about
   three-quarters of suspects are dealt with in six hours or under and about 95 per cent within
   24 hours. It is very rare for persons to be held for much longer than this without charge.'
4 Police and Criminal Evidence Act 1984 s 42(1). Note the time when detention begins is
   normally the time at which the detained person first arrives at the police station. But when
   he is arrested in one police area and taken to another area for questioning, time begins to
   run when he first arrives at a police station in the latter area: s 41(3).

Unless the magistrates are satisfied that each of these three conditions is proved, they must dismiss the application and the police must then either charge the suspect or release him (with or without bail). In no sense is a hearing under this procedure a formality. The application by the police must be on oath and supported by a written statement ('information') setting out:

(a) the nature of the offence for which the person to whom the application relates has been arrested;
(b) the general nature of the evidence on which that person was arrested;
(c) what enquiries relating to the offence have been made by the police and what further enquiries are proposed by them;
(d) the reasons for believing the continued detention of that person to be necessary for the purposes of such further enquiries[5].

Since the arrested suspect will be legally represented the police will be liable to be cross-examined. It will only be in the most unusual case that the magistrates should accede to such an application where a solicitor has advised the client not to answer further questions and the police have questioned a suspect for 36 hours and are still not in a position to charge; a competent solicitor would be bound to give such advice. If the magistrates were told by the solicitor that he had given that advice, it would be impossible for them to authorise continued detention on the grounds that it was 'necessary . . . to obtain such evidence by questioning him'; it would in effect be necessary for the police to show that other enquiries were under way but not completed which would affect their decision whether or not to charge.

If the suspect's lawyer comes to the conclusion that his detention is not justified in the sense that the conditions discussed above are not satisfied the decision of the superintendent or magistrates would be challenged by an application to the High Court for *habeas corpus*[6]. The procedure on an application for the writ to issue is set out in RSC Ord 54. The basic stages are as follows:

(i) an application is made by counsel appearing ex parte before a single High Court judge or (more usually) the Divisional Court on behalf of the detained person (or anyone else interested in securing his release). The application must be supported by affidavit evidence setting out the relevant facts and why it is claimed that the detention is unlawful. Three copies of the affidavit should be lodged at court;
(ii) assuming at this ex parte stage the court considers there is a serious issue as to the legality of the detention, the court will normally adjourn the application for notice to be given to the persons detaining the applicant and other concerned parties (usually the governor of the prison, the police and the magistrates). The court directs when the case will be reconsidered;
(iii) on the return day, the court considers the evidence submitted and hears counsel as to the legality of the detention[7].

---

5 Ibid s 43(4).
6 Ibid s 43(14).
7 See notes to RSC Ord 54 in the White Book.

It should be noted that when the Divisional Court is considering an application for *habeas corpus* it is not sitting as an appeal court; it is not sufficient for the applicant to show the decision is unfair; he must show it is illegal. It seems probable that the court will only act where it can show that the decision that the three detention conditions were satisfied was wrong in the sense that no police officer or magistrate properly understanding the evidence and directing himself as to the law and acting reasonably could have reached such decision[8].

CHILDREN AND YOUNG PERSONS

We shall consider later the special rules which relate to the trial and punishment of children (under 14) and young persons (under 17). At this stage, it may be convenient to summarise the rules which affect the investigation of crimes by juveniles and govern their arrest. These rules are in addition to the rules already discussed in this chapter.

(i) Arrest and initial detention
Juvenile offenders are not to be arrested[9] or interviewed[10] at their place of education save in exceptional circumstances. When a juvenile is brought to a police station under arrest the custody officer must contact 'the appropriate adult' (his parent or social worker) and ask that person to attend at the police station[11]. The juvenile must not be placed in the police cells unless no other secure accommodation is available[12].

(ii) Interrogation of juveniles
A juvenile, whether suspected of crime or not, must not be interviewed or asked to provide or sign a written statement in the absence of the appropriate adult (except in cases of grave urgency where an officer of the rank of superintendent or above authorises such interviewing)[13]. The juvenile, like every other arrested person, must be informed of his right to have a solicitor present at the police station; if the appropriate adult considers that legal advice should be taken, interviewing must not take place until such advice has been obtained.

(iii) Further detention
If the juvenile is charged he must either be released on bail[14] or taken into the care of the local authority[15].

---

8 By analogy with the principle in *Associated Provincial Picture Houses Ltd v Wednesbury Corpn* [1948] 1 KB 223, [1947] 2 All ER 680.
9 Code on Detention, Treatment and Questioning para 13D.
10 Ibid para 13.3.
11 Ibid para 13.6. 'Appropriate adult' is defined in the Code as '(i) his parent or guardian (or, if he is in care, the care authority or organisation) or (ii) a social worker or (iii) failing either of the above a named responsible adult who is not a police officer or employed by the police'.
12 Ibid para 8.8.
13 Ibid para 13.1 and Annex C.
14 His parents can be required to stand surety, eg Children and Young Persons Act 1969 s 28(2).
15 Police and Criminal Evidence Act 1984 s 58(6). Note: a juvenile can be detained if any of the conditions in s 31(1) apply or if such detention is 'in his own interests'.

Chapter 3

Magistrates' court jurisdiction

All criminal proceedings begin in a magistrates' court; in this chapter we shall consider:

(i)   the composition of the court;
(ii) the court's power to compel the attendance of the defendant;
(iii) how it is determined whether a case should be tried before the magistrates or sent for trial by a judge and jury at the Crown Court.

In Chapter Four we shall deal with the procedure whereby magistrates commit cases for trial at the Crown Court; in Chapter Six we shall look at the way in which a magistrates' court tries a case (ie *summary trial*).

MAGISTRATES AND THEIR CLERKS

Magistrates' courts are courts where the tribunal consists *either* of justices of the peace (who are unpaid laymen without any necessary legal qualifications) *or* of a stipendiary magistrate (who is a qualified lawyer paid a fixed salary for his work). Justices of the peace are appointed by the Lord Chancellor under s 6 of the Justices of the Peace Act 1979 to serve in one of the counties of England and Wales or in one of the London commission areas. The Lord Chancellor's Department is advised by committees of magistrates in the various counties of suitable persons to be appointed justices of the peace; in other words, existing magistrates themselves recommend new appointments to their number. In practice, the people who become magistrates are those who through work for the various political parties or through social service, have shown an interest in the welfare of the community. Justices therefore form a rather exceptional group of people and are not a simple cross-section of the community like a jury. (This fact is of significance when a lawyer has to advise his client whether or not to elect jury-trial; most experienced defence advocates consider that a random selection of members of the public is more likely to acquit than a bench of magistrates.)

Stipendiary magistrates sit in the very busy magistrates' courts in London and the large towns. The office was first created at the end of the eighteenth century to meet the need for efficient and qualified magistrates in the London courts. Stipendiary magistrates[1] are appointed from barris-

---

1 Until recently, and perhaps to some extent still today, the quality of stipendiaries has varied; in 1960 the Bow Group reported: 'A visit to many of the courts presided over by stipendiary magistrates will reveal justice being administered with speed, efficiency,

ters and solicitors with considerable experience of criminal practice; occasionally a stipendiary is appointed from the magistrates' courts service after long experience as a clerk.

Stipendiary magistrates usually sit alone (although sometimes they sit with justices of the peace); on the other hand, lay justices usually sit as a bench of two or three members. When they are trying an offence there must be at least two justices on the bench[2]; a single justice may, however, conduct committal proceedings[3].

Every magistrates' court has attached to it a legally qualified clerk and, usually, a number of assistant clerks. The clerk's functions in court are to advise on points of procedure and law; he also arranges the day-to-day administration of the court and deals with matters such as the issue of summonses and the grant of legal aid. Although justices of the peace receive basic training, they necessarily rely on the advice of their clerk on any legal or procedural points of complexity[4].

THE INFORMATION

Criminal proceedings[5] are commenced by the prosecution presenting to a magistrate an *information* alleging that the person named therein has committed some specific offence. Where the defendant has been arrested and charged by the police, a copy of the *charge sheet* is handed to the clerk and becomes the *information*. When the defendant has not been arrested (as, for example, will be the case with the vast majority of road traffic offenders), the police produce a written *information* to the court (see p 87 for an example). The magistrates, when they come to try the case against the defendant or to decide whether there is a sufficient case to commit him to the Crown Court, will use the *information* as the formal statement of the charge against him. Thus criminal proceedings in a magistrates' court are in law '*the hearing of an information*'.

Certain technical rules apply to the drafting of the information. It must give sufficient particulars to indicate the place, date and nature of the offence. Generally, however, defects and mistakes in setting out these

---

courtesy and good humour. . . . However, a visit to some other court of the same sort will reveal a very different state of affairs. Sufficient to say in them, both laymen and women are bullied and chivied and treated in a way which sometimes ignores even the most elementary rules of civilised behaviour; the sentencing of offenders tends to be haphazard and sometimes almost savage. One bad stipendiary magistrate sitting alone can do more harm than a dozen bad lay magistrates whose deficiencies will be tempered by right-thinking colleagues.'

2 Magistrates' Courts Act 1980 s 121.

3 Ibid s 4(1).

4 We discuss later (at p 158 below) the extent to which the court clerk may properly intervene to assist the magistrates. In practice, his knowledge of court procedure is more likely to be superior to that of any advocate appearing before the court. The barrister or solicitor starting to practise in the magistrates' courts would be well advised to inform the clerk before the justices sit of any procedural problem or particular point of law which is likely to arise. He may well find that the clerk can assist on the point of procedure and it is only common courtesy, since the clerk will in due course have to advise the justices as to the law, to inform him in advance of any point of law to be taken and the authorities relied upon.

5 Civil proceedings, such as matrimonial cases and care proceedings, are begun by a different process known as a *complaint*.

**PETTY SESSIONAL DIVISIONS
OF BARCHESTER**

IN THE COUNTY
OF BARSET

Date: 2nd January 1987

Accused: JOHN BOLD

Address: The Elms, Garden Drive, Barchester, Barset

Alleged offence: That on 1 January 1987 at High St,
                 Barchester, he wounded Albert Smith
                 with intent to cause him grievious
                 bodily harm contrary to section 18 of the
                 Offences against the Person Act 1861.

The information of: Police Constable 205 Robert ADAMS

Address: Police Station, Barchester

Telephone No.   54673

who (upon oath) states that the accused committed the
offence of which particulars are given above.
Taken (and sworn) before me

John Smith

Justice of the Peace

(Justices' Clerk)

INFORMATION

W 44 TP

matters can be amended[6]. More important, only one offence may be set out in any one information[7] (although several different informations may be set out in the same document[8]).

Example. If in the course of a fight D punched A on the nose and gave B a black eye, the prosecutor could not lay an information charging D with assault on A and B. He would have to set out two separate informations charging two separate offences of assault.

This principle (called 'the rule against duplicity') is of significance because the magistrates have no power to amend the information to cure duplicity once the trial has begun[9]. The test whether an information is bad for duplicity is to ask: 'Does the single count charge more than one activity even though that activity may involve more than one act?[10]'

There is a time limit so far as *summary offences* (eg careless driving) are concerned; the court will have no jurisdiction to hear the case if the *information* was laid more than six months after the offence was committed[11].

PROCESS

Laying the *information* is an ex parte action; in other words, proceedings in which only one side is involved. Once the *information* has been laid the court must then secure the attendance before it of the person charged. It has already been explained that where the police arrest a person and detain him after charging him they are under a statutory duty to bring him before the

---

6 Magistrates' Courts Act 1980 s 123(1): 'No objection may be allowed to any information . . . summons or warrant for any defect in it in substance or form or for any variance between it and the evidence at the hearing'. This section is not to be construed literally, it simply means the court has wide powers of amendment for any defect in it in substance or form or for any variation between it and the evidence at the hearing. See per Lord Parker CJ in *Hutchinson (Cinemas) Ltd v Tyson* (1969) 134 JP 202: 'It seems to me that one might find an information which was so defective, so fundamentally bad, that it could not be cured at all and the only proper course would be for the justices to dismiss the information. At the other end of the scale there may be informations which are deficient in some minor particular, a misdescription of premises or data, where there can be no prejudice and where no amendment or further particulars are required at all. In between there are informations, which are perfectly good as informations, albeit deficient and can be cured, not merely by a formal amendment, but by the delivery of particulars to supplement their contents.' See also *Wright v Nicholson* [1970] 1 All ER 12, [1970] 1 WLR 142.
7 Magistrates' Courts Rules 1981 r 12(1).
8 *DPP v Shah* [1984] 1 WLR 886.
9 See *Hargreaves v Alderson* [1964] 2 QB 159, [1962] 3 All ER 1919.
10 Per Lord Parker CJ in *Ware v Fox* [1967] 1 All ER 100, [1967] 1 WLR 379. The problem of duplicity arises in the same way in the rule that an individual count in an indictment may only charge one offence (see p 121 below). Practitioners in the magistrates' courts need to be aware of this problem in the case of offences involving a series of separate acts each of which alone would constitute an offence (eg *Jemmison v Priddle* [1972] 1 QB 489, [1972] 1 All ER 539, taking deer over a period – one offence; *Anderton v Cooper* (1980) 72 Cr App Rep 232, managing a brothel – one offence; *Horrix v Malam* [1984] RTR 112, incidents of careless driving over 35 minutes – not one offence; *R v Ballysingh* (1953) 37 Cr App Rep 28, shoplifting from different departments of a department store – not one offence; *R v Wilson* (1979) 69 Cr App Rep 83, planned shoplifting expedition – one offence although articles taken at different points in time).
11 Magistrates' Courts Act 1980 s 127. Note: this restriction does not apply to offences which are triable either way, such as theft. Note also that it is an abuse of the process of the court for the prosecutor to lay an information within the time period intending subsequently to decide whether or not to apply for a summons: *R v Brentford Justices, ex p Wong* [1981] QB 445, [1981] 1 All ER 884.

magistrates' court on the first sitting after he has been charged[12]. If he has been released on bail[13] then no problem occurs if he duly attends court and surrenders to his bail. Where, however (as will apply in the majority of cases), the accused has not been arrested (and so never subject to police bail) the court must issue process to secure his attendance.

In most cases (e g road traffic offenders) there is no reason to suppose that the accused will fail to appear before the court, so that it is sufficient that a formal document, called a *summons*, requiring his attendance, be sent to him.

As stated above, every magistrate is appointed with jurisdiction limited to a particular county or commission area. A justice of the peace (or magistrates' clerk) has power under s 1 of the Magistrates' Courts Act 1980 to issue a summons wherever:

(1) the offence was *committed* within that *county* (or commission area)[14];
(2) the offence is *indictable* and the accused *resides* within that *county* (or commission area)[15];
(3) it is necessary or expedient with a view to the better administration of justice that the accused should be *tried jointly with*, or at the same place as, some *other person* over whom the court has jurisdiction[16];
(4) he is *already due to appear* before the court for *some other offence* over which the court has jurisdiction and the subsequent offence is *summary*[17].

The effect of these complicated provisions can best be understood by noting the principal class of case over which the magistrates will normally have *no* power to issue a summons, namely *a summary offence not committed within their jurisdiction*.

Example 1. A steals a case at Southampton and returns home to Bristol. Both the magistrates at Southampton and Bristol will have jurisdiction to issue a summons since theft is an *indictable* offence.

Example 2. A drives his motor car without due care and attention in Southampton. Although he may live in Bristol, only the Southampton magistrates will have power to issue a summons since the offence is *summary*. This means that (unless A pleads guilty by post) he will have to travel to Southampton to answer the summons.

A summons may be served on a defendant in any one of the following ways:

(1) by personal delivery;
(2) by leaving it with some person for him at his last known or usual place of abode;

---

12 Police and Criminal Evidence Act 1984 s 46.
13 Ibid s 47.
14 Magistrates' Courts Act 1980 s 1(2)(a). Note: s 3 provides that where an offence has been committed on the boundary between two or more counties or commission areas or within 500 yards of such a boundary, or in any harbour, river, area of the sea or other water lying between them, the offence may be treated as having been committed in any of those areas. Similarly, where an offence is committed on a train or vehicle travelling from one place to another the offence will be treated as having been committed within the jurisdiction of any of the counties or commissions as are along the route of the journey.
15 Ibid s 1(2)(c).
16 Ibid s 1(2)(b).
17 Ibid s 2(6).

Copy to be retained by defendant

SUMMONS (M.C. Act 1980, s.1: M.C. Rules 1981 r.98)

.....Camberwell Green (Court 3).. Magistrates Court   (Court Code 2656)

Ref. Number   LS.M. 732

To
> Mr. Clive BARKER
> 106 High Street
> FARNHAM
> Surrey

You are hereby summoned to appear

on   5th April 1987   at 2.00 pm
before the Magistrates' Court
at 15 D'Eynsford Road, Camberwell, S.E.5
to answer to the following information laid
today
on 18th September 1986   at Streatham High Road S.W.16

Alleged   did drive a motor vehicle on a road without due care and
offence   attention. Contrary to Section 3 of, and Schedule 4 to,
the Road Traffic Act, 1972.

Informant   Police Constable James BUCKET (189L)
Address   Streatham Police Station

Date   13th February 1987   *Lionel Fang*
                        Metropolitan Stipendiary Magistrate/Justices' Clerk/Justice of the Peace

YOUR DRIVING LICENCE
MUST BE AT THIS COURT
BY THE DATE OF HEARING.
FAILURE TO COMPLY COULD
LEAD TO THE SUSPENSION OF
YOUR LICENCE AND A
FINE OF
UP TO £50.

STATEMENT OF FACTS (Magistrates' Courts Act, 1980, Section 12 (1)(b).)

IF YOU INFORM THE CLERK of the Court that you wish to plead guilty to the offence set out in the summons
served herewith, without appearing before the Court, and the Court proceeds to hear and dispose of the case in
your absence under Section 12 of the Magistrates' Courts Act 1980, the following Statement of Facts will be read
out in open Court before the Court decides whether to accept your plea.   If your plea of guilty is accepted the
Court will not, unless it adjourns the case after convicting you and before sentencing you, permit any other statement
to be made by or on behalf of the prosecutor with respect to any facts relating to the offence.

On 18th September 1986 at 14.20hrs you were the driver of an
Alfa Romeo index No. APB 267S travelling south on Oakfield Road
SW16. At the junction with Streatham High Road you turned right
and collided with a Lancia Fulvia JPA 955P travelling east
along the mian road. When asked by the Police Reporting
Officer what had happened, you said "The sun was in my eyes.
I just didn't notice him. He must have been going too fast".

PLEASE TURN OVER   Signed   ....*
                                                (On behalf of the Prosecutor)

IN THE COUNTY OF BARSET
PETTY SESSIONAL DIVISION OF BARCHESTER

Barchester Magistrates' Court (1873)

Date:	2nd January 1987
Accused:	JOHN BOLD
Address:	The Elms, Garden Drive, Barchester, Barset
Alleged offence:	That on 1 January 1987 at High St, Barchester, he wounded Albert Smith with intent to cause him grievous bodily harm contrary to section 18 of the Offences against the Person Act 1861

Information having been laid before me on oath (affirmation) by ROBERT ADAMS, P.C. 205 on 2nd January 1987 that the accused committed the above offence.

Direction: You, the constables of the Barchester Police Force, are hereby required to arrest the accused and to bring the accused before the above magistrates' court immediately (unless the accused is released on bail as directed below).

Bail: On arrest, after complying with the condition(s) specified on Schedule I hereto, the accused shall be released on bail (unconditionally), subject to the condition(s) specified in Schedule II hereto, and with a duty to surrender to the custody of the above magistrates' court on at 10 a.m.

John Smith

Justice of the Peace for the said Area.

Schedule I
Conditions to be complied with before release on bail
To provide   2   suret(y)(ies) in the sum of £2000   (each) to secure the accused's surrender to custody at the time and place appointed.

Schedule II
Conditions to be complied with after release on bail

To surrender passport to police

Warrant 1st instance

Form 4
CO 2472

*(3) by sending it to him by post in a letter addressed to him at his last
known or usual place of abode*[18].

The alternative form of process is by a *warrant* directing the police to *arrest*
the person named in the *information* and to produce him at court. This
procedure is only used in the following cases:

(1) where the charge is serious, or for some other reason it is thought
unlikely that the defendant will attend court voluntarily;
(2) where the police can prove that a summons has been served but the
defendant has failed to attend court;
(3) where the police have released a defendant on bail to appear at court
but he has failed to do so.

In practice, an application for a warrant is made by the police officer
concerned producing before a magistrate a written statement of evidence
stating shortly the facts alleged and verifying the statement on oath. A form
of warrant is set out on p 91. Where the magistrate feels it appropriate,
the warrant may be *backed for bail*, i e endorsed with a statement that the
police are to release the defendant on bail to attend the court at such time as
may be specified in the endorsement[19]. If the defendant fails to appear, he
will commit an offence under s 6 of the Bail Act 1976. The warrant may also
contain a direction that the arrested person is only to be released if he
obtains sureties to ensure his attendance at court.

JURISDICTION TO TRY OFFENCE CHARGED

When the accused appears before the magistrates' court its powers will be
either:

(1) to determine the issue whether the accused is guilty or not guilty of the
charge contained in the information (this is called *summary trial*). If the
accused admits his guilt, the issue will be to determine the appropriate
penalty; or
(2) to sit as examining justices to decide whether or not the accused should
be committed for trial to the Crown Court (this is called *committal
proceedings*).

It will be remembered that some cases (e g robbery) are so serious that even
if the accused intends to plead guilty, the magistrates' powers are limited to
deciding whether there is sufficient evidence to warrant committing the
defendant for trial before a jury at the Crown Court, while others (e g
driving without due care and attention) are comparatively trivial and can
only be heard in a magistrates' court. Between these extremes are many
different offences which can be tried either by the Crown Court or by a
magistrates' court. The basic division of offences is shown in the table
below:

18 Magistrates' Courts Rules 1981 r 99. Note that where the defendant is a company, service
is effected by delivering or sending the summons to the registered office.
19 Magistrates' Courts Act 1980 s 117. Note: he can enter into the recognizance without
attending a police station – i e 'doorstep bail'; see s 117(3) as substituted by Police and
Criminal Evidence Act 1984. This does *not* apply where sureties are required.

(1) Offences triable only on indictment
This category comprises:

(a) all common law offences – eg murder, manslaughter;
(b) offences created by statutes which only provide for a penalty on indictment – eg wounding with intent (Offences Against the Person Act 1861 s 18), robbery (Theft Act 1968, s 8), causing death by reckless driving (Road Traffic Act 1972 s 1).

(2) Offences triable either way
This category comprises:

(a) offences listed in Sch 1 of the Magistrates' Courts Act 1980 – eg most offences under the Theft Act 1968, unlawful wounding and assault occasioning actual bodily harm (Offences Against the Person Act 1861 ss 20 and 47), indecency between men (Sexual Offences Act 1956 s 13);
(b) offences where the penalty section provides they are punishable on indictment and summarily – eg living on the earnings of prostitution, importuning by a man (Sexual Offences Act 1956 ss 30 and 32), possession of a controlled drug (Misuse of Drugs Act 1971 s 5) reckless driving (Road Traffic Act 1972 s 2).

(3) Summary offences
This category comprises offences where the penalty section only provides for punishment on summary conviction – eg most offences under Road Traffic Act 1972, interference with vehicles (Criminal Attempts Act 1981 s 9), being found drunk (Licensing Act 1872 s 12), assault or obstruction of the police (Police Act 1964 s 51), public order offences (Public Order Act 1986).

It will be noted that there is no right of jury trial where a person is charged with assault on the police, obstruction or public order offences. In such cases the court is inevitably being asked to decide between the conflicting evidence of the police, on the one hand, and of the accused on the other. Such an issue is pre-eminently suitable for trial by jury. It is sometimes suggested that in inner urban areas coloured youths, for example, believe their conviction will be automatic because the magistrates simply will not be prepared to reject police evidence. While this criticism may well be unfair, the defendant in such a case is at a grave disadvantage because he will not have received advance information of the prosecution evidence (see p 155 below).

PROCEDURE WHERE OFFENCE TRIABLE EITHER WAY

If an offence can only be tried on indictment then, as stated below, the sole function of the magistrates is to hold *committal proceedings*; if the offence is summary the court proceeds at once to *summary trial*. Where, however, the offence is triable either way then:

(a) the court itself has to determine whether it would be appropriate to try the particular offence summarily;

(b) the defendant has to consent to the case being dealt with summarily.

The procedure which is followed when a magistrates' court is dealing with an offence triable either way involves the following stages[20];

(1) The court must first satisfy itself that the defendant is aware of his right to *advance disclosure* of the prosecution evidence (either in the form of a summary of the case or written statements from the witnesses). If a request for disclosure has been made to the prosecution, the court must ordinarily adjourn the proceedings if disclosure has not been made[1].

(2) The magistrates must then decide whether the case is *suitable for summary trial*[2]. This involves considering the seriousness of the offence[3] and the court's powers of sentencing. The maximum penalty a magistrates' court can impose for an offence triable either way is a sentence of six months' imprisonment or a fine not exceeding £2000 or both[4]. In making this decision the court is unaware of the accused's criminal record but if the magistrates do try the case and then discover the accused has previous convictions they may commit him to the Crown Court for sentence if they consider a more serious penalty is appropriate than they have power to impose[5]. In deciding whether the case is suitable for summary trial, the court must take into account representations made by the prosecutor and the defendant[6].

(3) If the magistrates decide that the case is appropriate for summary trial, the clerk must then explain to the defendant:

    (a) that he has the right to be tried by a judge and jury at the Crown Court; and

    (b) that if he is tried summarily by the magistrates they can nevertheless commit him to the Crown Court for sentence if they convict

20 The reader is asked to look back to p 8 in the case of Twist where the dialogue which takes place at this stage between the clerk of the court and the defendant is set out.

1 Magistrates' Courts (Advance Information) Rules 1985 rr 6(1) and 7(1).

2 Magistrates' Courts Act 1980 s 19(1). Note: if the prosecution is being conducted by the Director of Public Prosecutions the court is bound to sit as examining justices if the prosecution so applies: s 19(4).

3 For example, large scale theft or receiving should not be dealt with by the magistrates' court. Again, the Court of Appeal has said that offences of burglary at night are not normally appropriate for summary trial: See *R v Hardman* (1982) Times, 10 November. It should be noted that the Magistrates' Courts Act 1980 enables the court at any time up to the close of the prosecution case to discontinue a summary trial and to sit instead as examining justices. Such a course would be appropriate when the evidence shows the offence to be more serious than first thought. Conversely, where the court has begun to hear committal proceedings, it can (with the consent of the accused) proceed to try the case summarily.

4 Magistrates' Courts Act 1980 s 32; Criminal Penalties (Increase) Order 1984.

5 Magistrates Courts Act 1980 s 38; the Crown Court can pass any sentence which could have been imposed if the defendant had been committed for trial. This provision is discussed at p 221 below.

6 Such representations may be made by the defence advocate for two reasons: (i) if the client intends to plead guilty, he is likely to receive a lesser sentence at the magistrates' court, so that it is in his interests to seek to persuade the magistrates to deal with the case; (ii) if the client intends to plead not guilty and wishes to be tried by a jury, he is less likely to be subject to an adverse order for costs at the Crown Court if the magistrates declined jurisdiction than if the magistrates were prepared to try the case and he insisted on his right of trial by jury. For that reason, his advocate may feel it appropriate to try to persuade the court that this case is not suitable for summary trial.

and then, learning of his character and antecedents, come to the conclusion that greater punishment should be imposed than the court has power to inflict[7].

(4) The accused elects trial by jury or consents to summary trial.

Where the defendant says he is not guilty, the defence advocate will have to advise his client as to the respective merits of trial at the Crown Court and before the magistrates. Most practitioners agree that a defendant's chances of acquittal are higher before a jury (particularly if there is a conflict of evidence between him and the police) but there are other factors which may dispose the advocate to advise summary trial; for example, if the defence case is very weak, opting for trial at the Crown Court may mean the client receives a higher sentence; again, if the client is very distressed (eg shoplifters and people charged with offences involving indecency), it must be pointed out that there is usually a substantial waiting period before a case can be heard at the Crown Court.

A problem which sometimes arises in practice is that *after* an unrepresented accused has elected summary trial the magistrates grant legal aid and adjourn the case. When the accused sees his lawyer he may be advised that, on his version of events, he has a defence to the charge and would have a better chance of acquittal if he was to elect trial by jury. In such a case he may apply to change his election; the magistrates have a discretionary power to allow this to be done but if they refuse, the Divisional Court will only interfere if it can be shown that they were manifestly wrong in the way they exercised their discretion.

Example 1. Z was accused of shoplifting, elected summary trial and pleaded *not guilty*; the case was then adjourned for her to obtain legal representation. She consulted a solicitor and asked to change her election. The stipendiary magistrate refused and the Divisional Court declined to interfere with the exercise of his discretion[8].

Example 2. H and W were charged with stealing wood valued at £12. They elected to be tried summarily and pleaded *guilty*. They were granted legal aid because their mitigation showed a possible defence (ie they thought the wood had been thrown away). Having received advice they applied to change their election and claim trial by jury. The magistrates refused to allow them to change the election but the Divisional Court ordered that they should be allowed to change on the grounds that the original decision to opt for summary trial was made under a misapprehension that they had no defence[9].

Although in practice it is much easier to persuade a court to permit a change of election where the defendant initially pleaded guilty (under a mistake as to his legal position), it should also be a valid argument to show that the defendant (while always intending to contest the charge) did not fully appreciate the tactical implications of electing summary trial.

'If the accused demonstrates that his original choice was exercised when he did not properly understand the nature and significance of the choice which he was making, then it is as if he had never made that choice and ... Parliament

---

7 Magistrates' Courts Act 1980 s 20.
8 *R v Metropolitan Stipendiary Magistrate, ex p Zardin* (1971) referred to in the report of *R v Birmingham Justices ex p Hodgson* below.
9 *R v Birmingham Justices, ex p Hodgson* [1985] QB 1131, [1985] 2 All ER 193.

conferred on an accused the right to make that choice regardless of the justices' view about which was the more suitable court to deal with the case[10].'

Thus, for example, the Divisional Court has intervened where a 17-year-old defendant elected summary trial and pleaded not guilty without fully understanding the significance of his choice[11].

CRIMINAL DAMAGE CASES

A charge of criminal damage under s 1 of the Criminal Damage Act 1971 is only *triable either way* if the value of the propery destroyed or damage done exceeds £2000[12]. If the value of the property destroyed or cost of repairs does not exceed £2000 the case must be tried summarily. The magistrates have to decide as a preliminary point whether the value or cost of repairs is more than £2000. If the magistrates are uncertain whether the value of the property or cost of repairs exceeds £2000, the defendant is to be offered the right of summary trial on the basis that, if he is convicted, the maximum penalty will be three months' imprisonment and/or a fine of £1000 and that he *cannot* be committed to the Crown Court. Where the defendant is charged with two or more offences of criminal damage committed on the same occasion (or which are in some way linked) the offences are treated as summary unless the aggregate value of the property destroyed or the cost of the repairs exceeds £2000.

> *Example 1.* M is charged with damaging a padlock (value £5) and (ii) damaging the watch (value £15) of a police officer who tried to arrest him. If the first and second incident are linked, both charges must be treated purely as summary offences.[13]

Where the defendant is charged with criminal damage (and the value of the property damaged or the cost of repairs does not exceed £2000) but at the same time is charged with some other offence triable either way the criminal damage charge remains a summary offence unless there is a common link between the two offences and they constitute a series of offences of a similar character.

> *Example 2.* C is charged with burglary of a refreshment kiosk and causing criminal damage (amounting to £34) in breaking into it. The criminal damage charge would remain a summary offence because criminal damage is not an offence of a similar character to burglary.[14]

10　Ibid at 201 per McCullough J.
11　*R v Highbury Corner Metropolitan Stipendiary Magistrate, ex p Weekes* [1985] QB 1147, [1985] 2 WLR 643.
12　Magistrates' Courts Act 1980 s 22. Note: the magistrates merely have to hear representations, they are not obliged to hear evidence on the point; *R v Canterbury Justices, ex p Klisiak* [1982] QB 398, [1981] 2 All ER 129. Note also that there is no appeal to the Crown Court against their determination.
13　Magistrates' Courts Act 1980 s 22(11) – substituted by Criminal Justice Bill 1987, cl 35. Note the effect is to overrule the decision in *R v St Helens Justices, ex p McClorie* [1983] 1 WLR 1332.
14　Ibid cl 22(7). See *R v Considine* (1979) 70 Cr App Rep 239, [1980] Crim LR 179, CA and *R v Hatfield Justices, ex p Castle* [1980] 3 All ER 509, [1981] 1 WLR 267. Note: if the defendant elected trial by jury on the burglary charge, the magistrates could commit him for trial on the criminal damage charge under cl 36 of the Criminal Justice Bill 1987.

COMMITTAL FOR TRIAL OF SUMMARY OFFENCES

Clause 36 of the Criminal Justices Bill 1987 provides that where a person is committed to the Crown Court for trial for an offence triable either way, the court may also commit in respect of a summary offence provided:

(i) it is punishable with imprisonment or involves obligatory or discretionary disqualification from driving; and
(ii) it arises out of circumstances which are the same as or connected with those giving rise to the indictable offence.

An example would be where a defendant had taken a motor car without permission (which will become a summary offence) and used it for the purpose of carrying out a burglary (an offence triable either way).

CUSTODY TIME LIMITS

Section 22 of the Prosecution of Offences Act 1985 empowers the Home Secretary to provide time limits specifying the maximum period a person can be kept in custody before trial or committal. Regulations made in 1987 (SI 1987/299) provide such limits for cases proceeding in Avon, Kent, Somerset and West Midlands. If the prosecution are not ready to proceed within the specified period (70 days, except in West Midlands where the period is 98 days) the accused is to be given unconditional bail, unless the prosecution apply under s 23 of the Act for the court to extend the time limit and the court is satisfied that 'there is good or sufficient cause for so doing and that the prosecution has acted with all due expedition.'

SUMMARY

We have seen in this chapter:

(1) how proceedings are commenced by laying an information;
(2) how the accused is brought to court (ie by summons or warrant or from police detention);
(3) that in some cases, the magistrates will have no power to try the defendant and must begin committal proceedings;
(4) that in some cases, the magistrates alone have power to try the defendant and must embark on summary trial;
(5) that in many cases the magistrates have to decide whether they should try the accused summarily, and in all such cases they must first tell him of his right to elect jury trial, warn him of their power to commit to the Crown Court for sentence if they try and convict him, and ascertain whether he wishes to be tried summarily.

Chapter 4

Committal proceedings

RATIONALE

Whenever a person appears before a magistrates' court, charged either:

(1) with an offence which can only be tried by a jury (eg rape, arson, robbery), or
(2) with any offence triable either way which the magistrates have declined to deal with summarily (eg a serious theft charge), or
(3) with an offence for which he has the right to elect trial by jury (eg theft, reckless driving, assault occasioning actual bodily harm) and he has so elected,

then the magistrates' only function is to decide whether 'there is sufficient evidence to put the accused upon trial by jury for *any* indictable offence'[1].

The function of the magistrates' court is *not* to decide whether the accused is guilty of the offence charged for that would usurp the function of the trial jury: the court's task is simply to determine whether there is a case to answer, ie whether the evidence is sufficient to justify committing the accused to stand trial before a jury at the Crown Court. In other words, the committal proceedings are intended to act as a filtering process which will safeguard innocent persons from being sent for trial on insufficient evidence. Historically the function of the committal proceedings was rather different. Before there was an efficient police force, the justices of the peace took it upon themselves to investigate serious offences and interrogate suspects. In a sense, they acted like the 'juge d'instruction' in France today. In the nineteenth century, the grant of a statutory right to accused persons to remain silent before the courts destroyed the inquisitorial functions of the magistrates. At the same time, the establishment of a modern police force trained in the investigation of crime made it unnecessary for them to supervise criminal investigation themselves. However, the committal proceedings survived – no longer as a means of investigating a crime but as a safeguard to ensure that the citizen was not subjected to the criminal process except on evidence of sufficient weight to satisfy a magistrate that there was a case to answer.

---

1 Magistrates' Courts Act 1980 s 6(1). The magistrates exercising this jurisdiction are called 'examining justices'. Note that committal proceedings may be conducted by a single justice of the peace (s 4(1)).

Accordingly, the purpose of committal proceedings today is to test the strength of the prosecution case. At the same time, it provides a means by which the defence can hear the prosecution evidence and cross-examine prosecution witnesses before the trial at the Crown Court – in other words it provides the defence with a preliminary review of the prosecution evidence[2].

TWO TYPES OF COMMITTAL

In many cases the defence advocate, having considered written statements of the evidence, will accept that there is a 'case to answer'; in these circumstances, unless he wishes to test the evidence by cross-examination, he will agree to a formal committal (colloquially called 'a s 6(2) committal'). If however he decides the evidence does not disclose a 'case to answer' or he wishes to explore the evidence further by cross-examining the witnesses (and possibly asking questions which counsel would not wish to ask at the Crown Court without first knowing the answer) he will opt for 'an old-style committal'. We shall consider this form of committal first.

THE 'OLD-STYLE COMMITTAL' – PROSECUTION CASE

Full committal proceedings usually begin with a short address by the advocate for the prosecution explaining the nature of the evidence against the accused and how this evidence indicates the offence charged. The evidence which is then submitted to the magistrates may be either oral or written.

(a) Oral evidence. The witnesses are called by the prosecutor and examined orally by him, cross-examined by the defence advocate and then re-examined by the prosecution[3]. The clerk of the court records the evidence of the witnesses in the form of reported speech and the record is read over to the witness at the end of his evidence and he is asked to sign it. This written record of the evidence of a witness is known as a 'deposition'. The presiding magistrate must at the end of the proceedings sign a certificate authenticating all the depositions and written statements tendered at the committal[4].

2 But note the prosecution need not produce all their evidence at such proceedings even if the evidence called is that of a key witness (see *R v Epping Justices, ex p Massaro* [1973] QB 433, [1973] 1 All ER 101 – child victim of sexual assault not called by the prosecution at committal proceedings). The defence cannot insist that the prosecutor calls all the witnesses whose statements have been served: see *R v Grays Justices, ex p Tetley* (1979) 70 Cr App Rep 11. Note also that the Divisional Court will not interfere, at least while the committal proceedings are continuing, with a ruling by the magistrates that a particular line of cross-examination is irrelevant to the issue whether or not there is a case to answer (see *R v Wells St Stipendiary Magistrate, ex p Seillon* [1978] 3 All ER 257, [1978] 1 WLR 1002).
3 Objection can and should be taken by the defence advocate to inadmissible evidence: see per Kilner Brown J in *R v Colchester Stipendiary Magistrate, ex p Becks* [1979] QB 674, 143 JP 202: 'there is regrettably a tendency in committals . . . for quantities of irrelevant or inadmissible, or it may be highly prejudicial, material to be collected by prosecuting authorities and served without any attempt to remove such material before consideration by the court'. It is not clear whether examining magistrates have a discretion under s 78 of the Police and Criminal Evidence Act 1984 to exclude 'unfair evidence' in committal proceedings (see *R v Horsham Justices, ex p Bukhari* (1982) 74 Cr App Rep 291 (dock identification) as to the law before the Act).
4 Magistrates' Courts Rules 1981 r 7(3).

(b) Written evidence. The process described above is of course very lengthy and is a complete waste of time where the defence do not wish to explore or challenge the evidence of a particular witness at the committal proceedings. For this reason, s 102 of the Magistrates' Courts Act 1980 enables the court to receive a written statement which the police have earlier taken from a witness to save his attendance at the committal. The effect of s 102 is to provide that the written statement shall be admissible in committal proceedings as evidence to the like extent as oral evidence provided that:

'(a) the statement purports to be signed by a person who made it;
(b) the statement contains a declaration by that person to the effect that it is true to the best of his knowledge and belief and that he made the statement knowing that, if it were tendered in evidence, he would be liable to prosecution if he wilfully stated in it anything which he knew to be false or did not believe to be true;
(c) before the statement is tendered in evidence, a copy of the statement is given, by or on behalf of the party proposing to tender it, to each of the other parties to the proceedings; and
(d) none of the other parties, before the statement is tendered in evidence at the committal proceedings, objects to the statement being so tendered under this section.'

Thus this section enables a written statement to be used as a substitute for oral evidence at the committal proceedings. Section 102(5) provides that either the whole statement should be read aloud to the court or else the statement should be summarised and then handed in. It must be noted that such statements can only be used when the defence have not objected *before* the statement is read and even after it has been read the magistrates on application by either side or on their own motion may require the maker to attend to give oral evidence[5].

(c) Written statements from children and sick persons. In committal proceedings where the accused is charged with certain sexual offences against children, a statement taken earlier from a child should be produced as an exhibit without calling the child unless his evidence is necessary to prove identity or the defence require him to attend court[6]. In the case of a witness who is dangerously ill and unlikely to recover, a justice of the peace may take a deposition on oath from him which can be subsequently produced at the committal proceedings[7]. The accused has the right to attend at the taking of the deposition and to cross-examine the deponent[8].

SUBMISSION BY DEFENCE

At the conclusion of the prosecution evidence, the defence can submit that the evidence produced by the prosecution is not of sufficient weight to warrant committing the accused for trial. Such a submission is appropriate in two cases[9]:

5 Magistrates' Courts Act 1980 s 102(2)(d) and (4).
6 Ibid s 103.
7 Magistrates' Courts Act 1980 s 105.
8 Magistrates' Courts Rules 1981 r 33(1).
9 Cf the guidance given in respect of submissions of 'no case' in summary trials in *Practice Note* [1962] 1 All ER 448, [1962] 1 WLR 227.

(1) where the prosecution have failed to produce *any* evidence to establish an essential element of the offence (eg if, on a charge under s 1 of the Theft Act 1968 of stealing a bicycle, the police evidence showed the defendant had taken the bicycle in question but failed to show he intended permanently to deprive the owner – in other words, the case merely showed an unauthorised 'borrowing');

(2) where the prosecution evidence is so weak or has been so discredited by cross-examination that no reasonable jury could convict the accused (eg in a case turning on identification, where the sole witness turns out to be unsatisfactory).

The magistrates decide by a majority whether or not to uphold the defence submission. If the submission is upheld, the accused is discharged (unless the magistrates rule there is evidence sufficient to commit on some lesser charge)[10].

CHARGE AND ALIBI WARNING

At this stage, the clerk of the court reads over the charge to the accused and tells him of his right to remain silent or to give evidence from the witness-box (in which case he will be liable to cross-examination). In many cases, the accused person will decide to say nothing at all and 'reserve his defence' until he appears at the Crown Court. This is not in any sense an indication that he is guilty or that he has a weak case: it is merely that he sees no point in revealing the nature of his defence to the prosecution in advance. If, however, his case is very strong, it may well be sensible for him to give evidence at the committal proceedings, because this evidence may satisfy the magistrates that the prosecution case is too weak to warrant committal.

As already stated, the committal proceedings provide a means by which the defence hear all the prosecution evidence before the trial by jury. The prosecution have no such right to prior knowledge of the defence case. However, experience over the years indicated that the prosecution, in one particular sort of case, could be so seriously prejudiced by their lack of warning of the nature of the defence that injustice resulted. This was when the defendant raised an *alibi defence* – when he said he could not have committed the offence, because he was somewhere else when it was committed. Where a defence of this sort was raised without warning at the trial and witnesses were called to support it, the prosecution had no opportunity to make enquiries themselves to determine whether the alibi was true or had been manufactured by the accused and his friends. For this reason it is now provided that where an accused person wishes to raise an alibi defence at his trial he must, either at the committal proceedings or within seven days thereafter, give notice and particulars of his alibi[11]. Accordingly, at this stage of the committal, the clerk will ask the defence advocate whether an 'alibi warning' is appropriate and if so explain the effect of the rule to the

10 See *R v Cambridge Justices, ex p Fraser* [1985] 1 All ER 667, [1984] 1 WLR 1391, where the Divisional Court held that where the magistrates find there is no evidence of an offence which is only triable on indictment (such as aggravated burglary or wounding with intent) but hold the evidence discloses a case to answer for some lesser offence triable either way (eg burglary or unlawful wounding) they cannot proceed to try the lesser offence summarily but must commit the accused for trial for that offence.

11 Criminal Justice Act 1967 s 11. As to the meaning of 'alibi' in this context see p.146 below.

defendant so that if he gives evidence (or even if he does not) he can use this opportunity of announcing his alibi.

DEFENCE CASE AND SUBMISSION

It is now the turn of the defence to indicate their case. As stated above, in practice this will only be done where there is a reasonable likelihood that the magistrates will refuse to commit once they have heard the defendant's account of the matter. The defendant's advocate applies to address the court in an opening speech if he intends to call the defendant *and* witnesses to the facts[12]. This right is not very often exercised in practice because it gives the prosecution a right to address the court on the *facts* at the conclusion of the defence evidence – a right they do not otherwise have.

The defendant and his witnesses give evidence in exactly the same manner as the prosecution witnesses. Their evidence is subject to cross-examination, and recorded as depositions, which are read over to them and signed with any corrections they wish to make.

Once the defence evidence is complete, the accused's advocate may address the court and submit there is insufficient evidence to warrant committal. Once again, the magistrates are *not* considering the question whether the defendant is guilty or innocent: they are only considering whether there is a *case to answer*, but this time they do so on the totality of the evidence, bearing in mind the defendant's explanations of matters which were alleged by the prosecution witnesses[13].

If the magistrates decide not to commit the accused for trial, he is discharged. He may then apply for costs which, if awarded, will be paid out of central funds[14] or, where the magistrates decide that prosecution was brought in bad faith, by the prosecuting authority[15].

REPORTING

It is of importance to an accused man that the jury who eventually try him shall come to his case with an open mind[16]. In the past the press reported proceedings before examining magistrates so extensively that it was thought that this might sometimes have induced in the trial jury a predetermined opinion about the merits of the case. The report was generally one-sided because, as stated above, it frequently happens that the defence reserve their case so that only the prosecution evidence is heard at the magistrates' court[17]. For this reason, s 8 of the Magistrates' Courts Act 1980 now prohibits the publication by the press, television or radio, without the consent of the accused, of anything more than the formal details of the

12 Magistrates' Courts Rules 1981 r 7(11).
13 See *Re Roberts* [1967] 1 WLR 474.
14 Costs in Criminal Cases Act 1973 s 1(2).
15 Ibid s 2(4).
16 The publication of information about an accused person likely to interfere with the course of justice is a contempt of court (eg television or newspaper commentary on the case against a defendant); see *R v Savundranayagan and Walker* [1968] 3 All ER 439n, [1968] 1 WLR 1761 and Contempt of Court Act 1981 s 1. But the problem discussed here is not the publication of *commentary* but of reporting the *evidence* at the committal proceedings.
17 Prior to the Criminal Justice Act 1967 this had to be gone through in its entirety in open court.

committal and, in particular, prevents the publication of any account of the prosecution evidence[18].

Where there is only one defendant, these restrictions do not apply if he wishes the proceedings to be reported; similarly where there are several defendants and they all agree to the ban being lifted. Where however there is more than one defendant and one (but not all) wishes the restriction to be lifted he must satisfy the magistrates that such a course is necessary 'in the interests of justice'; only if a powerful case is made out should this be done where other defendants want the restriction to remain in force[19].

SHORT FORM OF COMMITTAL

It will be appreciated, that the committal proceedings so far described in this chapter necessarily take a great deal of time – particularly because the clerk of the court has to record all the oral testimony in the form of depositions. To some extent, the proceedings are shortened by reading aloud to the court statements taken before the proceedings began and submitted under s 102 of the Magistrates' Courts Act 1980. Nevertheless, the procedure is of little or no practical value in two important types of case:

(1) where the accused is charged with an offence over which the magistrates have no jurisdiction (eg robbery), but to which he intends to plead 'guilty' when he eventually appears at the Crown Court; *and*
(2) where, although the accused intends to plead 'not guilty' at the Crown Court, he accepts that there is obviously a 'case to answer'.

In these cases, if the accused is legally represented, he may agree that the magistrates should formally commit him to the Crown Court without their considering the evidence against him at all. This is the effect of s 6(2) of the Magistrates' Courts Act 1980 which provides:

'A magistrates' court inquiring into an offence as examining justices may, if satisfied that all the evidence before the court (whether for the prosecution or the defence) consists of written statements tendered to the court under s 102 below with or without exhibits, commit the accused for trial for the offence without consideration of the contents of those statements, unless –
(a) the accused or one of the accused has no solicitor acting for him in the case (whether present in court or not);
(b) counsel or a solicitor for the accused or one of the accused, as the case may be, has requested the court to consider a submission that the statements disclose insufficient evidence to put that accused on trial by jury for the offence.'

It should be noted that before this short form of committal can take place, the prosecution must have available their evidence in statements complying with the rules laid down in s 102 of the Magistrates' Courts Act 1980 and must have given copies of these statements to the defence advocate. It is the duty of the defence advocate to satisfy himself that these statements do, in fact, show a 'case to answer' before he agrees to a formal committal. This

18 Note: in rape cases the identity of the complainant and the defendant is not to be disclosed unless the Crown Court otherwise directs (for example, to assist in the production of witnesses for the defence): Sexual Offences (Amendment) Act 1976 s 4.
19 Magistrates' Courts Act 1980 s 8(2A). See *R v Leeds Justices, ex p Sykes* [1983] 1 All ER 460, [1983] 1 WLR 132 and *R v Horsham Justices, ex p Farquharson* [1982] QB 762, [1982] 2 All ER 269.

short form of committal (invariably called a 's 6(2) committal') is now used in a majority of cases but it should not be used unless it is clear that no benefit would be gained by the defendant by a full (or 'old-style') committal[20]. In cases where identification is in issue the prosecution should not proceed under s 6(2); instead the witnesses as to identity should be called to give oral evidence (although, if they have already attended an identification parade and not identified the accused, they should not be asked in court to make a dock identification)[1]. The procedure at a s 6(2) committal is set out in the table at p 108. Note that the alibi warning must still be given in appropriate cases.

THE APPROPRIATE CROWN COURT

Once the magistratates have decided to commit the accused to stand trial (whether as a result of an 'old-style' hearing of the evidence or because the accused's advocate has agreed to a 's 6(2) committal'), they then have to decide to which sitting of the Crown Court the accused should be sent for trial. Unlike the ancient criminal courts of Assize and Quarter Sessions (now abolished), the Crown Court has jurisdiction to try all offences wherever they may have occurred in England or Wales[2].

Three different classes of judges sit at the Crown Court, namely:

(1) *High Court judges* (normally judges of the Queen's Bench Division).
(2) *Circuit judges* (full time criminal judges or judges who divide their time between criminal work and the civil and divorce jurisdiction of the county courts).
(3) *Recorders* (barristers and solicitors who are in practice but sit for a number of weeks in every year as temporary judges trying criminal cases).

The Crown Court sits in many towns throughout the country. In the larger towns (eg Birmingham, Cardiff or Winchester) all three classes of judges will sit. In the smaller towns (eg Guildford or Newbury) circuit judges or recorders will sit. The work of the Crown Court is assigned between the various judges on the principle that the High Court judge should try the more serious or difficult cases. Directions[3] have been made under s 75 of the Supreme Court Act 1981, which in effect provide for *four* classes of offence as follows:

---

20 It is often forgotten that an old style committal gives one the opportunity to ask questions in cross-examination which one would not dare to ask in front of a jury lest, for example, the accused's previous convictions were disclosed in the answers; for example, in many criminal cases, it is helpful for the defence to probe the details of the police investigation by, for instance, asking what the police were told originally by the prosecution witnesses or as to conversations between the police and the accused not recorded in the committal statements.
1 Attorney General's Written Answer, Hansard, Vol 912 col 115, 27 May 1976. Reprinted in *Archbold* (42nd edn) para 14.1.
2 And, in certain cases, abroad. A definitive list of such appears set out in *Archbold* para 2–28 et seq.
3 See *Practice Note* [1971] 3 All ER 829, 56 Cr App Rep, 52, CA; *Practice Direction* [1978] 2 All ER 912, 67 Cr App Rep 114, CA.

Class 1: cases which must be tried by the High Court judge (eg murder, treason, offences under s 1 of the Official Secrets Act 1911).

Class 2: cases which should normally be tried by the High Court judge but which the High Court judge who is in charge of the circuit may assign to a circuit judge or recorder (eg manslaughter, infanticide, rape).

Class 3: cases which may be tried by either the High Court judge or a circuit judge or a recorder (eg possession of firearms with intent, arson with intent to endanger life).

Class 4: cases which will normally be tried by a circuit judge or recorder (eg wounding with intent, robbery, forgery, and all cases triable either way).

The directions also provide that if the magistrates feel a case which falls within *class 4* should be tried by a High Court judge, they should commit the accused to a place where a High Court judge will be sitting. The following considerations should influence the justices in favour of trial by a High Court judge, namely where:

(i)   the case involves death or serious risk to life (excluding cases of reckless driving, or causing death by reckless driving, having no aggravating features);

(ii)   widespread public concern is involved;

(iii) the case involves violence of a serious nature;

(iv)   the offence involves dishonesty in respect of a substantial sum of money;

(v)   the accused holds a public position or is a professional or other person owing a duty to the public;

(vi)   the circumstances are of unusual gravity in some respect other than those indicated above;

(vii) a novel or difficult issue of law is likely to be involved, or a prosecution for the offence is rare or novel[4].

It follows that in determining to which sitting of the Crown Court an accused man should be committed, the magistrates must decide two separate questions:

(1)   Into which class of case does the present offence fall?

(2)   Which is the nearest or otherwise most convenient sitting of the Crown Court which has jurisdiction to try cases in this class?

WITNESS ORDERS AND ANCILLARY MATTERS

When the accused is committed for trial, the magistrates must make appropriate orders to ensure the presence of the witnesses at the Crown Court. Under the Criminal Procedure (Attendance of Witnesses) Act 1965 the magistrates may order witnesses who have appeared before them or whose evidence has been tendered in statement form to appear at the court of trial. Disobedience of such an order is a contempt of the trial court which may issue a warrant ordering the arrest of the witness and his production before the court[5].

If, however, the accused intends to plead guilty so that no witnesses will be required at the Crown Court or if, although he intends to dispute the

4 Ibid.
5 Criminal Procedure (Attendance of Witnesses) Act 1965 s 94.

charge, a particular witness has given testimony which will not be substantially in dispute, eg in a theft case the statement of the loser, then the magistrates may make a *conditional witness order* whereby the witness need only attend the trial court if he subsequently is notified that his attendance is required. When such a *conditional order* is made, the magistrates must inform the accused of his right to require the attendance of that witness at the trial.

In addition to making the appropriate witness orders, the magistrates must deal with a number of other matters at the conclusion of the committal proceedings which can be conveniently summarised in note form:

(1) the name and address of the prosecution solicitor must be given to the accused so that he can send particulars of alibi defence to him, if not already given before the magistrates;

(2) the magistrates must decide who is to be responsible for the safe-keeping of any exhibits that have been produced. Where, as usually happens, the prosecution retain the exhibits they are under a duty:

    (a) to take all proper care to preserve the exhibits safe from loss and damage;

    (b) to co-operate with the defence in order to allow reasonable access to the exhibits for the purpose of inspection and examination;

    (c) to produce the exhibits at trial.

    Either side has the right to apply to the Crown Court for directions as to examination, etc of the exhibits[6].

(3) the prosecutor may apply for an order that his costs be paid out of central funds;

(4) the defendant may apply for bail (the principles to be applied are exactly the same as those discussed on p 196, below);

(5) the defendant may apply for legal aid to cover his trial at the Crown Court (again see the principles explained on p 207, below).

It might be convenient at this stage to set out in summary form the points so far discussed in this chapter. The plan can be used by the student when attending committal proceedings as an observer.

COMMITTAL FOR TRIAL

There are *two* different types of committal proceedings:

(1) where the magistrates *hear* and *consider* the evidence against the defendant and *decide* whether or not to commit him (Magistrates' Courts Act 1980, s 6(1));

(2) where the defendant has a solicitor acting for him and has been given copies of all statements made by prosecution witnesses and agrees that he should be committed for trial *without* the magistrates considering the evidence (Magistrates' Courts Act 1980 s 6(2)).

Procedure

(1) The charge is read to the defendants. In cases where a defendant has the right to be tried either by magistrates or jury this must be explained at this stage.

6 See *R v Lambeth Metropolitan Stipendiary Magistrates, ex p McComb* [1983] QB 551, [1983] 1 All ER 321.

(2)   The clerk explains the restriction on newspaper reporting and asks whether there is any application to lift reporting restrictions.

(3)   The clerk asks the prosecution if all the evidence is in the form of written statements and copies have been given to the defendants. If so, and each of the defendants has a solicitor acting for him, the clerk asks whether any defendant:
   (a) objects to any statement;
   (b) wishes to give evidence himself or call witnesses;
   (c) wishes to submit that there is insufficient evidence.
   If not, the court at once proceeds to give the alibi warning and commits for trial (see 14 (b) below).
   If the answer to either (a), (b) or (c) above is *yes*, or one or more of the defendants is not represented, then the proceedings continue as from stage 4, below.

(4)   Prosecutor opens case.

(5)   Prosecution present evidence which may be:
   (a) oral evidence taken down as a deposition (defence may cross-examine);
   (b) written statements under Magistrates' Courts Act 1980, s 102;
   (c) both oral evidence and written statements;
   (d) written statements from children (Magistrates' Courts Act 1980, s 103).

(6)   Defence may submit that there is insufficient evidence to commit. If accepted, the defendant is discharged and may apply for costs. If not accepted, proceed to item 7 below.

(7)   The charge is read over to the defendant who is told of his right to remain silent or give evidence.

(8)   Alibi warning given.

(9)   Defence solicitor or counsel may apply for leave to open the case *if* he is calling witnesses as to facts apart from the accused.

(10) Defence evidence called. Defendant gives evidence before his witnesses. This evidence is recorded as depositions.

(11) Prosecutor may make closing speech *if* (but *only if*) defence solicitor or counsel has opened.

(12) Defence counsel or solicitor may submit again that, now the accused's version has been heard, there is insufficient evidence to justify a committal.

(13) Magistrates decide whether or not to commit.

(14) (a) If they decide not to commit the defendant is discharged and may apply for costs.
   (b) If they decide to commit, then:
      (*i*)   They decide to which Crown Court the defendant should be committed and whether before High Court judge.
      (*ii*) Written notice repeating the alibi warning and stating address of prosecution solicitor is given to defendant.
      (*iii*) The court decides on types of witness order (ie full or conditional) if this has not already been done.
      (*iv*) Decision as to exhibits.
      (*v*)   Defendant applies for bail.
      (*vi*) Defendant applies for legal aid.

SERIOUS FRAUD CASES

The committal procedure described above does not apply in certain cases of serious fraud; instead the prosecution can serve notice transferring the case to the Crown Court under s 4 of the Criminal Justice Act 1987. It is necessary to look at these procedures in some detail.

A Serious Fraud Office has been set up with a Director and staff of lawyers which has the function of investigating any suspected offence which appears to the Director to involve serious or complex faud[7]. The Director has the power to give notice to a person under investigation requiring him to attend for questioning[8] and to produce documents[9]. As a result of their investigation the Director and his staff may initiate a criminal prosecution; alternatively, they may take over the conduct of a prosecution already under way[10].

Where a prosecution of a case of serious or complex fraud has been begun, the Director can serve notice transferring the case to the Crown Court. The following conditions must be satisfied:

(a) a person must have been charged with an indictable offence;
(b) the Director or a member of the Office must be satisfied that there is sufficient evidence for the person charged to be committed for trial and that the charge reveals a case of fraud of such seriousness and complexity that it is appropriate that the management of the case should without delay be taken over by the Crown Court;
(c) the magistrates' court has not begun to enquire into the case as examining justices[11].

The notice of transfer must specify the appropriate Crown Court and the charges in question and be accompanied by written statements of the evidence[12]. This power to serve notice of transfer may also be exercised by the DPP, the Commissioners of Inland Revenue and the Commissioners of Customs and Excise[13].

Once the case has been transferred to the Crown Court a preparatory hearing will normally take place[14]. At that stage the judge may rule that the written statements tendered do not reveal a case to answer[15]. The other directions which may be given at the preparatory hearing are discussed below (p 123).

VOLUNTARY BILL OF INDICTMENT

The procedure we have discussed above applies to more than 99 per cent of all cases which are sent for trial at the Crown Court. After the committal proceedings are concluded the prosecutor or an appropriate officer of the

---

7 Criminal Justice Act 1987 s 1(3).
8 Ibid s 2(2); failure to attend constitutes an offence under s 2(13).
9 Ibid s 2(3); if the documents are not produced or service of a notice would seriously prejudice the investigation, a warrant may be issued under s 2(5).
10 Ibid s 1(5).
11 Ibid s 4(1).
12 Ibid s 6(1), (2), (8) and (9).
13 Ibid s 4(2).
14 Ibid s 7.
15 Ibid ss 6(1) and 9(3). Note: oral evidence may only be given at the oral hearing with leave of the judge; s 6(2).

Crown Court within 28 days drafts and files a formal document containing the charges against the accused (called the *indictment*) and the case may then proceed.

There are, however, other means by which a person may be required to appear and stand trial at the Crown Court; for instance, a judge may send a witness for trial if he suspects the witness has committed perjury[16], or the Court of Appeal may order a new trial where the original trial has been a nullity[17]. The most important method is, however, by a *voluntary bill of indictment*, i e when a High Court judge orders the trial of an accused person at the Crown Court after an application has been made to him under s 2 of the Administration of Justice (Miscellaneous Provisions) Act 1933. This generally occurs in the following cases:

(1) Where magistrates have refused to commit a person for trial but the prosecution wish in effect to challenge this decision by applying directly to a judge for an order that the proposed defendant be tried.

(2) Where several persons have been committed for trial and it is desired that a co-defendant may be added without going through the formality of committing him (eg where A and B have been committed to the Crown Court charged with, for example, conspiracy and R is apprehended a short while before the trial is due to start).

(3) Where it is desired that two persons charged in different indictments should be tried together or that two offences charged against one person should be tried together (in these cases it is necessary for a new indictment to be preferred because of the technical rule that only one indictment may be tried at any one time).

The procedure adopted when it is desired to prefer a *voluntary bill* is set out in the Indictments (Procedure) Rules 1971[18]. Basically the applicant must prepare a written statement setting out why the application is made by this method and the result of any committal proceedings. This statement must be verified by an affidavit sworn by the applicant and accompanied by proofs of evidence, depositions and any written statements relating to the offence. The High Court judge considers the application in private although he may direct the applicant to attend. There is no provision for the proposed defendant to attend or make representations to the judge nor does the defendant have any right of appeal against the decision[19].

16 Perjury Act 1911 s 9.
17 Criminal Appeal Act 1964 s 5, Sch 2.
18 SI 1971/2084.
19 See *R v Raymond* [1981] QB 910, 72 Cr App Rep 151, CA.

Chapter 5

Trial at the Crown Court

The Crown Court was created by the Courts Act 1971 replacing the ancient courts of Assize and Quarter Sessions as a centrally administered criminal court of superior jurisdiction dealing with offences committed anywhere in England or Wales. The country has been divided into a number of circuits to each of which a Queen's Bench judge has been assigned with overall responsibility for the administration of the circuit. The court is responsible for hearing all trials on indictment (i e before a jury) and in addition sits to deal with cases committed for sentence by the local magistrates and to hear appeals from the magistrates' courts.

It has already been explained that the sittings of the Crown Court may be presided over by a High Court judge, a circuit judge or a part-time recorder[1]. The cases are assigned between them according to the gravity of the offence. The magistrates committing offenders for trial are required to determine the appropriate class of case and then commit to a convenient court where a judge competent to try that class of case will be sitting. If either prosecution or defence are dissatisfied with the magistrates' decision on this matter they may make application in open court to a High Court judge to vary the magistrates' order[2]. This would be done where, for instance, there was a real likelihood of local prejudice against the defendant.

JURISDICTION

The Crown Court has jurisdiction to deal with offences committed anywhere in England and Wales. In addition the court has jurisdiction over offences committed within territorial waters[3], and over British vessels on the high seas[4] and on oil rigs[5] and British aircraft[6]. Conversely, the Crown

---

1 See *Practice Note* [1971] 3 All ER 829, 56 Cr App Rep 52, CA (as amended *Practice Direction* [1978] 2 All ER 912, 67 Cr App Rep 114, CA) which is discussed at p 00 below.
2 Supreme Court Act 1981 s 76.
3 Territorial Waters Jurisdiction Act 1878 s 2.
4 The jurisdiction also covers a vessel on foreign rivers 'below the bridges, where the tide ebbs and flows and where great ships go': *R v Anderson* (1868) LR 1 CCR 161 (American killing a compatriot on a British ship below Bordeaux).
5 Offshore Activities: Oil and Gas (Enterprise) Act 1982.
6 Civil Aviation Act 1982 s 92.

Court has no jurisdiction over an offence committed abroad even by a British subject[7].

Problems arise (particularly because of the ease of modern travel and communications) where criminal activities involve more than one country: in such a case, the problem is whether a criminal offence has been committed within this country.

Example 1. T posted a letter in England addressed to a lady in Germany. The letter contained a demand for money under threat that if it was not forthcoming T would reveal to her husband that she had had an affair with another man. The question was whether T had made an 'unwarranted demand with menaces' (contrary to s 21(1) of the Theft Act 1968) *in England*. The House of Lords held that the offence was committed in England; per Lord Diplock: 'it is sufficient to constitute the offence of blackmail if *either* the physical acts are done *or* their consequences take effect in England or Wales'[8].

Example 2. D and other American citizens in Morocco planned to smuggle drugs to the USA via England. The drugs were imported into England en route for America (substantive offences were thereby committed under s 170 of the Customs and Excise Management Act 1979). The question was whether D and his associates had also committed the offence of conspiracy in this country given that the plot had been entirely worked out and agreed abroad. The House of Lords held[9] that a conspiracy was a continuing offence, so that where acts were committed in England in performance of an agreement made abroad, the persons involved were guilty of conspiracy in England. Lord Salmon[10] went further and suggested that so long as the plan remained in being, the persons concerned might be liable to be charged with conspiracy as soon as they arrived to carry out their purpose; it was not necessary that they should have committed some overt act within the jurisdiction.

Example 3. S (a well-known politician and businessman) flew to Miami where he faked his death by drowning. The news of his disappearance was broadcast in England and his wife innocently applied to be paid out under his life insurance policies. No money was in fact paid out. S was subsequently found in Australia and extradited to England charged with *attempting* to obtain money by deception. The issue was whether, since the only act by the defendant (i e faking his death) had occurred in America, he had committed any offence in England. The House of Lords held[11] that an offence had been committed in this country because the intended consequence of his actions abroad had been that money should be paid out in England. Per Lord Keith: 'an offence is committed if the *effects* of the act intentionally *operate* or *exist* within the jurisdiction'[12].

---

7   The only exceptions are treason (see *R v Casement* [1917] 1 KB 98) and certain cases where statute expressly gives jurisdiction to the court (e g Offences Against the Person Act 1861 s 9 – murder by a British subject).
8   *Treacy v DPP* [1971] 1 All ER 110 at 124.
9   *DPP v Doot* [1973] AC 807, [1973] 1 All ER 940.
10 Ibid at p 833: 'Suppose a case in which evidence existed of a conspiracy hatched abroad by bank robbers to raid a bank in London, or by terrorists to carry out some violent crime at an English airport, or by drug peddlers to smuggle large quantities of dangerous drugs on some stretch of the English coast. Suppose the conspirators came to England for the purpose of carrying out the crime and were detected by the police reconnoitring the place where they proposed to commit it, but doing nothing which by itself would be illegal. It would surely be absurd if the police could not arrest them then and there but had to take the risk of waiting and hoping to be able to catch them as they were actually committing or attempting to commit the crime.'
11 *DPP v Stonehouse* [1978] AC 55, [1977] 2 All ER 909.
12 Ibid at p 939.

ATTENDANCE OF THE DEFENDANT

If the defendant has been committed in custody to stand trial at the Crown Court, the court issues an order to the governor of the prison where he is detained directing that he shall be brought before the court. If the defendant has been released on bail, the court will inform him in advance of the likely date of his trial and (usually) the police call at his home on the day before the trial to check that he is aware of the time and place where the Crown Court will sit. If he fails to attend court, a *bench warrant* may be issued directing the police to arrest him and when he eventually appears the court will decide whether to treat his failure to appear as a criminal contempt of court[13].

THE INDICTMENT

An *indictment* is a formal document embodying the charge or charges brought by the Crown against the defendant. It is drafted either by the prosecution or by an officer of the court and may embody any charge which appears to be made out in the depositions and statements sent to the Crown Court after the committal. In other words, the charges need *not* be confined to those stated in the magistrates' court – for example, if a defendant is committed by the magistrates on a charge of malicious wounding[14] (which carries a maximum of five years' imprisonment), the prosecution may include a charge of wounding with intent to cause grievous bodily harm[15] (which carries a maximum of life imprisonment) provided such a charge is justified by the evidence in the committal statements.

Clause 37 of the Criminal Justice Bill 1987 provides that certain summary offences (common assault, taking a vehicle without authority, driving while disqualified and criminal damage) may be included in an indictment if they are founded on the same facts or evidence as a court charging in an indictable offence (or are part of a series of offences of the same or similar character).

The indictment may contain more than one charge and charge more than one person with the same or different offences. Each offence charged in the indictment is known as a *count*, and the *count* must contain a *statement of the offence* (including a reference to any statute creating the offence) and *particulars* stating: '(i) the party indicated, (ii) the party injured, and (iii) the facts and the intent that are necessary ingredients of the offence'. Rule 5(1) of the Indictment Rules 1971 provides

'. . . every indictment shall contain and shall be sufficient if it contains a statement of the specific offence with which the accused person is charged describing the offence shortly, together with such particulars as may be necessary for giving reasonable information as to the nature of the charge.'

It might be convenient at this stage to consider an example:

Example. On 2 January 1986 Oliver Twist is seen at King's Cross station stealing a gold watch from a passenger, but he runs off before he can be apprehended. The next day, just before midnight, the police acting on information received, arrive at a branch of Tellson's Bank in Southwark where they discover Oliver trying to open a safe. Outside the bank, they find Noah Claypole waiting for Oliver in a

---

13 Bail Act 1976 s 6(5). Note: the warrant may be backed for bail in cases where it appears the accused may have had reasonable cause to be absent.
14 Offences Against the Person Act 1861 s 20.
15 Ibid s 18.

INDICTMENT

No. 86 1217

THE CROWN COURT AT INNER LONDON SESSIONS HOUSE, NEWINGTON CAUSEWAY, LONDON SE1 6AZ

THE QUEEN   v   OLIVER TWIST, NOAH CLAYPOLE AND JOSEPH FAGIN

who are charged as follows:-

COUNT ONE   Statement of Offence:- THEFT, contrary to section 1 of the Theft Act 1968

Particulars of Offence:- OLIVER TWIST on the 2nd day of January 1986 stole a gold watch the property of Samuel Welles.

COUNT TWO   Statement of Offence:- TAKING A CONVEYANCE WITHOUT AUTHORITY, contrary to section 12(1) of the Theft Act 1968

Particulars of Offence:- OLIVER TWIST and NOAH CLAYPOLE on the 3rd day of January 1986, without the consent of the owner or other lawful authority, took a conveyance, namely a Ford Cortina motor car registration number PAA 531X for their own use.

COUNT THREE   Statement of Offence:- BURGLARY contrary to section 9(1)(a) of the Theft Act 1968

Particulars of Offence:- OLIVER TWIST on the 3rd day of January 1986 entered as a trespasser a building known as Tellson's Bank, Borough High Street, Southwark, London SE1 with intent to steal therein. NOAH CLAYPOLE at the same time and place did aid and abet counsel and procure OLIVER TWIST to commit the said offence.

COUNT FOUR   Statement of Offence:- HANDLING STOLEN GOODS contrary to section 22(1) of the Theft Act 1968

Particulars of Offence:- JOSEPH FAGIN, on a day between the 1st and 4th days of January 1986, dishonestly received certain stolen goods, namely a gold watch the property of Samuel Welles, knowing or believing the same to be stolen goods.

COUNT FIVE   Statement of Offence:- HANDLING STOLEN GOODS, contrary to section 22(1) of the Theft Act 1968

Particulars of Offence:- JOSEPH FAGIN, on a day unknown before the 4th day of January 1986 dishonestly received certain stolen goods, namely a Phillips video recorder, knowing or believing the same to be stolen goods.

Dated: 16th April

John Smith

Officer of the Crown Court

Ford Cortina. Oliver, when he is interviewed by the police, admits that he and Noah took the Cortina from outside a discotheque in Hammersmith earlier that evening. He also tells the police that he sold the gold watch to his landlord, Mr Fagin. The police obtain a warrant under s 26 of the Theft Act 1968 to search Fagin's house at Saffron Hill and there find the gold watch. They also discover a brand new video recorder; Fagin tells them he bought it from a man in a public house for £150.

The appropriate indictment is set out opposite.

A number of points emerge from a study of this indictment: in particular, it will be noted that the one indictment contains no less than five different charges and involves three individuals. We discuss below the rules concerning the question of *joinder* of charges and defendants within the same indictment. However, three points should be made at this stage:

(a) Joint enterprise. Where two or more persons participate in different ways in the furtherance of a criminal enterprise they are all guilty of the offence; thus, for example, where at a robbery one man produces a gun and threatens a cashier and another waits outside in a vehicle to enable his confederate to escape, they are each guilty of the offence of robbery. This is the effect of s 8 of the Accessories and Abettors Act 1861 which provides:

> 'Whosoever shall aid, abet, counsel or procure the commission of an indictable offence . . . shall be liable to be tried, indicted and punished as a principal offender.'

Thus in count two the particulars of offence do not distinguish between the role played by Oliver and Noah in taking the motor car; it makes no difference which of them actually gained entry into the car or drove it away provided they were both present and acting as part of a joint enterprise when the car was taken. Although this is the normal way of indicting participants, there will be cases where it is better to draft the particulars so as to show clearly the role of the participants; a form of words which can be used in such a case as shown in count three[16].

(b) Particulars of date and place. Where (as in counts four and five) the exact date when an offence occurred is not known, it is usual to charge that the offence took place 'on a day between' two dates; for example, where the date of loss and recovery are known it is proper to allege a receiving on a day between the day *before* the goods were stolen and the day *after* they were recovered. Generally, it is not essential that the prosecution prove the offence occurred when alleged in the indictment, but where it becomes clear from the evidence at the trial that the offence occurred on some other date, the indictment should be amended and if necessary (e g where the defence is alibi) an adjournment granted[17]. Statements as to the location of the offence are again not essential averments unless the offence can only be committed at a particular type of location (e g burglary, which can only be committed in a 'building', or carrying an offensive weapon, which can only be committed in a 'public place')[18].

16 See observations of Lord Edmund-Davies in *DPP for Northern Ireland v Maxwell* [1978] 3 All ER 1140 at 1148.
17 See *R v Dossi* (1918) 13 Cr App Rep 158; *R v Browning* [1974] Crim LR 714, CA.
18 Prevention of Crime Act 1953, s 1 and see *R v Allamby and Medford* [1974] 3 All ER 126, [1974] 1 WLR 1494 (no evidence kitchen knives were to be used as offensive weapons at the date and place alleged, although admissions they were intended to be so used on an earlier occasion and different location).

(c) Particulars of ownership. Generally, on a charge of theft or receiving, the name of the loser should be stated in the particulars[19]. However, where the owner's identity is unknown (as in count five) then it is proper to allege the goods in question were the property of a person unknown. In such a case, the prosecution will of course have to prove by circumstantial evidence that the property in question has been stolen; thus, in count five (the charge of receiving the video recorder), it will be necessary for the prosecution to produce evidence (e g Fagin's explanation of the circumstances by which he acquired the video recorder) from which the only reasonable inference is that it has been stolen[20].

JOINDER AND SEVERANCE

In the examples above, three defendants are charged with five different offences in one indictment. It is now necessary to look at the rules concerning the *joinder* of different offences and different defendants in the same indictment; frequently, it is in the interests of a defendant to apply that separate offences should be tried before different juries or that he be tried separately from his co-defendants: this process by which an indictment is split up is called *severance*.

(a) Separate trial of different charges
Section 4 of the Indictments Act 1915 states that different offences may be joined on one indictment subject to the provisions of rules of court. The relevant rule is r 9 of the Indictment Rules 1971 which provides:

> 'Charges for any offences may be joined in the same indictment if those charges are founded on the same facts, or form or are a part of a series of offences of the same or similar character.'

In a case as the example discussed above, the court would therefore have to ask itself:

(1) are the charges *founded on the same facts*; or
(2) are they *a part of a series of offences of the same character*; or
(3) are they a part of *a series of offences of a similar character*?

In order to answer these questions it is necessary to know something of the case law which has grown up around r 9.

The first question is when are charges 'founded on the same facts'? The answer is to ask whether the charges have a common factual origin.

> *Example.* B was charged with affray arising out of an incident at a discotheque. In another court he was charged with attempting to pervert the course of justice: the allegation was that about two months after the affray he had offered the manager of the discotheque £1000 to change his evidence. He appealed against his convictions on the ground that the two charges should not have been joined on the same indictment. Per Shaw LJ: 'The phrase "founded on the same facts" does not mean that for charges to be properly joined on the same indictment, the facts in relation to the respective charges must be identical in substance or virtually contemporaneous. The test is whether the charges have a common factual origin. If the charge is one that could not have been alleged but for the facts which give

---

19 See *R v Gregory* [1972] 2 All ER 861, 56 Cr App Rep 441, CA.
20 See *R v Fuschillo* [1940] 2 All ER 489 27 Cr App Rep 193; 26 cwt of sugar found in F's shop during wartime rationing; F said 'this means going away'. No direct evidence of sugar being stolen. Held, jury could infer the sugar had been stolen.

rise to . . . the primary charge, then it is true to say for the purposes of rule 9 that those charges are founded, that is to say have their origin, in the same facts and can legitimately be joined in the same indictment[1].'

In the example we have just used in this chapter, there is no doubt that count two (charging taking a car without authority) and count three (burglary at the bank) would be properly joined in the same indictment because the vehicle was to be used for the purposes of removing the property stolen during the burglary.

The second question is what is meant by a *series of offences*; for example, could two charges be properly described as a *series*?

Example. K was charged with the murder of C at a public house in Whitechapel in March 1966; he was charged in a second count in the same indictment with the murder of M at his home in October 1967. He appealed on the grounds that these two charges should not have been included in the same indictment. Per Widgery LJ: 'It may be true that the word "series" is not wholly apt to describe less than three components, but so to limit its meaning in the present context would produce the perverse result that whereas three murders could be charged in the same indictment two could not. The construction of the rule has not been restricted in this way in practice during the fifty years which have followed the passage of the [Indictments] Act and it is too late now to take a different view[2].'

The third question is what is meant by 'offences of a *similar* character'; the House of Lords has said that one has to look to see if there is a common link or 'nexus' both as to the facts and as to the legal type of offence.

Example 1. L was charged with (1) attempting to steal from a public house in West London and (2) robbery (snatching back a pound note in the course of an argument and punching a barman) on a different occasion at a different public house in the same general area. The trial judge held the two counts were properly joined in the same indictment and refused an application for severance. The House of Lords upheld his decision. Per Lord Pearson: 'in my opinion, there was in the present case a sufficient nexus between the two offences to make them a "series of offences of . . . a similar character" within the meaning of the rule. They were similar both in law and fact. They had the same essential ingredient of actual or attempted theft, and they involved stealing or attempting to steal in neighbouring public houses at a time interval of only 16 days[3].'

Example 2. H was charged with conspiracy to defraud and obtaining property by deception (both offences involving the theft and use of cheque and credit cards). After his arrest the police searched his house and found property which had come from a recent burglary. He was therefore also charged with receiving stolen goods

1 *R v Barrell and Wilson* (1979) 69 Cr App Rep 250, [1979] Crim LR 663, CA. Note: an argument that the judge should have exercised his discretion to order severance notwithstanding the joinder was permissible under r 9 was rejected on the basis that the evidence of the affray would have been admissible if the count of perverting the course of justice had been tried separately and vice versa. See also *R v Bell* (1984) 78 Cr App Rep 305, CA.

2 *R v Kray* [1970] 1 QB 125, [1969] 3 All ER 941. An argument that the judge should have nonetheless ordered separate trials was also rejected: 'severance is not appropriate where two cases exhibit unusual common features which render a joint trial desirable in the general interests of justice, regard being had to the interests, not only of the accused in question, but also of others accused, the Crown, the witnesses and the public. These two cases did exhibit such features, the two murders having many unusual factors in common.' (The court also held that the interest of the press in the affair was so great that if the two murders had been tried separately the publicity attending the first trial would have made a fair trial of the remaining charge impossible.)

3 *Ludlow v Metropolitan Police Comr* [1970] 1 All ER 567 at 574. The House of Lords also held that the judge had not erred in the exercise of his discretion to refuse separate trials.

and a count in respect of this charge was added to the indictment. The Court of Appeal held that this was a misjoinder; there was not a sufficient nexus merely because all the offences involved a dishonest state of mind[4].

Where different offences are properly joined in the same indictment under r 9, the trial judge still has a discretion to order separate trials if fairness to the accused requires it:

'Where, before trial, or at any stage of a trial, the court is of opinion that a person accused may be prejudiced or embarrassed by reason of being charged with more than one offence on the same indictment or that for any other reason it is desirable to direct that the person should be tried separately for any one or more offences charged in an indictment, the court may order a separate trial of any count or counts of such indictment[4].'

It seldom happens that there is any serious dispute over whether the provisions of r 9 have been satisfied, but it does often happen that counsel for the defendant argues that his client would be prejudiced by facing trial on more than one charge at the same time. Such an application seldom succeeds for the reasons set out by Lord Pearson in *Ludlow*'s case:

'the manifest intention of the Act is that charges which either are founded on the same facts or relate to a series of offences of the same or a similar character properly can and normally should be joined in one indictment and *a joint trial of the charges will normally follow*, although the judge has a discretionary power to direct separate trials . . . The judge has no duty to direct separate trials under s 5(3) unless in his opinion there is some special feature of the case which would make a joint trial of the several counts prejudicial or embarrassing to the accused and separate trials are required in the interests of justice[5].'

This means that in practice the fact that evidence on one count is inadmissible on another count is *not* in itself a sufficient reason to order separate trials[6].

'Every trial judge is familiar with the requirement, where more counts than one of a similar kind are joined in an indictment, of adding a warning to the jury that they must not add all the counts together and convict because there is more than one count in the indictment, or use the evidence on one count as evidence on the other . . . Juries have shown themselves well able over the years to follow such a direction and apply it[7].'

The courts will normally only order separate trials where either:

(1) the evidence on one or more charges is of a scandalous nature[8]; or
(2) the trial of the charges together would raise such a multiplicity of issues as to confuse the jury.

---

4 *R v Harward* (1981) 73 Cr App Rep 168, [1981] Crim LR 403.
5 [1970] 1 All ER 567 at 575.
6 See *R v Blackstock* (1979) 70 Cr App Rep 34: evidence on one count of robbery not admissible on second count alleging a robbery which had occurred on a subsequent occasion, but trial judge properly exercised his discretion to refuse defence application for severance.
7 Ibid per Roskill LJ at p 37.
8 *R v Novac* (1976) 65 Cr App Rep 197. In cases where the prosecution allege separate acts of sexual misconduct, a separate trial of each allegation is usually necessary unless the evidence on one count is admissible on the others under the 'similar fact' test: see *DPP v Kilbourne* [1973] AC 729, [1973] 1 All ER 440; *Boardman v DPP* [1974] 3 All ER 887 at 896 and *R v Scarrott* [1978] QB 1016, [1978] 1 All ER 672.

(b) Separate trial of different defendants

It is permissible to charge two or more persons in the same indictment where:

(1) they have jointly committed an offence; or

(2) they have committed separate offences which are linked together in some way so that it is in the interests of justice that they should be tried together.

It is necessary to consider these rules in a little detail. Firstly, when can it be said that two or more persons have committed the same offence? If, for example, two men burgle a house together as part of a preconceived plan – a 'common enterprise' – there is no problem. In other cases, however, it may not be clear whether they are jointly committing one offence or separately committing different offences.

Example. John and his brother Frank are charged in one count with wounding V with intent contrary to s 18 of the Offences Against the Person Act 1861. The evidence shows that John stabbed V once in the back and that thereafter Frank stabbed V a number of times. Frank pleads guilty. Is it necessary that John was acting *in concert* with Frank in striking the *initial* blow for him to be guilty of the offence as charged on the indictment? The answer is no.

'Where a number of acts of a similar nature committed by one or more defendants were connected with one another, in the time and place of their commission or by their common purpose, in such a way that they could fairly be regarded as forming part of the same transaction or criminal enterprise, it was the practice, as early as the eighteenth century, to charge them in a single count of an indictment. Where such a count was laid against more than one defendant, the jury could find each of them guilty of one offence only; but a failure by the prosecution to prove the allegation, formerly expressly stated in the indictment but now only implicit in their joinder in the same court, that the unlawful acts of each were done jointly in aid of one another did not render the indictment ex post facto bad or invalidate the jury's verdict against those found guilty ... I conclude, therefore, that whenever two or more defendants are charged in the same count of an indictment with any offence which men can help one another to commit it is sufficient to support a conviction against any and each of them to prove *either* that he himself did a physical act which is an essential ingredient of the offence charged *or* that he helped another defendant to do such an act, *and,* that in doing the act or in helping the other defendant to do it, he himself had the necessary criminal intent[9].'

The second problem arises where two defendants commit clearly separate offences but they are in some way linked; when can the defendants be joined in the same indictment and be tried together?

Example. W and L went to a nightclub but refused to pay for the drinks they had consumed. A (the receptionist) then attacked W and C (the doorman) attacked L. A and C were charged in separate counts in the same indictment. A was convicted and appealed on the grounds there was no general power to try offenders charged with *separate* offences together. His appeal was dismissed. Per Sachs J: 'As a general rule it is, of course, no more proper to have tried by the same jury several offenders on charges of committing individual offences that have nothing to do with each other, than it is to try before the same jury offences committed by the same person that have nothing to do with each other. Where, however, the matters which constitute the individual offences of the several offenders are upon the available evidence so related, whether in time or by other factors, that the

9 Per Lord Diplock in *DPP v Merriman* [1973] AC 584 at 607, [1972] 3 All ER 42.

interests of justice are best served by their being tried together, then they can properly be the subject of counts in one indictment and can, subject always to the discretion of the court, be tried together. Such a rule, of course, includes cases where there is evidence that several offenders acted in concert, but it is not limited to such cases. Again, while the court has in mind the classes of case that have been particularly the subject of discussion before it, such as incidents which . . . are contemporanous (as where there has been something in the nature of an affray), or successive (as in protection racket cases), or linked in a similar manner (as where two persons individually in the course of the same trial commit perjury as regards the same or a closely connected fact), the court does not intend the operation of the rule to be restricted so as to apply only to such cases as have been discussed before it[10].'

The above rules determine when two defendants can be joined in the same indictment; in every case it must be remembered that the ultimate decision depends on the court's assessment of what are the interests of justice. This is essentially a matter for the discretion of the trial judge; and the Court of Appeal will be very reluctant to interfere with his decision.

The problem of separate trials occurs acutely where the defence of one defendant involves an attack on the character of the co-defendant, or where one defendant has made a statement to the police implicating his co-defendant.

Example. B and D committed a burglary at a country house. They both told the police in interview that they had been tipped off by a confederate, L, that the owners would be absent at the material time. All three were charged in one count with conspiracy to burgle. The evidence against L was of association with B and his being the only person who was aware the owners would be away at the material time. L's counsel applied for a separate trial on the grounds that the jury trying L should not be aware of the incriminating statements made by B and D to the police (which were of course inadmissible evidence against him). The application was refused and L was convicted. He appealed to the Court of Appeal. Per Lord Widgery CJ: 'The judge declined to order separate trials and we think that he was right. It has been accepted for a very long time in English practice that there are powerful public reasons why joint offences should be tried jointly. The importance is not merely one of saving time and money. It also affects the desirability that the same verdict and the same treatment shall be returned against all those concerned on the same offence. If joint offences were widely to be treated as separate offences, all sorts of inconsistencies might arise. Accordingly it is accepted practice, from which we certainly should not depart in this Court today, that a joint offence can properly be tried jointly, even though this will involve inadmissible evidence being given before the jury and the possible prejudice which may result from that. Of course the practice requires that the trial judge in such a case should warn the jury that the evidence is not admissible . . . However, the question of severance is primarily one for the trial judge. The discretion was properly exercised in the present case, and notwithstanding the fact that there must have been some risk of prejudice the decision of the judge, we think, was right. Of course if a strong case is strong enough, if the prejudice is dangerous enough, if the circumstances are particular enough, all rules of this kind must go in the interests of justice, but this is not the sort of case in which the ordinary rule of practice in our judgment will operate unduly to the detriment of

10 Per Sachs LJ in *R v Assim* [1966] 2 QB 249, [1966] 2 All ER 881, 50 Cr App Rep 224.

the accused and therefore it is a case in which we should apply the ordinary rule[11].'

Although it is sometimes possible to edit out references to a co-accused from a statement,[12] there is nonetheless a very real problem in the type of case discussed above that once the jury have heard the damning (but inadmissible) piece of evidence it will influence them, however much the judge directs them to ignore it.

It may be worth considering, finally, the example of an indictment given at the beginning of this chapter (p 114). It will be seen that in count one T is charged with stealing a watch and in count four F is charged with receiving it. This joinder would obviously be permissible because the offences are directly linked within the principles of *Assam*. However, there is no link between those offences and the fifth count alleging a quite separate handling, and one would expect an application for that count to be tried separately to succeed. Indeed, it would have been better for count five to have been put on a separate indictment.

THE DUPLICITY RULE

Although, as we have just seen, more than one offence may be charged in an indictment, each individual *count* of the indictment must only charge *one offence*.

> *Example.* A group of pickets visited seven building sites in Shrewsbury and Telford in order to induce workmen to support their cause. The prosecution alleged that at each site fighting and intimidation occurred. The pickets were charged on a count which alleged that they 'together with others . . . on September 6, 1972 on divers building sites in the county of Salop unlawfully fought and made an affray'. Particulars of the charge showed that the prosecution were alleging that the pickets had travelled from site to site and that separate fights had occurred at each site. The Court of Appeal quashed the conviction on this count on the grounds it was bad for duplicity: 'The count charging affray . . . when read with the particulars delivered . . . shows on the face of it that there were clearly defined and separate places at which the affray was said to have taken place; the separate places were situate some distance apart; the "times" of fighting and making affray referred to in the particulars did not form a continuous period. On the face of count three, as particularised, there was indicated a number of activities of the same kind rather than one activity[13].'

Although in the above example it is fairly easy to see that a number of separate offences rather than one continuing offence had occurred, there are many cases where the analysis is much more difficult. One activity may involve incidents which would each constitute a separate offence and yet the whole incident may properly be regarded as one activity and charged as one offence:

> *Example.* D was charged in one information alleging that he killed two red deer without a gaming licence. He appealed to the Divisional Court on the grounds that the information disclosed two separate offences. [The duplicity rule applies to informations laid before a magistrates' court in exactly the same way as it applies to the counts in an indictment.] Per Lord Widgery CJ: 'It is legitimate to charge in a single information one activity even though the activity may involve more than one act. One looks at this case and asks oneself what was the activity

11 *R v Lake* (1976) 64 Cr App Rep 172 at 174.
12 See, for example, *R v Rogers and Tarren* [1971] Crim LR 413.
13 Per James LJ in *R v Jones* (1974) 59 Cr App Rep 120.

with which the appellant was being charged. It was the activity of shooting red deer without a gaming licence, and although as a nice debating point it might well be contended that each shot was a separate act, indeed that each killing was a separate offence, I find that all these matters, occurring as they must have done within a very few seconds of time and all in the same geographical location are fairly to be described as components of a single activity, and that made it proper for the prosecution in this instance to join them in a single charge[14].'

Where it is arguable from the particulars stated in the indictment that two offences are being charged on one count, counsel for the defence should move to quash the indictment before the charge is put to his client[15]. If the argument succeeds it will usually be open to the prosecution to apply to amend the indictment so as to provide separate counts for each offence:

'Where, before trial, or at any stage of a trial, it appears to the court that the indictment is defective, the court shall make such order for the amendment of the indictment as the court thinks necessary to meet the circumstances of the case, unless, having regard to the merits of the case, the required amendments cannot be made without injustice . . .'[16]

A similar problem may arise where the evidence on a count on its face apparently disclosing only one offence shows that the prosecution are alleging that several offences have occurred. Suppose D is charged with stealing different items (a watch, a book and a bottle of wine) from a department store. On the face of it the count in the indictment is only charging one offence. Once the prosecution evidence has been given it may, however, be apparent that there have been three separate takings. Objection can be taken at the close of the prosecution case. (The objection is usually described as 'for duplicity' although more accurately it should be said to be for 'a divergence or departure' from the offence alleged[17].) Two cases illustrate this problem:

Example 1. B was charged in one count with stealing an ashtray, a cushion, a knife and a carton containing six glasses from a department store in Birmingham. The Court of Appeal held that separate takings (from different departments in the store) should have been charged on separate counts[18].

Example 2. W was charged with stealing a bottle of aftershave lotion and a number of gramophone records from Boots' Chemists shop in Southampton. The Court of Appeal held that the separate takings could be charged on one count as constituting a single activity – i e a shoplifting expedition. The defendant was not pre-

14 Per Lord Widgery CJ in *Jemmison v Priddle* [1972] 1 QB 489 at 494, 56 Cr App Rep 229 at 234. And see *DPP v Merriman* [1973] AC 584, 56 Cr App Rep 766. Per Lord Morris of Borth-y-Gest at 593, 775: 'In my view such questions when they arise are best answered by applying common sense and by deciding what is fair in the circumstances.'

15 A motion to quash the indictment would also be the appropriate procedure if the defence counsel wished to submit that the count disclosed no offence known to law or that the court had no jurisdiction over the offence charged.

16 Indictments Act 1915 s 5.

17 See *R v Greenfield* [1973] 3 All ER 1050, 57 Cr App Rep 849 where the court said 'Duplicity in a count is a matter of form; it is not a matter relating to the evidence called in support of the count.'

18 *R v Ballysingh* (1953) 37 Cr App Rep 28, CCA. The court went on to apply the proviso and dismissed the appeal because B's counsel had agreed at the trial that there was no prejudice in the separate takings being charged on one count.

judiced in any way by the inclusion of the separate takings in one count because his defence was the same – ie that he had paid for all the items[19].

If a successful argument based on duplicity is addressed to the court at the close of the prosecution case, the prosecution must either seek leave to amend the indictment by setting out separate counts or elect to proceed on only one of the offences disclosed by the evidence[20].

A closely similar problem may arise where the defendant is charged with stealing but the evidence discloses merely a general deficiency in cash receipts.

Example. T was manager of a store. A stock check showed a large quantity of stock had disappeared over several months and was not accounted for in the receipts. T was charged with stealing the proceeds. Per Hallett J: 'if the evidence for the prosecution makes it clear that there has been a fraudulent conversion of either the whole or part of a general balance at one time, it is proper to charge the conversion of a general balance on a day between the specified dates'[1].

In all the cases where the duplicity argument is raised after evidence has been called the question seems to be whether, notwithstanding the possibility that the accused's acts could constitute more than one offence there is anything unfair to him in treating the matter as one criminal activity.

PRACTICE DIRECTIONS

In serious or complex cases the practice has developed of holding a pre trial hearing at which the court can give 'practice directions'; the idea is that such a hearing can be used to determine preliminary procedural matters and narrow the issues before the hearing. The procedure is set out in Practice Rules 1977; in outline these provide that:

(i) the judge can review in chambers details of the likely pleas, the witnesses who will be likely to attend, the question of admissions of fact, the possibility of agreeing schedules, the pagination of bundles of documents and the probable length of the trial;
(ii) the judge can give directions in open court relating to severance of the indictment and as to amendment and particulars of the counts.

Frequently at this stage the prosecution will agree to provide a case summary setting out how the case will be put (often this will be the draft of the opening speech). Ideally, this summary should be provided before the practice direction hearing; in reality this is often not possible. Also ideally, the judge who conducts the practice direction should be the judge who will try the case, but again this may well not be practicable.

SERIOUS FRAUD CASES

When a serious or complex fraud case has been committed to the Crown Court (or transferred under s 4 of the Criminal Justice Act 1987) there will inevitably be preparatory hearings conducted by the judge who will try the

19 *R v Wilson* (1979) 69 Cr App Rep 83, CA.
20 Ibid per Browne LJ at 85.
 1 *R v Tomlin* [1954] 2 QB 274, 38 Cr App Rep 82. See also *R v Balls* (1871) LR 1 CCR 328 (treasurer of Provident Society stealing subscriptions) and *R v Lawson* [1952] 1 All ER 804, 36 Cr App Rep 30 (solicitor stealing from clients' account).

case. The procedure set out in ss 8 and 9 of the Act envisage the following stages:

(i)   the arraignment will take place and pleas will be recorded;
(ii) the prosecution will be ordered to serve a *case statement* setting out the facts which they will seek to establish by reference to specific witnesses and exhibits;
(iii) after the prosecution *case statement* has been served the judge may direct the defendant to serve 'a statement in writing setting out in general terms the nature of his defence and indicating the principal matters on which he takes issue with the prosecution'.

It would appear that the prosecution's case statement and (with his consent) the defendant's statement will be made available to the jury. Section 10 provides the sanction where the defence fails to comply with the direction or departs from the statement; the judge and the prosecution (with permission from the judge) can comment and the jury may draw such inference as appears proper.

THE ARRAIGNMENT

The trial of an accused person on indictment begins by the Clerk calling upon him by name, reading over the indictment to him and asking him whether he pleads guilty or not guilty to the indictment. When the indictment has been read over to him the accused may take any one of the following courses:

(1) Plead guilty to the offence(s) charged or plead guilty to some lesser offence not charged in the indictment.
(2) Plead *autrefois acquit* or *autrefois convict*.
(3) Stand silent.
(4) Plead 'not guilty'.

We must now consider these possibilities in some detail.

PLEA OF GUILTY

The defendant must plead guilty in person[2]. The decision must be his own and although it may be proper for counsel to give him strong advice on this point (including telling him that the courts treat a plea of guilty showing contrition as a mitigating factor), nothing must be done which in any sense pressurises him into a plea of guilty[3].

It frequently happens that an accused person is charged in the alternative in an indictment with offences of different degrees of seriousness. In such a case the prosecution may be prepared to accept a plea of guilty to the less serious offence charged subject to the approval of the trial judge. The proper course is for the judge himself to order that a verdict of 'not guilty' be recorded on the more serious count.

It may also happen that an accused person, although intending to plead

2 A limited company or corporation enters a plea in writing: Criminal Justice Act 1925 s 33(3).
3 *R v Turner* [1970] 2 QB 321, [1970] 2 All ER 281. Cf *R v Peace* [1976] Crim LR 119, CA. Where an accused person pleads guilty albeit unhappily and reluctantly, after receiving strong advice from counsel, the Court of Appeal will not treat the plea entered as a nullity unless the court is satisfied that he did not make a voluntary and deliberate choice.

'not guilty' to an offence charged in the indictment would be prepared to plead 'guilty' to some lesser offence *not* appearing on the indictment.

> *Example.* A in a family quarrel seizes a bread knife and stabs his brother B causing serious injuries. A is charged in one count with wounding with intent to cause grievous bodily harm – a serious offence which is punishable with a maximum of life imprisonment. A tells counsel that he did not intend to cause his brother serious injuries of the type which transpired. Counsel advises him to plead 'not guilty' to the charge in the indictment but 'guilty' to unlawful wounding – a lesser offence punishable with a maximum of five years' imprisonment.

In such circumstances the accused can plead guilty to the lesser offence even though it does not appear on the indictment provided that a jury could lawfully convict him of such an offence at his trial[4]. Generally, the jury can bring in a verdict of guilty of a lesser offence than that charged wherever *the allegations in the indictment amount to or include (expressly or by implication) an allegation of another offence falling within the jurisdiction of the court*[5]. The correct practice in these cases is for defence counsel to inform the prosecution in advance of the defendant's intention to plead guilty to a lesser offence not appearing on the indictment. It is then the duty of prosecuting counsel to decide whether it would be proper to accept such a plea. For instance, in the example above, the plea would probably have been accepted although the position would have been different if a flick-knife had been used because that would have indicated a much more deliberate assault. If the prosecution accept the plea, counsel must explain to the trial judge why they feel that this is appropriate and the judge must approve the course proposed. The plea of guilty to a lesser offence not on the indictment is a *conditional* plea until such time as it is accepted by the judge. This means that if the judge refuses to accept a plea to a lesser offence so that the trial continues and the defendant is then acquitted, he cannot be sentenced on the basis of his plea to the lesser offence[6].

Once a plea of guilty to the offence charged or to a lesser offence has been accepted and recorded, the court proceeds at once to sentence (without of course empanelling a jury to hear the evidence). The procedure on sentence is described in Part three of this book[7].

It will be appreciated that there may be circumstances in which counsel wish to discuss informally with the judge whether a plea to a lesser offence would be acceptable to the court. There will be other occasions where counsel for the defence would like an indication of the probable sentence if the defendant pleads guilty. Such discussions (which do not take place in open court) would be objectionable if the defendant was left with the impression that the outcome of the case had been negotiated in private. Again the procedure would be oppressive if, for example, the defendant was pressurised into a plea of guilty because the judge had intimated he would receive a custodial sentence if he fought the case. For these reasons the Court of Appeal has laid down very strict rules as to the circumstances in which such private discussions should take place:

---

4 Criminal Law Act 1967 s 6(1)(b).
5 Ibid s 6(3). On a charge of reckless driving or causing death by reckless driving the jury may find the defendant guilty of careless driving although that offence does not otherwise fall within the jurisdiction of the Crown Court: Criminal Law Act 1977 Sch 12.
6 *R v Hazeltine* [1967] 2 QB 857, [1967] 2 All ER 671.
7 See p 221 below.

'There must be freedom of access between counsel and judge. Any discussion, however, which takes place must be between the judge and both counsel for the defence and counsel for the prosecution . . . It is of course imperative that so far as possible justice must be administered in open court. Counsel should, therefore, only ask to see the judge when it is felt to be really necessary and the judge must be careful only to treat such communications as private where, in fairness to the accused person, this is necessary.

The judge should, subject to the one exception referred to hereafter, never indicate the sentence which he is minded to impose. A statement that on a plea of Guilty he would impose one sentence but that on a conviction following a plea of Not Guilty he would impose a severer sentence is one which should never be made. This could be taken to be undue pressure on the accused, thus depriving him of that complete freedom of choice which is essential. Such cases, however, are in the experience of the Court happily rare. What on occasions does appear to happen however is that a judge will tell counsel that, having read the depositions and antecedents he can safely say that on a plea of Guilty he will for instance make a probation order, something which may be helpful to counsel in advising the accused. The judge in such a case is no doubt careful not to mention what he would do if the accused were convicted following a plea of Not Guilty. Even so, the accused may well get the impression that the judge is intimating that in the event a severer sentence, maybe a custodial sentence, would result, so that again he may feel under pressure. This accordingly must also not be done.

The only exception to this rule is that it should be permissible for a judge to say, if it be the case, that whatever happens, whether the accused pleads Guilty or Not Guilty, the sentence will or will not take a particular form, eg a probation order or a fine, or a custodial sentence. Finally, where any such discussion on sentence has taken place between judge and counsel, counsel for the defence should disclose this to the accused and inform him of what took place[8].

AUTREFOIS ACQUIT AND CONVICT

At this stage[9] it is open to the defendant to object that he has already been tried for the same or substantially the same offence. It is a fundamental rule of the common law that no man can be charged twice with the same offence:

> *Example*. A is charged with murdering B, by burning down a house knowing that B was inside it. The jury acquit him. He then sells an account of the case to a Sunday newspaper under the headline 'I did it but I was too clever for them.' Also, new evidence comes to light to show that A bought a can of paraffin on the day in question. Nevertheless, if A is again indicted for murdering B, he can successfully plead his previous acquittal as a bar to the proceedings.

This is known as a plea of *autrefois acquit* (or *convict*). The rule applies not only to the specific offence for which the defendant was charged, but to every offence of which he could have been convicted at his trial. Thus, in the above example A could not be subsequently charged with *manslaughter*

---

8 *R v Turner* [1970] 2 QB 321, 54 Cr App Rep 352. Note in *Turner* it was suggested that the defence solicitor should, if he wished, be present at such discussions; this does not happen in practice.

9 Note it is also possible at this stage for the accused to *plead to the jurisdiction*. This plea, which is virtually obsolete, is used in exactly the same circumstances as a motion to quash the indictment. Another possible objection (which is never now employed in practice but appears in the old cases) is to *demur* to the charge. By a *demurrer* the defendant would admit the facts alleged by the prosecution but say that in law they did not constitute the offence with which he was charged.

(because this was a possible alternative verdict at his first trial) but he could be charged with *arson* (which is not an alternative verdict on a murder charge)[10]. The plea will only succeed where there has been a determination of the defendant's guilt – where the jury fail to agree or the Court of Appeal orders a new trial, the plea cannot succeed[11].

If an accused person is acquitted of an offence, he cannot subsequently be tried for some other more serious offence where his guilt can only be established by proving that the first offence was committed:

> *Example.* A is charged with assault occasioning actual bodily harm, and is acquitted. He cannot subsequently be tried on a charge of unlawful wounding arising out of the same incident, since that offence could only be proved by showing he was guilty of the first offence[12].

On the other hand, if an accused person is *convicted* of an offence, this does *not* act as a bar to a prosecution for a more serious offence arising out of the same incident:

> *Example.* A is charged with wounding B with intent to cause him grievous bodily harm, and is convicted. B dies within a year and a day of the attack. A cannot plead *autrefois convict* to a charge of murdering B[13].

The theory behind the *autrefois acquit* and *autrefois convict* rule is discussed at great length in the speeches of *Connelly v DPP*[14], which is the leading case on the subject. In *Connelly*'s case the facts were as follows:

> The prosecution alleged that C had committed murder while in the course of robbery. C was tried for murder only. At his trial he put forward a defence of alibi claiming that the evidence of identification was mistaken. He also contended that, in any event, the evidence did not establish that the man identified as him had an intent to kill the deceased. C was convicted but his conviction was quashed on appeal. He was then indicted for the robbery. His plea of *autrefois acquit* was rejected because (a) he could not have been convicted of robbery at the first trial and so was never in jeopardy and (b) the quashing of a conviction by the Court of Appeal on the ground of misdirection does not constitute an 'acquittal'.

The case is important because it highlights the problem which could arise if genuine acquittals were to be challenged by fresh indictments. Suppose Connelly's sole defence to the murder charge had been alibi and he had been acquitted by the jury. Their verdict would necessarily have meant that the prosecution had failed to prove his presence at the scene of the crime. Could he thereafter have been prosecuted for robbery? If he had been so prosecuted the plea of *autrefois acquit* would still not have been available to him because he would not have been liable to conviction for that offence at the first trial. Lord Devlin suggested that the problem could be solved by the court staying proceedings on the second indictment if it thought a second trial would be oppressive:

> '. . . the judges of the High Court have in their inherent jurisdiction, both in civil and in criminal matters, power (subject of course to any statutory rules) to make and enforce rules of practice in order to ensure that the court's process is used fairly and conveniently by both sides. I consider it to be within this power for the

---

10 And he could be convicted of perjury: see *HM Advocate v Cairns* 1968 JC 37.
11 *R v Shipton, ex p DPP* [1957] 1 All ER 206n, [1957] 1 WLR 259; *Connelly v DPP* [1964] AC 1254, [1964] 2 All ER 401.
12 *R v Miles* (1890) 24 QBD 423.
13 *R v Thomas* [1950] 1 KB 26, [1949] 2 All ER 662.
14 [1964] AC 1254, [1964] 2 All ER 401.

court to declare that the prosecution must as a general rule join in the same indictment charges that "are founded on the same facts, or form or are a part of a series of offences of the same or a similar character" [see Indictment Rules r 9]; and power to enforce such a direction (as indeed is already done in the civil process) by staying a second indictment if it is satisfied that its subject matter ought to have been included in the first. I think that the appropriate form of order to make in such a case is that the indictment remain on the file marked not to be proceeded with[15].'

A similar point arises where a defendant who has been acquitted after giving evidence of his innocence (eg an alibi) is subsequently indicted for perjury on the grounds of new evidence showing that what he said at the trial was false.

Example. H was acquitted at his trial of driving while disqualified but subsequently charged with perjury on the basis of evidence clearly showing his defence at the first trial to have been untrue. The House of Lords upheld his conviction but both Lord Edmund-Davies and Lord Salmon held that in a proper case the Crown Court had the power to prevent the prosecution proceeding in circumstances which would amount to oppression and would therefore be an abuse of process of the court[16].

It would seem that the facts of a previous acquittal cannot be used by the Crown to establish guilt under the similar fact principle however overwhelming the evidence may be.

Example. In 1980 A arrived at Gatwick Airport with a case containing packages of cannabis wrapped in plastic bags bearing the name of a trading company in Lagos. She claimed that the packages had been put into her case without her knowledge and was acquitted of illegal importation contrary to s 170(2) of the Customs and Excise Management Act 1979. In 1982 she again arrived at Gatwick with a case containing cannabis wrapped in identical bags bearing the name of the same trading company. *Quaere* whether evidence of the earlier importation is admissible?

It would seem that the evidence of the earlier importation would be inadmissible to the extent that the prosecution were asserting expressly or by implication that she was guilty of the earlier offence:

'The effect of a verdict of acquittal pronounced by a competent court on a lawful charge and after a lawful trial is not completely stated by saying that the person acquitted cannot be tried again for the same offence. To that it must be added that the verdict is binding and conclusive in all subsequent proceedings between the parties for the adjudication[17].'

If a plea of *autrefois acquit* or *convict* is raised, a jury has to be empanelled to try the issue[18].

DEFENDANT REMAINING SILENT

When an accused person remains silent, and makes no answer to the question whether he be 'guilty' or 'not guilty', the question arises whether

15 [1964] AC 1254 at 1360, [1964] 2 All ER 401 at 446.
16 *DPP v Humphreys* [1977] AC 1, 63 Cr App Rep 95.
17 *Sambasivam v Malaya Federation Public Prosecutor* [1950] AC 458 per Lord MacDermott at 479 (evidence of confession of charge on which S had been acquitted wrongly admitted at trial on another charge).
18 A written plea is put in as follows: 'AB says that the Queen ought not further to prosecute the indictment against him, because he has been lawfully convicted of the offence charged therein'.

he is deliberately refusing to answer (*mute of malice*) or, usually because of mental illness, is unable to understand what is going on (*mute by visitation of God*). If the prosecution deny that he is unable to answer to the arraignment, this issue must be determined by a jury. The prosecution must prove beyond reasonable doubt that he is deliberately not answering. The procedure adopted is the same as at the trial of the general issue, i e the prosecution call evidence which is subject to cross-examination, the defence may call evidence in rebuttal, counsel address the jury and the judge directs the jury as to the law and summarises the evidence. If the defendant is found to be *mute of malice*, the court enters a plea of Not Guilty and proceeds to try the general issue with a new jury. If the defendant is found to be *mute by visitation of God*, the court will then have to determine, either with the same or a new jury, whether he is fit to plead.

FITNESS TO PLEAD

This issue may arise as stated above because of a finding by a jury that the defendant is *mute by visitation of God* but it more frequently arises because, before the arraignment, the prosecution (or the defence or indeed the court itself) have specifically raised the question of the defendant's mental state. This issue once raised can only be determined by a jury. They have to decide whether the accused person is capable of understanding, and pleading to the indictment, and fit to stand trial in the sense of comprehending what is occurring, and communicating with his legal advisers. If the prosecution allege that the defendant is unfit to plead, and the defence dispute this, the onus is on the prosecution to prove their contention beyond reasonable doubt; conversely, if the contention is put forward by the defence, the onus is on them to prove their case but only on a balance of probabilities[19]. The issue may be determined at once, but the court has a power under the Criminal Procedure (Insanity) Act 1964[20], to postpone the determination of this question until any time up to the opening of the case for the defence. The reason the court has been given this power is that, if an accused is found to be unfit to plead, the court must direct that he be detained in a mental hospital[1] specified by the Secretary of State even though *he has not been convicted of any offence*. To avoid this grave consequence, the court should generally postpone the decision of fitness to plead until the prosecution case has been heard, thereby giving the defence an opportunity to test the evidence and, if appropriate, submit there is insufficient evidence to warrant a conviction[2].

THE JURY

Once the defendant has pleaded 'not guilty' to any count on the indictment, a jury must be empanelled to try him. The jury panel will normally have been outside the court during the arraignment, because if the defendant

19 *R v Podola* [1960] 1 QB 325, [1959] 3 All ER 418.
20 Section 4(2).
 1 The effect of the order is as if he had been made subject to a restriction order without limitation of time: see Criminal Procedure (Insanity) Act 1964 Sch 4 and p 267 below.
 2 See *R v Webb* [1969] 2 QB 278, [1969] 2 All ER 626 and *R v Burles* [1970] 2 QB 191, 54 Cr App Rep 196.

pleads 'guilty' to some charges, and 'not guilty' to others, the jury must not normally be told that he has admitted his guilt of these offences[3].

The qualification for jury service is now set out in s 1 of the Juries Act 1974, which in effect provides that a person is liable for jury service if:

(1) he is registered as a parliamentary or local government elector, and
(2) he is not less than 18 years old, and not more than 65, and
(3) he has been ordinarily resident in the United Kingdom for a period of at least five years since his thirteenth birthday, and
(4) he does not fall within the classes of persons who are ineligible or disqualified from jury service:
  (a) Persons ineligible
  (i) past and present members of the judiciary including justices of peace;
  (ii) other persons who are or have been within the last ten years concerned with the administration of justice (eg barristers, solicitors, policemen);
  (iii) the clergy;
  (iv) the mentally ill.
  (b) Persons disqualified[4]
  (i) persons who have at any time been detained during Her Majesty's pleasure, sentenced to a term of imprisonment or youth custody, of five years or more;
  (ii) persons who within the last ten years have been sentenced to a term of imprisonment, borstal training, youth custody, detention or have been made the subject of a community service order or have been placed on probation within the last five years.

Jurors are summoned to attend the Crown Court by a notice sent to them at the address shown in the jury list. Failure to attend for jury service is an offence punishable as contempt of court by a fine of up to £400[5]. However, a juror may apply for any good reason to the officer of the court responsible for summoning the panel to be excused from attending at court[6]. Certain persons are excusable as of right from jury service, for instance, members of Parliament, of the armed services and of the medical and other similar professions[7]. In addition, persons who have served on a jury within the two years preceding the service of the summons are required to be excused[8].

Before the jurors are selected, counsel are entitled to see a list showing the names of all the jurors on the panel together with their addresses[9]. In addition counsel for the prosecution will usually have been told by the police of any criminal convictions recorded against the jurors and (in a proper case) will have communicated this to the defence counsel. This is

---

3 This is part of the important, and basic, principle in the English law of evidence that the prosecution are not allowed to present evidence showing the accused to be a man of bad character.
4 The police check the jury panels to determine whether any disqualified persons have been selected. In *R v Mason* [1981] QB 881, 7 Cr App Rep 157 this practice was expressly approved by the Court of Appeal.
5 Juries Act 1974 s 20(1).
6 Ibid s 9(2).
7 Ibid Sch 1 Pt III.
8 Ibid s 8(1). Note: a judge may direct that jurors serving in a long trial be excused for a longer period.
9 Ibid s 5(2).

normally the only information counsel have as to the persons who are going to decide the case[10].

A panel of more than 12 jurors is brought into court, and the clerk selects 12 jurors by ballot. Immediately after this is done, the defendant is told that the jurors whose names are called out will form the jury to try him, but that he has the right to challenge the jurors before they take the oath. Now, in the USA, challenging prospective jurors is often a matter of great importance because counsel are entitled to examine the jurors before deciding whether or not to object, and thus have the opportunity in advance of ascertaining whether the juror is likely to be prejudiced. The converse is true in England, where counsel are not permitted to question jurors before challenging them[11]. This means, in effect, the challenging depends largely upon the personal idiosyncracies of counsel for the defence[12], or upon his desire to exclude a particular juror because of his appearance[13].

The rules relating to challenges are complex and archaic, but they can be summarised as follows:

(1) Either side may challenge the *array*, ie challenge the whole body of jurors on the ground that *the person responsible for summoning the jurors in question is biased or has acted improperly*[14].

(2) Either side may challenge individual jurors for *cause*, ie because the juror is disqualified or ineligible or because he is partial[15] or might be partial.

(3) Each defendant (but not the prosecution) has the right to make three peremptory challenges, ie challenges for which no reason need be given[16].

(4) The prosecution may require that individual jurors should *stand by,* ie be excluded unless it is impossible to form a jury from the panel of prospective jurors without calling on them[17].

Generally, there will be sufficient jurors present in court to form a jury of 12 persons even after some of them have been challenged. Where, however, a jury cannot be formed the court may require qualified persons present in

---

10 In cases involving national security or terrorism, the Attorney General may authorise a check of Special Branch records. See *A-G's Guidelines on Jury Checks* (1981) 72 Cr App Rep 14.

11 There is a very rare exception to this where there has been such pre-trial publicity relating to the defendants, that there is a real possibility that the jurors may be prejudiced: see *R v Kray* (1969) 53 Cr App Rep 412.

12 In fraud cases it was common for counsel to challenge bank managers, accountants and persons of kindred occupations. This is no longer possible because the jury list does not now disclose the juror's occupation.

13 Juries Act 1974 s 12(6).

14 This challenge is known as *propter affectum*.

15 This challenge is called a challenge for favour.

16 Juries Act 1974 s 12(1), as amended by Criminal Law Act 1977 s 43. This is, in effect, how defence counsel can exclude persons he feels would be unsympathetic to the accused.

17 See *R v Mason* [1981] QB 881, 71 Cr App Rep 157. Counsel for the prosecution was aware because of the police Criminal Records Office check on the potential jurors that some had convictions (although not such as to disqualify them). Per Lawton LJ: 'We can see no reason why information about such convictions should not be passed on to prosecuting counsel. He may consider that a juror with a conviction for burglary would be unsuitable to sit on a jury trying a burglar; and if he does so he can exercise the Crown's rights. Many persons, but not burglars, would probably think that he should.' The defence have no similar right: *R v Chandler* (No 2) [1964] 2 QB 322, [1964] 1 All ER 761. The Crown should not exercise this right unless there are cogent reasons for believing the juror is unfit to serve.

the vicinity of the court to be called upon to serve[18]. This procedure is traditionally called *praying a tales*.

Once a jury of 12 persons has been duly sworn, the clerk of the court reads the indictment to them, tells them that the defendant has pleaded 'not guilty' to the indictment and that it is their charge to say, having heard the evidence, whether he be 'guilty' or 'not guilty'.

THE COURSE OF THE TRIAL: THE OPENING SPEECH

After the defendant has been put in charge of the jury, counsel for the prosecution opens the case by telling the jury the essential matters alleged against the defendant and how such facts would amount to the offence charged. At the same time, he must tell the jury that the burden of proof rests on the prosecution to establish the defendant's guilt beyond reasonable doubt. The function of prosecution counsel (both at the Crown Court and before magistrates), is quite different from that of counsel in a civil case who must do all that he properly can do to further the interests of his client. In a criminal trial, the prosecuting counsel stands as the representative of the Crown, a 'minister of justice', whose only function is to lay the facts of the case dispassionately before the court and to use his skills in order to assist in ascertaining where the truth lies.

'It is not his duty to obtain a conviction by all means; but simply to lay before the jury the whole of the facts which compose his case, and to make those perfectly intelligible, and to see that the jury are instructed with regard to the law and are able to apply the law to the facts[19]'.

An important aspect of this duty is the requirement on the prosecution to make available 'unused material' (i e statements, notes and documents not contained in the committal papers) which might have some bearing on the offences charged or the surrounding circumstances of the case. It has long been the rule that if prosecuting counsel knows of a credible witness who can speak to material facts which tend to show the defendant to be innocent he should either call that witness himself or inform the defence of his availability to support their case[20]. Guidelines by the Attorney General on disclosure of 'unused material' however take the matter much further; as a general rule the defence should be shown all statements or documents in the prosecution's possession which *might* have some relevance to the case. There are, however, exceptional cases where the prosecution are not obliged to make such disclosure:

'There is a discretion not to make disclosure – at least until Counsel has considered and advised on the matter – in the following circumstances:
(i)　There are grounds for fearing that disclosing a statement [prior to commit-

18　Juries Act 1974 s 6(1).
19　Sir J Holker A-G 1880 cited *Kenny* (17th edn) p 569, and see Lord Birkett *The Art of Advocacy* 'the duty of prosecuting counsel is to act as a minister of justice in the fullest sense. He must make sure that the evidence is relevant and admissible and is presented without bias. He must also make sure that the evidence in favour of the prisoner is before the court and is given the same prominence and emphasis as the evidence tendered to show his guilt.' (Republished in *Six Great Advocates*, Penguin Books, 1961.)
20　See *Dallison v Caffery* [1965] 1 QB 348 at 369. Lord Denning MR suggested that in such a case the witness's statement should be given to the defence. Although this will usually be the case, there may be circumstances where this will not be appropriate: see *R v Bryant* (1946) 31 Cr App Rep 146 and the *A-G Guidelines* below.

tal] might lead to an attempt being made to persuade a witness to make a statement retracting his original one, to change his story, not to appear at Court or otherwise to intimidiate him.

(ii) The statement (eg from a relative or close friend of the accused) is believed to be wholly or partially untrue and might be of use in the cross-examination if the witness should be called by the defence.

(iii) The statement is favourable to the prosecution and believed to be substantially true but there are grounds for fearing that the witness, due to feelings of loyalty or fear, might give the defence solicitor a quite different, and false, story favourable to the defendant. If called as a defence witness upon the basis of this second account, the statement to the police can be of use on the cross-examination.

(iv) The statement is quite neutral and there is no reason to doubt its truthfulness – eg "I saw nothing of the fight" or "He was not at home that afternoon". There are however grounds to believe that the witness might change his story and give evidence for the defence – eg purporting to give an account of the fight or an alibi. Here again, the statement can properly be withheld for use on cross-examination (NB. In cases (i) to (iv) the name and address of the witness should normally be supplied).

(v) The statement is, to a greater or lesser extent, "sensitive" and for this reason it is not in the public interest to disclose it. Examples of statements containing sensitive material are as follows: (a) it deals with matters of national security; or it is by, or discloses the identity of, a member of the Security Services who would be of no further use to those Services once his identity became known. (b) It is by, or discloses the identity of, an informant and there are reasons for fearing that disclosure of his identity would put him or his family in danger. (c) It is by, or discloses the identity of, a witness who might be in danger of assault or intimidation if his identity became known. (d) It contains details which, if they became known, might facilitate the commission of other offences or alert someone not in custody that he was a suspect; or it discloses some unusual form of surveillance or method of detecting crime. (e) It is supplied only on condition that the contents will not be disclosed, at least until a subpoena has been served upon the supplier – eg a bank official. (f) It relates to other offences by, or serious allegations against, someone who is not an accused, or discloses previous convictions or other matters prejudicial to him. (g) It contains details of private delicacy to the maker and/or might create risk of domestic strife[1].'

It is the duty of prosecuting counsel to inform the defence in advance of the bad character or criminal record of any prosecution witnesses[2] and to inform the defence of any statement made by a prosecution witness which substantially conflicts with what he says in evidence[3].

THE PROSECUTION EVIDENCE

The prosecution must secure the attendance of any witnesses whose depositions or statements were tendered at the committal proceedings[4], unless those witnesses were made subject to a conditional witness order and no notice has been served by the defence. Where the prosecution, after taking

1 *Practice Note* [1982] 1 All ER 734, 74 Cr App Rep 302.
2 *R v Collister* (1955) 39 Cr App Rep 100; *R v Paraskeva* (1982) 76 Cr App Rep 162, [1983] Crim LR 186, CA (robbery and assault – sole witness had a spent conviction for theft which was not revealed to the defence; Court of Appeal quashed conviction; per O'Connor LJ: 'It cannot be said that it was not a relevant matter for the jury to be told that one man had been dishonest in the past.')
3 *Baksh v R* [1958] AC 167, [1958] 2 WLR 536, PC.
4 *R v Oliva* [1965] 3 All ER 116, [1965] 1 WLR 1028.

reasonable steps, are unable to secure the attendance of a witness, the court has a discretionary power to allow the case to proceed but must not exercise its discretion in favour of such a course unless it is satisfied that no injustice would thereby be done[5]. The prosecution are not compelled to rely solely on the evidence tendered at the committal proceedings, but if they choose to use additional evidence, they must serve a Notice of Additional Evidence containing a statement from the witness on the defence, and to the court[6]. If this is not done, the defence are entitled to ask for an adjournment in order to consider the additional evidence.

EVIDENCE OF CO-DEFENDANT'S PLEA

Where the guilt of the defendant can only be established by proving that some other person has committed an offence, that fact can be proved by producing a certificate of conviction.

> *Example.* Fagin is charged with handling a stolen gold watch. The prosecution must prove the watch has been stolen. They can do this by producing a certificate showing Twist was convicted of stealing the watch. It does not matter whether Twist pleaded guilty or was found guilty after a trial.

This is the effect of s 74(1) of the Police and Criminal Evidence Act 1984 which provides:

> 'In any proceedings the fact that a person other than the accused has been convicted of an offence by or before any court in the United Kingdom shall be admissible in evidence for the purpose of proving, *where to do so is relevant to any issue in those proceedings*, that that person committed that offence, whether or not any other evidence of his having committed that offence is given.'

Section 74(2) provides that the fact of conviction is evidence that the other person has committed the offence 'unless the contrary is proved', (presumably, on a balance of probabilities). It should be noted of course that the fact of conviction must be relevant to some issue in the subsequent proceedings. A question arises whether where two defendants are charged on an indictment and one pleads guilty, the fact of his conviction can be used as evidence by the Crown. In the example above, it would clearly be nonsensical if the prosecution were not allowed to prove Twist's conviction for theft because they had both been charged in the same indictment. Where, however, two or more defendants are charged with jointly committing the same offence it may be that s 74 applies.

> *Example.* A, B, C and D are charged with conspiring to pervert the course of justice by persuading W not to give evidence at the trial of A's son. D pleads guilty. A, B and C plead not guilty. They deny that they at any time entered into any agreement with D or with each other. It would be surprising if the Crown could prove the fact of a conspiracy by merely giving evidence of D's plea. It would be absurd if this evidence cast a burden of proof on the defence to disprove a conspiracy.

It is submitted that in the above example this absurd result could be avoided by the court declining under s 78 to admit evidence on the ground that to do so would be unfair.[6a]

Where the court rules that the fact of a co-defendant's plea of guilty

---

5   *R v Shaw* [1972] 2 All ER 704, [1972] 1 WLR 676.
6   Normally such statements comply with the Criminal Justice Act 1967 s 9.
6a See s 78 and *R v Robertson* [1987] QB 920, [1987] 3 All ER 231.

should not be disclosed to the jury, it may make an order under s 4(2) of the Contempt of Court Act 1981 postponing the publication of any report of the plea (or mitigation or sentence) until the conclusion of the trial of the co-accused[7].

EXAMINATION IN CHIEF AND CROSS-EXAMINATION[8]

Prosecuting counsel calls his own witnesses and examines them *in chief*. Now, since *examination in chief* is designed to elicit evidence favourable to one's own case, two important restrictions are placed on the advocate's conduct of the examination. The first rule is that counsel must not prompt his own witness on contentious matters. He therefore must not ask 'leading questions' – i e questions framed so as to suggest a particular answer. He is also not allowed to refer his own witness to any statement the witness has made (for example at the committal proceedings). This is very inconvenient where the witness has simply forgotten some detail or is so overwhelmed by the atmosphere of the court that he cannot recollect. There are two partial exceptions to this rule:

(a) The witness may 'refresh his memory' by referring to any notes or documents including a witness statement made either at the time of the matter in question or shortly afterwards while the events were fresh in his memory[9]. It is under this exception that police officers are allowed to refer to their note books (see below).
(b) The witness may be shown his statement to the police *before* he comes into court[10]. This is permissible even though he would not be allowed to read from the statement in court as described above. Where a witness has been shown his statement in advance this fact should always be disclosed to the defence[11]. (There will be cases where prosecuting counsel should not permit the witness to be shown his statement – e g where there was good cause to believe the statement was fabricated.)

The second rule is that counsel may not contradict the testimony of his own witness by referring to a *prior inconsistent statement*[12]; thus, if the witness says something quite different from what is contained in counsel's proof of evidence, he must accept the answer given, and is not allowed to refer the witness to what he had said when the proof was taken.

7 See *Practice Note* [1983] 1 All ER 64, [1982] 1 WLR 1475 and *R v Horsham Justices, ex p Farquharson* [1982] QB 762, [1982] 2 All ER 269.
8 The rules here explained apply equally to summary trials before magistrates and to committal proceedings. They also apply equally to the examination and cross-examination of defence witnesses. On this point generally see *Cross on Evidence* (4th edn) pp 195 et seq. See also the trial of Oliver Twist, p 31 above.
9 See *A-G's Reference (No 3 of 1979)* (1979) 69 Cr App Rep 411, [1979] Crim LR 786, CA.
10 See *R v Richardson* [1971] 2 QB 484, [1971] 2 All ER 773 where the Court of Appeal approved the following observation in the Hong Kong case *Lau Pak Ngam v R* [1966] Crim LR 443: 'Testimony in the witness-box becomes more a test of memory than of truthfulness if witnesses are deprived of the opportunity of checking their recollection beforehand by reference to statements or notes made at a time closer to the events in question.'
11 *Worley v Bentley* [1976] 2 All ER 449, 62 Cr App Rep 239, DC.
12 Except in the very unusual case of a witness who can be shown to be 'hostile' in the sense of showing bias against the party calling him.

Cross-examination is designed
(1) to elicit evidence favourable to the defence case, and
(2) to discredit the testimony of the witness.

In *cross-examination* the converse rules to those described above apply. Thus *leading questions* are perfectly permissible and counsel may refer the witness to any *prior inconsistent statement* he has made and ask him to explain why his evidence is now different. Indeed the technique of discrediting a witness by reference to earlier inconsistent statements is one of the most important devices in cross-examination – the reason being that both statements cannot be correct and the discrepancy may suggest that other points of the witness's evidence may be incorrect. It will be appreciated that defence counsel is greatly assisted in conducting such a cross-examination by the depositions and committal statements he has before him.

It should be noted that it is the duty of counsel for the defence to *put his case* to the prosecution witnesses, ie to cross-examine them on all points where the defence case differs from the evidence of the witness. It is however very easy in a long cross-examination for counsel to omit to put certain points; if subsequently the accused is challenged when he gives evidence and it is suggested that he has fabricated this evidence because otherwise these points would have been raised by defence counsel, counsel should at once inform the prosecution of the mistake he has made and if possible show the written instructions which he omitted to put. If in fact counsel for the defence was never told of the point (either in conference or in written instructions) there is nothing he can do at this stage. It may be, however, that prosecuting counsel are too ready to attack a defendant's evidence on the basis he is speaking of matters upon which the prosecution witnesses were not challenged; in real life it does quite often happen that defence counsel and solicitors have simply not explored with sufficient depth before the trial parts of the case which at the time did not seem of crucial importance.

After *cross-examination* is concluded, counsel for the prosecution may re-examine his witness. Such *re-examination* is designed to obviate the effects of *cross-examination* and must be confined to points arising therefrom and not used as a means of producing new evidence which should have been led *in chief*.

POLICE EVIDENCE

Although the police are entitled to no special credence when giving evidence, they in fact enjoy one very substantial advantage over almost every other witness, including the defendant, in that they are aware of and thus able to exploit the rule (see above) that witnesses are entitled to refresh their memory from any notes made by them at the time of, or shortly after, the events recorded occurred. In practice, police officers invariably record in their note books details of all crimes which they investigate, including a note of any oral statements made by the defendant, and are given permission by the trial judge to refer to these notes when they give evidence. It should be noted that counsel for the defence is entitled to call for and examine the officer's note books (whether used to refresh memory *in* court or not)[13]; the note books do *not* become exhibits unless counsel for the

13 *Owen v Edwards* (1983) 77 Cr App Rep 191.

defence applies to make them so or cross-examines the officers on passages the officer has not referred to the way the note has been written out as opposed to the contents[14].

It often happens that the principal evidence against an accused man is not evidence of eye witnesses but the police record of interviews they have conducted with him. The Code of Practice on Detention, Treatment and Questioning (Code C) provides that as a general rule an arrested person is not to be questioned until he has had access to a solicitor and that he has the right to have a solicitor present at any interview (paras 6.3 and 6.5; see p 76 above). It is likely, however, that there will still be a good many cases where an interview is conducted in the absence of a solicitor. An important safeguard for the suspect is provided by the rule that all interviews are to be recorded contemporaneously either by tape recording or in a 'written interview record':

'11.3 (a) An accurate record must be made of each interview with a person suspected of an offence, whether or not the interview takes place at a police station
(b) If the interview takes place in the police station or other premises:
   (i) the record must state the place of the interview, the time it begins and ends, the time the record is made (if different), any breaks in the interview and the names of all those present; and must be made on the forms provided for this purpose or on the officer's pocket book or in accordance with the code of practice for the tape recording of police interviews with suspects;
   (ii) the record must be made during the course of the interview unless in the investigating officer's view this would not be practicable or would interfere with the conduct of the interview, and must constitute either a verbatim record of what has been said or, failing this, an account of the interview which adequately and accurately summarises it.

11.4 If an interview record is not made during the course of the interview it must be made as soon as practicable after its completion.

11.5 Written interview records must be timed and signed by the maker.

11.6 If an interview record is not completed in the course of the interview the reason must be recorded in the officer's pocket book.

11.7 Any refusal by a person to sign an interview record when asked to do so in accordance with the provisions of this code must itself be recorded.'

It should be noted that in practice where a contemporaneous note has been taken and signed by the defendant, Crown Court judges treat that interview record as if it were an exhibit and copies are given to the jury.

Tape recording of interviews has been carried out in experimental schemes by a number of police forces and by the Customs. It seems likely that the Code of Practice will provide:

(a) that a transcript should *not* normally be made; but
(b) the interviewing officer should prepare a witness statement setting out the relevant questions and answers (either in précis form or as a note of both questions and answers); and
(c) points of challenge can be resolved by agreement of the parties after checking the tape or alternatively played aloud to the jury.

There will, however, be many cases where it will be desirable for the jury to

---

14 See *R v Bass* [1953] 1 QB 680, 37 Cr App Rep 51; *R v Callum* [1975] RTR 415, [1976] Crim LR 257, CA; *R v Britton* [1987] 2 All ER 412, [1987] 1 WLR 539, CA.

hear the whole or a substantial part of the tape in order to judge what really took place at the interview.

Where the interview is not recorded on tape or set out in a written record signed by the defendant, the defence advocate will have to take particular care to check the police statements with his client in detail noting down not only those parts which he says the police have misrecorded but also noting carefully what it is alleged they have left out. These points of challenge must be put to the police witnesses[15].

CONDITIONALLY BOUND WITNESSES

In addition to the oral evidence, the prosecuting counsel (or the clerk of the court) will read aloud to the jury the written statements or depositions of witnesses in respect of whom *conditional witness orders* were made, i e evidence which is in effect not in dispute. Additional written statements may be served on the defence after the committal proceedings which under s 9 of the Criminal Justice Act 1967 will be admissible at the trial unless the defence serve notice of objection within seven days[16]. In all these cases the evidence is, of course, read by agreement.

DOCUMENTARY EVIDENCE

The basic rule of evidence for centuries has been that evidence cannot be given unless it can be tested by cross-examination. For this reason, when in the past a prosecution witness was overseas, or unavailable, his statement could not be read to the jury. The Criminal Justice Bill 1987 gives the court the power to admit such evidence. Clause 21(1) provides:

> 'a statement made by a person in a document shall be admissible in criminal proceedings as evidence of any fact of which direct oral evidence by him would be admissible.'

Note that the evidence in question would have to be admissible if the witness had attended court and given his evidence from the witness box; a written statement by him saying what someone else had told him about the facts in issue will still be inadmissible.

> *Example 1.* George writes to his former employer (a building contractor) stating 'Oliver took supplies from the stores and always told me they were for use on the sites'. Oliver is now charged with stealing from the stores and George has emigrated to Australia. George's letter to his employer would be admissible

15 The only safe course is to make the defendant describe in conference everything that has happened from the moment the police first arrived to interview him to his eventual release from custody. This can be a long and painstaking process but is really essential if the case is to be properly prepared. As stated above, a standard technique of checking police evidence is to compare what is contained in the witness statement or written interview record with the period during which the interview was conducted. It will often be found that there is a startling discrepancy which indicates either that the police have made a précis of a much longer conversation or have omitted large sections of what was said. Note however, that extreme caution must be used in cross-examining on this point because if the police are asked what else was said at such an interview they may remember conversations highly prejudicial to the defendant. Such matters may be better probed at committal proceedings than at the trial itself.

16 Criminal Justice Act 1967 s 9(2)(d), but the court may on application or on its own motion require the maker of the statement to attend and give oral evidence.

under cl 21 (subject to the courts' discretionary power to exclude it, discussed below).

Example 2. George writes a letter to his former employers stating 'Harry used to tell me that Oliver had been taking supplies from the stores'. This letter would be inadmissible because George, if called as a witness, could not give evidence of what he had been told by a third party.

This rule that documents are only admissible as 'first hand hearsay' is very inconvenient in the case, for example, of business documents where the compiler of the document may have acted on the information given to him by different persons over a period of time.

Example 3. At Oliver's trial, the prosecution wish to put in as evidence the store records complied by Frank, on the basis of dockets and delivery notes provided by many different workmen.

Clause 22(1) of the Criminal Justice Bill 1987 provides a solution for this problem:

'a statement in a document shall be admissible in criminal proceedings as evidence of any fact of which direct oral evidence would be admissible, if the following conditions are satisfied –
(a) the document was created or received by a person –
   (i) in the course of a trade, business, profession or other occupation; or
   (ii) as the holder of a paid or unpaid office; and
(b) the information contained in the document was supplied by a person (whether or not the maker of the statement) who had, or may reasonably be supposed to have had, personal knowledge of the matters dealt with'.

(Subclause (2) goes on to provide that the information may be supplied indirectly, i e through a chain of persons).

The main problem with these new provisions will be that the evidence cannot be tested by cross-examination. For this reason, cl 23 provides that the court is to have a discretion to exclude such evidence if it is of the opinion that in the interests of justice it ought not to be admitted. Where such a point is raised by the defence the court is bound to have regard:

'(a) to the nature and source of the document containing the statement and to whether or not, having regard to its nature and source and to any other circumstances that appear to the court to be relevant, it is likely that the document is authentic;
(b) to the extent to which the statement appears to supply evidence which would otherwise not be readily available;
(c) to the relevance of the evidence that it appears to apply to any issue which is likely to have to be determined in the proceeding; and
(d) to any risk, having regard in particular to whether it is likely to be possible to controvert the statement if the person making it does not attend to give oral evidence in the proceedings, that its admission or exclusion will result in unfairness to the accused or, if there is more than one, to any of them.'

In the first example above, one would expect the defence to have objected to the admissibility of George's letter on the ground that it contained key evidence and his counsel would not be able to cross-examine the witness.

A special rule applies when the written statement has been made specifically for the purpose of criminal proceedings (e g witness statement taken by the police). In such a case, cl 24 provides that the statement:

'shall not be given in evidence . . . without leave of the court, and the court shall not give leave unless it is of the opinion that the statement ought to be admitted in the interests of justice; and in considering whether its admission would be in the interests of justice, it shall be the duty of the court to have regard –

(i)   to the contents of the statement;

(ii) to any risk, having regard in particular to whether it is likely to be possible to controvert the statement if the person making it does not attend to give oral evidence in the proceedings, that its admission or exclusion will result in unfairness to the accused or, if there is more than one, to any of them; and

(iii) to any other circumstances that appear to the court to be relevant'.

The way in which this provision may work can be seen in the example below.

Example 4. Oliver's former employer has made a statement to the police that he saw Oliver loading a quantity of the firm's stores into the boot of his car. At the hearing the witness does not attend because he is on an extended stay abroad. The prosecution must apply under cl 24 for leave to adduce the statement in evidence and if leave is granted it becomes evidence under cl 21. However, Oliver's counsel can oppose the application on the grounds that this is critical evidence which should not be admitted unless it can be tested by cross-examination.

COMPUTER RECORDS

Section 69 of the Police and Criminal Evidence Act 1984 provides that computer print-outs are to be admissible in evidence provided the party putting in the print-out can establish that the computer has been functioning properly and that there has been no opportunity for tampering with the data.

Example. In a Customs prosecution it is necessary to prove when a particular airline ticket was issued in Colombia. A print-out showing the date and time of issue will be admissible provided witness statements are obtained from the airline staff able to give evidence that '(a) there are no reasonable grounds for believing that the computer [statement] is inaccurate because of improper use of the computer, and (b) at all material times the computer was operating properly or, if not, that any respect in which it was not operating properly or was out of operation was not such as to affect the production of the document or the accuracy of its contents'.

OBJECTIONS TO EVIDENCE

In a criminal trial before a jury, the defence counsel will have studied the depositions and statements, and may have come to the conclusion that certain items of evidence are inadmissible.

Example. A is charged with burglary. The only issue is as to identity. One witness says in his statement that he had been told that A was seen at the house in question. Such evidence would be inadmissible as hearsay.

In such a case, the usual practice is for defence counsel to indicate to prosecuting counsel before the trial begins that he will take objection to this evidence. It may be that prosecuting counsel will accept that it is inadmissible, in which case, he will simply agree that it should be excluded and, through his solicitor, warn the witness that the particular part of his original statement is not to be mentioned in court. If, however, counsel do not agree, the question of admissibility becomes an issue for the trial judge to decide. Prosecuting counsel will omit all reference to the evidence under objection in his opening speech. When the relevant witness is about to be called, he will indicate to the judge that both counsel wish to seek his guidance on a point of law and the judge will ask the jury to retire. The reason for this is that there is no point in objection being taken to the evidence if the jury hear it while the argument over admissibility is proceeding[17]. When the objection can be indicated by reference to the deposition, or written statement, the judge merely hears counsel's argument and gives his ruling[18]. When, however, as sometimes happens, the matter in dispute is not apparent from the depositions (as for instance where objection is taken to a confession) the defence indicate the nature of the objection and then all relevant witnesses (including the accused), are examined as to the matter in issue and the judge decides whether to admit the evidence in question.

This procedure of a 'trial within a trial' is called a *voire-dire*.

Example. C, a Malaysian student, is arrested by the police in a highly drunken state following a fight in a Soho restaurant in which a man is killed and several persons are seriously wounded. His clothes are blood-stained. C is detained for 34 hours without being charged, notification to his relatives is refused, access to a solicitor is refused and he is interviewed on four separate occasions wearing nothing but a blanket. On the fourth interview he admits having thrown a bottle during the fight. He now says that he only made this admission because he believed the investigating officers were about to beat him up. He is charged with affray.

The admissibility of such a statement (as we have seen on p 74 above) may be challenged under s 76 of the Police and Criminal Evidence Act 1984, which provides:

'If in any proceedings where the prosecution proposes to give in evidence a confession made by an accused person, it is represented to the court that the confession was or may have been obtained –
(a) by oppression of the person who made it; or
(b) in consequence of anything said or done which was likely, in the circumstances existing at the time, to render unreliable any confession which might be made in consequence thereof,
the court shall not allow the confession to be given in evidence against him except in so far as the prosecution proves to the court beyond reasonable doubt that the confession (notwithstanding that it may be true) was not obtained as aforesaid.'

Counsel for the defence will be entitled to rely on the apparent breaches of the Code of Practice in support of an argument that the conduct of the interview was oppressive[19].

It will be appreciated that in order to exclude the confession it is necessary for the defence to cross-examine the officers (who may have convincing reasons why some of the provisions of the Code could not be complied with and who will certainly deny any oppressive behaviour); it will also be

17 Contrast the position in a magistrates' court where a successful objection to evidence may be a pyhrric victory unless the court orders a new bench to try the case.
18 See p 33 in the trial of Twist above.
19 See Police and Criminal Evidence Act 1984 s 67(11). The relevant breaches would appear to be of Code C para 5 (right not to be held incommunicado), para 6 (right to legal advice), para 8.5 (conditions of detention) and also s 41 of the Act (limits on period of detention without charge). The facts of the problem are taken from a case tried at the Central Criminal Court in January/February 1983. See *R v Fulling* [1987] QB 426 [1987] 2 All ER 65.

necessary to call the defendant to give his account of the matter. If the submission fails, the cross-examination of the police will have to be repeated[20] before the jury (although the officers will have been forewarned of the questions they will be asked and the prosecutor will have had advance notice of what the defendant will say).[1] For this reason, experienced defence advocates will sometimes not take the point of admissibility until the close of all the evidence. The position has been explained as follows[2]:

'1   In the normal situation which arises at the vast majority of trials where the admissibility of a confession statement is to be challenged, defending counsel will notify prosecuting counsel that an objection to admissibility is to be raised, prosecuting counsel will not mention the statement in his opening to the jury, and at the appropriate time the judge will conduct a trial on the *voire-dire* to decide on the admissibility of the statement; this will normally be in the absence of the jury, but only at the request or with the consent of the defence: see *R v Anderson* (1929) 21 Cr App Rep 178.

2   Though the case for the defence raises an issue as to the voluntariness of a statement ... defending counsel may for tactical reasons prefer that the evidence bearing on that issue be heard before the jury, with a single cross-examination of the witnesses on both sides, even though this means that the jury hear the impugned statement whether admissible or not. If the defence adopt the tactic, it will be open to defending counsel to submit at the close of the evidence that, if the judge doubts the voluntariness of the statement, he would direct the jury to disregard it, or, if the statement is essential to sustain the prosecution case, direct an acquittal. Even in the absence of such a submission, if the judge himself forms the view that the voluntariness of the statement is in doubt, he should take the like action *proprio motu*.'

ADMISSIONS

In a criminal trial, the prosecution must prove every relevant matter beyond reasonable doubt. However, in many cases the real issue is quite narrow so that much of the prosecution evidence, although relevant, is not contentious. In these circumstances, as explained above, the defence may agree that such evidence should be read aloud from the depositions or statements. The defence may also decide to admit certain facts:

Example 1. Where, at a trial, a photograph is produced showing the scene of the alleged crime, counsel may decide to admit it to save the time and expense of a photographer attending to give formal evidence of taking the photograph and having the untouched negative in his possession.

Example 2. Where, in a complicated fraud case, the prosecution produce a schedule summarising the salient points made in thousands of pages of documents exhibited, the defence may be prepared to admit the schedule as an accurate summary of those documents.

Section 10(1) of the Criminal Justice Act 1967 provides that *any fact of which oral evidence may be given in any criminal proceedings may be admitted for the purpose of those proceedings by, or on behalf of, the prosecutor or defendant, and the admission by any party of any such fact shall as against that party be conclusive evidence in those*

20   This is because the defendant is entitled to raise the same points again before the jury on the issue of what *weight* should be given to the confession (even though the judge has ruled it admissible): see *Prasad v R* [1981] 1 All ER 319, [1981] 1 WLR 469, PC.

1   Note: the prosecutor during the *voire-dire* is not allowed to ask the defendant whether the confession is true: see *Wong Kam-ming v R* [1980] AC 247, [1979] 1 All ER 939, PC.

2   Per Lord Bridge in *Ajodha v The State* [1981] 2 All ER 193 at 202.

proceedings of the fact admitted. Such an admission may be made at the trial by counsel for either side, or may be made before the proceedings – in which case, if made by a defendant, it must be in writing and approved by his counsel or solicitor[3]. It seems that an admission cannot be made by an unrepresented defendant. An admission may be withdrawn by leave of the court[4], for example, where subsequent investigation showed the defendant that the facts might not be as admitted.

DEFENCE SUBMISSION

When the prosecution evidence has been concluded, it is open to counsel for the defence to invite the trial judge to direct the jury that as a matter of law they should acquit the defendant either:

(1) because the prosecution have failed to produce any evidence to establish some essential ingredient of the offence; or
(2) because the evidence produced is so weak or so discredited by cross-examination that no reasonable jury could convict.

It can be seen that this is exactly the same submission that can be made to the magistrates at the committal proceedings.

It is important to note that a judge is not entitled to withdraw a case from the jury merely because he has doubts as to the validity of the prosecution evidence – he has to come to the conclusion that no reasonable juryman could believe the evidence:

'It cannot be too clearly stated that the judge's obligation to stop the case is an obligation which is concerned primarily with those cases where the necessary minimum evidence to establish the facts of the crime has not been called. It is not the judge's job to weigh the evidence, decide who is telling the truth, and to stop the case merely because he thinks the witness is lying. To do that is to usurp the function of the jury . . .'[5]

The circumstances where it is proper for the judge to uphold a submission have been summarised as follows:

'How then should the judge approach a submission of "no case"? (1) If there is no evidence that the crime alleged has been committed by the defendant, there is no difficulty. The judge will of course stop the case. (2) The difficulty arises where there is some evidence but it is of a tenuous character, for example because of inherent weaknesses or vagueness or because it is inconsistent with other evidence. (a) Where the judge comes to the conclusion that the Crown's evidence, taken at its highest, is such that a jury properly directed could not properly convict on it, it is his duty, on a submission being made, to stop the case. (b) Where, however, the Crown's evidence is such that its strength or weakness depends on the view to be taken of a witness's reliability, or other matters which are generally speaking within the province of the jury and where on one possible view of the facts *is* evidence on which a jury could properly come to the conclusion that the defendant is guilty, then the judge should allow the matter to be tried by the jury . . . There will of course, as always on this branch of the law, be borderline cases. They can safely be left to the discretion of the judge[6].'

3 Criminal Justice Act 1967 s 10(2).
4 Ibid s 10(4).
5 Per Lord Widgery CJ in *R v Barker* (1977) 65 Cr App Rep 287 at 288.
6 Per Lord Lane CJ in *R v Galbraith* [1981] 2 All ER 1060 at 1062.

A very difficult problem arises where at the close of the prosecution case the evidence is equally consistent with the defendant having committed one of two alternative counts (e g theft or handling). The best view seems to be that a submission should be upheld[7], unless in fact the counts are not truly alternative (i e on any basis the defendant would be guilty of at some stage appropriating the goods for his own use and therefore stealing them)[8]. Even if the judge is not prepared to rule that no reasonable jury could convict on the evidence, he may still be prepared to remind the jury of their right to stop the case and acquit the defendant at any stage during the defence case[9].

THE CASE FOR THE DEFENCE

Counsel for the defence is entitled to an opening speech before calling evidence if he is calling the defendant and other witnesses as to the *facts*. When he is only calling the defendant or only the defendant and character witnesses, he is *not* entitled to make an opening speech.

Counsel for the defence, once he has received clear instructions from his client, is under a duty to put the defendant's case fearlessly and must not allow his personal opinion or any intimations of judicial displeasure to deflect him from his course. If, for example, the defence case involves serious imputations being made upon the behaviour of the investigating police officers, it is counsel's duty to present that case to the very best of his ability and if necessary to pursue the point by rigorous cross-examination. He is, of course, under a duty to avoid wasting time by repetition or prolixity and he must not be made the instrument of unnecessary attacks on the witnesses; indeed, anything in the nature of hectoring or bullying a witness will be counter-productive with the jury. But, subject to the above qualifications, it cannot be too much stressed that it is the duty of counsel for the defence to use every proper line of questioning and argument to secure the acquittal of his client[10].

The defendant is not obliged to give evidence at his trial; instead he may remain silent and so avoid cross-examination by counsel for the prosecution. The defendant, if he gives evidence, is in the same position as any other witness, save that he may not be cross-examined as to *credit* (i e to show he has committed other offences or he is of bad character and so should be disbelieved) unless[11]:

(1) *the proof that he has committed, or been convicted of such other offence, is admissible evidence to show that he is guilty of the offence wherewith he is then charged*; or

(2) *he has personally, or by his advocate, asked questions of the witnesses for the*

---

7 See *Tsang Ping Nam v R* [1981] 1 WLR 1462, 74 Cr App Rep 139 (D made statement to police accusing officers of corruption but gave contrary evidence at trial; either his statement or his evidence was untrue but prosecution could not show which was false: D could not be convicted of either making a false statement or perjury). But see, on receiving, the contrary dicta of Winn LJ in *R v Plain* [1967] 1 All ER 614, 51 Cr App Rep 9.

8 *Stapylton v O'Callaghan* [1973] 2 All ER 782, DC but cf *R v Brown* (1983) 79 Cr App Rep 115.

9 Cf Dicta of Roskill LJ in *R v Falconer-Atlee* (1973) 58 Cr App Rep 348 (judge should take it on himself to direct acquittal) and dicta in *Barker* and *Galbraith* above.

10 See the statement of the Chairman of the Bar (1976) 62 Cr App Rep 193 which affirms the above principles and which was issued after the Bar Council had rejected complaints made by Melford Stevenson J in a case where the defence of certain terrorists involved the allegation that fingerprints had been 'planted' by the police.

11 Criminal Evidence Act 1898 proviso (f) to s 1.

prosecution with a view to establish his own good character, or has given evidence of his good character, or the nature or conduct of the defence is such as to involve imputations on the character of the prosecutor, or the witnesses for the prosecution; or

(3) *he has given evidence against any other person charged with the same offence.*

The effect of this crucial provision can be summarised by saying that the prosecuting counsel may cross-examine an accused person as to his character only when:

(1) the defendant suggests he is of good character; or
(2) he attacks the prosecution witnesses[12]; or
(3) he gives evidence against the co-defendant; or
(4) in one of the rare cases where the prosecution can prove previous convictions as part of their case[13].

The judge has a discretion to prevent prosecuting counsel[14] embarking on such cross-examination notwithstanding that the case falls within the statute. Accordingly, the course normally taken is for the judge to direct the jury to withdraw while he considers an application by the prosecuting counsel to cross-examine the accused as to his character. It sometimes happens, particularly where the evidence against the accused is entirely that of police officers, that the defendant simply cannot put forward his defence (eg that an alleged oral admission has been fabricated or that goods have been 'planted' on him) without casting imputations on the character of the prosecutor. The Court of Appeal has given guidance as to how the judge's discretion should be exercised, in the following terms:

'First [the discretion should be exercised in favour of the defendant] if there is nothing more than a denial, however emphatic or offensively made, of an act or even a short series of acts amounting to one incident or in what was said to have been a short interview. . . . The position would be different however if there were a denial of evidence of a long period of detailed observation extending over hours and . . . where there were denials of long conversations. Secondly, cross-examination should only be allowed if the judge is sure that there is no possibility of mistake, misunderstanding or confusion and that the jury will inevitably have to decide whether the prosecution witnesses have fabricated evidence. Defendants sometimes make wild allegations when giving evidence. Allowance should be made for the strain of being in a witness box and the exaggerated use of language which sometimes results from such strain or lack of education or mental instability. Particular care should be used when a defendant is led into making allegations during cross-examination. The defendant, who, during cross-examination is driven to explaining away the evidence by saying it has been made up or planted on him, usually convicts himself without having his previous

12 Note that an emphatic denial of what is said by a witness will not in itself be an attack on his character; the accused must go further and, in effect, be alleging deliberate fabrication. See *Selvey v DPP* [1970] AC 304, [1968] 2 All ER 497; *R v Tanner* (1977) 66 Cr App Rep 56. But counsel cannot evade the operation of s 1(f) by carefully avoiding putting an explicit allegation of misconduct, if such an allegation is the only inference that can be drawn from the questioning – see *R v Britzman and R v Hall* [1983] 1 All ER 369, 76 Cr App Rep 134, CA.
13 Eg to negative a defence of innocent association in a case of indecency or rape.
14 But *not* counsel for a co-defendant where evidence has been given by the accused against him: *Murdoch v Taylor* [1965] AC 574, [1965] 1 All ER 406. See *R v Varley* [1982] 2 All ER 519, CA for guidelines as to when the right to cross-examine a co-accused on his character arises.

convictions brought out. Finally, there is no need for the prosecution to rely upon section 1(f)(ii) if the evidence against a defendant is overwhelming[15].'

ALIBI DEFENCE

As we have seen earlier[16] s 11(1) of the Criminal Justice Act 1967 provides that:

'On a trial on indictment the defendant shall not without the leave of the court adduce evidence in support of an alibi unless, before the end of the prescribed period, he gives notice of particulars of the alibi.'

It should be noted that although the particulars should be given either at the committal proceedings, or within seven days thereafter, the Crown Court may still grant leave to the defendant to pursue an alibi defence where there is some valid reason for his failure to supply particulars[17], but when such leave is granted, the prosecution will be entitled to an adjournment if they need time to check the alibi.

The question has arisen as to what exactly is meant by an *alibi defence*. Section 11(8) provides that:

'"evidence in support of an alibi" means evidence tending to show that by reason of the presence of the defendant at a particular place or in a particular area at a particular time he was not, or was unlikely to have been, at the place where the offence is alleged to have been committed at the time of its alleged commission.'

This definition seems clearly to cover the case where the defendant says he was not present at the place where the crime was committed, when it was committed[18].

Example. A is charged with the murder of B, by shooting him in London at 10.30 pm on 1 January 1979. His defence is that he was staying in a hotel in Edinburgh at the material time. This is clearly an alibi defence of which particulars would have to be served on the prosecution.

This position is more difficult where the offence is of a continuing nature or where the evidence in question is not of the actual offence itself but of an act preparatory thereto.

Example. A is charged with murdering B by administering poison to him on 1 January 1979 at B's home in London. A principal item of evidence is that on 31 December 1978 he was seen buying poison at a chemist's shop in London. A claims that he spent the whole day on 31 December in Manchester.

It is submitted that in the example above the evidence is not *in support of an alibi* within the meaning of s 11(8) because that section contemplates a specific offence at a particular place at a particular time[19].

Where the Crown wish to call evidence to rebut a defence of alibi, this may be done either before or after the evidence in support of the alibi is given[20].

15 See *R v Britzman and R v Hall* above.
16 See p 102 above.
17 Such as that he has only recently taken legal advice: see *R v Sullivan* [1971] 1 QB 253, [1970] 2 All ER 681.
18 Cf the famous definition of Sergeant Arabin 'the prisoner was not there when he did it': *R v Parish Dighton* (1835) Arab 16 AP.
19 See *R v Hassan* [1970] 1 QB 423, [1970] 1 All ER 745.
20 Section 11(4).

SPEECHES AND SUMMING-UP

At the conclusion of the evidence, counsel are entitled to address the jury. The prosecution are heard first so that the defence always have the last word[1].

It is then the duty of the trial judge to sum up the evidence to the jury. Counsel for the defence should pay particular attention to what is said and take a careful note, because he will need this record to advise his client on the merits of an appeal[2]. It is not possible to summarise here all the matters which may be referred to, but counsel should check to see whether the judge deals with the following points:

(1) He must explain to the jury in unequivocal terms that although they accept his directions as to the law they are the sole judges of fact and are free to disregard any comment he may make on the facts.

(2) He must both at the beginning of the summing-up and throughout his review of the evidence explain that the burden of proof rests on the prosecution to prove the case beyond reasonable doubt (ie so that the jury are satisfied that they feel sure). He must not, when he comes to review the defence case, suggest that it is for the defendant to prove his defence to be true[3].

(3) When the accused faces several charges the judge must make it clear to the jury that they are to consider each case separately and the judge himself must in his summing-up deal quite separately with each charge.

(4) Where more than one person is standing trial the judge must:
  (a) Warn the jury to consider the case of each defendant separately.
  (b) Point out where the evidence given is relevant to the case against only one defendant. This is particularly important where police interviews are concerned because whatever one defendant may tell the police in the absence of his co-defendant[4] is inadmissible hearsay against the other.
  (c) Warn the jury, where one defendant has pleaded guilty and given evidence for the prosecution against the other, that it is dangerous to convict on such evidence unless it is corroborated[5].
  (d) Warn the jury where one defendant has given evidence on his own behalf which implicates the other defendant that they should treat with caution such testimony[6].

(5) Where the prosecution case depends wholly or substantially on the correctness of the identification which the defence say is mistaken the judge should[7]:
  (a) warn the jury of the special need for caution before convicting,

1 Criminal Procedure (Right of Reply) Act 1964.
2 Transcripts of the summing-up will not be available for a very considerable time after the period in which to file notice of appeal has expired. In addition, a single judge of the Court of Appeal will not grant bail on the basis of misdirection unless there is a clear note before him of the passages of which complaint is taken.
3 When the defence is alibi or self-defence, it is particularly important to see that the judge, when reviewing the defence case, does not use words to suggest that the defendant has to satisfy the jury on any matter
4 Eg 'it was [co-defendant] that stole the television I didn't have anything to do with it'.
5 And the judge must indicate what parts of the evidence are capable in law of amounting to corroboration: *R v Charles* (1976) 68 Cr App Rep 334.
6 *R v Prater* [1960] 2 QB 464, [1960] 1 All ER 298.
7 *R v Turnbull* [1977] 2 QB 224, [1976] 3 All ER 549.

(b) explain the reasons why such caution is necessary (eg the fact that a mistaken but honest witness will necessarily give an impression of candour which may mislead the jury into believing him accurate), and

(c) refer to the possibility of mistake by the witnesses[8].

He should go on to examine closely the circumstances in which the identification came to be made and remind the jury of any specific weaknesses which had appeared in the identification evidence.

The judge will conclude his summing-up by telling the jury that they must endeavour to reach a unanimous verdict and that circumstances have not yet arisen under which he could accept a majority verdict[9]. Note that if defence counsel considers an error has occurred in the summing-up generally he should merely note this for reference at a later stage when he has to consider grounds of appeal: it is not his role to draw the attention of the judge to the error that has occurred[10].

THE VERDICT

After the conclusion of the summing-up, the jury are not normally allowed to separate until they have returned a verdict or have been discharged because there is no chance of agreement. The jury must feel absolutely free to deliberate and it is improper for the court to seek to hurry them or in any way put pressure on them to return a verdict.

> *Example.* At 2.38 pm after a little over two hours' retirement, the trial judge told the jury 'In ten minutes I shall leave this building and, if by that time you have not arrived at a conclusion in this case, you will have to be kept in all night and we will resume this matter tomorrow.' The jury retired and returned a verdict of guilty in six minutes.

The conviction was quashed by the Court of Appeal[11]. Indeed, since *R v Bushell*[12] where a jury were imprisoned for contempt for acquitting the Quaker William Penn on a charge of unlawful assembly (and were not released until an order of *habeas corpus* was issued by Lord Vaughan CJ) the

---

8 The jury should be told to look specifically at (a) the length of the initial observation, (b) proximity of the witness to the person purported to have been identified as the accused, (c) the lighting, (d) whether the witness had ever seen the person before, (e) the time which elapsed between the initial observation and the identification of the accused, and (f) any discrepancy between the accused's appearance and the description given to the police.

9 *Practice Direction* [1967] 3 All ER 137, [1967] 1 WLR 1198.

10 See *R v Cocks* (1976) 63 Cr App Rep 79 where James LJ at p 82 says 'defending counsel owes a duty to his client and it is not his duty to correct the judge if the judge has gone wrong . . . if prosecuting counsel listening to the summing-up appreciates that there has been some misdirection of law or fact then he has a right, if he thinks fit, to raise the matter with the judge and so obtain any correction necessary before the judge retires'. The position is different where a procedural irregularity has occurred. See Appendix C of the Code of Conduct for the Bar (1985) para 154: 'If some procedural irregularity comes to the knowledge of defence counsel before the verdict is returned, he should inform the court as soon as practicable and should not wait with a view to raising the matter later on appeal. Defence counsel is not under any duty to draw matters of fact or law to the attention of the court at the conclusion of the summing-up, but he may do so if he believes it would be to the advantage of his client.'

11 *R v McKenna* [1960] 1 QB 411, [1960] 1 All ER 326.

12 (1670) 6 State Tr 999.

right of the jury to absolute freedom in their deliberations has been considered a most important constitutional safeguard for the subject[13].

MAJORITY VERDICTS

Section 13 of the Criminal Justice Act 1967 enables the court to accept a majority verdict provided that the following conditions are satisfied:

(1) the jury have had not less than two hours[14] for deliberation or such longer period as the court thinks reasonable having regard to the nature and complexity of the case; and
(2) at least ten of the jurors (or nine if there are only ten jurors) agree on the verdict.

If the verdict is 'guilty', the foreman must be asked to state the number of jurors who respectively have agreed to or dissented from the verdict. Practice Directions[15] have been given to ensure that a majority verdict should not be accepted until the judge is satisfied that the jury cannot reach a verdict on which they are all agreed.

VERDICT OF GUILTY OF A LESSER OFFENCE

Section 6(3) of the Criminal Law Act 1967[16] enables a jury to return a verdict of 'not guilty' of the offence charged in the indictment, but 'guilty' of some lesser offence, provided that the allegations in the indictment amount to or include (expressly or by implication) an allegation of another offence.

SPECIAL VERDICTS

It is open to the jury to return a verdict whereby they merely state findings of fact and leave the court to give judgment whether on this finding the defendant is guilty or not of the offence.

> *Example.* D and S, the master and mate of the yacht *Mignonette*, were indicted for murder of the cabin boy. The jury found a special verdict by which they declared that the prisoners had been ship-wrecked and had killed the boy and eaten him and would probably not otherwise have survived. The judge reserved the judgment for the decision of the Divisional Court of the Queen's Bench Division who held that the special verdict amounted to a finding of guilty of murder[17].

13 But as to the value of the jury as protectors of the liberty of the subject see RM Jackson (1938) CLJ 367, and the discussion by WR Cornish in *The Jury* (Penguin Books, 1968) pp 138–162.
   As to the general question of how juries reach this decision, see the important research conducted by the Oxford Penal Research Unit summarised in *The Jury at Work* by Sarah McCabe and Robert Purves (Blackwell, Oxford 1972).
14 In fact, the court should never accept a majority verdict unless at least two hours and ten minutes have elapsed: *Practice Direction* [1970] 1 WLR 916, 54 Cr App Rep 373.
15 See *Practice Direction* [1967] 3 All ER 137, 51 Cr App Rep 454.
16 It should be noted that these provisions do not apply to murder charges where, however, alternative verdicts for some lesser offences are possible. Note also that handling stolen goods is *not* an alternative verdict on a charge of theft. The alternative verdict must be for an offence falling within the jurisdiction of the Crown Court, except in the case of reckless driving where an alternative verdict can be returned of careless driving: see Criminal Law Act 1977 Sch 12.
17 *R v Dudley and Stephens* (1884) 14 QBD 273.

This procedure is now never used because, since the establishment of the Court of Criminal Appeal in 1904, it is no longer necessary for such legal argument to be reserved.

However, a special verdict is still returned in one type of case, namely where the jury find the defendant *insane, so as not to be responsible, according to law, for his actions at the time when the act was done or omission made*[18], in which case they return a special verdict that the accused is *not guilty by reason of insanity*.

FINALITY OF VERDICT

The verdict of a jury is complete once it is announced and the Court of Appeal will not consider evidence to show what has occurred in the jury room or that some jurors were not in agreement with the verdict announced[19]. The reason for this has been explained as (a) securing a finality to the proceedings and (b) removing jurors after a case is concluded from threats or pressure to say they were not in agreement with the verdict[20].

CONTEMPT OF COURT

The Crown Court has power to punish as contempt conduct calculated to interfere with the due administration of justice[1]. The correct procedure where such conduct is reported to the court is for the alleged contemnor to be remanded until the case against him is presented by the prosecuting authorities and his representation by counsel is arranged. The proceedings will however be summary, ie determined by a judge and not by a jury. Examples of such cases are:

(1) The publication of matter which creates 'a substantial risk that the course of justice in the proceedings in question will be seriously impeded or prejudiced'[2]. This is why the newspapers in this country are not allowed to comment on proceedings until they are completed.
(2) Failure of witnesses[3] and jurors to attend court.
(3) Threats to witnesses or parties either before, during or after the case in question[4].
(4) Publication of matters which the court has directed should be kept confidential (eg the identity of witnesses in blackmail cases)[5], provided such publication interferes with the administration of justice[6].

---

18 Trial of Lunatics Act 1883 s 2, as amended by Criminal Procedure (Insanity) Act 1964 s 1.
19 *R v Roads* [1967] 2 QB 108, [1966] 2 All ER 84.
20 Note: under s 8(1) of the Contempt of Court Act 1981 it is a contempt of court 'to obtain, disclose or solicit any particulars of statements made, opinions expressed, arguments advanced or votes cast by members of a jury in the course of their deliberations in any legal proceedings'.
1 Courts Act 1971 s 4(8).
2 *A-G v Times Newspapers* [1974] AC 273, [1973] 3 All ER 54. Contempt of Court Act 1981 s 2 makes such conduct an offence of strict liability.
3 Criminal Procedure (Attendance of Witnesses) Act 1965 s 3.
4 Eg *Moore v Clerk of Assize, Bristol* [1972] 1 All ER 58, [1971] 1 WLR 1669, where a witness was threatened after she had given her evidence. See Contempt of Court Act 1981 s 11.
5 *R v Socialist Worker Printers Publishers Ltd, ex p A-G* [1975] QB 637, [1975] 1 All ER 142 where a journalist published details of the identity of victims of alleged blackmail after the court had directed their names should not be revealed.
6 *A-G v Leveller Magazine Ltd* [1979] AC 440, [1979] 1 All ER 745, HL.

Such contempt can be punished by imprisonment and a fine. In exceptional cases where the contempt occurs in the face of the court and is of extreme gravity the court can deal with the matter at once; this would apply, for example, where a deliberate disturbance was actually created in the courtroom; in other cases the right course is for the matter to be put over so that the court is not acting as both prosecutor and judge and so that the accused can be legally represented. The principles have been summarised by Lord Denning MR as follows:

'The new Crown Court is in being. The judges of it have not yet acquired the prestige of the red judge when he went on assize. His robes and bearing made everyone alike stand in awe of him. Rarely did he need to exercise his great power of summary punishment. Yet there is just as much need for the Crown Court to maintain its dignity and authority. The judges of it should not hesitate to exercise the authority they inherit from the past. Insults are best treated with disdain – save where they are gross and scandalous. Refusal to answer with admonishment – save where it is vital to know the answer. But disruption of the court or threats to witnesses or to jurors should be visited with immediate arrest. Then a remand in custody and, if it can be arranged, representation by counsel[7].'

7 *Balogh v St Albans Crown Court* [1975] QB 73, [1974] 3 All ER 283, where a solicitor's clerk introduced a cylinder of 'laughing gas' into the courthouse intending to enliven the proceedings and was sent to prison by Melford-Stevenson J. Note: in that case the Court of Appeal held that he had not committed a contempt because he had not proceeded so far with his plan to be guilty of the offence or even an attempt. He was accordingly released.

Chapter 6

Trial before magistrates

We have already seen that there are some offences which can only be tried by magistrates' courts (eg careless driving, assaulting or obstructing a police officer), and other offences (eg theft, assault occasioning bodily harm) which may be tried before magistrates provided certain conditions are fulfilled.

We must now examine the procedure by which a magistrates' court tries a criminal case. Such proceedings are known as *summary trial*. We shall see that this procedure is a modification of the rules which apply to jury trial at the Crown Court.

ADVANCE INFORMATION TO DEFENCE

Where the defendant is charged with an offence triable either way (eg theft or assault occasioning actual bodily harm) the prosecuting authority must serve a notice on him explaining his right to request information of the evidence against him. If a request is made by the defendant, the prosecutor must serve on him as soon as practicable either:

(a) a copy of those parts of every written statement which contain information as to the facts and matters of which the prosecutor proposes to adduce evidence in the proceedings; or

(b) a summary of the facts and matters of which the prosecutor proposes to adduce evidence in the proceedings[1].

This procedure does *not* apply to cases where the offence is purely summary (although such a charge, for example assault on the police, may sometimes lead to custodial sentences). In such a case, however, most prosecuting counsel and solicitors will provide at least a basic outline of the evidence to the defence advocate.

In addition, the defence must be told in every case:

(i) the identity and address of any person from whom the prosecution have taken a statement[2];

---

1 Magistrates' Court (Advance Information) Rules 1985, SI 1985/601 (made under s 144 of the Magistrates' Courts Act 1980).
2 See *R v Leyland Justices, ex p Hawthorn* [1979] QB 283, [1979] 1 All ER 209. The prosecutor is not obliged to provide a copy of the statement taken: *R v Bryant* and *R v Dickson* (1946) 31 Cr App Rep 146. See further the *Practice Note* [1982] 1 All ER 734, 74 Cr App Rep 302.

(ii) details of any previous convictions of the prosecution witnesses[3].

PLEA

A summary trial begins with the clerk reading the substance of the charge over to the defendant and asking him whether he pleads 'guilty or not guilty'[4]. A plea of 'guilty' can only be accepted if it is unequivocal. One of the problems facing a busy magistrates' court is that many of the defendants appearing before them will have little or no knowledge of the law and will be without legal assistance. For this reason, the greatest care must be taken to ensure that every defendant understands what it is alleged he has done and that, if he purports to plead 'guilty', that he is really admitting that the allegation is true. Even if the defendant pleads 'guilty', the Crown Court will set aside his plea if in substance his mitigation amounts to a defence to the charge.

> *Example.* A is charged with theft of a motorbike. He elects summary trial and pleads guilty. By way of mitigation he says that he was only borrowing the bike and would have returned it. The Crown Court must set aside such a plea of guilty because his mitigation is an allegation of facts which, if true, amount to a defence[5].

If the defendant enters an unequivocal plea of 'guilty', the court passes at once to the process of sentence (which is discussed at p 223 in Part three of this book). If his plea is obviously equivocal, the court itself enters a plea of 'not guilty'[6].

PLEA OF GUILTY BY POST

In Chapter 2, we saw that, generally, summary offences can only be tried in the county (or commission area) in which it is alleged that they were committed. Thus, for instance, a man who drove past a red traffic light in Newcastle would have to attend before the magistrates for that city if he wished to contest the charge, even if he lived in Penzance. Partly for this reason, and partly because many summary offences are minor in character and only carry a small fine, Parliament has provided a means by which offenders *who wish to plead guilty*, may be invited to do so by post without the necessity of attending court[7]. The Magistrates' Courts Act 1980 s 12 provides that where a summons has been issued in respect of a summary offence which is not punishable with more than three months' imprisonment, the prosecution may serve on the defendant:

(1) a statement of the facts alleged against him, and
(2) a statement of the procedure for dealing with the case in his absence.

The defendant or his solicitor may notify the court of his desire to plead

---

3 *R v Collister* (1955) 39 Cr App Rep 100; *R v Paraskeva* (1982) 76 Cr App Rep 162.
4 The plea must be entered personally by the accused; thus, where a plea of 'guilty' was entered by a solicitor without the question being put to the defendant, the Divisional Court set aside the plea: *R v Wakefield Justices, ex p Butterworth* [1970] 1 All ER 1181.
5 *R v Durham Quarter Sessions, ex p Virgo* [1952] 2 QB 1, [1952] 1 All ER 466 and see cases cited at p 221 below.
6 Where it appears that he is suffering from mental disorder, the court may under the Mental Health Act 1959 s 60(2), hear the case against the defendant as if he had tendered a plea of not guilty and make a hospital order if it finds that he has committed the acts charged.
7 See summons on p 90 below.

guilty, and the court will proceed with the case in his absence. The prosecution will not be permitted to give any evidence of the facts of the case except for the statement already sent to the defendant. He may send to the court a written statement of any matters which he thinks they should take into account in determining sentence. The court will normally pass sentence in his absence but, if they desire more information or if they are considering a severe penalty (such as disqualification from driving), they must adjourn for the defendant to attend in person[8].

ABSENCE OF DEFENDANT

It frequently happens in practice that defendants fail to attend court on the date fixed for the hearing. Where this happens the court will take one of the following courses:

(i)   issue a warrant[9] (which may be backed for bail) requiring the defendant to attend on a stated day; this would be necessary where the offence was indictable or triable either way or where there was any likelihood of his receiving a custodial sentence;

(ii) proceed to try the case in his absence; this procedure is only available in the case of a summary offence; the prosecution must prove service of the summons upon him[10]. Any conviction will be automatically set aside if the defendant makes a statutory declaration to the effect that he was unaware of the proceedings and serves this declaration on the clerk to the justices within 21 days of the date upon which he first has knowledge of the proceedings[11];

(iii) adjourn the case and give notice to the defendant of the new hearing date[12] (this would be appropriate where, for example, he was ill and could not attend court).

SUMMARY TRIAL

Where the defendant pleads 'not guilty', the magistrates must then determine the issue of his guilt or innocence applying the same rules of evidence and the same standard of proof as would be applied by the Crown Court dealing with the trial of an indictable offence. The court may only try one information at one time, unless the accused agrees that more than one charge should be heard together[13].

(a) The opening speech
The prosecution will be represented by counsel, or by a solicitor from the Crown Prosecution Service. He has the right to make an opening speech

8 Magistrates' Courts Act 1980 s 11(4).
9 Magistrates' Courts Act 1980 s 13(1).
10 Ibid s 11(1) and (2).
11 Ibid s 14.
12 Note that the clerk must given written notice of the time and place of the resumed hearing under r 99 of the Magistrates' Courts Rules 1981, SI 1981/552 (which provides that proof of receipt is not necessary where the notice is sent by the registered post or recorded delivery). In the absence of such notice, any resumed trial is a nullity: see *R v Seisdon Justices, ex p Dougan* [1983] 1 All ER 6, [1982] 1 WLR 1476.
13 *Brangwynne v Evans* [1962] 1 All ER 446, [1962] 1 WLR 267, but note an information may charge two or more persons with *jointly* committing *one* offence in which case they must be tried together.

but, unlike counsel for the prosecution in a trial by jury, he generally has no right to a second speech at the end of the defence evidence[14].

(b) The prosecution evidence

Once the prosecutor has opened his case, he calls for witnesses. The same rules as to examination in chief, cross-examination and re-examination apply as in a trial on indictment at the Crown Court (see p 135 above). There are, however, a number of points which apply to summary trial which should be noted:

(i) *Limited disclosure of evidence.* Where the court is trying an offence which is *summary only* (eg most road traffic cases and assault or obstructing the police) the defence advocate will *not* be entitled to a statement of the prosecution evidence under the advance information rules. Even where the offence is *triable either way* (eg theft or assault occasioning actual bodily harm), the advocate may only have received a summary of the evidence. Although it may be possible for the advocate to make a shrewd guess at what will be said by the prosecution witnesses, there will be occasions when the evidence takes him by surprise. In such cases, it will be necessary for the advocate to ask for an opportunity to take his client's instructions on the evidence (in particular, so that he can put the points of challenge to the prosecuting witnesses). Normally, this can be done by the court rising for a few minutes. In extreme cases, the defence may properly ask for an adjournment to produce rebutting evidence.

(ii) *Objections as to the admissibility of evidence may be pointless.* We have already explained that at the Crown Court the defence will be aware from the committal statements of the points of objection which they wish to make (eg as to hearsay evidence or disclosure of prejudicial material). The question of admissibility is determined by the trial judge in the absence of the jury so that, if the objection succeeds, they remain unaware of the inadmissible evidence. In a magistrates' court, the position is different (a) because the same tribunal has to determine questions of admissibility as will eventually decide the facts, and (b) because the defence may be unaware of the inadmissible evidence until it has already been given. It may be, therefore, that the effect of an objection, even if it is decided in favour of the defendant, will be merely to place a spotlight on the objectionable evidence. Such an objection is seldom worthwhile except:

(1) where the inadmissible evidence is serious (eg improperly adduced evidence of the defendant's previous convictions) so that it is necessary to make sure that the bench exclude it from their consideration in determining whether the offence is proved. (Note in an extreme case it may be necessary to ask for the case to be reheard before a new bench); or

(2) where the piece of evidence in question is the *only* evidence to prove one essential element of the offence (or to establish a chain of events which the prosecution have to prove) so that if the court excludes it, the defence will be able to submit 'no case to answer'.

14 See the Magistrates' Courts Rules 1980.

(iii) Procedure for determining admissibility of confessions. Where the defence challenge the admissibility of a confession on the grounds that it was obtained by oppression or is unreliable, s 76 of the Police and Criminal Evidence Act 1984 provides that:

> 'The court shall not allow the confession to be given in evidence . . . except in so far as the prosecution proves to the court beyond reasonable doubt that the confession . . . was not obtained as aforesaid.'

These words require the magistrates, if the defence so request, to determine as a preliminary issue (if necessary by hearing evidence from the police and the defendant at a 'trial within a trial') whether or not to admit the confession. The former practice was for the court to hear all the evidence and only determine at that stage whether or not to exclude the confession[15].

(c) Submission of no case

Once the prosecution case is closed the defence may make legal submissions of 'no case to answer' and, since these are matters of law, the prosecution may reply. The principles in determining such submissions have already been discussed[16] but it is worth setting out here the *Practice Note*[17] issued by the Divisional Court to guide magistrates as to when a submission is appropriate:

> 'A submission that there is no case to answer may properly be made and upheld:
> (a) when there has been no evidence to prove an essential element of the alleged offence[18];
> (b) when the evidence adduced by the prosecution has been so discredited as a result of cross-examination or is so manifestly unreliable that no reasonable tribunal could safely convict on it.
> Apart from these two situations a tribunal should not in general be called on to reach a decision as to conviction or acquittal until the whole of the evidence which either side wishes to tender has been placed before it. If, however, a submission is made that there is no case to answer the decision should depend not so much on whether the adjudicating tribunal (if compelled to do so) would at that stage convict or acquit, but on whether the evidence is such that a reasonable tribunal might convict. If a reasonable tribunal might convict on the evidence so far laid before it, there is a case to answer.'

(d) Defence case

At this stage the defendant has the right either to remain silent or give evidence from the witness-box (in which case, of course, he is liable to be cross-examined). After he has given his evidence, his witnesses are called. In very exceptional cases, where the defence have produced evidence or made allegations which the prosecution could not have foreseen, the court

---

15 See *R v Liverpool Juvenile Court, ex p R* [1987] 2 All ER 688, [1987] 3 WLR 224.
16 See p 143 above.
17 [1962] 1 All ER 448, sub nom Practice Direction [1962] 1 WLR 227. Note that the magistrates may ask the advocate whether he is reserving the right to call evidence if they are against his submission: *R v Gravesend Justices, ex p Sheldon* [1968] 3 All ER 466, [1968] 1 WLR 1699.
18 Where the submission is made on the basis that there is no evidence to prove some essential matter, the court has a discretion to permit the prosecution to reopen its case but should not normally exercise that discretion unless the matter is purely formal: the power is not to be exercised to enable the prosecution to call evidence available from the outset which goes to a substantial part of their case and which by mistake has not been adduced: see *R v Pilcher* (1974) 60 Cr App Rep 1, [1974] Crim LR 613, CA.

may permit the prosecutor to call evidence in rebuttal[19]. Finally, the defence advocate addresses the magistrates.

(e) The decision

The court decides by a majority: there is no need for unanimity. If the magistrates are equally divided, a new trial will be ordered. Note that magistrates are *not* entitled to make a finding of guilty of a lesser offence not specifically charged. They are entitled to ask their clerk to advise them privately on points of law but they must not seek or listen to his views on the issues of fact and it is improper for them to request the clerk to retire with them when no issues of law arise in the case. The reason for this was explained by Lord Goddard CJ as follows:

> 'I think that it has been said more than once in this court that it is not right that the justices' clerk should retire with them. It has been often said that the decision must be the decision of the justices, not the decision of the justices *and* the clerk, still less the decision of the clerk; and if the clerk retires with the justices, the inevitable conclusion that people will form is that he may influence the justices, or may take some course which is for the justices alone to take. Justices can always send for the clerk if they require advice on a point of law, because that is what the clerk is there for; but it is not desirable, and is irregular, for a clerk to retire with justices as a matter of course when they are considering the facts[20].'

A *Practice Direction*[1] issued by the Divisional Court provides that the clerk is to:

(i) advise the magistrates on questions of law, mixed fact and law, or practice and procedure;

(ii) refresh their memory as to any matters of evidence and draw attention to any issues involved in the matters before the court;

(iii) assist the magistrates from his notes if they are in any doubt as to the evidence which has been given. The magistrates should ordinarily do this in open court to avoid any suspicion that the clerk has been involved in deciding issues of fact.

Lay justices do not normally give reasons in open court for their finding, although some metropolitan stipendiary magistrates do this as a matter of course. It is submitted that in any case of substance, reasons for the decision should be given. Justice requires not only a fair decision, but a reasoned decision and the expression of those reasons. It is very seldom in a county court, where the judge must give an oral judgment, that one finds the bitterness and suspicion that sometimes arises when a bench of magistrates return with the laconic comment 'case proved'[2].

---

19 See *R v Harris* [1927] 2 KB 587: 'Matters arising *ex improviso* which no human ingenuity can foresee.' This does *not* enable the prosecution to call evidence (such as an analyst's certificate) which they forgot to put in during their case: see *Piggott v Sims* [1973] RTR 15, [1972] Crim LR 595.

20 *R v East Kerries Justices, ex p Mundy* [1952] 2 QB 719 at 723. See also *R v Barry (Glamorgan) Justices, ex p Kashim* [1953] 2 All ER 1005, [1953] 1 WLR 1320; *R v Guildford Justices, ex p Harding* (1981) 145 JP 174.

1 [1981] 2 All ER 831, [1981] 1 WLR 1163.

2 The converse point of view was expressed by Lord Mansfield: 'Consider what you think justice requires and decide accordingly. But never give your reasons; for your judgment will probably be right, but your reasons will certainly be wrong.' Cited in Grierson *Confessions of a Country Magistrate* (Gollancz, 1972).

THE ADVANTAGES AND DISADVANTAGES OF SUMMARY TRIAL

The principal advantages to a defendant of summary trial are speed and cost. A trial on indictment will invariably take several months before it comes on. In a magistrates' court, even a contested case can usually be disposed of within a few weeks of the arrest or process. In addition, proceedings before magistrates are inexpensive. An unsuccessful defendant will be faced with a bill for his own costs (or legal aid contribution), and probably a contribution towards the costs of the prosecution which together may total about £200. At the Crown Court, he may have to pay double or treble this amount. However, as indicated above, a defendant at a magistrates' court is at a substantial tactical disadvantage when he has no advance notice of the evidence against him. The other disadvantage in summary proceedings, from the point of view of the defendant, is that in most cases, where there is a conflict of evidence between the police and the defendant, there is a greater likelihood of conviction before a bench of magistrates than a jury. This statement is in a sense impossible to prove, but it appears to be the settled conclusion of the majority of experienced defence lawyers.

JUVENILE COURT PROCEEDINGS

SEPARATE COURT SYSTEM

The basic rule is that a person who has not attained the age of 17 must be tried in a juvenile court. The court consists of three magistrates who must not all be of the same sex and who have special experience of young persons and children in trouble. The law channels juvenile offenders to the juvenile court by excluding them from the jurisdiction of the adult courts. Thus, s 46 of the Children and Young Persons Act 1933 sets out the general rule that no charge against a child or a young person[3] can be heard by an adult magistrates' court and s 24 of the Magistrates' Courts Act 1980 effectively abolishes their right to claim jury trial at the Crown Court[4].

A problem occurs, however, where a juvenile commits an offence with an adult offender.

Example. John (aged 16) and Alan (aged 18) are jointly charged with taking a motor car without the owner's consent contrary to s 12 of the Theft Act 1968.

In such a case, both boys will be brought before the adult magistrates' court, which has sole jurisdiction to entertain proceedings where a juvenile is charged jointly with a person over 17 (and which may assume jurisdiction

---

3 A child is a person over ten but under 14; a young person is a juvenile who is over 14 but has not attained the age of 17. Criminal proceedings cannot be brought against a person under the age of ten.

4 In cases which would be punishable by a sentence of over 14 years if the defendant was an adult the magistrates have in theory the power to commit to the Crown Court for trial; if the juvenile is charged with murder or causing death by reckless driving the juvenile court must commit him for trial to the Crown Court. Note that if the defendant attains 17 after being charged but before the juvenile court has determined the mode of trial (in effect his first appearance other than a formal remand) he has the right to elect jury trial; see *R v Islington North Juvenile Court, ex p Daley* [1983] 1 AC 347, [1982] 2 All ER 974.

where they are charged as accomplices[5]). Once they appear before the adult magistrates' court there are a number of possibilities:

(i) Alan (the adult) elects summary trial and pleads 'not guilty'. John will be tried with him at the magistrates' court but the court has only very restricted powers of punishing him if they convict him. Unless the adult court decides to grant an absolute or conditional discharge, or fine John, or bind over his parents to exercise proper control of him, they *must* remit his case for sentence by the juvenile court[6]. The adult court may *not* make a supervision order or detention centre order or commit John to the Crown Court for sentence.

(ii) Alan elects summary trial and pleads 'guilty'. If John also admits to the charge, the magistrates' powers of sentence are as set out above. If John denies the charge the adult court is empowered to remit his case to the juvenile court[7] and normally should do so unless it is clear from the outset that if the case is proved against John it would be appropriate to deal with him in one of the limited ways discussed above.

(iii) Alan elects trial by jury. The magistrates have a discretion whether to remit John to the juvenile court or commit him to the Crown Court with Alan[8]. They should commit if they consider it 'necessary in the interests of justice to commit them both for trial'. If John indicates that he admits the charge it will often be appropriate to remit his case to the juvenile court. If, on the other hand, the juvenile disputes the charge it will usually be appropriate to commit him for trial to the Crown Court to avoid the undesirable situation where different tribunals come to different decisions on the same evidence. If the juvenile is convicted at the Crown Court that court may remit him for sentence to the juvenile court, but this would normally not be appropriate because the sentencing powers of the Crown Court and the juvenile court are, broadly speaking, the same[9].

CARE PROCEEDINGS

The Children and Young Persons Act 1969 envisaged that the normal form of proceedings against juveniles (and eventually the only form against children under 14) would be *care proceedings* before the juvenile court. These are civil proceedings by which the court is asked to make an order placing a child, or young person, under the care[10] or supervision[10] of the local authority. Although it is unlikely that criminal proceedings will be replaced by care proceedings in the foreseeable future, it is worth understanding how

5 Children and Young Persons Act 1933 s 46.
6 Ibid s 56(1), as amended by Children and Young Persons Act 1969 s 7(8). The adult court can also award costs against him, and disqualify him from driving without remitting the case to the juvenile court.
7 Magistrates' Courts Act 1980 s 29.
8 Ibid s 24(1). If the juvenile is also charged with some related offence (ie in a case involving a joint assault on B, the juvenile is also charged with assault on A) the magistrates may commit the juvenile to stand trial on the related charge as well.
9 Children and Young Persons Act 1933, s 56(1): see *R v Lewis* (1984) 148 JP 329, CA.
10 As to the meaning and effect of such orders, see Part three pp 263–264 below.

the proposed system would operate. Before an order can be made, the juvenile court must be satisfied[11]:

(1) that one or more specific conditions have arisen, for example, that the child is being ill-treated or is not receiving full-time education or *is guilty of an offence, excluding homicide*; and

(2) that he is in need of care, or control, which he is unlikely to receive unless the court makes an order in respect of him.

It will be noticed that the consequence is that in some *but not all* care proceedings, the court will have to determine the question of criminal liability as a preliminary point before it goes on to consider whether the juvenile is in need of care.

> *Example.* Peter (15) is charged by the police with burglary and theft. He has four previous findings of guilt for similar offences. He lives with his mother who is divorced, and is looking after five younger children. He is at the moment under a supervision order, but has not been responding to the advice of the supervising officer. The police, having consulted the local children's department, initiate care proceedings.

In Peter's case, the proceedings will fall into two quite distinct stages:

(i) The issue whether Peter is guilty of the offence charged. This must be determined according to the strict rules of evidence followed in the adult criminal courts. No mention may be made of his previous findings of guilt. The court must be certain beyond reasonable doubt before they find that he has committed the offence. If they do find the offence made out they must announce their decision before moving on to the second stage. If they acquit, he is discharged and the proceedings are at an end.

(ii) The issue whether Peter is in need of care and control. At this stage, the local children's department present their evidence to substantiate the need to take the child into care. The child, and his parents, must be afforded opportunity to cross-examine the department's witnesses, and to present their side of the case. The standard of proof is the civil standard of a balance or probabilities.

CRIMINAL PROCEEDINGS

As stated above, it is intended that eventually the *only* proceedings against children under 14 will be care proceedings. The theory is that offences committed by children should only result in court action where there is also present a lack of proper care and control at home. However, a 'young person' over 14, and for the time being, children over ten, may be and almost invariably are brought before the juvenile court on a straight-forward criminal charge. The proceedings then follow the rules described above for summary trial, subject to the safeguards mentioned later.

---

11 Children and Young Persons Act 1969 s 1(2), which is set out in Appendix 1 below.

QUALIFIED INFORMANTS AND CAUTIONING

Section 5 of the Children and Young Persons Act 1969[12] provides that proceedings against juveniles can only be brought by 'qualified informants', which generally means police officers and local authorities. The informant must be satisfied before initiating proceedings that the case falls within the types of cases listed by the Secretary of State as being appropriate for prosecution *and* that it cannot be more adequately dealt with by the child's parents or teacher or by a caution from the police. It should be observed, at this point, that the police in some localities operate *juvenile bureaux* which screen complaints against juveniles and frequently direct that a caution should be administered to a child in the presence of a parent, rather than a prosecution. Such cautions will only be administered, however, where every juvenile concerned in the offence admits complicity[13].

PROCEDURAL SAFEGUARDS

When the young offender is brought before the juvenile court, the law imposes certain rules to protect him from exposure to adult criminals and from publicity, and to enable him to understand what is happening.

Children and young persons must be kept separate from adult offenders at the police station and when detained by order of the court[14]. Ideally, juvenile courts should sit in separate buildings from the adult magistrates' courts. This is possible in large cities (for example, the juvenile court complex for Central London in Marylebone) but would be impracticable elsewhere. Where, however, the same building is used for both courts, the juvenile court must not sit in a room where an adult court has sat within the last hour[15].

The only persons who are permitted to be present at juvenile court proceedings are members and officers of the court, parties to the case, newspaper reporters and specially authorised persons (such as law students)[16]. Although the press may be present, it is an offence to publish the name, address or school of the juvenile or to include in any report of the proceedings matters calculated to lead to the identification of the child[17].

The parents of the child are required to attend court with him[18]. Indeed, as we shall see later, the court may dispose of the case by binding them over to exercise proper control of the child. The procedure, though formal, must be explained in simple terms to the child. The charge must be put in straightforward language, the oath is a promise to tell the truth, and if the case is proved, no conviction is recorded but merely a 'finding of guilt'.

As mentioned earlier, the actual proceedings to determine guilt follow exactly the pattern already described for a summary trial.

---

12 This provision has not yet been brought into force, except for sub-s (8) which requires the police to notify the local authority social services department of prosecutions against juveniles.
13 See article by Tuth and Criller 'Police cautioning of juveniles: the practice of diversity' [1983] Crim LR 587 which points out the wide diversity of police practice.
14 Children and Young Persons Act 1933 s 31.
15 Children and Young Persons Act 1933 s 47(2).
16 Ibid s 31.
17 Ibid s 49.
18 Ibid s 34. The summons will be directed to both the child and his parent or guardian: see Magistrates' Courts (Children and Young Persons) Rules 1970 r 26.

Chapter 7

Appeals from magistrates' courts

APPEAL TO THE CROWN COURT AGAINST CONVICTION

By s 108 of the Magistrates' Courts Act 1980, a defendant who pleads *not* guilty before a magistrates' court may appeal against his conviction to the Crown Court. The prosecutor has no such right.

> *Example*. Albert is charged with assault on the police. There is no right of jury trial so the case has to proceed summarily. Albert pleads not guilty. There is a substantial dispute as to the facts. The magistrates believe the police and convict Albert. He may appeal as of right to the Crown Court.

The procedure is governed by rr 6–8 of the Crown Court Rules 1982. The appellant must serve notice of appeal on both the clerk to the magistrates and the prosecutor within 21 days of the date upon which the magistrates passed sentence. The Crown Court may extend the period in proper cases.

In criminal cases, the notice of appeal to the Crown Court need *not* set out grounds of appeal[1] although in practice this is often done.

The appeal is heard by a circuit judge or recorder, sitting with a bench of magistrates. There is no jury. The form of the appeal is by way of a complete *rehearing* of the case so that evidence may be adduced which was not before the magistrates. The prosecutor opens, and calls his witnesses. The appellant may then submit that there is no case to answer. If no submission is made, or such a submission fails, the appellant may then remain silent, or give evidence on oath. He may call witnesses to give evidence. Finally, the appellant or his advocate may address the court. The prosecutor has no right to a second speech save on points of law which have arisen. It can be seen that the procedure is exactly the same as at a summary trial before a magistrates' court.

Once an appeal against conviction has been heard, then, although the appeal did not purport to challenge the sentence, the question of punishment becomes at large. This means that the Crown Court may, of its own motion, consider the sentence passed below and impose instead any sentence which could have been imposed by the magistrates. Thus the appellant who wishes to challenge his conviction may find that his appeal against conviction is dismissed and even (in rarer cases) that a more severe sentence is imposed upon him by the Crown Court than he received at first instance.

---

1 Supreme Court Act 1981 s 48(4).

NOTICE OF APPEAL

To the Clerk of the Magistrates' Court sitting at the Court House, High Street, Barchester, Barset, and to the Crown Prosecutor, Crown Prosecution Service, Barchester Branch Office, 5th. Floor, Worley House, 225 High Road, Barchester.

I, Albert Smith

Of 23 Acacia Avenue, Plumpstead, Barset (at present in custody at HM Prison, Barchester)

Do hereby give each of you notice that it is my intention to appeal to the Crown Court at Barchester against:-

*my conviction and/or

*the sentence passed on me and/or

*the order made against me

by the said Magistrates Court on the 2nd day of April 1987

for having on the 23rd day of March 1987

at Market Street, Barchester

state shortly the particulars of the offence assaulted Ernest Boot, a police officer, in the execution of his duty contrary to section 51 of the Police Act 1964

when I was:-
(state sentence or order) sentenced to 3 months imprisonment

The general grounds of appeal are:- that the said Ernest Boot was not at the material time acting as a police officer in the execution of his duty

*and that I am not guilty of the offence and

*that my sentence was too severe.

Dated this 5th day of April 1987

Signed Dodson and Fogg
Solicitors for the Appellant

*Delete as appropriate

APPEAL PROCEDURE

1. Notice of appeal must be given in writing. It must set out the general grounds of the appeal and must be signed by you or your solicitor.

2. Two copies of this notice must be given to the Clerk of this Court and one copy must be given to the prosecutor or complainant who brought the proceedings against you.

3. The copies may be delivered by hand or may be sent by registered post addressed to the person concerned at his last or usual place of abode, and must reach the other party and this court within 21 days of the day on which the decision being appealed against was given.
   If notice is not given within the prescribed period of 21 days an application for an extention of the time limit may be made in writing to the Chief Clerk, Barchester Crown Court, Lordship Lane, Barchester, Barset, and must state the reasons why an application for an extension of the time limit is being made.

4. After the written notices have been delivered, if you are in custody, you may apply to this court to be released on bail pending the hearing of the appeal.

5. Notice of the date of hearing will be sent to you by the Chief Clerk of the Crown Court.

6. If, after giving notice of appeal, you wish to abandon your appeal you may do so by giving written notice to the Crown Court at Barchester and to the Clerk of this Court. Such notice must be given not later than the third day before the date fixed for the hearing of your appeal.

7. You are also required to notify the Crown Court of the name of any solicitor you instruct to act for you in your appeal. If you change your solicitor, the name and address of the new solicitor must be given to the Crown Court. If you change your address you must also notify the Crown Court.

APPEAL TO THE CROWN COURT AFTER AN EQUIVOCAL PLEA

We have already said that to be effective a plea of 'guilty' before a magistrates' court must be unequivocal. Where, therefore, the plea was equivocal or matters arose during the hearing which showed the defendant was not in reality admitting guilt, he may apply to the Crown Court to set aside his conviction, and remit the case to the magistrates with a direction to enter a plea of 'not guilty', and proceed to summary trial. This procedure is only available in the very rare cases where something said at the magistrates' court shows the accused was not really admitting his guilt: the Divisional Court has explained what should happen at the Crown Court:

'First of all they should hear evidence from, or on behalf of the defendant . . . as to the basis on which the allegation of equivocality is founded. In the great majority of cases the evidence will fall far short of demonstrating any equivocality at all. It is the plea which must be equivocal; in other words the equivocality must be shown by what went on before the magistrates' court . . . The fact that the defendant has subsequently thought better of the plea or has in some way changed his mind, is not sufficient on its own. It must be apparent to the justices that the defendant is saying "I am guilty but" . . . If there is no such evidence, then that is the end of the matter . . . But there may be the very rare case when the appellant in the Crown Court does produce some prima facie evidence, and credible evidence, tending to show that the plea before the justices was equivocal. It is essential that in those rare cases, when there is some prima facie and credible evidence, that the Crown Court should seek help from the magistrates' court as to what happened at the original hearing. The chairman of the bench or the clerk . . . should swear on affidavit as to what happened in the magistrates' court for the benefit of the Crown Court, and only after considering such an affidavit should the Crown Court come to a conclusion about equivocality or otherwise[2].'

The Crown Court also has power to set aside an unequivocal plea where the plea was entered because of threats from a third party[3]. It is doubtful whether the power exists where the plea is unequivocal but entered into under a mistaken apprehension of law[4].

APPEAL TO THE CROWN COURT AGAINST SENTENCE

A defendant may appeal as of right to the Crown Court against any

---

2 Per Lord Lane CJ in *R v Rochdale Justices, ex p Allwork* [1981] 3 All ER 434. On this point see Supreme Court Act 1981 s 48(2)(b) (for the power to remit) and the following cases: *R v Durham Quarter Sessions, ex p Virgo* [1952] 2 QB 1, [1952] 1 All ER 466 (D charged with theft; in mitigation he said he took the articles by mistake); *S v Recorder of Manchester* [1971] AC 481, [1969] 3 All ER 1230 (educationally subnormal boy pleaded guilty at a juvenile court to sexual assault; at adjourned hearing it transpired from reports that he had in the past confessed to crimes he did not commit). Note: where the magistrates do not proceed to sentence themselves but instead commit to the Crown Court for sentence it would seem the Crown Court may remit the case for hearing on the basis of a not guilty plea if anything transpires at the Crown Court which indicates the defendant is not in fact accepting guilt (i e even if there was nothing to suggest this at the magistrates' hearing). See *R v Mutford and Lothingland Justices, ex p Harber* [1971] 2 QB 291, [1971] 1 All ER 81.
3 *R v Crown Court at Huntingdon, ex p Jordan* [1981] QB 857, [1981] 2 All ER 872 (wife threatened by husband to plead guilty). Quaere would this apply if the police had put pressure on an unrepresented defendant to plead guilty (e g by promises that there would be no publicity or that the defendant would only receive a light sentence on a guilty plea).
4 *R v Crown Court at Snaresbrook, ex p Gavi Burjore* (20 December 1979, unreported) but cited in *ex p Jordan*.

sentence or order made by a magistrates' court, except against an order for costs[5]. The time for appeal is 21 days from the date of sentence. As explained above, even though no appeal is entered against sentence, the Crown Court has the power to review sentence when it is dealing with an appeal against conviction only.

The Crown Court, in reviewing sentence, must hear the antecedents of the appellant, consider all the relevant reports on him and afford him an opportunity to address the court in mitigation. The court may pass any sentence, or make any order which the magistrates could have made[6]. This means that the Crown Court may *increase* the sentence passed by the inferior court[7]. The power to increase sentence is not very frequently exercised and it would appear only to be appropriate where new matters have come to light during the hearing of the appeal, or the sentence imposed by the magistrates was manifestly wrong in principle.

APPLICATION TO THE HIGH COURT FOR JUDICIAL REVIEW

Where a magistrates' court[8] acts without jurisdiction or commits a serious procedural error or fails to observe the rules of natural justice, either the prosecutor or the defendant may apply to the Divisional Court for judicial review. That court may make one or more of the following orders:

(i) An order of certiorari. Historically the High Court supervised the lower courts by requiring them to submit their records and quashing decisions where the record disclosed some procedural error. In a sense, certiorari is still used today for this purpose, i e correcting procedural and jurisdictional mistakes by magistrates' courts:

> *Example.* G pleaded guilty by post to a driving offence but, because of his record, was liable to mandatory disqualification. The magistrates proceeded to disqualify him. The Divisional Court quashed the order because the magistrates should, under s 11(4) of the Magistrates' Courts Act 1980, have adjourned the case to give him an opportunity to be present and put forward any mitigation. (Note in such a case, the Divisional Court might have quashed the magistrates' decision, proceeded itself to pass an appropriate sentence and amended the decision of the magistrates accordingly: Supreme Court Act 1981 s 43.)[9]

Certiorari is also used where the magistrates have failed to observe the rules of natural justice, or where the behaviour of the court or its officers raises a reasonable suspicion in the minds of those present that they were biased against the defendant[10].

---

5 See Magistrates' Courts Act 1980 s 108. In such a case he may still appeal against the *conviction* which resulted in the order in question.
6 Save that the Crown Court cannot increase its powers by committing the appellant to itself under Magistrates' Courts Act 1980 s 37 or s 38; see *R v Bullock* [1964] 1 QB 481, [1963] 3 All ER 506.
7 Note: the Court of Appeal has *no* such power in reviewing appeals against sentences imposed by the Crown Court.
8 Or the Crown Court when not dealing with a trial on indictment: Supreme Court Act s 29(3).
9 See *R v Llandrindod Wells Justices, ex p Gibson* [1968] 2 All ER 20, [1968] 1 WLR 598.
10 Per Edmund Davies LJ in *Metropolitan Properties Co (FGC) Ltd v Lannon* [1969] 1 QB 577, [1968] 3 All ER 304. A more limited test, that there should be a reasonable likelihood of bias, is propounded by Devlin J in *R v Barnsley Licensing Justices, ex p Barnsley and District Licensed Victuallers Association* [1960] 2 QB 167, [1960] 2 All ER 703.

IN THE HIGH COURT OF JUSTICE   86A

Applicant's Ref. No.	NOTICE OF APPLICATION FOR LEAVE TO APPLY FOR JUDICIAL REVIEW (ORDER 55 rule 3(2))	Crown Office Ref. No.

This form must be read together with Notes for Guidance obtainable from the Crown Office.

To the Master of the Crown Office, Royal Courts of Justice, Strand, London
                                                              WC2A 2LL

Name, address and description of applicant(s)	Jack Dawkins 80 Saffron Hill, London EC1
Judgment, order, decision or other proceeding in respect of which relief is sought	Refusal of Legal Aid Order

Relief Sought

1) an order of <u>Certiorari</u> to remove into the Queen's Bench Division for
   the purpose of its being quashed the decision of Lionel Fang, Esq,
   (one of Her Majesty's Metropolitan Stipendiary Magistrates sitting at
   Bow Street Magistrates Court) dated 20th October 1986 refusing to
   make a legal aid order in favour of the applicant under section 28(2)
   Legal Aid Act 1974;

2) an order of <u>Mandamus</u> directed to the said Lionel Fang, Esq, requiring
   him forthwith to grant such order to the Applicant.

Name and address of applicant's solicitors, or, if no solicitors acting, the address for service of the applicant	Parker and Co. 2 Field Court, Gray's Inn, London WC1

Signed   Parker and Co. | Dated **27th October 1986**

Example. The clerk to the justices was a local solicitor. He retired with the magistrates to advise them on law. His firm had acted for one of the parties although he had no personal knowledge of this. The Divisional Court issued an order of certiorari. Per Lord Hewart CJ: 'justice should not only be done, but should manifestly and undoubtedly be seen to be done'[11].

(ii) An order of mandamus. This is an order directing the lower court to take a particular course which it has declined to take.

Example. D was convicted of assault and theft and committed to the Crown Court for sentence. On his appearance at the Crown Court a detention centre order was made. It was then discovered that he wished to appeal against his conviction but the Crown Court declined to hear an application for leave to appeal out of time on the grounds it was *functus officio.* The Divisional Court held that the Crown Court did have power to hear the appeal and issued an order of mandamus directing it to hear the application[12].

(iii) An order of prohibition. This is an order forbidding the magistrates taking some course they are proposing to take.

Example. D was arrested when under 17 but by the time he appeared before the juvenile court (other than on formal remands) he had attained 17. He insisted the case should be dealt with at the adult court (where he would have the right to elect trial by jury). The juvenile court insisted it would proceed to try the case. The court would *prohibit* the juvenile court from proceeding to try the case[13].

It is worth observing that judicial review is appropriate, not only where a specific charge is being tried, but wherever anybody is charged with the duty to act judicially[14]. Thus, judicial review can be used to control the administrative tribunals which administer social welfare legislation and, more important for present purposes, magistrates and area committees determining the right to legal aid[15]. In practice, it is difficult to challenge such decisions because of the very wide area of discretion given to those who originally decide the matter; in practice the applicant will usually allege that the decision should be reviewed under what is called the *Wednesbury* principle.

Wednesbury Corporation granted a licence under the Sunday Entertainments Act 1932 to a cinema to be open on Sunday but imposed a condition that no children should be admitted whether or not accompanied by an adult. The Court of Appeal declined to set aside the condition as unlawfully imposed. Per Lord Green MR:

'When an executive discretion is entrusted by Parliament to a local authority, what purports to be an exercise of that discretion can only be challenged in the courts in a very limited class of case. It must always be remembered that the court is not a court of appeal. The law recognises certain principles on which the discretion must be exercised, but within the four corners of those principles the discretion is an absolute one and cannot be questioned in any court of law. What

11 *R v Sussex Justices, ex p McCarthy* [1924] 1 KB 256.
12 *R v Crown Court at Croydon, ex p Bernard* [1980] 3 All ER 106, [1981] 1 WLR 116.
13 *R v Islington North Juvenile Court, ex p Daley* [1983] 1 AC 347, [1982] 3 All ER 974. Note: in that case the juvenile court had proceeded to hear the case so the orders sought were certiorari to quash the conviction and mandamus to compel them to send the case to the adult magistrates' court.
14 *R v Electricity Comrs, ex p London Electricity Joint Committee Co (1920) Ltd* [1924] 1 KB 171.
15 See p 207 below, where the authorities on legal aid are discussed.

then are those principles? They are perfectly well understood. The exercise of such a discretion must be a real exercise of the discretion. If, in the statute conferring the discretion, there is to be found, expressly or by implication, matters to which the authority exercising the discretion ought to have regard, then, in exercising the discretion, they must have regard for these matters. Conversely, if the nature of the subject matter and the general interpretation of the Act make it clear that certain matters would not be germane to the matter in question, they must disregard those matters . . . Counsel for the plaintiffs did not suggest that the authority were directing their minds to a purely extraneous and irrelevant matter, but he based his argument on the word "unreasonableness" which he treated as an independent ground for attacking the decision of the authority. Once, however, it is conceded, as it must be conceded, that the subject matter of the condition was one which it was competent for the authority to consider there, in my opinion, is an end of the case, because, once that is granted, counsel must go so far as to say that the decision of the authority is wrong because it is unreasonable, and then he is really saying that the ultimate arbiter of what is and is not reasonable is the court and not the local authority. It is just there, it seems to me, that the whole argument entirely breaks down . . . Theoretically it is true to say . . . that, if a decision on a competent matter is so unreasonable that no reasonable authority could ever have come to it, then the courts can interfere. That, I think, is right, but that would require overwhelming proof, and in this case the facts do not come anywhere near such a thing[16].'

An application for judicial review comprises two stages:

(1) The ex parte stage. The applicant must persuade the court that he may have an arguable case; this is, therefore, a screening process. Generally, leave should be granted unless it is clear the applicant would be bound to fail at a full hearing:

'The whole purpose of requiring that leave should first be obtained to make an application for judicial review would be defeated if the court were to go into the matter at any depth at that stage. If, on a quick perusal of the material then available, the court thinks that it discloses what might on further consideration turn out to be an arguable case in favour of granting to the applicant the relief claimed, it ought, in the exercise of a judicial discretion, to give him leave to apply for that relief[17].'

(2) The inter partes stage. Once leave is granted, the applicant serves notice of motion on the magistrates, prosecution (or defence) and any other interested parties and a hearing takes place before a Divisional Court (comprising two or three judges).

We now set out the procedure which applies to an application in a criminal matter: this procedure is to be found in RSC Ord 53:

(1) The applicant prepares an application for leave to apply for judicial review. He must use (or adapt) High Court Form 86A (see p 167). At the same time he prepares an affidavit setting out the relevant facts.
(2) The application form and affidavit (plus two copies) are lodged at the Crown Office and a fee is paid. This application must be lodged as soon as possible after the decision, and in any event within three months.

16 *Associated Provincial Picture Houses Ltd v Wednesbury Corpn* [1947] 2 All ER 680 at 682–83.
17 *IRC v National Federation of Self-Employed and Small Businesses Ltd* [1982] AC 617, [1981] 2 All ER 93.

(3) The applicant now has a choice – he can either make a 'paper applica-
     tion' (ie agree that the application be considered privately by a judge
     reading the papers) or he can ask for the application to be listed for
     hearing before a single judge. Unless the matter is very clear, it is better
     to opt for a hearing before a judge where one can answer any doubts the
     judge might have about the merits of the case. If leave is refused, the
     applicant may renew his application to a Divisional Court.
(4) If leave is granted, the applicant must within 14 days serve *notice of
     motion* on all the persons affected and deliver a copy of the notice and an
     affidavit proving service at the Crown Office.
(5) At this stage the respondents (magistrates or prosecution) may file
     evidence by affidavits. These must be lodged within 21 days of the date
     of service of the notice of motion.
(6) When an application is ready to be heard it will be entered in the
     warned list and the applicant or his solicitor informed. The application
     will be heard by a Divisional Court (comprising two or more judges).

In a criminal case either side can appeal to the House of Lords from the
decision of the Divisional Court provided (i) the court certifies that a point
of law of general public importance is involved in the decision and (ii) the
court of the House of Lords grants leave[18].

It should be noted that the Divisional Court will not hear an application
for review if the applicant has in the meantime appealed to the Crown
Court[19]. This is a sensible rule where the Crown Court is being asked to
determine the same question as the Divisional Court, but seems unjust
where the applicant wishes to complain (a) that the first court acted
improperly, and (b) that they also came to the wrong conclusion on the
facts. In Canada[20] and New Zealand[1] the courts have held that where there
is evidence that the inferior tribunal has acted improperly so that its
proceedings are a nullity, the person aggrieved should have the right to
apply that the proceedings be quashed before appealing against the decision as being incorrect on the facts. At present, however, the position is that
the Divisional Court automatically adjourns any application for leave to
apply for review once a notice of appeal to the Crown Court has been served
and the application generally becomes otiose once the Crown Court has
heard the case because any procedural irregularity or bias will have been
cured.

APPEAL ON POINT OF LAW TO THE HIGH COURT

Either party to criminal proceedings before a magistrates' court can challenge the decision of the court on a point of law by requiring the court to *state
a case* for the determination of the High Court[2].

> *Example.* Benjamin, is charged with driving a motor vehicle on a public place
> while under the influence of drink, contrary to s 5 of the Road Traffic Act 1972.
> The uncontested evidence is that he drove a car around Gray's Inn Square
> after consuming a substantial amount of drink and crashed at the gateway which

18 Administration of Justice Act 1960 s 1(1), (2).
19 *R v Banes, ex p Lord Vernon* (1910) 102 LT 860.
20 *R v Alberta Law Society, ex p Demco* (1967) 64 DLR (2d) 140.
 1 *McCarthy v Grant* [1959] NZLR 1014.
 2 Magistrates' Courts Act 1980 s 111.

leads through to Gray's Inn Road. The sole issue is whether a square within the precincts of an inn of court is a public place within the meaning of the section. The magistrates convict him.

In this case, Benjamin has a choice: he can, if he wishes, appeal to the Crown Court for a complete rehearing of his case; on the other hand, since the only issue is a point of law, he may choose instead to appeal directly to the High Court. If he applies to the magistrates to state a case, his right of appeal to the Crown Court ceases.

Appeal by way of case stated falls into four distinct stages:

(i) Application to the magistrates to state a case. The appellant must send a request in writing within 21 days of the final proceedings in the magistrates' court, asking the court to draw up a statement of the case. The court is bound to do this, unless the application is frivolous. The appellant may be required to enter into a recognizance to prosecute the appeal without delay.

(ii) Drawing up of the statement[3]. The clerk to the justices (or sometimes the parties themselves) then prepares a statement containing:

(a) a recital of the charges against the defendant;
(b) the findings of fact upon which the magistrates based their decision;
(c) the point of law raised and the authorities cited to the court; and
(d) the decision of the magistrates on the point of law.

The statement concludes with the *question* which the High Court is asked to determine. The case is sent to the parties who then have 21 days to suggest alterations in the clerk's draft.

(iii) Transmission of the case to the High Court. The justices sign the case which is then sent by their clerk to the appellant. Within four days, the appellant must serve all the parties with a *notice of appeal* and a copy of the *statement* signed by the magistrates. Within ten days, he must lodge the statement at the Crown Office in the High Court[4].

(iv) Hearing of appeal. The appeal is then listed for hearing before three judges of the Queen's Bench Division sitting as a *Divisional Court.* The appellant is not allowed to introduce any evidence on the appeal and is bound by the findings of fact in the statement. The appeal consists purely of legal argument between counsel as to whether the magistrates' decision on the legal point was correct. The Divisional Court may affirm, reverse or amend the decision appealed against. Where the prosecution successfully appeal, the Court will remit the matter to the magistrates with a direction to convict and proceed to sentence. A further appeal lies to the House of Lords if the Divisional Court certifies that a point of law of general public importance is involved in the decision, and leave is granted by that court or by the House of Lords[5].

It was noted above that a convicted defendant at a magistrates' court may, instead of asking for a case to be stated, decide to appeal to the Crown

3 Magistrates' Court Rules 1981 r 77.
4 See RSC Ord 56 r 6.
5 Administration of Justice Act 1960 s 1, and see *Gilberg v Miller* [1961] 1 All ER 618n, [1961] 1 WLR 459 – only the Divisional Court can certify there is a question of law of general public importance.

In the High Court of Justice

Queen's Bench Division

(Divisional Court)

Between:

Benjamin Charleston   Appellant

and

Eric Drake   Respondent

Case stated by Justices of the Peace for the Inner London Commission Area in respect of their adjudication as a Magistrates' Court sitting at Clerkenwell in the London Borough of Camden.

CASE

1. The Appellant was charged in an information preferred by the Respondent that on the 10th day of May 1986 he drove a motor vehicle on a public place namely Gray's Inn Square in Holborn whilst unfit through drink contrary to section 5 of the Road Traffic Act 1972.

2. The Appellant pleaded not guilty to the charge.

3. We found the following facts:-

   (a) The Respondent who is a police officer observed the Appellant driving an Austin 1100 motor vehicle from a stationary position to the gateway of Gray's Inn Square at about ten o'clock in the evening of the 10th day of May 1986.

   (b) The said vehicle collided with the north corner of the gate.

   (c) The Appellant is a law student who on the evening in question had consumed two glasses of sherry, a bottle of claret and numerous glasses of port wine.

   (d) The Appellant was seen by the Respondent to stagger from the car and was unable to stand upright whilst speaking to the officer without clutching the door of the car.

   (e) The Appellant was (as he candidly admitted to us) drunk and unfit to drive.

(f) Gray's Inn Square is an area surrounded on three sides by professional and residential chambers and on the south side by the Hall and Chapel of the Inn. There is direct entrance through a gateway to Gray's Inn Road but the gate is locked each evening at eight o'clock. However members of the public are permitted to walk through the Inn to Holborn during the day and evening and gain access through an open gate leading into Holborn. Many members of the public use this route during the daytime but very few in the evenings.

4. The Appellant contended that the said square was not a "public place" because members of the public were only admitted on sufferance. The Prosecution contended that since the public had access in fact to the Square it was a "public place" within the meaning of the Act.

5. We were referred to the following authorities:-

R v Collinson (1931) 23 Cr App Rep 49

R v Waters (1963) 47 Cr. App. Rep 149

Harrison v Hill (1932) J C 13

Buchanan v Motor Insurers' Bureau [1955] 1 All E R 607

6. We agreed with the Prosecution's contention and accordingly convicted the Appellant of the offence charged in the information.

QUESTION

The question for the opinion of the High Court is whether, upon the above-mentioned statements of fact, we came to a correct determination and decision in point of law, and, if not, the Court is respectfully requested to reverse or amend the same or to remit the matter to us with the opinion of the Court thereon.

Court. Such a course is appropriate where he feels that he might succeed on an issue of fact, or where the facts as they appeared at the magistrates' court do not clearly lead to the proposition of law he wishes to establish. If, subsequently, the judge and magistrates sitting at the Crown Court find against him, he may require them to state a case to the Divisional Court[6].

6 Courts Act 1971 s 10(2) and (3).

Chapter 8

Appeal from the Crown Court

(Before studying this subject the reader is advised to read quickly through the example appended at the end of the chapter.)

APPEAL AGAINST CONVICTION

A defendant who has been convicted at the Crown Court may appeal against his conviction to the Criminal Division of the Court of Appeal. He may appeal as *of right* on any question of law alone (eg whether certain evidence infringed the hearsay rule or whether the judge properly defined the ingredients of the offence to the jury). In cases which involve questions of fact alone (eg whether the jury should have convicted on the evidence at all) or which involve questions of mixed fact and law (eg whether a statement was voluntary), the defendant can only appeal if he obtains *either* a certificate from the trial judge that the case is fit for appeal *or* leave from the Court of Appeal[1].

The Court of Appeal may only allow the appeal on one of the following general grounds[2]:

(1) *That the conviction should be set aside on the ground that under all the circumstances of the case it is unsafe or unsatisfactory.* (For example: where the issue of identity is crucial, and the conviction turns upon a single identification some time after the event[3].)

(2) *That the judgment of the court of trial should be set aside on the ground of a wrong decision of any question of law.* (For example: where the trial judge has misconstrued the provisions of a statute.)

(3) *That there was a material irregularity in the course of the trial.* (For example: where the trial judge constantly interrupted proceedings, or wrongly

---

1 This is a rough paraphrase of the Criminal Appeal Act 1968 s 1. The Court of Appeal may also grant leave on any other ground which appears to it to be a sufficient ground for appeal (eg misbehaviour by the trial judge).

2 Criminal Appeal Act 1968 s 2(1) (as amended by Criminal Law Act 1977 s 44). Note a conviction based on a plea of guilty will be unsafe or unsatisfactory if it appears that (i) the appellant did not understand the charge against him or (ii) did not intend to admit his guilt or (iii) upon the admitted facts, he could not in law have been convicted of the offence charged: see *R v Forde* [1923] 2 KB 400.

3 It has been said that a conviction is 'unsafe or unsatisfactory' if the Court of Appeal is left with 'a lurking doubt' about the appellant's guilt; see *R v Pattinson* and *R v Laws* (1973) 58 Cr App Rep 417.

ordered two defendants to be tried together, or wrongly admitted evidence of the accused's previous convictions.)

It will be appreciated that many individual complaints may fit into more than one of the general grounds set out above (for example, absence of corroboration).

The Court of Appeal is not bound to quash the appellant's conviction even if they hold that a defect has occurred in the trial. Thus, the court may substitute a conviction for some other offence of which the jury could have found the appellant guilty if the court is of opinion that the jury must have been satisfied of facts which could prove him guilty of this other offence[4]. An example where this power would be exercised is where the evidence does not justify a conviction for the completed offence, but amply justifies a conviction for attempt.

The Court of Appeal may also dismiss an appeal where, although there has been a wrong decision on a point of law or an irregularity in the trial, the court '*considers that no miscarriage of justice has actually occurred*'[5]. Thus, for example, where an item of evidence has been wrongly admitted, the court will exercise the proviso and dismiss the appeal if it feels that the jury would inevitably have convicted the defendant even if that evidence had not been given[6].

It should be noted that in practice it is very difficult in the absence of new evidence to challenge the actual verdict of the jury; the Court of Appeal may interfere if the jury have been misdirected or heard inadmissible evidence, but the court will only in the most exceptional case review the jury's decision on the evidence. This unfortunately may have led to miscarriages of justice. The point has been explained by Professor Glanville Williams as follows:

'it is far easier for a person convicted by a jury to take and win an appeal on an unmeritorious point of procedure or evidence than it is for him to reopen on appeal the really serious question of his guilt. While the jury system encourages the unmeritorious appeals, to which an easy ear is given, it discourages those on questions of substance[7].'

Where new evidence has become available since the trial (whether documents, expert testimony or witnesses as to the facts) the Court of Appeal may receive such evidence if:

(1) It appears to the court that it is likely to be credible, and would have been admissible at the trial if then available.
(2) The court is satisfied that there is a reasonable explanation for the failure to adduce such evidence in the court below[8].

If the court feels that such evidence could have caused the jury to reach a different verdict they will quash the conviction, or (if new evidence is the only ground of the appeal) order a new trial[9].

The court may also order a new trial where an irregularity has occurred

4 Criminal Appeal Act 1968 s 3(1).
5 Proviso to Criminal Appeal Act 1968 s 2(1).
6 *R v Parker* (1960) 45 Cr App Rep 1.
7 *The Proof of Guilt* (3rd edn, Stevens, 1963).
8 Criminal Appeal Act 1968 s 23.
9 Ibid s 7(1).

before the actual hearing of evidence commenced which was so grave as to render the first trial a nullity. The order is by a writ *venire de novo*.

It should however be noted that where a material irregularity occurs between the time the trial commenced and the verdict of the jury, the Court of Appeal has no power to order a new trial; it must quash the conviction[10].

The same rights of appeal are conferred upon a person who has been found not guilty by reason of insanity[11]. In such a case, in addition to its normal powers to allow the appeal and quash the conviction, the court may also substitute a verdict of guilty if it is of the opinion that the accused committed the offence but was not insane[12]. Similarly, a defendant who has been found unfit to plead may appeal against this finding to the Court of Appeal[13]. If this issue was determined before the arraignment a successful appellant is remitted to the Crown Court to stand trial. If the issue was determined after arraignment he may be sent back to the Crown Court for trial or the court may, even if it is of opinion that the finding was correct, quash the finding and order an acquittal to be recorded if it thinks that he should have been acquitted at the close of the prosecution case and before the issue of fitness was tried[14].

APPEAL AGAINST SENTENCE

A defendant may appeal to the Court of Appeal from the Crown Court against:

(1) any sentence passed on his conviction on indictment[15]; and
(2) certain sentences passed after he has been committed to the Crown Court following his conviction at a magistrates' court[16].

Appeal against sentence however only lies with leave of the Court of Appeal[17]. The court may quash the sentence imposed by the Crown Court and in its place substitute any sentence which that court could have imposed[18]. It will not, however, exercise this power merely because each of the members of the court would have imposed a different sentence from the court below. Before the Court of Appeal will interfere with the sentence, it must be shown to be *manifestly excessive* in view of the circumstances of the case or *wrong in principle*[19]. Where the Court of Appeal varies a sentence it

10 *R v Rose* [1982] AC 822, [1982] 2 All ER 731, HL (where the judge had applied improper pressure on the jury to return a verdict in a murder trial).
11 Criminal Appeal Act 1968 s 23.
12 Ibid s 13(4).
13 Ibid s 15.
14 Ibid s 16. See p 129 above and *R v Webb* [1969] 2 QB 278, [1969] 2 All ER 626.
15 Ibid s 9.
16 Ibid s 10 – this covers two cases: (a) where the magistrates commit to the Crown Court because they feel the defendant merits a sentence they cannot impose eg committals under the Magistrates' Courts Act 1980 ss 37 and 38 and (b) where he is committed because his summary conviction is a breach of a conditional discharge or probation order made by the Crown Court in earlier proceedings, or involves the activation of a suspended sentence imposed earlier by the Crown Court. Appeal will only lie where the Crown Court imposes a sentence exceeding six months' imprisonment or youth custody, or makes a recommendation for deportation or orders disqualification from driving or brings into effect a suspended sentence.
17 Criminal Appeal Act 1968 s 11(1).
18 Ibid s 11(3).
19 *R v Ball* (1951) 35 Cr App Rep 164.

must so exercise its powers that, *taking the case as a whole, the appellant is not more severely dealt with on appeal than he was dealt with by the court below*[20].

APPEALS ON COSTS AND LEGAL AID CONTRIBUTIONS

It should be noted that an appeal will lie to the Court of Appeal with leave against an order requiring a defendant to pay costs (since this is deemed to be part of his sentence[1]) but no appeal will lie against an order that he contribute to the costs of his representation under the Legal Aid Act[2] nor against a refusal to award costs to an acquitted defendant[3]. Nor in these cases will the Divisional Court have power to order judicial review since these are matters relating to 'trial on indictment'[4].

APPLICATION FOR LEAVE TO APPEAL

It can be seen above that, except in the case of an appeal against conviction on a pure question of law (or with a certificate from the trial judge), the appellant must obtain leave to appeal from the Court of Appeal. He must within 28 days[5] of his conviction or sentence, file an *application for leave* and *notice of grounds of appeal* with the registrar of the Court[6]. The relevant form can be seen in the example at the end of the chapter. The application is placed before a single judge of the Court. The single judge may exercise any of the following powers at this preliminary stage[7].

(1) Extend the time for making an application for leave to appeal.
(2) Grant leave to appeal.
(3) Order the appellant's release on bail (or vary or revoke bail granted by the Crown Court).
(4) Direct that the appellant be granted legal aid for the appeal.
(5) Give leave for the appellant to be present at the appeal.
(6) Order a witness to attend for examination by the Court of Appeal.

An appellant may apply to the full court against any decision of the single judge. This means that a person whose application for leave to appeal is refused by the single judge may pursue his application before the full court. The idea of the review by a single judge is that:

(1) He should be able to give directions on preliminary matters such as bail and the preparation of the case for appeal.
(2) He should act as a screening process to filter out obviously hopeless appeals.

It should be noted that where (e g because transcripts are not available) the single judge thinks there might be merit in the application, he may refer the application for leave to the full court and order transcripts and grant legal aid for counsel to represent the applicant.

20 Criminal Appeal Act 1968 s 11(3).
 1 Ibid s 50(1); *R v Hayden* [1975] 2 All ER 558, [1975] 1 WLR 852.
 2 *R v Crown Court at Cardiff, ex p Jones* [1974] QB 113. [1973] 3 All ER 1027.
 3 *Ex p Meredith* [1973] 2 All ER 234, [1973] 1 WLR 435.
 4 See the Supreme Court Act 1981 s 28.
 5 Criminal Appeal Act 1968 s 18.
 6 Counsel are expected to obtain and study the official publication *A Guide to Proceedings in the Court of Appeal Criminal Division* (reproduced (1983) 77 Cr App Rep 138).
 7 Criminal Appeal Act 1968 s 31.

In order to discourage appellants who have no chance of success, the single judge or the full court (on a renewed application) may direct that time spent in custody pending the hearing shall not count towards sentence[8]. Although this power is more frequently exercised by the full court where an application is renewed after being rejected by the single judge, the court has emphasised that the single judge is also entitled to exercise this power:

'In order to accelerate the hearing of those appeals in which there is some merit, single judges will give special consideration to the giving of a direction for loss of time, whenever an application for leave to appeal is refused. It may be expected that such a direction will normally be made unless the grounds are not only settled and signed by counsel, but also supported by the written opinion of counsel . . . Counsel should not settle grounds, or support them with written advice, unless he considers that the proposed appeal is properly arguable[9].'

PROCEDURE ON APPEAL

After leave is granted, the registrar may invite counsel to supplement the grounds of appeal by reference to passages from the transcript or to decided cases. In such a case he prepares 'perfected grounds of appeal' (as in the example at p 184 below). In rare cases, examination of the transcript may reveal an entirely new point; in such a case, an application must be made for leave to amend the grounds of appeal.

The hearing of the appeal is by a court of three judges (who will be judges of the Court of Appeal or the Queen's Bench Division). The judges will have received a note on the case prepared by a barrister employed by the Court of Appeal. This note will set out a summary of the facts and arguments. The note is *not* made available to counsel although obviously it *could* have had an important influence on the single judge and members of the court when reading through the papers before the hearing. The Court will also have before it the observations of the single judge; he decides whether these should be shown to counsel who will conduct the appeal. Counsel on behalf of the appellant and the respondent address the court, and the decision is by a majority. Where the appellant shows that a submission of no case to answer was wrongly overruled, the court *will not* look at any evidence given subsequently at the trial[10]. Further appeal lies to the House of Lords at the instance of either side in the exceptional case where the court certifies that a point of law of general public importance is involved, and either the Court of Appeal or the House of Lords grants leave[11].

REFERENCES BY THE SECRETARY OF STATE OR THE ATTORNEY GENERAL

The Home Secretary may refer to the Court of Appeal any case where an accused person has been convicted or found not guilty by reason of insanity, or found to be under a disability[12]. This power has been used where, for

8 Ibid s 29.
9 *Practice Note* [1980] 1 All ER 555, 70 Cr App Rep 186.
10 *R v Cockley* (1984) 79 Cr App Rep 181.
11 Criminal Appeal Act 1968 s 33. See *Practice Direction* [1979] 1 WLR 497 as to the procedure on applying for leave to the House of Lords. Procedure in the House of Lords is explained in a booklet *Directions as to Procedure Applicable to Criminal Appeals* (1982) which is obtainable from the judicial office.
12 Criminal Appeal Act 1968 s 17.

example, grave public concern has arisen as to conviction after the defendant has been hanged (eg Timothy Evans's case).

Although the Crown has no right to appeal against a verdict of 'not
guilty', it may happen that during the trial the judge will have ruled on
some important point of law, and the prosecution wish to challenge this
ruling. In such a case, the Attorney General may refer the point of law to the
Court of Appeal for their advisory opinion upon it[13].

When a sentence passed by the Crown Court has given rise to criticism
on the grounds that it is inadequate for the offence in question, under the
Criminal Justice Bill 1987 the Attorney General can refer the case to the
Court of Appeal 'to obtain their opinion on the principles which should be
observed in sentencing in similar cases in the future'[14].

APPEALS FROM THE CROWN COURT BY WAY OF CASE STATED ETC

Where the Crown Court is sitting to hear appeals from magistrates' courts,
its decisions thereon cannot be challenged in the Court of Appeal.
However, the appellant has the right to apply for a case to be stated for the
determination of a point of law by a Divisional Court of the Queen's Bench
Division[15]. This form of procedure has been discussed in the preceding
chapter. The Divisional Court also has the power to supervise proceedings
on appeal to the Crown Court by way of judicial review[16].

EXAMPLE OF APPEAL CASE

(Study carefully the facts given below. Some of these matters we have
already considered in the text. Then look at the standard appeal form and
finally consider the draft grounds of appeal.)

R V VINCENT DUBOIS

Vincent, who is aged 18 and is a French national, was charged in an
indictment which contained two counts:

(1) unauthorised possession of a controlled drug, cannabis resin, contrary
    to s 5(2) of the Misuse of Drugs Act 1971; and
(2) dishonestly receiving a stolen colour television set contrary to s 22 of
    the Theft Act 1968.

At his trial, he applied for each count to be tried separately[17]. This application was refused. The prosecution called a police officer who said that he
searched Vincent's flat and found a packet containing a few grains of
cannabis resin hidden under a cushion. The officer agreed that at the
material time a party was going on and a number of young people were
present. He also found a colour television set in the bedroom. He arrested
Vincent and took him to the police station. A second officer was called who
said that Vincent had told him at the station that, although he knew
nothing of the cannabis, he had bought the television knowing it was stolen.

13 Criminal Justice Act 1972 s 36(1).
14 Criminal Justice Bill 1987 cl 38(1).
15 Supreme Court Act 1981 s 28(1).
16 Ibid s 29(3).
17 See p 116 above and *Ludlow v Metropolitan Police Comr* [1971] AC 29, [1970] 1 All ER 567.

Before the police officer gave evidence, the defence submitted in the absence of the jury that the alleged confession had been obtained by an improper inducement, namely by an offer to allow Vincent to see his girlfriend, if he co-operated[18]. This allegation was denied by the police. The judge held that (a) such a promise would not render a confession inadmissible and (b) that in any event he accepted the police evidence that no such promise was made. At the close of the prosecution case, the judge rejected a defence submission[19] that there was insufficient evidence of possession by Vincent of the cannabis for a jury to convict. Vincent then gave evidence-in-chief, and said that he had bought the television set from a man in a public house whom he would not recognise again. The judge remarked, 'How often we have heard that story!' The judge then held that the allegation of an improper inducement to confess amounted to an attack on the character of a prosecution witness and gave permission to the prosecution to cross-examine Vincent about his previous convictions[20]. Vincent had, in fact, two previous convictions for unlawful sexual intercourse. In his summing-up, the judge told the jury that they should convict if they felt 'satisfied that he has committed the offences'. He said it was 'quite simply a question whether you accept his story or the police officer's evidence'[1]. The judge made no reference to the defence case that the television set had been acquired innocently. The jury convicted Vincent on both counts. A social enquiry report recommended probation. The judge sentenced him to:

(1) six months' youth custody on count one;
(2) six months' youth custody consecutive on count two.

The judge also recommended that he should be deported on completion of his sentence. After the trial was over a young man, Gilbert Fournier, contacted the defence solicitors and told them that he had brought the cannabis to the party, and had slipped it out of his pocket and put it under a cushion when the police arrived.

18 See p 74 above.
19 See p 143 above.
20 See p 144 above and proviso to Criminal Evidence Act 1898 s 1(f).
 1 See p 147 above.

SEE NOTES ON BACK	**CRIMINAL APPEAL ACT, 1968**		(See R2 Form 2)
COURT OF APPEAL CRIMINAL DIVISION **N**	NOTICE OF APPLICATION FOR LEAVE TO APPEAL AND OF OTHER APPLICATIONS (See Note 7)	To the Registrar, Criminal Appeal Office **REF. No.** Royal Courts of Justice, Strand, LONDON, W.C.2A 2LL	

Write legibly in black   **PART 1**

Particulars of APPELLANT	FULL NAMES Block letters	FORENAMES	SURNAME	Age on Conviction
		VINCENT	DUBOIS	18

	ADDRESS If detained give address where detained	H.M. PRISON, WANDSWORTH	Index number if detained 245617

COURT where tried and/or Sentenced. (see note 3)	DATES of appearances at the Court including dates of conviction (if convicted at the Court) and sentence. 22–24 June 1986	Name of Court CROWN COURT, SOUTHWARK
		Name of Judge HIS HON. JUDGE ARCHBOLD, Q.C.

Particulars of OFFENCES of which convicted. (State whether convicted on indictment or by a magistrates Court) and particulars of SENTENCES and ORDERS.	OFFENCES	Convicted on INDICTMENT or by MAGISTRATES COURT	SENTENCES AND ORDERS
	POSSESSION OF CLASS B CONTROLLED DRUG	I	6 MONTHS Y.C.
	HANDLING STOLEN GOODS	I	6 MONTHS Y.C. CONSECUTIVE RECOMMENDED DEPORTATION

Offences TAKEN INTO CONSIDERATION when sentenced. NONE	TOTAL SENTENCE 12 MONTHS Y.C.

PART 2

The appellant is applying for:—   (*Delete if inapplicable)

~~*EXTENSION of time in which to give notice of application for leave to appeal.~~

*LEAVE to appeal against CONVICTION.

*LEAVE to appeal against SENTENCE.

*LEGAL AID.

see note 8

*BAIL.

*LEAVE to be present at hearing.

*LEAVE to call WITNESSES.

Dodson and Fogg Solicitors (Signed) (Appellant)	Date 4/7/86	Address of person signing on behalf of Appellant. (See Note 6) 13 Old Square, Gray's Inn, WC1.

This notice was handed in by the appellant today. (Signed) (Officer)	Date	**N** Received in the Criminal Appeal Office. FORMS N.G. Date
E.D.R.		

Form 1458 31431—5-5-70 XBD

SEE NOTES ON BACK	**CRIMINAL APPEAL ACT, 1968**		(See R2 Form 3)
COURT OF APPEAL CRIMINAL DIVISION	**G**	Grounds of Application for Extension of Time Leave to Appeal Against Conviction Leave to Appeal Against Sentence	To the Registrar, Criminal Appeal Office REF. No. Royal Courts of Justice, Strand, LONDON, W.C.2A 2LL

Write Legibly in Black

FULL NAMES OF APPELLANT Block letters	FORENAMES VINCENT	SURNAME DUBOIS

Give the Name and Address of the Solicitor and/or Counsel (if any) who represented the Appellant at the Trial

SOLICITOR	DODSON & FOGG OLD SQUARE, GRAY'S INN	COUNSEL P.Q. BYLE

List of Documents sent with this Form which the Appellant wishes to be returned. Criminal Appeal Forms will **NOT** be returned

THE APPLICATIONS ARE FOR:—

EXTENSION of time in which to give notice of application for leave to appeal against:— *CONVICTION and *SENTENCE (*Delete if inapplicable)	Delete this section if no extension required

LEAVE TO APPEAL AGAINST CONVICTION for the following offences:— 1. POSSESSION OF CONTROLLED DRUG 2. HANDLING STOLEN GOODS	Delete this section if there is no application against conviction

LEAVE TO APPEAL AGAINST THE FOLLOWING SENTENCES OR ORDERS:— 1. SIX MONTHS YOUTH CUSTODY ON COUNT 1 2. SIX MONTHS YOUTH CUSTODY ON COUNT 2 RECOMMENDATION FOR DEPORTATION	Delete this section if there is no application against sentence

THE GROUNDS ARE AS FOLLOWS:— (Include reasons for delay if extension asked for)

If Grounds of Appeal have been settled and signed by Counsel they should be sent with this Form (see note 14)

SETTLED BY COUNSEL – SEE
SEPARATE SHEET

Continue (and sign) on Page 3 if necessary.

I HAVE READ FORM A A Dodson & Fogg (Solicitors) (Signed) (Appellant)	Date 4/7/86	Address of person signing on behalf of Appellant (See Note 13) 13 Old Square, Gray's Inn, WC1
		G	FOR USE IN THE CRIMINAL APPEAL OFFICE Received

Form 1457 31430—4-5-70 XBD

GROUNDS OF APPEAL

The grounds of appeal against conviction are:

1. The learned judge failed to order that each count of the indictment should be tried separately and the appellant was thereby prejudiced (p 2 A–C) (Reference will be made to Indictment Rules 1971, rule 9 and Ludlow v Metropolitan Police Commission (1970) 54 Cr App Rep 233 HL)

2. The learned judge erred in that he permitted one Thomas Boot a police officer to give evidence of a statement made to him by the appellant in consequence of an improper inducement. (p 16 A–D) (Police and Criminal Evidence Act 1984, s76)

3. Upon a submission by defence counsel at the conclusion of the prosecution evidence that there was insufficient evidence to go before the jury on the unlawful possession of drugs charge as set out in count 1 of the indictment, the learned judge failed to withdraw that count from the jury. The appellant now relies upon the submissions made by defence counsel at the trial. (p 19C–22D)

4. The learned judge improperly interrupted the appellant's evidence-in-chief to indicate his disbelief of the appellant's account of purchasing the television set the subject of the handling charge as set out in count 2 of the indictment. (. 28C)

5. The learned judge erred in that he permitted the prosecution to cross-examine the appellant upon his previous convictions. (p 30B–32C) (Reference will be made to Clark (1955) 39 Cr App Rep 120)

6. The learned judge in his summing-up misdirected the jury in that:-
   (i) he failed to direct them properly or adequately upon the burden and standard of proof; and (p 38C)
   (ii) he failed to direct them upon the appellant's defence to the second count namely that he had acquired the television set innocently. (p 40A)

7.   The appellant desires to call one Gilbert Fournier to give evidence
before this Honourable Court that unbeknown to the appellant he brought
the cannabis resin the subject of count one into the appellant's flat
and concealed it beneath a cushion.   This witness came forward after
the appellant was convicted.

The grounds of appeal against sentence are:

1.   The sentence of six months youth custody (on the count under s 5(2)
of the Misuse of Drugs Act 1971) was excessive since only a small quantity
of cannabis resin was found and there was no evidence to suggest that
the appellant was engaged in selling drugs or was an habitual taker of
drugs.

2.   The sentence of six months youth custody (on the count under s 22
of the Theft Act 1968) was excessive since the appellant has never before
been convicted of an offence of dishonesty.

3.   The learned judge failed to give sufficient consideration to the
appellant's youth.

4.   The learned judge failed to give sufficient weight to the recommendation
of probation contained in the Social Enquiry Report as an alternative
to a custodial sentence.

5.   The recommendation for deportation was unduly severe for the reasons
set out in paragraphs 1-4 herein.

Joseph Soap
Counsel for the Appellant

Chapter 9

Bail

A person is *bailed* when he is released from custody to attend at a court, or at a police station, at a specified date and time. If he fails to attend without reasonable cause he commits an offence[1]. This obligation may be under-written by *sureties*, who stand to forfeit fixed sums on the failure of the person bailed to attend as promised.

POLICE BAIL

(a) Where a person has been arrested without a warrant
As we have seen (p 63 above), whenever an arrested person is brought to a police station the custody officer is responsible for considering whether or not he should be granted bail. In some cases, the custody office will grant bail to the arrested person conditional on his returning to the police station when enquiries are completed[2]. This power might be used, for example, where a substance believed to be a drug has to be sent for analysis. Usually the arrested person is detained on the authority of the custody officer for questioning and for other enquiries to be carried out to see whether there is sufficient evidence to charge. During this period the question of release from custody has to be considered every six hours and the arrested person or his solicitor is entitled to make oral or written representations (see p 80 above). The maximum period of police detention without charge is 36 hours (unless a magistrates' court issues a warrant of further detention). In the ordinary case, long before this period has elapsed, the police will have taken a decision whether or not to charge.

If the police decide to charge the detained person, the custody officer must release him on bail unless:

'(i)   his name or address cannot be ascertained or the custody officer has reasonable grounds for doubting whether a name or address furnished by him as his name or address is his real name or address;
(ii)   the custody officer has reasonable grounds for believing that the detention

1 Bail Act 1976 s 6(1). The offence is triable summarily by a magistrates' court or can be dealt with by the Crown Court as a criminal contempt: see *R v Harbax Singh* [1979] QB 319, [1979] 1 All ER 524. Note: if the magistrates try the offence summarily they may commit to the Crown Court for sentence under s 6(6) either because they feel their powers of punishment are inadequate or because it is appropriate that the matter should be considered together with other offences for which they intend to commit for trial.
2 Police and Criminal Evidence Act 1984 ss 37(2) and 47(3).

of the person arrested is necessary for his own protection or to prevent him from causing physical injury to any other person or from causing loss of or damage to property; or

(iii) the custody officer has reasonable grounds for believing that the person arrested will fail to appear in court to answer to bail or that his detention is necessary to prevent him from interfering with the administration of justice or with the investigation of offences or of a particular offence[3].'

It should be noted that the custody officer is entitled to require sureties to secure the attendance of the person charged at court. If the suspect is not given police bail then he must be brought before a magistrates' court 'as soon as is practicable and in any event not later than the first sitting after he is charged with the offence'[4]. If no court will sit on the day on which he is charged or the next day, then the custody officer must notify the clerk of the court who will arrange a special sitting. (There is an exception where the next day would be Sunday or a bank holiday.) These provisions are slightly modified where the person charged is to appear before a magistrates' court in some other area.

(b) Where a person is arrested on warrant
The police must obey the terms of the warrant. It may have been *backed for bail* by the magistrate who issued it, ie it may contain a direction to the police to release the arrested person on bail with or without sureties[5].

BAIL AT REMAND HEARINGS

(1) The power to remand an offender
Although very straightforward cases (particularly where the defendant pleads guilty) may be disposed of by a magistrates' court in a single sitting, usually the court will have to adjourn the case (possibly for some time) before it can be heard; if the defendant is convicted, there may be a further adjournment while reports are prepared. Where the defendant has been summonsed to court in respect of a summary offence (eg careless driving) normally no question of bail will arise; the court simply adjourns and requests him to attend at the next hearing. However, in more serious cases, the court will not simply adjourn; it will instead *remand* the defendant – in theory authorise his continued status as an arrested person. He may be remanded in custody or on bail but he is no longer a free agent. The position is as follows:

(i)   in cases which must be tried on indictment at the Crown Court, the court *must* remand the defendant (Magistrates' Courts Act 1980 s 5);

(ii)   where the defendant is charged with an offence triable either way (eg theft), the court must remand him if he was initially arrested by the police (albeit later released on bail). In other cases (eg where a summons has been served) the court may remand but does not have to do so (Magistrates' Courts Act 1980 s 18(4));

(iii) in summary cases, as stated above, the defendant is not usually remanded; but the court may do so where the charge is serious (eg assault on the police).

3 Ibid s 38. Note a juvenile may also be detained if the custody officer has reasonable grounds for believing this is in his own interests.
4 Ibid s 46.
5 Magistrates' Courts Act 1980 s 117.

It will be appreciated that the question of bail only arises if there is a remand. Before considering the principles which govern this decision, it may be convenient to note at this stage the *length of remands*. The basic rule is that a remand in custody must not exceed eight clear days[6]; if the defendant is remanded on bail, the length of remand may exceed that limit provided both the defendant and the prosecutor consent[7]. Where a defendant is remanded in custody and it is clear the case cannot be heard for several weeks he may agree that he should not be brought back from prison every week but that he should be formally remanded in his absence[8]. This procedure, however, is only permitted where the defendant has a solicitor acting for him and even then the defendant can only be remanded in his absence on three successive occasions. If the defendant is serving a prison sentence for some other offence, a different rule applies: he may be remanded in custody for up to 28 clear days[9]. Where a defendant has been convicted after a summary trial, a remand for reports may be for up to four weeks, unless he is in custody, in which case the remand period must not exceed three weeks[10].

(2) The objections to bail
Section 4 of the Bail Act 1976 enacts the basic principle that until a person has been convicted of an offence he should be granted bail; in reality, if the police object to bail, the defendant is likely to have a difficult task persuading a magistrates' court that he should be released. It is, therefore, necessary to look at the legal framework which governs this decision in some detail. The starting point is Sch 1 para 2 of the Bail Act 1976[11] which provides:

> 'The defendant need not be granted bail if the court is satisfied that there are substantial grounds for believing that the defendant, if released on bail (whether subject to conditions or not) would –
> (a) fail to surrender to custody, or
> (b) commit an offence while on bail, or
> (c) interfere with witnesses or otherwise obstruct the course of justice, whether in relation to himself or any other person.'

The primary purpose of bail is to secure the attendance of the defendant at court at the specified time. It follows that the principal questions which are relevant in an enquiry into whether or not to grant bail are those designed to ascertain whether he is likely to attend trial. The court is expressly required by Sch 1 para 9 of the Bail Act 1976 to consider the following matters:

(a) The nature and seriousness of the offence or default (and the probable method of dealing with the defendant for it). The more serious the charge, usually the

---

6 Ibid s 128(6).
7 Ibid s 128(6)(a).
8 Ibid s 128(1)(a)(b)(c); (3A)–(3E).
9 Ibid s 131.
10 Ibid s 10(3).
11 Note: the court may also refuse bail if it is satisfied that the defendant should be kept in custody for his own protection (para 3) – the power is sometimes used, for example, where the accused is charged with sexual offences on children whose parents would be likely to attack the defendant. Note also Pt II of Sch 1 of the Bail Act 1976 provides that in the case of offences which are not punishable with imprisonment the court must normally grant bail.

greater is the incentive to abscond; conversely, where the defendant is charged with a minor offence, the risk of his absconding may be negligible. The court is directed to consider the likely method of dealing with the offender. The Home Office working party on bail gave the following advice to magistrates in considering this point:

'The court should also have regard to the likely sentence if the defendant is convicted, since his perception of the likely consequences of a conviction may be expected to have a considerable influence on his reaction to bail. The defendant will have much less incentive to abscond if the likely penalty is a fine or probation than if a custodial sentence is in prospect. If a person is remanded in custody and subsequently receives a sentence of imprisonment, the time spent on remand counts towards the sentence by virtue of s 67 of the Criminal Justice Act 1967. If, however, he does not receive a sentence of imprisonment, he cannot of course gain "credit" for his period in custody. Although it is wrong to assume that when a custodial remand is followed by a non-custodial sentence bail should have been granted initially, it is clearly desirable that, where an eventual custodial sentence is unlikely, bail should be granted unless there are strong grounds for a remand in custody. We would suggest that in a borderline case the court might give the defendant the benefit of the doubt, if a non-custodial sentence seems the likeliest outcome.

   This is not to say that a person who is likely to receive a custodial sentence if convicted should necessarily be refused bail. It has been suggested that, where a defendant is likely to receive a custodial sentence, it is doing him no kindness to give him a preliminary period of liberty. We do not think that this is a conclusive argument; much depends on whether the likely sentence of imprisonment will be short or long, since there is a danger, if the sentence is likely to be short, that the period on remand may exceed it. It seems to us, therefore, that the likely sentence if the defendant is convicted should be considered more in relation to the danger of his absconding than as a factor in its own right.'

(b) The character, antecedents, associations and community ties of the defendant.
Previous convictions do not, in themselves, amount to a valid reason for refusing bail, unless they point to the likelihood of the accused receiving a custodial sentence and, therefore, amount to a reason why he should not appear. This might be the case where, for example, the accused is at present subject to a suspended sentence. The Home Office working party commented:

'The [defendant's antecedents] are a valuable guide, but need to be interpreted with some care. If the defendant has abused the grant of bail in the past or is already on bail in respect of another charge, these facts should count strongly against him. In other cases, however, the defendant's previous convictions may not provide a reliable guide to his likely reaction to the grant of bail, unless, for example, they disclose a large number of serious offences. A long string of petty offences does not automatically justify a remand in custody. Clearly, a man who, although convicted on a number of occasions in the past, has always answered his bail, is likely to be a good bail risk.'

   The defendant's home circumstances and employment position are clearly of great importance. A defendant who has a stable home environment and a job is likely to receive bail even on a serious charge. Conversely, a defendant who is both out of work and without regular accommodation is likely to be treated as a poor bail risk (although his advocate may persuade the court to grant bail on the basis that he will reside at a bail hostel).

(c) The defendant's record as respects the fulfilment of his obligations under previous grants of bail in criminal proceedings. This is really self-evident. If the advocate is faced with a record which shows a previous failure to surrender to bail, he must obtain a full explanation from his client and the police about the circumstances of that default and will have to try to persuade the court that there are good reasons why it would not be repeated.

(d) The strength of the evidence of his having committed the offence or having defaulted. However serious the charge, the court should be reluctant to remand a defendant in custody if the evidence against him is tenuous. On the other hand, where the evidence is compelling, such as a signed confession, this, in conjunction with other matters, may indicate a likelihood that the defendant will eventually be given a custodial sentence and so will have an incentive not to stand trial.

As stated at the beginning of this section, bail may also be refused for reasons not primarily concerned with the likely attendance of the defendant at court. These reasons are:

(i) The likelihood of the defendant interfering with police witnesses[12]. It is submitted that compelling evidence should be produced in support of such a contention, which is easily made and almost impossible to rebut. The Home Office report comments:

> 'The possibility of the defendant interfering with witnesses arises less frequently and will usually be relevant only when the alleged offence is comparatively serious and there is some other indication, such as a past record of violence or threatening behaviour by the defendant[13].'

The defence advocate who is faced with such an objection which is not supported by evidence should remind the magistrates of their powers to impose conditions to bail which may go a long way to meeting the objection (see below). It is also true that any sophisticated criminal who is detained in custody can still make arrangements, if he wishes to do so, with his friends for them to contact the witnesses[14].

(ii) The likelihood of the defendant committing further offences[15]. Magistrates tend to have experience of offenders committing further offences on bail (in particular, defendants charged with robbery and burglary). This experience tends to make them give credit to police objections that a defendant (*not* already on bail for some other offence) should be refused bail because he is likely to commit an offence. It may be that this objection is accepted too frequently – it involves (a) the magistrates assuming without considering the evidence that the defendant is guilty of the present offence and (b) further assuming that he will go on to commit some other offences.

---

12 Bail Act 1976 Sch 1 Pt I para 2(c).
13 Cited in Harris *Criminal Jurisdiction of Magistrates* (10th edn).
14 Note: it is, of course, never a valid objection that the defendant wishes to have the police witnesses interviewed. See Lord Devlin *The Criminal Prosecution in England* (OUP, 1960) p 80: 'The power of refusing bail is not to be used simply to deny to the accused the same freedom of inquiry that the prosecution has.' Where a solicitor wishes to interview a police witness he should normally give notice to the police and permit an officer to attend the interview.
15 Bail Act 1976 Sch 1 Pt 1 para 2(b).

Although there will be some cases (eg serious violence between neighbours or a defendant whose record shows he is a professional housebreaker[16]) where a remand in custody is justified for this reason, the magistrates should normally require very strong grounds for refusing bail on this ground.

(3) The power to impose bail conditions

Section 3 of the Bail Act 1976 provides that a court releasing a defendant on bail may include special conditions for three purposes:

(1) *to ensure his attendance at trial*, eg that he should reside at a bail hostel or at a particular address or surrender his passport or report daily to a police station. If it appears he is unlikely to remain in Great Britain until the time appointed for him to surrender, he may be required before release on bail to provide security, eg to deposit a fixed sum of money;
(2) *to secure the interests of justice*, eg that he should not personally contact a prosecution witness; and
(3) *to prevent crime*, eg in an assault case that he should not go into a specified district in which the complainant lives.

These conditions give the court a great deal of flexibility in determining bail, and achieving the desired result which is, of course, the eventual attendance of the accused at his trial.

In addition to the above conditions, the magistrates may order the defendant to provide *sureties* who agree to forfeit a specified sum if the defendant fails to attend. Section 8(2) of the Bail Act provides:

'In considering the suitability . . . of a proposed surety, regard may be had (amongst other things) to –
(a) the surety's financial resources;
(b) his character and any previous convictions of his; and
(c) his proximity (whether in point of kinship, place of residence or otherwise) to the person for whom he is to be surety.'

(4) The procedure at the remand hearing

There are no statutory rules which describe the procedure to be adopted at a bail hearing. The procedure which ought to be followed is:

(i) The prosecuting solicitor indicates to the court the nature of the objections to bail. Sometimes, the officer in the case will take the oath and confirm the objections; the rules of evidence do not apply so he is entitled to put forward matters which are entirely hearsay[17].
(ii) The defence advocate can cross-examine the officer as to the police objections to bail. Considerable care has to be taken in conducting such a cross-examination as the officer's answers may reinforce the case he has put forward.
(iii) The defence advocate addresses the bench. He may (but rarely does) call his client. He may also call any sureties and anyone else who can speak for his client.

In practice, it may be that no officer will be present to give evidence in support of the objections.

---

16 As in *R v Phillips* (1947) 111 JP 333, 32 Cr App Rep 47 where the Court of Appeal criticised magistrates who had released on bail a professional burglar.
17 See *Re Moles* [1981] Crim LR 170.

The court is required to record all decisions relating to bail (see bail record p 194 below). If bail is refused (or conditions are imposed or varied) it must state its reasons. In theory, where an appeal is taken from a decision by a magistrates' court, the record will be of value to the defendant in formulating his arguments; in practice, the courts simply restate the nature of the police objection and give no reasons why they accept the objection as being well-founded. The value of the bail record is, therefore, minimal.

A magistrates' court is required to grant legal aid to a person who appears in pursuance of a remand in custody if he was not represented on the previous remand[18].

Where the magistrates grant bail subject to the defendant providing sureties but (as often happens) the sureties are not present at court, the recognizance of the sureties may be taken late by the clerk of the court or a police inspector[19]; if he is not prepared to accept the surety in question as suitable, the question is referred to the court granting bail or the surety's local court[20].

SUBSEQUENT APPLICATIONS

It will be appreciated that weeks may go by between the initial appearance of a defendant at a magistrates' court and his eventual trial or committal. During that period (unless he agrees to the contrary) he must be produced before the court every eight days and further remanded. The question arises whether he is entitled to make a fresh bail application on each remand. This important point was considered by the High Court in *R v Nottingham Justices, ex p Davies*[1]. The Nottingham Magistrates' Court adopted a policy of refusing to hear further bail applications after they had once heard a 'full application' unless there were 'new circumstances'. The High Court upheld this practice. Per Donaldson LJ:

> 'On [the previous occasion] the court will have been under an obligation to grant bail unless it was satisfied that a Sch I exception was made out. If it was so satisfied, it will have recorded the exceptions which in its judgment were applicable. The "satisfaction" is not a personal intellectual conclusion by each justice. It is a finding by the court that Sch I circumstances then existed and it is to be treated like every other finding of the court. It is res judicata or analogous thereto. It stands as a finding unless and until it is overturned on appeal . . . It follows that on the next occasion when bail is considered the court should treat, as an essential fact, that, at the time when the matter of bail was last considered, Sch I circumstances did indeed exist. Strictly speaking, they can and should only investigate whether the situation has changed since then.'

The rule that the magistrates will not hear repeated bail applications at remand hearings is qualified in the following ways[2]:

(1) It only applies after a *full* bail application has been made presenting all the relevant facts to the court. The Nottingham magistrates excepted

---

18 Legal Aid Act 1974 s 29(1)(c). The same requirement applies where the defendant is to be remanded in custody for reports.
19 Bail Act 1976 s 8(3).
20 Ibid s 8(5).
 1 [1981] QB 38, [1980] 2 All ER 775.
 2 See Andy Hall 'Nottingham JJs Revisited' [1984] LAG Bulletin 76 for a highly informative discussion of the problem posed by this case.

IN THE COUNTY OF BARSET
PETTY SESSIONAL DIVISION OF BARCHESTER

Barchester Magistrates' Court (1892)

Accused: **William Sikes**   Date of Birth: **15.7.44**

                                                            Offence: **Conspiracy to steal**

DECISION

THE ACCUSED IS:-

☑ Remanded to appear before the Barset Court at 10 a.m. on **14th January 1986**
☐ Committed to appear before the Crown Court as notified.
☐ Granted un/conditional bail.
☑ Refused bail.

Exception(s) to bail		Reason(s) for applying exception(s)	
Para 2(a) Fail surrender.	☑	☑ Nature & gravity of offence & probable sentence.	
2(b) Commit offence.	☑	☐ Character/antecedents.	
2(c) Interfere with etc.	☑	☐ Lack of community ties.	
3 Own protection/Welfare.	☐	☐ Previously failed to surrender to custody.	
4 Serving sentence.	☐	☐ Behaviour towards/proximity to prosecution witnesses.	
5 Insufficient info.	☐		
6 Current bail breach.	☐		
7 Cannot complete report/enquiries.	☐	☐	

CONDITIONS TO BE COMPLIED WITH BEFORE RELEASE ON BAIL
To provide   surety(ies) in the sum of £   (each) to secure the accused's surrender to custody at the time and place appointed.
☐ Surrender passport.
☐ Provide security in the sum of £

CONDITIONS TO BE COMPLIED WITH AFTER RELEASE ON BAIL
☐ To reside at
☐ Report to   Police station between   Twice/Daily
☐ Curfew between   p.m. and   a.m. daily.
☐ Not to communicate or interfere with prosecution witnesses.

The above conditions were imposed on the grant of bail for the following reasons:-
        ☐ To ensure surrender to custody.
        ☐ To prevent the commission of further offences.
        ☐ To protect witnesses.
        ☐

Accused agreed to remands in absence:- YES/NO

- -

I HEREBY CERTIFY that, at a hearing this day, the court heard full argument on an application for bail made by (on behalf of) the accused, before refusing the application and remanding the accused in custody under Section **5** of the Magistrates' Courts Act 1980.

☑ The court has not previously heard full argument on an application for bail by or on behalf of the accused in these proceedings.

☐ The court has previously heard full argument from the accused on an application for bail, but is satisfied:

    ☐ that there has been the following change in his circumstances:

    ☐ that the following new considerations have been placed before it:

BY ORDER OF THE COURT   *John Smith*

CLERK OF THE COURT   Date: **8th Jan 86**

from their policy the situation where on the first remand a bail application was made by a duty solicitor who would not be aware of the full facts, and this exception was expressly approved by the High Court. Where an advocate (*not* the duty solicitor) is instructed to make a bail application on the first remand, he should make it clear to the court that he is necessarily doing so on incomplete information. In some cases, he may remind the court that they are entitled under para 5 of Sch 1 to state that they are refusing bail because sufficient information is not yet available for them to be able to decide. If they certify that is the reason for refusing bail, a second application can always be made[3].

(2) The rule does not apply where there has been a change of circumstances, for example:

    (a) sureties may have come forward, accommodation or employment may be available to the defendant; these are highly relevant matters in considering any objection based on lack of community ties;

    (b) once the committal papers (or advance information statements) have been served, the defence may be justified in asking the court to reconsider an objection under Sch 1 para 9(a) on the grounds of 'the nature and seriousness of the offence . . . and the probable method of dealing with the defendant for it';

    (c) an objection on the basis that the defendant would interfere with witnesses may have to be reconsidered once police enquiries have progressed and statements have been taken[4];

    (d) if there has been delay while the prosecution is getting its case ready for trial, that is a valid reason for renewing a bail application: 'it is well established that it is a proper exercise of judicial discretion to decide that the prosecution has unreasonably delayed in the preparation of its case and that, on that account, the accused should no longer be remanded in custody'[5].

(3) The rule does not apply where relevant matters were not drawn to the attention of the court on the previous occasion. Donaldson LJ in *ex p Davies* stated the position as follows: 'The court, considering afresh the question of bail, is both entitled and bound to take account . . . of circumstances which, although they then existed, were not brought to the attention of the court. To do so is not to impugn the previous decision of the court and is necessary in justice to the accused[6].'

APPEALS

A defendant who is *refused* bail at a remand hearing has a right of appeal:

(a) To the *Crown Court*[7]. The defendant's solicitor submits a notice of application[8] accompanied by a certificate from the magistrates' court that a full bail application has been made[9]. A specimen form of notice is set out at p 202. It should be noted that it is important to take great care

3 Ibid.
4 Per Donaldson LJ in *R v Nottingham Justices, ex p Davies* [1980] 2 All ER 775 at 779.
5 Ibid at 779.
6 Ibid at 779.
7 The right is conferred by Supreme Court Act 1981 s 81 (as amended by Criminal Justice Act 1982 s 60).
8 Crown Court Rules 1982, SI 1982/1109 r 19.
9 The certificate is issued under Bail Act 1976 s 5(6A).

in setting out the grounds upon which the application is made; the Crown Court judge may well form a provisional view on the basis of reading the papers in advance. The notice of application is served on the prosecutor (with prior notice of sureties) at least 24 hours before the application is to be heard. The actual hearing is in chambers and either counsel or a solicitor may represent the defendant. A legal aid certificate granted for the purpose of the proceedings at the magistrates' courts will cover representation at the Crown Court.

(b) To the *High Court*[10]. An alternative method of appeal is to apply to a judge in chambers in the High Court. The procedure is governed by RSC Ord 79 r 9; the application is by summons supported by an affidavit which sets out the objections to bail, the answers thereto and details of previous applications. Legal aid is only available through the civil scheme and, although a local area office may be prepared to grant an emergency certificate, it may be this would not be granted because of the speedy alternative of using the magistrates' court certificate for an application to the Crown Court. There is one case, however, where the Crown Court is *not* an alternative forum and that is where the magistrates have granted bail but subject to conditions (including sureties) which the defendant cannot satisfy: in that situation, an application to vary the terms can only be made to the High Court. We set out at pp 199–201 a precedent of the summons to be used and affidavit in support.

The practitioner will realise that there is a risk in appealing against the decision of a magistrates' court in that, if the appeal is refused, it may be almost impossible to persuade the magistrates later that there has been a change in circumstances:

> 'Careful thought must be given to venue and timing of challenges to justices' determinations. A refusal of bail by a higher tribunal is likely to be taken as the "final word" by magistrates. New circumstances which have arisen since that time may not impress justices whose earlier decision to detain in custody has been vindicated. A further summary application, even if permitted, is likely to fail. Accordingly, over-enthusiasm on the part of clients is best tempered by objective advice. A good rule of thumb, except in the most urgent or convincing cases, is not to apply elsewhere until all possibility of reconsideration in the lower court has been exhausted[11].'

BAIL AT COMMITTAL

Where a magistrates' court commits for trial, it has to determine whether or not the defendant should be kept in custody pending his appearance at the Crown Court[12]. If the defendant is already on bail, the court will usually grant fresh bail and if sureties are required they will have to be taken again. If the defendant is in custody, the question arises whether the committal stage represents a change of circumstances within the rule in *R v Nottingham Justices, ex p Davies*. The answer is that in almost every case it will justify a fresh application, because the committal papers will have shown the case in a new light. In *R v Reading Crown Court, ex p Malik*[13], Donaldson LJ said:

10 Criminal Justice Act 1967 s 22.
11 Andy Hall 'Bail: Appeals' [1984] LAG Bulletin 145.
12 Magistrates' Courts Act 1980 s 6(3).
13 [1981] QB 451 at 454.

'Although there may be exceptional cases[14], as a general rule the moment of committal for trial must, in our judgment, be an occasion upon which an accused person is entitled to have his right to bail fully reviewed. In any particular case, the eligibility of the accused for bail may or may not have improved, but it is almost inevitable that there will have been a change in circumstances. For example, the court will be in a much better position to assess "the nature and seriousness of the offence": para 9(a) of Sch 1 to the Bail Act 1976. In addition the strength of the prosecution case can for the first time be fully assessed, both by the committing court and by the accused himself. This can be very material in considering the likelihood that the accused may fail to surrender to custody: Sch 1 para 2(1).'

Where bail is refused at the committal proceedings, the defendant may appeal to the Crown Court or to a High Court judge in chambers. The procedure is as discussed above at p 195[15].

BAIL AT THE CROWN COURT

Once the defendant attends the Crown Court for his trial, the question arises whether he should be granted bail during his trial. There are two points to note:

(a) The original grant of bail by the magistrates' court will normally have directed his appearance at every time and place to which, during the course of the proceedings, the hearing may be from time to time adjourned. This means that it is not necessary for the sureties to be retaken when he appears at the Crown Court.

(b) The Crown Court may, however, vary or withdraw bail.

The practice to be followed at the Crown Court has been summarised as follows:

'Once a trial has begun, the further grant of bail, whether during the short adjournment or overnight, is in the discretion of the trial judge. It may be a proper exercise of this discretion to refuse bail during the short adjournment if the accused cannot otherwise be segregated from witnesses and jurors.

An accused who was on bail while on remand should not be refused overnight bail during the trial, unless in the opinion of the judge there are positive reasons to justify this refusal. Such reasons are likely to be: (1) that a point has been reached where there is a real danger that the accused will abscond, either because the case is going badly for him or for any other reason; (2) that there is a real danger that he may interfere with witnesses or jurors. There is no universal rule of practice that bail shall not be renewed when the summing-up has begun. Each case must be decided in the light of its own circumstances and having regard to the judge's assessment from time to time of the risks involved.

Once the jury has returned a verdict, a further renewal of bail should be regarded as exceptional[16].'

14 Such a case was *R v Slough Justices, ex p Duncan and Embling* (1982) 75 Cr App Rep 384 where the defence accepted there had been no change of circumstances at the committal stage.
15 If the defendant is committed to the Central Criminal Court, a bail application only lies to that court.
16 *Practice Note* [1974] 2 All ER 794, [1974] 1 WLR 770, CA.

BAIL ON APPEAL FROM THE CROWN COURT

Where a person intends to appeal to the Court of Appeal against conviction or sentence, he may apply to the trial judge at the Crown Court for a certificate:

(a) that there are proper grounds for appeal against conviction[17], or

(b) that there are such grounds for appeal against sentence[18].

If the judge grants such a certificate, he may also grant the defendant bail pending his appeal. The judge will normally require a draft of the proposed grounds of appeal. The following guidance has been given as to how the judge should approach such an application:

> 'The first question is whether there exists a particular and urgent ground of appeal. If there is no such ground there can be no certificate and if there is no certificate there can be no bail. A judge should not grant a certificate with regard to sentence merely in the light of mitigation to which he has in his opinion given due weight, or in regard to a conviction on a ground where he considers the chance of a successful appeal is not substantial[19].'

The Court of Appeal (including the single judge) has power under s 19 of the Criminal Appeal Act 1968 to admit appellants on bail pending their appeal. This power is rarely exercised but is appropriate, for example, where a short sentence has been passed so that, if the appellant has to remain in custody, a successful appeal would be otiose. More commonly, in such cases the court directs expedition of the appeal. It is worth noting that the single judge may decline to consider an application for bail pending an appeal against conviction on the grounds of misdirection unless either a transcript is available or counsel is able to produce a clear note of the summing-up. Appellants who were legally aided at the trial will find that their certificate does not cover applications to the single judge for bail. This means that they will either have to instruct a solicitor to act privately for them or hope the registrar will instruct counsel on their behalf.

17 Criminal Appeal Act 1968 s 1(2) and Supreme Court Act 1981 s 81(1B).
18 Criminal Appeal Act 1968 s 11(1A).
19 *Practice Note* [1983] 3 All ER 608, [1983] 1 WLR 1292, CA.

IN THE HIGH COURT OF JUSTICE

QUEEN'S BENCH DIVISION

IN THE MATTER OF AN APPLICATION FOR BAIL BY

WILLIAM SIKES

Let all parties concerned attend the Judge in Chambers

on the 12th   day of January 1986, at   10.30 a.m.   on

the hearing of an application on behalf of William Sikes to

be granted bail as to his commitment on the 4th January 1986 by

the Magistrates' Court sitting at Barchester Magistrates Court.

Dated the   9th   day of January 1986.

This Summons was taken out by Messrs. Dodson and Fogg of

3 Freeman's Court, London EC2A 2CV., Solicitors for the said

WILLIAM SIKES

IN THE HIGH COURT OF JUSTICE

QUEEN'S BENCH DIVISION

In the Matter of an Application for Bail by

WILLIAM SIKES

Affidavit of Joseph Fogg

I, EDWARD FOGG, of 3 Freeman's Court, Cornhill, London EC2,
a Solicitor of the Supreme Court, MAKE OATH and SAY as follows:-

1. I am a solicitor of the Supreme Court and am instructed
   in the conduct of his defence by the above-named Applicant,
   Mr William Sikes, and am duly authorised to make this
   affidavit on his behalf.

2. The Applicant was arrested on 3rd January 1986 and
   subsequently charged with conspiracy to handle stolen
   goods.

3. The Applicant appeared at Barchester Magistrates Court
   on 4th January 1986 when he was remanded in custody until
   8th January. On that date he further appeared before
   the said Magistrates Court when the solicitor for the
   Crown Prosecution Service opposed bail on the following
   grounds:-

   (a) the Applicant was likely to abscond because of the
       nature and gravity of the offence;

   (b) He was likely to interfere with witnesses;

   (c) He was likely to commit further offences.

   The magistrates refused his application for bail and he
   was remanded to 14th January. A copy of the bail record
   is now produced and shown to me marked "JFI".

4. The Applicant, who disputes the charge and will plead
   'not guilty', has a fixed address at Sunnyfields Farm,
   Plumstead where he has lived with his wife and daughters
   for the last seven years. He is prepared to surrender
   his passport to the police and report on a daily basis
   to Plumstead Police Station. The following persons
   are prepared to stand as sureties (each in the sum of
   £10,000) to secure his attendance at trial:-

        (a) Mr Joseph Fagin
            10 Saffron Hill, London WC1
            (his former employer)

   (b) Mr Matthew Pocket
       5 Peabody Road, Rochester
       (his brother in law)

5. I understand from Chief Inspector Bucket who is in charge of the
   police investigation that substantial inquiries have now been
   undertaken and witnesses interviewed since the Applicant's
   arrest and that the prosecution will be in a position to serve
   the committal statements within the next week. I further
   understand that this evidence comprises statements from
   the losers of the property the subject matter of the charge
   and statements from police officers. In the circumstances
   I would respectfully submit that there is no likelihood
   of the Applicant being able to interfere with witnesses
   (even if he wished to do so).

6. I would further submit that (although the Applicant has
   previous convictions) there is no evidence to support the
   allegation that he would commit further offences.

7. In the circumstances I would respectfully apply to this
   Honourable Court to admit the Applicant to bail on such
   terms and conditions as it sees fit.

SWORN by the above named

deponent EDWARD FOGG at

2 New Street, London EC1

this 9th day of January 1986   *Edward Fogg*

Before me   Benjamin Simms

A Solicitor

NOTICE OF APPLICATION RELATING TO BAIL TO BE MADE
TO THE CROWN COURT

AT   THE CENTRAL CRIMINAL COURT, OLD BAILEY, LONDON EC4

CROWN COURT NO.   Not applicable

[OR]

SERIAL NO. AND   2656

NAME AND LOCATION OF MAGISTRATES COURT   Camberwell Green Magistrates Court

Note: The appropriate office of the Crown Court should be consulted about the time and place of
      the hearing before this notice is sent to the other party to the application.
      A copy of this notice should be sent to the Crown Court.
      In the case of an application for bail in the course of proceedings being held before
      Magistrates the certificate prescribed by Section 5(6)A of the Bail Act 1976 (as amended)
      should accompany this notice when it is lodged at the Crown Court office.

TAKE NOTICE that an application relating to bail will be made to the
Crown Court

at .The Central Criminal Court, Old Bailey, London, EC4

on .14th April 1987

at .10 a.m./p̶m̶.

on behalf of the defendant/a̶p̶p̶e̶l̶l̶a̶n̶t̶/p̶r̶o̶s̶e̶c̶u̶t̶o̶r̶/r̶e̶s̶p̶o̶n̶d̶e̶n̶t̶.

1. Defendant/a̶p̶p̶e̶l̶l̶a̶n̶t̶ (block letters please)

   Surname .. MAGWITCH .... Date of birth ... 19/3/63 ....

   Forename .. ABLE ....

   Home Address .. 27A THEOBALDS ROAD ....

                   LONDON WC1
   ....

2. Solicitor for the applicant

   Name .. JOSIAH JAGGERS ....

   Address .. JAGGERS AND CO ....

            LITTLE BRITAIN, LONDON EC2
   ....

3. If defendant/a̶p̶p̶e̶l̶l̶a̶n̶t̶ is in custody state:

   place of detention .. H. M. Prison Wormwood Scrubs ....

   prison number (if applicable) ..... Y46275 ....

   length of time in custody .. since arrest by police on 2/3/87 ....

   date of last remand ...... 6th April 1987 ....

4. State the particulars of proceedings during which the defendant/appellant was committed to custody or bailed (un)conditionally including:

(a) the stage reached in the proceedings as at the date of this application:
Remanded in custody pending committal proceedings to be heard on
15 May 1987

(b) the offences alleged:
That on 2/3/87 at New Cross Road, London SE4, he attempted to murder
John Compeyson

(c) (If the application relates to a case pending before Magistrates) Give details of next appearance:
Place Camberwell Green Magistrates Court
Date 1st May 1987 (not to be produced before then) Time 10.30 a.m.

5. Give details of any relevant previous applications for bail or variation of conditions of bail:
A full application was made to Camberwell Green Magistrates Court
on 1st April 1987

6. Nature and grounds of application:
(a) State fully the grounds relief on and list previous convictions (if any):
The charge is contested. The applicant surrendered himself to the police station and has given particulars of alibi to the prosecution. The evidence in the case relies upon a night time identification by the victim and one other witness. He has resided at 27a Theobalds Road, London WC1 since his return from Australia in 1985 and has been in regular employment; his employers are willing to continue to employ him if he is admitted to bail. He has had no convictions since 1963. (A list of convictions is attached).

(b) Give details of any proposed sureties and answer any objections raised previously:
The following persons are prepared to stand surety:-
1. Mr Phillip Pirrip, 20 James Street, London WC1
2. Mr Joe Gargery, The Old Forge, Queenborough, Kent
The Applicant would comply with any conditions as to residence, reporting and curfew and his passport has already been seized by the police. He would undertake not to contact any prosecution witness.

Chapter 10

Costs and legal aid

COSTS

In civil proceedings the party who wins is normally entitled to an order that his costs should be paid by the losing side. In criminal proceedings the position is different because:

(1) although an award of costs is often made against a defendant after conviction, such an order will be worthless if the defendant is going to prison or is impecunious. In such circumstances, the court frequently makes no order as to costs – although special provision is made for indemnifying a private prosecutor;

(2) if the defendant is acquitted, this does not normally mean the prosecution were at fault in bringing the case. For this reason, the costs of successful defendants are ordered to be paid out of central funds and not by the prosecutor.

The law concerning costs in criminal cases is contained in ss 16–21 of the Prosecution of Offences Act 1985.

DEFENDANT'S COSTS ORDER

Section 16 provides that the court may order the payment of the defendant's costs out of central funds in any of the following cases:

(a) *In the magistrates' court* where:
    (i) the information is not proceeded with;
    (ii) the magistrates sitting as examining justices decide the defendant should not be committed for trial;
    (iii) the magistrates try the information and acquit the defendant (this applies whether the charge is triable either way or is only summary).

(b) *Before the Crown Court* where:
    (i) the prosecution offer no evidence;
    (ii) the defendant is acquitted of any count on the indictment;
    (iii) on appeal, his conviction by the magistrates is set aside;
    (iv) on appeal against sentence, a less severe punishment is imposed.

(c) *In the Court of Appeal* where the defendant is successful in his appeal.

(d) On determination of any appeal by the *Divisional Court* or *House of Lords*.

The order for costs is to be for the payment out of central funds of 'such amount as the court considers reasonably sufficient to compensate him for any expenses properly incurred by him in the proceedings' (s 16(6)); the court, however, has a discretion to specify the payment of a specific sum where it 'is of the opinion that there are circumstances which make it inappropriate that the person in whose favour the order is made should recover the full amount'. Note that the defendant cannot recover his loss of earnings while attending court. A *Practice Note* [1982] 3 All ER 1152, [1982] 1 WLR 1447, CA sets out what would appear still to be the relevant principle under the new Act:

'Whether to make such an award is a matter in the unfettered discretion of the court in the light of the circumstances of each particular case. It should be accepted as normal practice that such an award be made unless there are positive reasons for making a different order. Examples of such reasons are:

Where the defendant's own conduct has brought suspicion on himself and has misled the prosecution into thinking that the case against him is stronger than it is the defendant can be left to pay his own costs. Where there is ample evidence to support a conviction but the defendant is acquitted on a technicality which has no merit. Here again the defendant can be left to pay his own costs. Where the defendant is acquitted on one charge but convicted on another. Here the court should make whatever order seems just having regard to the relative importance of the two charges and the conduct of the parties generally'.

Where a magistrates' court refuses to award costs, it is, in theory, possible for the defendant to apply to the High Court for leave to challenge their decision by a judicial review. In practice, since questions of costs are 'discretionary', the High Court will only grant leave where it is clear the magistrates proceeded on some wholly wrong basis. Where the Crown Court refuses to award costs after a trial on indictment, there is no method of appealing against the decision.

It should be noted that where the defendant is legally aided, the court usually makes no order for costs (but directs instead that any contribution by him towards the legal aid costs be refunded under s 8(5) of the Legal Aid Act 1982). The court may, however, make an order in favour of a defendant who is legally aided; in such a case, any expenses incurred on his behalf under the legal aid order are disregarded in determining the amount of the award of costs (s 16(8) of the Prosecution of Offences Act 1985).

COSTS OF PRIVATE PROSECUTOR

A private person who brings a private prosecution for an indictable offence (eg a store prosecuting a shop-lifter) is entitled to apply for an order that his costs be paid out of central funds whether or not the prosecution is successful (s 17 of the Prosecution of Offences Act 1985). This section does *not* apply to the Crown Prosecution Service, Customs and Excise, Civil Service or local authority prosecutions.

AWARD OF COSTS AGAINST ACCUSED

A defendant may be ordered under s 18 of the Prosecution of Offences Act 1985 to pay the prosecution costs where:

(a) he is convicted at a magistrates' court;
(b) he is convicted before the Crown Court;
(c) the Crown Court dismisses an appeal against conviction or sentence.

(There is a similar power in the Court of Appeal, although in practice there will be few cases where it would be appropriate to make an order.)

The court must specify in the order the amount of costs to be paid. No appeal to the Crown Court lies against an order for costs alone (although if an appeal is taken against conviction or sentence, the matter is at large). An appeal will lie to the Court of Appeal against an order for costs made by the Crown Court after a trial on indictment; leave must be obtained as in the case of an appeal against sentence (see *R v Hayden* [1975] 2 All ER 558, [1975] 1 WLR 852).

LEGAL AID

In civil cases legal aid is available through a scheme run by the Law Society which operates independently of the courts. In criminal cases the courts themselves determine whether an accused person should receive legal aid. Emergency legal aid is available under the Duty Solicitor Scheme for persons detained in custody by the police and for defendants on their initial appearance at the magistrates' court; thereafter legal aid is provided on the basis of a certificate assigning the case to a specific solicitor. The principal occasions when some form of legal aid is available are shown in the table below.

(1) On *arrest and detention*: we have already seen (p 68 above) that where a person is questioned or detained by the police he has the right to consult a solicitor privately under s 58 of the Police and Criminal Evidence Act 1984; legal advice is available to him through the Duty Solicitor Scheme under s 1 of the Legal Aid Act 1982.

(2) On *initial remand hearings*: an accused person is also entitled to advice from the court duty solicitor when he appears on remand at a magistrates' court. The duty solicitor will (a) represent the defendant on a bail application, (b) represent a defendant in custody who wants to plead guilty at once, (c) appear for a fine defaulter who is at risk of going to prison, (d) assist other defendants on matters such as completing legal aid forms.

(3) *Magistrates' court proceedings* (including juvenile courts): on application to court – can be granted by clerk but only refused by magistrates (Legal Aid Act 1974 s 28(2), (3)). Note: where committal proceedings are held, the court can make a *through* order, ie direct that legal aid be available for both the magistrates' court proceedings and the subsequent proceedings before the Crown Court (Legal Aid Act 1982 s 2).

(4) *Crown Court proceedings*: can be granted either by magistrates' court committing defendant to Crown Court (or from whom appeal has been taken) or by Crown Court. The order covers *advice* on appeal to the Court of Appeal (Legal Aid Act 1974 s 28(5)–(7)).

(5) *High Court judge in chambers – bail*: can only be obtained in practice through the services of the Official Solicitor who then acts for the applicant. For this reason, where magistrates refuse bail an application is usually made to the Crown Court; legal aid order granted in the magistrates' court covers an application by a solicitor to a Crown Court judge (Legal Aid Act 1974 s 30(1A)).

(6) *Court of Appeal*: can only be obtained through the single judge or full court. Usually the Registrar of the Criminal Division of the Court is directed to act for the appellant (Legal Aid Act 1974 s 28(8)).

(7) *Case stated to High Court and application for prerogative orders*: in these cases legal aid is available under the civil scheme (Legal Aid Act 1974 Sch 1).

Whenever a court has power to make a legal aid order it has to consider:

(a) the nature of the charge to determine whether it warrants legal aid, and
(b) the means of the defendant.

If there is any doubt whether a legal aid order should be made it should be resolved in the applicant's favour[1].

The Widgery Committee (1966)[2] recommended that legal aid should be granted (subject to the applicant's means) in the following cases:

(1) where the charge is a grave one in the sense that the accused is in real jeopardy of losing his liberty or livelihood or suffering serious damage to his reputation; or
(2) where the charge raises a substantial question of law; or
(3) where the accused is unable to follow the proceedings and state his own case because of his inadequate knowledge of English, mental illness or other mental or physical disability; or
(4) where the nature of the defence involves the tracing and interviewing of witnesses or expert cross-examination of a witness for the prosecution; or
(5) where legal representation is desirable in the interests of someone other than the accused as, for example, in the case of sexual offences against young children where it is undesirable that the accused should cross-examine the witness in person.

It should be noted that:

(a) the courts cannot pass a sentence of imprisonment on a person who has not already been to prison unless he has been offered legal aid (or is ineligible because of his means): Powers of Criminal Courts Act 1973 s 21;
(b) the courts cannot pass a youth custody sentence or make a detention centre order unless the defendant has been offered legal aid (or is ineligible because of his means): Criminal Justice Act 1982 s 3.

Where legal aid is refused by a magistrates' court, or by a single magistrate or the clerk, the defendant has the right to have the decision reviewed by the area criminal legal aid committee; the following conditions must be satisfied before a review is available:

(1) the offence charged must be indictable;
(2) the refusal must be on the ground that legal aid was not required in the interests of justice;
(3) the application for legal aid was made at least 21 days before any date fixed for the committal or summary trial[3].

The committee considers the application afresh and either refuses it or makes a legal aid order. The committee must give specific reasons for its decision (which can be examined on an application for judicial review)[4]. There is no provision for review where legal aid is refused by the Crown Court.

In many cases (eg all summary cases) review by the area committee will not be available. In theory, the decision of the magistrates is subject to challenge by way of judicial review. Similarly, the decisions of the Crown Court (*except* where dealing with a case on indictment[5]) are subject to review. However, in practice, it is difficult to persuade the Divisional Court to review the decision.

1　Legal Aid Act 1974 s 29(6).
2　Cmnd 2934 of 1966.
3　Legal Aid in Criminal Proceedings (General) Regulations 1968, SI 1968/1231 reg 6E(2).
4　See *R v No 14 (London West) Legal Aid Area Committee, ex p Bunting* (1974) 118 Sol Jo 259.
5　*R v Crown Court at Chichester, ex p Abodunrin* [1984] Crim LR 240.

Example 1. H was an undergraduate who was alleged to have been in possession of a small quantity of cannabis; the charge was nonetheless serious so far as he was concerned because he did not want a criminal record. In addition, his defence involved the difficult point of when a trace can be evidence of possession. The Divisional Court refused to grant judicial review against the refusal of a legal aid order. Drake J rejected counsel's submissions that 'in any case involving difficult facts or difficult points of law . . . it must be mandatory on the court to grant a legal aid order because it would be in the interests of justice to make an order and contrary to those interests to refuse to do so'[6].

Example 2. L, a serving soldier, was charged with three charges of indecent exposure. The magistrates refused legal aid. The Divisional Court granted judicial review on the basis that his career was at stake. Per Mann J: 'in exercising [their] discretion, they will have regard to the Widgery criteria. Among the matters which they can take into account under the Widgery criteria are threats to a person's livelihood . . . the identification of a person as a serving soldier, without more, should have led the justices to grant legal aid[7].'

Quite apart from the question whether the particular case is sufficiently serious to merit legal aid, the court considering such an application has to decide whether the applicant could in fact afford to pay for legal representation himself and, if he could not, whether he should none the less contribute something towards the cost of his representation. The system which has been developed (and which is set out in the Legal Aid in Criminal Proceedings (General) Regulations 1968) provides that:

(1) the applicant submits a written statement of means to the court (reg 4);
(2) the court determines the amount of any contributions he should make (reg 18);
(3) the court then makes a legal aid contribution order (reg 20); the defendant may under the order be required to pay a specific sum at once or instalments or both (reg 22);
(4) if the defendant is in due course acquitted, the court which disposes of the case can direct that his contribution be repaid (Legal Aid Act 1982 s 8(5)).

It should be noted that, where, during the course of a case, the defendant's solicitor wishes to incur unusual expenditure, he must apply to the area criminal legal aid committee for authority; thus reg 14D provides:

'(1) Where it appears to a legally assisted person's solicitor necessary for the proper conduct of proceedings in a magistrates' court or in the Crown Court to incur costs by taking any of the following steps –
   (a) obtaining a report or opinion of one or more experts or tendering expert evidence;
   (b) employing a person to provide a report or opinion (otherwise than as an expert);
   (c) bespeaking transcripts of shorthand notes or tape recordings of any proceedings, including police questioning suspects; or

---

6 *R v Crown Court at Cambridge, ex p Hagi* (1979) 144 JP 145. It should be pointed out that in fact the judges of the Divisional Court, while declining to order judicial review, expressed their concern that the defendant should be unrepresented and suggested a fresh application be made to the Crown Court in the light of their comments. The application was made and granted.
7 *R v Briggs Justices, ex p Lynch* (1984) 148 JP 214.

   (d) performing an act which is either unusual in its nature or involves
        unusually large expenditure;
   he may apply to the appropriate legal aid committee for authority to do so.
   (2) If a criminal legal aid committee authorises the taking of any step specified in
        para (1), it shall authorise the maximum fee for any such report, opinion,
        expert evidence, transcript or act.'

It should also be noted that where the defendant wishes to change the
solicitor assigned to him under the order (or the solicitor wishes to cease
acting) an application must be made to the court to amend the legal aid
order (s 31 of the Legal Aid Act 1974). In a magistrates' court, the application is made to the clerk to the justices. If the application is not granted, the
application is referred to the area committee (reg 14). There is no review,
however, where the application to change solicitor is made within 14 days of
the date fixed for the hearing.

We conclude this section with an example to show how the legal aid
system works in serious criminal cases.

Example. Christopher is arrested by the police on suspicion of using a firearm with
intent to endanger life (Firearms Act 1968 s 16). He is detained at the police
station for questioning and is told of his right to obtain legal advice (Code C para
6). The duty solicitor attends at the police station. This assistance is available
under the scheme established under s 1(1)(aa) of the Legal Aid Act 1982. The
next day he is charged and brought before the local magistrates' court and he asks
the solicitor who has assisted him at the police station to represent him. The
solicitor prior to the hearing submits an application for legal aid and a statement
of means and the clerk grants legal aid subject to a contribution order (Legal Aid
Act 1974 s 28(2)). The magistrates refuse to grant bail and the solicitor under the
same legal aid order applies successfully to the Crown Court (s 30(1A)). At the
committal proceedings, the court makes a new legal aid order to cover representation at the Crown Court (s 28(5)): this would not have been necessary if a
'through' order had been made in the initial application (see Legal Aid Act 1982
s 2). Before the trial at the Crown Court, the solicitor realises that a gun expert
will be necessary and secures authority from the area criminal legal aid committee for the expenditure (reg 14D). At the Crown Court, Christopher is
acquitted and the judge orders that he be repaid the amount he has paid by way of
legal aid contribution (Legal Aid Act 1982 s 8(5)).

Form 1

Application for Legal Aid

PLEASE USE BLOCK CAPITALS AND CROSS OUT ANYTHING WHICH DOES NOT APPLY

1 Name .... CHARLES RYDER

   Permanent Address ..... 136 BAYSWATER ROAD LONDON W1

   .... Date of Birth 15/7/67

   Present Address (where different from above) ....

      LAZARUS COLLEGE CAMBRIDGE

2 I apply for legal aid for the purpose of proceedings before the .... CAMBRIDGE

   (Magistrates') (Juvenile) Court (on behalf of my child (name)) ....

   The case is due to be heard on ... 1ST JUNE 87 ... at .... 10.00 .... am/~pm~

3 Is any other person charged with you (your child) in these proceedings? ~Yes~/No.

   If so, whom ....

4 The Solicitor I wish to act for me (my child) is (state name and address)

   ..... JOHN BROWN, CHADWICK AND CO

   ..... DOWNING STREET CAMBRIDGE

   If you do not give the name of a solicitor the Court will select the solicitor assigned to you. (If you have been (your child has been) charged with another person or persons, the Court may assign a solicitor other than the solicitor of your choice.)

5 Describe shortly what it is you are (your child is) accused of doing, e.g. "stealing £50 from my employer", "kicking a door causing £50 damage", etc.

   ..... UNLAWFUL POSSESSION OF CONTROLLED DRUG

   ....

   ....

The following pages have been completed with a statement of my means (parent's means).

I understand that the Court may order me to make a contribution to the costs of legal aid or to pay the whole costs if it considers that my means enable me to do so and if I am under 16, may make a similar order with respect to my parents.

Signed...... *Charles Ryder* .... Date... 20th MAY 1987

3

Form 1   (continued)

Reasons for wanting Legal Aid

When deciding whether to grant you legal aid, the Court will need to know the reasons why it is in the interests of justice for you to be represented. You are therefore REQUESTED to complete the remainder of this form to avoid the possibility of legal aid being refused because the Court does not have sufficient information about the case. IF YOU NEED HELP IN COMPLETING THIS FORM, AND ESPECIALLY IF YOU HAVE PREVIOUS CONVICTIONS, YOU SHOULD SEE A SOLICITOR. He may be able to advise you free of charge or at a reduced fee.

6   I am in real danger of a custodial sentence for the following reasons: (Give brief reasons. You should consider seeing a solicitor before answering this question.)

N/A

7   I am subject to a *(tick the box(es) applicable)*

☐ suspended or partially suspended   ☐ supervision order
☐ sentence of imprisonment   ☐ deferred sentence
☐ conditional discharge   ☐ community service order
☐ probation order   ☐ care order

(Give brief details so far as you are able, including the nature of the offence and when the order was made. You should consider seeing a solicitor before answering this question.)

N/A

8   I am in real danger of losing my livelihood or suffering serious damage to my reputation because (Give brief reasons)

I AM AN UNDERGRADUATE AT LAZARUS COLLEGE. I AM LIABLE TO BE SENT DOWN OR SUSPENDED BY THE COLLEGE AUTHORITIES IF I AM CONVICTED. IN ADDITION I WILL BE UNABLE TO TAKE UP A VISA TO STUDY IN USA.

9   I have been advised by a solicitor that a *substantial* question of law is involved. (Give brief details. You will need the help of a solicitor to answer this question.)

WHETHER A PERSON IS IN POSSESSION OF A QUANTITY OF CANNABIS WHEN HE IS AWARE OF THE POSSIBILITY OF THE PRESENCE OF A TRACE OF THE DRUG IN HIS PREMISES.

4

10   I shall be unable to follow the proceedings because:
(a) My knowledge of English is inadequate   YES/NO
(b) I suffer from a disability, namely...

N/A

---

11   Witnesses have to be traced and interviewed on my behalf (State circumstances)

MY ROOMS WERE USED IN THE WEEK PRIOR TO MY ARREST BY FRIENDS FROM FRANCE. THEY HAVE TO BE TRACED AND MAY BE CALLED AS WITNESSES.

---

12   The case involves expert cross-examination of a prosecution witness. (Give brief details)

I CHALLENGE THE RECORD OF INTERVIEW BY PC BUCKET AND THE DETAILS OF HIS EVIDENCE AS TO THE SEARCH CARRIED OUT AT MY ROOM.

---

13   The case is a very complex one (for example mistaken identity) explain briefly (to answer this question you may need the help of a solicitor)

THE CASE INVOLVES CHALLENGING THE PROSECUTION EVIDENCE THAT A SUFFICIENT QUANTITY OF CANNABIS WAS IN FACT FOUND FOR THE CHARGE OF POSSESSION TO BE MADE OUT.

---

14   Any other reasons. (Give full particulars)

I AM ADVISED BY MY SOLICITORS THAT THE POLICE CONTRAVENED PROVISIONS OF THE POLICE AND CRIMINAL EVIDENCE ACT 1984 AND THE CODES OF PRACTICE IN THE CONDUCT OF THE SEARCH AND INTERVIEW I NEED A SOLICITOR'S ASSISTANCE TO PUT FORWARD THESE POINTS.

NOTE: If you plead NOT GUILTY, neither the information in this Form nor in Form 5 will be made known to the Magistrates who will try your case unless they convict you. If you are acquitted, only the financial information you have given in Form 5 will be given to them.

5

Form 5

Statement of Means

To apply for criminal legal aid you MUST complete this form. If you are not yet sixteen, then your mother or father may also be asked to complete one. If you have applied for legal aid for a child, and your child is sixteen years old or over, then *you* do not need to fill in this form. *Your child* should complete it, giving details of his or her *own income.*

This information is needed before legal aid can be granted, so to avoid any delay in your application being considered, please complete this form as fully and as carefully as possible.

BEFORE COMPLETING THIS FORM YOU SHOULD READ THE WARNING AND DECLARATION ON PAGE 9.

PLEASE USE BLOCK CAPITALS

Section 1—Personal Details

1. Full name ...... CHARLES RYDER
2. Date of birth 15/7/67
3. Home address ...... 136 BAYSWATER ROAD, LONDON W1

4. Marital status *(please tick one box)*

   ☐ single   divorced ☐
   ☐ married   widow(er) ☐
   ☐ married but separated

5. Occupation *(state 'unemployed' is appropriate)*
   List here *all* your jobs, including any part-time work and your employer's name and address. (If you have more than one job, give the name and address of each employer; if self-employed state 'self'.)

   ...... UNDERGRADUATE

Section 2—Personal Details (Dependant Child)

If legal aid is being sought for a dependent child, and he or she is not yet sixteen, please answer the following questions about him or her.

1. Full name ...... N/A
2. Date of birth ......
3. Home address *(If different from yours)* ......

4. Your relationship to him or her *(e.g. father)* ......

Section 3—Financial Details

Part A—Income
Please give below details of your net income *(i.e. after the deduction of tax and national insurance)* from all sources for the three months immediately before this form is completed. If you are married and living with your wife or husband, then you have to provide details of his or her income as well. The court may ask you to provide proof of the information you give in this form.
Your contribution, if any, will be assessed and collected on a *weekly* basis, so if you are paid monthly, please give *weekly* figures.

1. Do you receive Supplementary Benefit?
   ☐ Yes—*You do not need to complete the rest of this form, simply turn to the declaration on page nine and sign it.*
   ☑ No—*Please go on to question two.*

2. Do you receive Family Income Supplement?
   ☐ Yes—*There is no need to complete any more of Part A, so please turn to Part B—Capital and Savings.*
   ☑ No—*Please go on to question three.*

6

Form 5   (continued)

Section 3—Financial Details (continued)

3.   Please give details of your INCOME in the table below:

Description of Income	Amount		Remarks
	Your income	Income of wife/husband	
(a) Weekly earnings or salary, including over-time, commission or bonuses. (Please give net figures.) Please attach with this form your last six wage slips. If you do not have that many, please attach as many as you can.	NONE		
(b) If your earnings change from week to week, give the amounts for the last 13 weeks. (If you do not have this information, please give the amounts for as many weeks as you can, and at least the last six weeks. You should if possible attach wage slips.)			
(c) Income from any part-time job not included at (a) above. (Please give gross and net figures.)	NONE		
(d) Income from state benefits—e.g. family allowance (please specify below here).	NONE		
(e) Gross income from sub-letting house, rooms, etc.	NONE		
(f) Any other income (please give details below here).	£50 pw		STUDENT GRANT
(g) If in a business of your own, please attach the most recent accounts available.	N/A		

Important: If the information you have given in the table above is going to change soon, please give details of the changes in section 5 of this form.

Part B—Capital and Savings

Please give details of all your capital and savings. If you are married and living with your husband or wife, also give details of his or her capital and savings. You should give particulars of savings with the National Savings Bank or with other banks, National Savings Certificates, cash stocks and shares or any other investments. Please also give details of any property you own, such as houses or flats apart from the house or flat in which you live.

1.   Please give details of your CAPITAL and SAVINGS in the table below:

Description of CAPITAL and SAVINGS	Amount		Remarks
	You	Husband/Wife	
(a) Do you own house property (apart from your main or only dwelling)? (Answer YES or NO)	YES/NO	YES/NO	
(b) If YES state: (i) The value (i.e the approximate selling price) (ii) The amount of any outstanding mortgage			
(c) Give details of your savings. (State saving Institution below here)			
Give details of any articles of value that you own (e.g. jewellery, furs, paintings) with their approximate value	NONE		

7

Form 5　(continued)

Section 4—Allowances and Deductions

In assessing your means for legal aid purposes, the court will make allowances for the cost of supporting your husband or wife, children and any other dependent relatives, and also for your accommodation costs and travelling expenses. If there are any other expenses which you think the court should make allowance for, please give details at question 4 below.

1.　Please give the NUMBER of dependants who are *LIVING WITH YOU.*　N IA

Husband or wife	Children 18 and over	Children 16 and 17	Children 11 to 15	Children under 11	Other *(specify below)*

2.　If you pay maintenance to a dependant who does not live with you, please give details of the amounts you pay to support them.

Age of dependant	Your relationship to him or her	Amount you pay per week
	N JA	

3.　You may claim for the HOUSING EXPENSES of you and your wife or husband. Please give the amounts you pay each week. If you own more than one house, only give details connected with the house in which you live. If you are paying the housing expenses of (a) dependant(s) who do(es) not live with you, please give both amounts.

Description of payment	Amount per week	Amount per week for dependant(s)
Rent		
Mortgage repayment		
Ground rent		
Service charge		
Rates		
Board and lodging	£25	
Bed and breakfast		

4.　The TRAVELLING EXPENSES of you and your husband or wife may be taken into account. You may claim for the actual amounts that you and your husband or wife spend per week travelling to and from your place(s) of employment.

	You	Your husband or wife
Amount spent	N IA	

5.　Please give details of any OTHER EXPENSES which you think the court should know about.

Description of expenditure	Amount spent per week
GENERAL LIVING EXPENSES	£60 PER WEEK

8

Form 5   (continued)

Section 4—Allowances and Deductions (continued)

6. Allowance for contributions in respect of LEGAL ADVICE AND ASSISTANCE under the "green form" scheme. You may already have been given some advice and assistance by a solicitor under the "green form" scheme, and you may have paid, or been asked to pay, a contribution towards that advice. If this is the case, then the amount of your legal aid contribution will be reduced by the amount of "green form" contribution you have paid.

Name and address of the solicitor who gave the advice and assistance	Amount of contribution paid (or to be paid)
JOHN BROWN CHADWICK & CO DOWNING STREET CAMBRIDGE	£30

Section 5—Further Information

This part of the form is set aside for you to give any financial information that you think the court should have when deciding upon your application for legal aid. You may also use this part of the form to tell the court of any future changes in circumstance that might alter your financial position.

I RECEIVE NO FINANCIAL SUPPORT FROM EITHER OF MY PARENTS AND LIVE ON MY STUDENT GRANT AND SUCH CASUAL WORK AS I AM ABLE TO OBTAIN DURING VACATIONS.

Continue on page 10 if necessary

Section 6—Declaration

WARNING

Anyone who has knowingly or recklessly made a statement which is false in any way, or has knowingly withheld information is liable to be prosecuted and, if convicted, to either imprisonment for a term not exceeding four months, or to a fine or both. After your application has been considered by the court, you may be asked to give further information or to clarify information that you have already given. In particular you may be required to provide documentary proof of the information you have given (e.g. wage slips, rent books, etc.).

I declare that to the best of my knowledge and belief, I have given a complete and correct statement of my income, savings and capital (and that of my husband or wife)* (and that of my child)**.

Date 20th MAY 1987   Signed Charles Ryder

* Delete if you are not living with your husband or wife, or if you are single.
** Delete if legal aid is not sought for your child.

9

Part three

Sentencing

Chapter 11

The process of sentencing

CROWN COURT JURISDICTION

The Crown Court has the power to sentence offenders in the following circumstances:

(1) where a defendant has been found guilty by a jury after his trial on indictment;
(2) where a defendant has pleaded guilty to the indictment;
(3) where a defendant has appealed against a conviction or sentence by a magistrates' court;
(4) where a defendant has been convicted by a magistrates' court and has been *committed* by that court *for sentence* at the Crown Court.

This latter category represents an important part of the business of the Crown Court and must be considered in a little detail. Broadly speaking, such committals for sentence fall within one of two groups: the defendant is *either* committed because the magistrates think that he should receive a more substantial punishment than they can impose *or* because the Crown Court has to reconsider the punishment imposed for earlier offences. The most common forms of committal from magistrates' courts are shown in the table below:

Group I (where magistrates think offender deserves punishment or treatment they cannot order)	(1) *Section 38 committals*: where a person not less than 17 is convicted of an offence *triable either way* if, on obtaining information about his *character* and *antecedents*[1] the court is of opinion that they are such that greater punishment should be inflicted for the offence than the

---

1 *Antecedents* include, for example, the nature of the defendant's occupation. In *R v Lymm Justices, ex p Brown* [1973] 1 All ER 716, the Divisional Court held that the magistrates had rightly committed the defendant for sentence on the basis that his position as an airport policeman was a relevant factor to be considered in sentencing. But the mere fact that the magistrates, having heard all the evidence, think the offence is more serious than when they agreed to try it summarily will not justify a committal. See also *R v Warrington Justices, ex p Mooney* (1980) 2 Cr App Rep (S) 40 and *R v Derby and South Derbyshire Magistrates, ex p McCarthy* (1980 2 Cr App Rep (S) 140.

court has power to inflict, it may commit him to the Crown Court who may sentence him as if he had been convicted on indictment. (Magistrates' Courts Act 1980 s 38.)

(2) *Committed by juvenile court*: If a juvenile court considers an offender aged 15–16 years should serve a term of youth custody in excess of 6 months it can commit him to the Crown Court. (Magistrates' Court Act 1980 s 37.)

(3) *Mentally sick offenders*: where a magistrates' court thinks that the appropriate method of dealing with an offender is an order committing him to hospital together with an order *restricting* the circumstances in which he can be released, they must commit him to the Crown Court. (Mental Health Act 1983 s 43.)

Group II
(where a defendant has to be dealt with further by the Crown Court for earlier offences)

(1) *Breach of a probation order or conditional discharge*: where a defendant has been convicted by a magistrates' court while subject to a conditional discharge or probation order imposed by the Crown Court or is otherwise in breach of such a probation order the magistrates may commit him to the Crown Court to deal with him for the breach of probation or conditional discharge. (Powers of Criminal Courts Act 1973 ss 6(4) and 8(6).)

(2) *Conviction for further offence committed during operational period of suspended sentence imposed by Crown Court*: where a defendant has been given a suspended sentence by the Crown Court and he is convicted by a magistrates' court of an offence committed during the period of suspension, the magistrates must either commit

him to the appropriate sitting of
the Crown Court or notify that
court of the conviction. (Powers of
Criminal Courts Act 1973
s 24(2).)

It often happens that offenders appearing before a magistrates' court are
charged with several offences, some of which are purely summary and some
triable either way, ie triable summarily with the consent of the accused.
Although magistrates have no power to commit for sentence an offender
who is convicted of a purely summary offence, s 56 of the Criminal Justice
Act 1967[2] enables them to commit him for sentence for such an offence if
they are already committing him in respect of some other offence which
though triable either way has been tried summarily. A similar power under
s 56 exists where a summary conviction for an offence triable either way
occurs during the operational period of a suspended sentence earlier
imposed by a magistrates' court.

Example. A is charged with taking a motor car without lawful authority contrary
to s 12 of the Theft Act 1968. This is an offence triable either way. The accused
elects summary trial and pleads 'guilty'. He is also charged with careless driving
which is a purely summary offence. He pleads guilty to that charge. These
offences were committed during the operational period of a suspended sentence
imposed by a magistrates' court. The magistrates can:

(1) commit him under s 38 for the offence of taking a motor vehicle;
(2) commit him under s 56 for the summary offence of careless driving;
(3) commit him under s 56 for the Crown Court to deal with the suspended
sentence.

Where a magistrates' court commits for subsidiary offences under s 56,
the powers of the Crown Court are limited to the punishments which the
magistrates could have imposed. The reason for subsidiary committals is
merely to enable one court to deal at the same time with all the outstanding
offences against the defendant.

PRESENTATION OF PROSECUTION CASE

Where a defendant pleads 'guilty', or has been committed for sentence,
prosecuting counsel outlines the circumstances of the offence to the court
but *does not call evidence*. If the defendant does not dispute the facts against
him this course presents no problem. Where, however, the defendant
admits his guilt but substantially challenges the prosecution account of the
case very severe problems can arise.

Sometimes the problem can be resolved by the prosecution framing an
indictment with alternative counts so that a jury can determine whether the
prosecution version of events is correct. If this is possible, this course *must* be
taken.

Example. C pleaded guilty to buggery with a youth of 19 which is an offence under
s 12 of the Sexual Offences Act 1956 (even if the youth consents). The
prosecution maintained that there was no consent but the youth concerned was

---

2 As amended by the Criminal Law Act 1977 s 46.

forced to submit by terrifying violence. This was contested by the defence. The judge heard evidence and proceeded to sentence on the basis there had been no consent. The House of Lords held this was wrong. Section 12 creates a number of offences, including a specific offence of buggery without consent, and the prosecution should have charged that specific offence so that a jury could have tried the issue whether or not there had been consent[3].

Another example where it would be possible to frame alternative counts in an indictment so that a jury could determine which version of events was correct would be where the prosecution alleged that the accused had wounded intending to cause substantial harm (s 18 of the Offences Against the Person Act 1861) but the defendant, while admitting the wounding, maintained that he had no intent to cause the degree of harm that resulted (and so would only be guilty under s 20).

In very many cases, however, the factual dispute between the prosecution and the defence cannot be resolved by framing alternative counts on an indictment.

Example. Benjamin is charged with unlawful wounding of Eric. The prosecution say that Benjamin, without any provocation, picked a fight with Eric, knocked him to the ground and kicked him in the head while he was lying on the floor. Benjamin admits the assault but says that Eric provoked him beyond endurance and started hitting him and shouting that he was too cowardly to fight back. He then lost control and knocked Eric to the ground and kicked him. Although Benjamin must plead guilty to the offence under s 20 of the Offences Against the Person Act, sentence will obviously depend very much on which version of events the court accepts.

The Court of Appeal has given guidance as to how the issue can be determined where it is not possible to frame alternative counts for a jury:

'The method . . . which could be adopted by the judge in these circumstances is himself to hear the evidence on one side and another, and come to his own conclusion, acting, so to speak, as his own jury on the issue which is the root of the problem. The [other] possibility in these circumstances is for him to hear no evidence but to listen to the submissions of counsel and then come to a conclusion. But if he does that, then . . . where there is a substantial conflict between the two sides he must come down on the side of the defendant. In other words, where there has been a substantial conflict, the version of the defendant must so far as possible be accepted[4].'

Where the court is proceeding to sentence after trial, it will have already heard all the evidence for and against the defendant and so the prosecution will not outline the facts again. The problem discussed above may, however, still occur because the verdict is merely a statement of the defendant's guilt and *not* a reasoned judgment. Thus, it may be that the jury find the defendant guilty, even though they reject the prosecution account of the case. The trial judge, in sentencing the defendant, must make his own decision on the evidence as to what were the true circumstances of the

---

3 *R v Courtie* [1984] AC 463, [1984] 1 All ER 740 per Lord Diplock. 'The question whether the other man had consented or not was one of fact and if, in a trial on indictment, it was disputed, it was a question to be determined by the jury on admissible evidence adduced before them and not to be determined by anyone else.'

4 Per Lord Lane CJ in *R v Newton* (1982) 77 Cr App Rep 13 at 15. It should be noted that what the court must not do is to empanel a jury to try the issue where it is not possible to frame alternative counts: see *R v Milligan* [1982] Crim LR 317.

offence. His decision on this matter can be challenged in the Court of Appeal[5].

THE DEFENDANT'S CHARACTER AND RECORD

The prosecution next present evidence of the defendant's previous convictions and of his general character[6]. A document containing this information is presented to the court and to defence counsel. (The form in common use is set out on pp 22 and 23 in Part one of this book.)

The general rules of evidence do not apply to such information, unless the defendant requires that his previous convictions should be strictly proved. Where the defendant is alleged to be in breach of an order of probation, or conditional discharge, or to have committed an offence during the operational period of a suspended sentence, the circumstances of the earlier conviction must be outlined to the court and he must be asked whether he specifically admits the conviction. If he does not, they must be proved by the production of a certificate of conviction[7].

The prosecution also outline evidence of the defendant's character, for instance, his education, employment, income, commitments and family circumstances. It used to be the practice to include information prejudicial to the accused, such as 'known to associate with violent criminals'. This practice is improper and should never be followed[8].

TAKING OTHER OFFENCES INTO CONSIDERATION

Where a defendant is convicted of a specific offence (or offences) he may ask the court in assessing sentence to take into account other offences which he has committed but for which he has not been tried.

> *Example.* Donald is charged in an indictment containing one count of burglary. He pleads guilty to that count and wishes to admit 20 other offences of a similar nature.

The court will normally accede to such a request. It then passes on the defendant a sentence for the count charged which reflects the fact that the defendant himself admits other offences. He cannot be sentenced to a higher term than the maximum for the offence on the indictment and, although an offence 'taken into consideration' is not technically a conviction, in practice he will never be prosecuted for the offences he has

---

5 *R v Gormley* (1966) 110 Sol Jo 51.
6 See *Practice Direction* [1966] 2 All ER 929, [1966] 1 WLR 1184. Note that although the provisions of the Rehabilitation of Offenders Act 1974 do not strictly apply to criminal proceedings, in practice the courts do not normally consider 'spent' offences. See *Practice Note* [1975] 2 All ER 1072. 'After a verdict of guilty the court must be provided with a statement of the defendant's record for the purposes of sentence. The record supplied should contain all previous convictions, but those which are spent should, so far as is practicable, be marked as such. No one should refer in open court to a spent conviction without the authority of the judge, which authority should not be given unless the interests of justice so require. When passing sentence the judge should make no reference to a spent conviction unless it is necessary so to do for the purpose of explaining the sentence to be passed.'
7 See Police and Criminal Evidence Act 1984 s 73 as to the method to be followed.
8 *R v Robinson* (1969) 53 Cr App Rep 314.

admitted. The procedure in effect enables a convicted defendant to 'wipe the slate clean'.

The procedure in these cases is that the police prepare beforehand a schedule of offences which the defendant wishes taken into consideration stating the date, type of offence and the value of any property concerned. The defendant signs the list if he agrees with that which is set out therein. The defendant's advocate must go through the schedule with the defendant before the hearing to make sure he is accepting that he has committed all the offences listed (and not merely assisting the police to clear their record of unsolved crimes). At the trial, the judge (or presiding magistrate in a magistrates' court) is given the schedule and then asks the defendant if he admits the offences set out and wishes them taken into consideration when sentence is passed[9].

THE SOCIAL ENQUIRY REPORT

In most cases at the Crown Court, and most serious cases at magistrates' courts, a report by an experienced social worker is made available to the tribunal before sentence is passed. The court already has an outline of the accused's background from the police antecedent report, but the social enquiry report is an in-depth enquiry into the defendant's circumstances in order:

(1) to indicate the factors which may have led him into trouble (eg a bad home background, sickness, loss of job);
(2) to suggest his likely response to various sentences (eg probation, suspended sentence).

Most courts pay great attention to such reports; their importance in the process of sentencing cannot be exaggerated. Such reports are generally obligatory in juvenile courts[10], and must normally be obtained by courts imposing immediate custodial sentences on offenders under 21[11] or sentencing adults to imprisonment who have not already served a term[12]. It is surprising that as a general rule, the defence advocate is usually not supplied with a copy of the report before the actual hearing although it is known that the defendant intends to plead guilty.

In theory, the person who has made these reports is available to the court for cross-examination by the defence counsel. In practice (certainly in London) the authors of the reports are not usually present when the report is considered and only in the most exceptional case will the court be asked to adjourn so that they can be present and questioned about what they have said.

---

9 Note: if the defendant has been committed to the Crown Court for sentence having asked in the magistrates' court for offences to be taken into consideration, he must be asked again at the Crown Court whether he still wishes the offences to be taken into consideration. If he does not, those offences are to be ignored: *R v Davies* (1980) 72 Cr App Rep 262.
10 Children and Young Persons Act 1933 s 35(2).
11 Criminal Justice Act 1982 s 2(2).
12 Powers of Criminal Courts Act 1973 s 20A.

PLEA IN MITIGATION

Before sentence the court must allow the defendant or his advocate to plead in mitigation. The plea is one of the most difficult of the arts of the advocate. A knowledge of the tribunal is essential – a suggestion which may appear perfectly sensible to one judge may seem to another judge to be ludicrous beyond belief. The purpose of the plea is to direct the court's attention to such matters as:

(1) *Those circumstances of the offence* which can properly be said to be mitigating – eg that an act was impulsive and not carefully planned, that the accused was gravely provoked, that he was led into trouble by more experienced malefactors or that he only took a peripheral part in the offence.
(2) *Conduct after the offence which indicates contrition* – eg that the defendant made a full and frank confession to the police or has made restitution to his victim.
(3) *The factors in his personal life which indicate an ability to reform* – eg that he has not been in serious trouble before or that he has kept out of trouble for some substantial period since his last conviction or that he has been in regular employment.

No list of these matters could be exhaustive. As a general rule it is sensible for the defence advocate to indicate to the court the sentence or order for which he is contending – although some judges prefer that such a suggestion should be referred to obliquely rather than explicitly stated.

One of the curious features of the English system of sentencing is that the defendant (unless he contests the case and gives evidence) will speak entirely through his advocate. At, for example, the large London Crown Courts a judge may sentence a dozen men in a day without ever hearing any of them give their own account of the charges against them and without questioning any of them. Indeed it is considered wrong for the judge to speak personally to the defendant without requesting counsel's agreement. The result is that the judge has to form an opinion based on depositions, reports and counsel's advocacy and without speaking to the man whose character he is trying to assess. In fact, of course, one can often learn a great deal more about a man in a few moments' questioning than in pages of reports. For this reason, counsel experienced in criminal trials, when they believe their client's personality and desire for reform would impress the court, sometimes apply to call the defendant to give evidence at this stage. Again if the accused's account of the offence, although tantamount to an admission of guilt, differs from that given by the prosecution and is likely to be credible, it may be worth calling him to put forward his version of the facts. It should be remembered, however, that, where the accused is not likely to impress the particular judge deciding the case, such a course may well be counter-productive.

SENTENCE

There is no statutory code which sets out the matters which should determine the appropriate sentence for the defendant, nor would it seem that such a code was a realistic possibility. It seems fairly clear however, that each of the following matters is of relevance:

(1) *The court's duty to protect the public*: the courts claim that this is their primary duty. Thus, there will be some offences (serious breaches of public duty by a responsible official or vicious crimes of violence) where the court's duty to protect society overrides the personal circumstances of the defendant. The same is true where the defendant's record shows that he is of particular danger to other people (eg persistent sex offenders).

(2) *The punishment of the offender*: Victorian judges (such as Fitzjames-Stephen) firmly believed that the courts were bound to express society's loathing of crime by punishing the offender – in the sense of inflicting suffering on him as retribution for his offence. Such a theory is seldom used to justify sentences today although, of course, it could be said to be the concealed rationale of many sentences which are ostensibly supported on other grounds.

(3) *The reform of the defendant*: in modern times the courts and Parliament have increasingly come to recognise that crime may be the product of poverty and misfortune. The result has been that the courts are now normally concerned that the sentence passed will help to achieve the reform of the offender.

(4) *Deterrence*: the courts have persistently increased sentences where particular crimes have become prevalent in order to discourage other offenders (eg the sentences of imprisonment passed during 1985 on persons involved in supplying class A drugs such as heroin and cocaine).

The eventual sentence may be the product of two or more of the above factors.

When the court passes sentence on an offender the judge will usually deliver a homily which indicates the matters which he has considered in determining the correct sentence. However, this is nothing like a reasoned explanation by the court of the sentence it has imposed. It is submitted that the absence of a short but clear explanation is to be regretted and that natural justice requires that a man who is being sentenced should hear a reasoned judgment indicating what the court has felt were the essential factors in his case and why the sentence imposed is considered appropriate.

SUMMARY OF PROCEDURE AT CROWN COURT AND MAGISTRATES' COURT

It might be helpful at this stage to repeat in summary form the procedure at the Crown Court on sentence:

(1) Where defendant pleads guilty or appeals against sentence or has been committed for sentence, prosecution explain their version of the facts.

(2) Police give evidence of defendant's previous convictions and general character. Defendant asked to admit breaches of probation and conditional discharge and suspended sentences.

(3) Defendant may ask for other outstanding offences to be taken into consideration.

(4) Social enquiry and other reports.

(5) Plea in mitigation.

(6) Sentence.

The procedure at a magistrates' court is in practice identical to that which has been described as operating in the Crown Court. *Note* – where sentences of imprisonment are imposed on an offender charged with more than one offence the sentences may be consecutive (ie run after one another) or concurrent (run together).

Powers available to all courts

Age group	Non-custodial	Custodial

10 and under 14	Absolute/conditional discharge
	    Bind over ⎱
	    Fine ⎬ normally to be paid by parent or guardian.
	    Compensation Order ⎰
	Supervision Order (with or without added requirements).
	Attendance Centre Order (for boys in most areas; girls only in some).
	Care Order (to which a charge and control condition may be attached following a subsequent offence).	

14 and under 17	Absolute/conditional discharge
	    Bind over ⎱
	    Fine ⎬ normally to be paid by parent or guardian.
	    Compensation Order ⎰
	Supervision Order (with or without added requirements).
	Attendance Centre Order (for boys in most areas; girls only in some).
	Care Order (to which a charge and control condition may be attached following a subsequent offence).
	Community Service Order (for 16 year olds only).
		Detention Centre Order (for boys only)
		
		Youth Custody (for 15 and 16 year olds only)

17 and under 21	Absolute/conditional discharge
	    Bind over
	    Fine
	    Compensation Order.
	Probation Order (with or without added requirements).
	Attendance Centre Order (in some areas only).
	Community Service Order.
		Detention Centre Order (for boys only)
		
		Youth Custody

21 and over	Absolute/conditional discharge
	    Bind over
	    Fine
	    Compensation Order.
	Probation Order (with or without added requirements).
	Community Service Order.
		Imprisonment

Source: *The Sentence of the Court* (4th edn, 1986) HMSO. Reproduced with the permission of the Controller of Her Majesty's Stationery Office.

Chapter 12

Imprisonment

RESTRICTIONS ON IMPRISONMENT

The ultimate sanction of the criminal law is the deprivation of the offender's liberty. Such a course inevitably creates substantial problems. Firstly, it normally involves hardship and suffering to the offender's family and his dependants. Secondly, the offender is placed into a close-knit society of fellow criminals so that, particularly if he is not yet an experienced wrongdoer, he is liable to corruption. Finally, there is the disruption to the offender's own life: upon his release, he may find that his family has broken up, that he has nowhere to live, and that there is no place for him with his former employers. These circumstances may lead him back to crime. Since young offenders and persons who have not been to prison before are particularly vulnerable in these respects, the law places a number of restrictions on the powers of the criminal courts to impose sentences of imprisonment. These restrictions can be summarised as follows:

(1) No person under the age of 21 can be sent to prison[1]. This rule does not prevent the court remanding a young offender to prison pending the final disposal of his case. (It should, of course, be noted that the court may send such an offender to a custodial regime such as a detention centre or youth custody where he may find the conditions more onerous than they would be in prison.)

(2) No adult is to be sentenced to imprisonment who has not already served a prison term unless the court is 'of opinion that no other method of dealing with him is appropriate'[2].

(3) The court is not to come to such a conclusion unless it has first obtained a social enquiry report[3]. In some cases, the court may sentence without such a report if it is of opinion it is unnecessary to obtain one; this would be the case in the Crown Court where the only possible disposal was imprisonment. It could very seldom be the case in a magistrates' court and for that reason, when magistrates sentence to imprisonment

---

1 Criminal Justice Act 1982 s 1(1).
2 Powers of Criminal Courts Act 1973 s 20(1). Note: this provision is wider than appears from the text, in that it applies not only to a court passing an immediate sentence but also to courts passing suspended sentences.
3 Powers of Criminal Courts Act 1973 s 20A(1).

without obtaining a report, they must state their reasons for doing so in open court[4].

(4) The court is not to pass a sentence of imprisonment on a person who has not already been to prison unless he is legally represented[5]. This rule does not apply if he refuses legal aid or is ineligible because of his means.

RESTRICTIONS ON LENGTH OF SENTENCE

As a general rule a magistrates' court can only sentence an offender to a maximum term of *six months* for any one offence[6]. Where magistrates are dealing with more than one offence the total of the individual terms imposed must not exceed 12 months[7]. The minimum term which can be imposed by a magistrates' court is five days[8]; if the magistrates wish to impose a shorter period, they must order the offender to be detained in police custody (for up to four days) or in the courthouse or police station (up to 8.00 pm on day of sentence)[9].

The maximum powers of the Crown Court are normally set out in the statute creating the offence in question. In murder cases the court is obliged to pass a sentence of imprisonment for life, although the judge may recommend a minimum period which should elapse before the Secretary of State considers the release of the defendant on licence[10]. As stated above, in other cases the maximum term is normally defined by statute. Some examples are given in the table below:

Offence	Max Term	Statute
Manslaughter	Life	Offences Against the Person Act 1861 s 5
Wounding with intent	Life	Ibid s 18
Unlawful wounding	5 years	Ibid s 20 (as amended by Criminal Justice Act 1948 s 1(1))
Assault, occasioning actual bodily harm	5 years	Ibid s 47
Common assault	1 year	Ibid s 47
Assault on police	6 months	Police Act 1964 s 51
Carrying offensive weapons	2 years	Prevention of Crime Act 1953
Robbery	Life	Theft Act 1968 s 8
Burglary	14 years	Ibid s 9(4)
Theft	10 years	Ibid s 7
Obtaining property by deception	10 years	Ibid s 15
Obtaining pecuniary advantage by deception	5 years	Ibid s 16
Taking a conveyance	3 years	Ibid s 12(2)
Obtaining services by deception	5 years	Theft Act 1978 ss 1 and 4
Making off without payment	2 years	Theft Act 1978, ss 3 and 4

4 Ibid s 20A(3).
5 Ibid s 21(1).
6 Magistrates' Courts Act 1980 s 31(1).
7 Ibid s 133(2) – one of the offences must have been triable either way.
8 Ibid s 132.
9 Ibid ss 134 and 135.
10 Murder (Abolition of Death Penalty) Act 1965.

Offence	Max Term	Statute
Handling stolen goods	14 years	Theft Act 1968 s 22(2)
Going equipped to steal	3 years	Ibid s 25
Criminal damage	10 years	Criminal Damage Act 1971 s 4
Arson	Life	Ibid s 4
Rape	Life	Sexual Offenders Act 1956 s 37
Unlawful intercourse with girl under 16	2 years	Ibid s 37
Unlawful intercourse with girl under 13	Life	Ibid s 37
Possession of class A controlled drug (eg heroin, cocaine)	7 years	Misuse of Drugs Act 1971 s 5(2)
Possession of class B drug (eg cannabis or amphetamine)	5 years	Ibid s 5(2)
Possession of class A or B drug with intent to supply others or supplying the same	Life	Controlled Drugs (Penalties) Act 1985 s 2(1)

The table above sets out examples of the *maximum* sentences which the Crown Court can impose. Where an offender is convicted of conspiracy[11] or of an attempt, the sentence passed must not be greater than for the substantive offence[12].

The actual use of imprisonment can be seen from the table on p 235 which shows the number of persons sentenced to imprisonment by the courts in 1984 in various categories of indictable offence. It will be seen from the table that the majority of the prison population are serving sentences for burglary or offences of dishonesty (but with a sizeable proportion for offences of violence). The average cost of keeping an offender in prison in 1982/83 was £11,336 per annum. In 1984 28.1 per cent of all adults convicted at the Crown Court were sent to prison.

THE PRISON SYSTEM

Once the court has sentenced an offender to a term of imprisonment, the regime to which he is to be subjected is entirely a matter for the Home Office and the Prison Service. All prisoners are sent initially to a *local prison* (such as Wormwood Scrubs or the old county gaols like Oxford Prison). If a prisoner is serving a short-term sentence of, for instance, six months, he will normally serve the whole of his sentence in the local prison. For other offenders, the local prison acts as a classifying centre from which they are sent to long-term prisons. Conditions in local prisons are generally recognised to be unsatisfactory. The prisoners are kept two or three to a cell, often without sanitation. They may be confined to these cells for up to 16 hours in every day and have only the most limited opportunities for association and recreation.

11 See Criminal Law Act 1977 s 3.
12 Criminal Attempts Act 1981 s 4.

Long or medium-term prisoners are sent from the local prison to *closed* or *open* prisons. Over 80 per cent of such prisoners will go to *closed* prisons for the whole of their term. These establishments vary among themselves in the type of regime and degree of security to which the prisoner is subjected. Less than 20 per cent of convicted prisoners are sent for the whole, or part of their sentence, to *open* prisons. These prisons are run more along the lines of army camps so that the prisoners eat together, have substantial periods of recreation and sleep in unlocked dormitories or cubicles[13].

All prisoners automatically receive one-third remission of sentence at the commencement of imprisonment[14]. They may subsequently lose part, or all, of this remission for misbehaviour. Thus, the prisoner knows at the commencement of his sentence that he will be released after serving two-thirds of the term imposed by the court provided he does not lose remission. The rules made under the Prison Act 1952 provide that offences against discipline are to be heard in the first instance by the prison governor (who can order forfeiture of remission for up to 28 days). More serious cases are referred to the Board of Visitors[15] who can order forfeiture of remission for a period of 180 days[16].

On release, all prisoners are entitled to make use of the after-care facilities provided by the probation service, but few do so in fact. As stated earlier, the prisoner is particularly vulnerable on his release because he may have little money, he may well be unable to find employment by himself and he may find that his family unit has broken up. Since the after-care system is voluntary, many ex-prisoners do not take advantage of it and are without supervision when they are particularly in need of help and particularly liable to get into further trouble. One attempt to solve this has been the hostel system, whereby prisoners prior to release are allowed to work out in the community. The other method is the parole system.

13 As to conditions in prison see Cross *Punishment, Prison and the Public* (Stevens, 1971); Tony Parker *The Frying Pan* (1970); *People in Prison* (1969) Cmnd 4214.

14 Prison Rules 1964, SI 1964/388, r 5 (does not apply to life prisoners or sentences of under 35 days).

15 The Board has a dual function. Under s 6(3) of the Prison Act 1952 the members are 'to pay frequent visits to the prison and hear any complaints which may be made by the prisoner and report to the Secretary of State any matter which they consider it expedient to report': they also have the function of adjudicating on serious breaches of discipline. It should be noted that under r 47 of the Prison Rules 1964 an offence against discipline occurs where a prisoner makes 'any false or malicious allegation against an officer' or repeatedly makes 'groundless complaints'. One therefore has at present the situation where the complaints tribunal may later be punishing an unsuccessful complainant by depriving him of his liberty.

16 Note: the Divisional Court may interfere with the findings of the Board of Visitors where there has been a failure to observe the rules of natural justice by, for example, not providing the opportunity to a prisoner to call witnesses or not considering applications for legal representation in serious cases: see *R v Hull Prison Board of Visitors, ex p St Germain* [1979] QB 425, [1979] 1 All ER 701, CA and *R v Secretary of State for the Home Department, ex p Tarrant* [1985] QB 251, [1984] 1 All ER 799. Judicial review is not available in respect of decisions by the governor – the prisoner's remedy is to appeal to the Board of Visitors: *R v Deputy Governor of Camp-hill Prison, ex p King* [1985] QB 735, [1984] 3 All ER 897, CA.

Sentences of Imprisonment Passed by Magistrates' Courts and Crown Court in 1984

Category of offence	Total no of offenders	Total sentences unsuspended	Total partially suspended	Total suspended	Unsuspended %	Partially suspended %	Suspended %
Violence	47,900	4,200	500	3,100	9	1	7
Sexual offences	5,600	1,000	200	500	20	3	8
Burglary	72,800	9,900	800	4,100	14	1	6
Robbery	4,300	1,500	100	100	36	2	2
Theft and handling	219,200	12,700	1,300	10,800	6	1	5
Fraud and forgery	25,800	3,000	600	3,100	12	2	12
Criminal damage	11,500	800	100	500	7	1	4
Motoring	29,200	2,600	100	2,500	9	0	9
Other offences	33,600	3,500	300	1,600	10	1	5
Total of offences	449,800	39,400	3,900	26,300	9	1	6

Source: *Judicial Statistics* (1984)

THE PAROLE SYSTEM

Since it is difficult, if not impossible, to train a person to become a responsible member of society in the wholly artificial and restricted environment of a prison, and a sudden transition from prison to society without support may actually impair the chances of reforming the offender, Parliament has introduced a system whereby an offender may be permitted to serve part of his sentence under supervision in the community. This provision has the advantage that the total period of imprisonment is reduced while the offender is assisted in settling back into normal life.

Section 60 of the Criminal Justice Act 1967 enables the Home Secretary to release a prisoner who has served at least one-third of his sentence (or six months if that expires later) on a licence which will last until he would otherwise have been granted remission[17]. The procedure is that each prison has attached to it a *local review committee* which normally includes the governor, a magistrate and a probation officer. This committee will consider the cases of all prisoners who are about to be eligible for parole or who have been refused parole in the previous year and are eligible to be reconsidered. The local committee then reports to the *Parole Board* (which must include a judge, a psychiatrist, a person experienced in the after-care of prisoners and a criminologist) which makes the final recommendation to the Home Secretary. Provision has been made in the Act of 1972 for the Home Secretary to release certain classes of offenders on the recommendation of the *local review committee* alone[18]. It should be noted that the Home Secretary is not bound by the recommendations of the Parole Board and may still refuse to release a prisoner despite a recommendation. In 1983 the then Home Secretary announced that parole would be withheld from prisoners serving five years' imprisonment or longer for offences of violence or drug trafficking. The substantial criticism which can be made at the way in which the system operates at present is that the prisoner who is unsuccessful is not told why his application for parole has been refused although he knows he can make a further application. This lack of information (together with the fact that most prisoners because of discretionary parole are unaware when their sentence will end) contributes to the tension and unhappiness of the prison community.

If the paroled prisoner after release does not co-operate with the supervising officer, for instance by wilfully failing to keep in regular employment or associating with criminals, the Board may recommend his recall to prison and the Home Secretary may revoke his licence[19]. In extreme cases, the Home Secretary may revoke the licence without a recommendation from the Board. Where the paroled prisoner is convicted of further offences by the Crown Court, that court may revoke his licence. If he is convicted of an indictable offence tried summarily by a magistrates' court, they may commit him to the Crown Court for revocation of his licence.

---

17 Criminal Justice Act 1967 s 61 empowers the Secretary of State to release on licence persons sentenced to imprisonment for life or detained under the Children and Young Persons Act 1933 s 53.
18 Criminal Justice Act 1972 s 35. As to the operation of the system, see Sarah McCabe 'The Powers and Purposes of the Parole Board' [1985] Crim LR 489.
19 Criminal Justice Act 1967 s 62(1).

THE ACTUAL LENGTH OF SENTENCE

The above discussion shows that, in effect, the sentence imposed by the court is a statement of the maximum length of time for which the prisoner can be detained. From this there is an automatic reduction of one-third remission for good conduct and a possible further one-third reduction under the parole scheme. If the offender has spent time in custody on remand before being sentenced, that time counts in calculating his release date and his eligibility for remission unless he was at the same time in custody on other charges.

NEED FOR SHORTER SENTENCES

Until recently the courts worked on the basis that short-term sentences (ie sentences for a few months) were not usually appropriate even for first offenders and so it very seldom happened that a judge, having decided to impose a custodial sentence, would specify a term less than six months. However it is now generally recognised that:

(1) it is the first few weeks of a man's sentence which are most likely to have a deterrent effect upon him, and

(2) there is no evidence to suggest that further periods spent in prison are reformative (although they may, of course, be necessary for other reasons).

For this reason the Advisory Council on the Penal System have recommended to the Home Secretary and to the courts that greater use should be made of short-term sentences and that, as a general matter of policy, the length of all short and medium-term sentences should be reduced:

> 'While a much higher proportion of offenders than ever before is being dealt with by non-custodial methods, there has not been any corresponding reduction in the average length of sentence served by those offenders who receive terms of immediate imprisonment. Given, however, that there is no reason to suppose that longer sentences have a greater impact upon the prisoner than shorter ones, the general rule which we advocate for all courts to follow is to stop at the point where a sentence has been decided upon and consider whether a shorter one would not do just as well . . . Research findings up till now indicate that shorter sentences are no less effective than longer ones. Unless and until there is evidence to the contrary, it will be both logical and economical to reduce the length of sentences in the middle and lower ranges. A general lowering of sentence lengths need not disturb the relativity of individual sentences; existing distinctions between different offenders and different offences could still be successfully maintained. Although in our final report we hope to make recommendations for a new system of maximum penalties, at this juncture we wish merely to pose a few simple questions. Are there not cases of two years' imprisonment where 18 months or 15 or even less, might safely be passed, and sentences of 12 months when six months would do just as well? And for the offender going to prison for the first time, should not an even shorter sentence suffice?'

This recommendation has now been implemented by the courts; in the important case of *Bibi*[20] Lord Lane gave the following general guidance to sentences:

20 *R v Bibi* (1980) 71 Cr App Rep 360, [1980] Crim LR 732.

'It is no secret that our prisons at the moment are dangerously overcrowded, so much so that sentencing courts must be particularly careful to examine each case to ensure, if an immediate custodial sentence is necessary, that the sentence is as short as possible, consistent only with the duty to protect the interests of the public and to punish and deter the criminal.

Many offenders can be dealt with equally justly and effectively by a sentence of six or nine months' imprisonment as by one of 18 months or three years. We have in mind not only the obvious case of the first offender for whom any prison sentence however short may be an adequate punishment and deterrent, but other types of case as well.

The less serious types of factory or shop-breaking; the minor cases of sexual indecency; the more petty frauds where small amounts of money are involved; the fringe participant in more serious crime: all these are examples of cases where the shorter sentence would be appropriate.

There are, on the other hand, some offences for which, generally speaking, only the medium or longer sentences will be appropriate. For example, most robberies; most offences involving serious violence; use of a weapon to wound; burglary of private dwelling-houses; planned crime for wholesale profit; active large scale trafficking in dangerous drugs. These are only examples. It would be impossible to set out a catalogue of those offences which do and those which do not merit more severe treatment. So much will, obviously, depend upon the circumstances of each individual offender and each individual offence.

What the court can and should do is to ask itself whether there is any compelling reason why a short sentence should not be passed. We are not aiming at uniformity of sentence; that would be impossible. We are aiming at uniformity of approach.'

SUSPENDED SENTENCES

(a) When appropriate

A court which imposes a sentence of imprisonment for a term of two years or less may order that such sentence should not come into effect if the defendant refrains from the commission of further offences during a stated period. It has already been said that imprisonment is in reality the ultimate sanction of the criminal law. The suspended sentence must, therefore, be seen as the last chance offered to the offender before this ultimate sanction is brought into effect. For this reason a suspended sentence must not be passed unless the court has already determined that all other forms of non-custodial sentence are inappropriate. Thus, s 22(2) of the Powers of Criminal Courts Act 1973 provides that an offender shall not be dealt with by means of a suspended sentence 'unless the case appears to the court to be one in which a sentence of imprisonment would have been appropriate in the absence of any power to suspend such a sentence'[1].

(b) The power to suspend a sentence

The basic power is contained in s 22(1) of the Powers of Criminal Courts Act 1973, which enables the court to order that a sentence of two years' imprisonment or less may be suspended for a period of not less than one year and not exceeding two years. The section provides:

1 See *R v O'Keefe* [1969] 2 QB 29, [1969] 1 All ER 426: the court must initially decide that none of the non-custodial remedies (fine, probation, etc) are appropriate; it must then decide the appropriate length of sentence for the offence and if that sentence is less than two years, it should then consider whether or not immediate imprisonment is necessary.

'. . . a court which passes a sentence of imprisonment for a term of not more than two years for an offence may order that the sentence shall not take effect unless, during a period specified in the order, being not less than one year or more than two years from the date of the order, the offender commits in Great Britain another offence punishable with imprisonment and thereafter a court having power to do so orders . . . that the original sentence shall take effect. . .'

Where a suspended sentence is passed on an offender the court must explain to him in ordinary language that if, during the operational period of the suspended sentence, he commits any further offence punishable with imprisonment, then, whatever happens to him for the subsequent offence, he will normally have to serve the term of the sentence at present suspended. It should be noted, therefore, that the sentence which is to be suspended must be appropriate for the offence in question; it should not be made larger than it would otherwise be because it is to be suspended[2].

Where a defendant is charged with two or more offences, the question arises whether the court can pass a suspended sentence for one offence and some other sentence for the other offences. The Court of Appeal has laid down the following guidelines[3]:

(1) The court should not pass a suspended sentence for one offence if at the same time:
   (a) it is passing an immediate custodial sentence,
   (b) it is proposing to make a community service order for another offence[4], or
   (c) it is proposing to deal with the other offence by way of a probation order[5].
(2) The court may pass a suspended sentence for one offence and at the same time deal with another offence by way of:
   (a) fine (but special care must be taken to see the fine is well within the offender's means)[6],
   (b) another suspended sentence (which may be concurrent or consecutive)[7].

(c) Commission of further offence

The basic rule is that where an offender commits an offence during the operational period of a suspended sentence, that sentence *must* be brought into effect, to run consecutively to any other sentence of imprisonment imposed at the same time. If this was not so, the concept of a suspended sentence as the ultimate punishment short of immediate imprisonment would lose most of its effect.

Where the offender has committed a further offence, the correct procedure is for the court to determine first the appropriate sentence for

2 See Advisory Council's *Interim Report on the Penal System* (1977) para 14: 'Are not many suspended sentences longer than the sentence would have been if it had been immediate, and in many such cases, does not the eventual activation of the suspended sentence without any reduction in its length create a situation where the total sentence is too long?'
3 *R v Sapiano* (1968) 52 Cr App Rep 674.
4 *R v Starie* (1979) 68 Cr App Rep 239. As to the imposition of a community service order on a person already subject to a suspended sentence, see [1979] Crim LR 731 (commentary).
5 Powers of Criminal Courts Act 1973 s 22(3).
6 *R v King* [1970] 2 All ER 249, 54 Cr App Rep 362.
7 *R v Wilkinson* [1970] 3 All ER 439, [1970] 1 WLR 1319. Note the sentences must state whether the terms are to be concurrent or consecutive; if consecutive, they must not exceed two years in aggregate.

that further offence[8]. The court will then deal with the suspended sentence and *must* make an order that the suspended sentence should take effect (with the original term unaltered) unless the court is of opinion that it would be unjust to do so in view of all the circumstances including the facts of the subsequent offence, and where it is of that opinion, the court should state its reasons (s 23(1)).

In the exceptional cases where the court determines that it would be unjust to bring the suspended sentence into force it may:

(1) order the sentence should take effect but for a lesser term;
(2) vary the original sentence by imposing a new operational period expiring not later than two years from the date of the variation;
(3) make no order at all.

Where the court imposes a new operational period or decides to make no specific order it may at that time add to the suspended sentence a supervision order[9]. It is not possible to give a comprehensive definition of the circumstances where the court would consider it unjust to bring a suspended sentence into effect. If the court is not imposing a custodial sentence for the further offence, it will probably be disposed to find a reason for not activating the suspended sentence – particularly if the subsequent offence is of a different character from the offence for which the suspended sentence was given[10]. However, the mere fact that the subsequent offence is of a different type from the first offence is not *of itself* a ground for not bringing the suspended sentence into effect[11]. It should be noted that, where the court imposes probation for the subsequent offence, this does not rank as a 'conviction', and so no question arises of activating the suspended sentence[12].

The Crown Court has power to bring into effect a suspended sentence passed by any court. Magistrates may bring into effect suspended sentences imposed by themselves or some other magistrates' court. Where, however, they have convicted a person who is under a suspended sentence imposed by the Crown Court, they cannot deal with that sentence themselves but must either commit him to the Crown Court or notify that court of his subsequent conviction.

(d) Suspended sentence supervision orders
Where a suspended sentence is imposed, the court works on the basis that the threat of imprisonment hanging over the offender may in itself be a sufficient deterrent to keep him out of trouble. Experience suggests that in the case of socially inadequate offenders and those who have serious personal, domestic or employment problems, the suspended sentence deterrent is not likely to be effective unless it is coupled with support and assistance from the probation service. For this reason, s 26 of the Powers of Criminal Courts Act 1973 enables the court to order that an offender upon

8 See *R v Ithell* [1969] 2 All ER 449, [1969] 1 WLR 272.
9 Powers of Criminal Courts Act 1973 s 26(10). See below.
10 See *R v Moylan* [1970] 1 QB 143, [1969] 3 All ER 783.
11 *R v Saunders* (1970) 54 Cr App Rep 247.
12 *R v Tarry* [1970] 2 QB 560, [1970] 2 All ER 185. This is because a suspended sentence will only be brought into effect if the defendant is *convicted* of a subsequent offence; where a person is found guilty of an offence but is placed on probation or given an absolute or conditional discharge he is deemed in law *not* to have been convicted: Powers of Criminal Courts Act 1973 s 13.

whom has been passed a suspended sentence of not less than six months' imprisonment shall be placed under the supervision of a supervising officer. The offender is under a duty to keep in touch with the supervising officer in accordance with his instructions. If he disobeys these instructions, or fails to notify any change of address, he may be brought before his local magistrates' court and fined up to £400. However, there is no power to punish him if he fails to take the advice offered, or to keep in regular employment, or generally to be of good behaviour. To this extent, supervision differs from a probation order and must be seen merely as an ancillary to the suspended sentence, and not as a form of punishment or treatment, in itself.

PARTLY SUSPENDED SENTENCES

Where a court decides that an offender must be sent to prison, it may order that only part of the term imposed need be served and that the remainder may be held in suspense. Section 47 of the Criminal Law Act 1977[13] provides that:

(a) the total term of the sentence must be not less than three months and not more than two years;
(b) the part of the sentence to be served immediately shall be not less than 28 days;
(c) the part held in suspense shall be not less than one-quarter of the whole term.

If during the period of suspension the offender is convicted of a further offence the court may order him to serve the suspended portion of his sentence in addition to any other sentence then passed[14]. If this would be unjust in view of all the circumstances (including the facts of the subsequent offence) the court may instead order that he serves a shorter term or make no order at all (in which case the suspended sentence remains in force).

The power is intended to be used as an alternative to a normal sentence of imprisonment and not as an alternative to a wholly suspended sentence. In other words, the court must have decided that the offence is too grave to deal with by a suspended sentence before it passes on to consider a partly suspended sentence. The Court of Appeal has provided guidelines as to how the courts should approach a case where a partly suspended sentence seems appropriate[15]:

'Before imposing a partly suspended sentence the court should ask itself the following question: first of all, is this a case where a custodial sentence is really necessary? If it is not, it should pass a non-custodial sentence; but if it is necessary then the court should ask itself, second, this: can we make a community service order as an equivalent to imprisonment, or can we suspend the whole sentence? That problem requires very careful consideration. It is easy to slip into a partly

13 As amended by the Criminal Justice Act 1982 s 30.
14 Criminal Law Act 1977 s 47(3). Note: if the partly suspended sentence was imposed by the Crown Court and during the suspension period the offender is convicted of a further offence by a magistrates' court, that court must either commit him (in custody or on bail) to the Crown Court to deal with the partly suspended sentence or notify the Crown Court (Criminal Law Act 1977 Sch 9 para 2). If the offender is convicted by a magistrates' court during the period of suspension of a sentence imposed by another magistrates' court, the court considering the further offence can deal with the partly suspended sentence.
15 *R v Clarke* [1982] 3 All ER 232, (1982) 75 Cr App Rep 119, CA.

suspended sentence because the court does not have the courage of its own convictions. That temptation must be resisted. If it is possible to make a community service order or to suspend the whole of the sentence, then of course that should be done. If not, then the third point arises: what is the shortest sentence the court can properly impose? In many cases, of which an obvious example is the case of the first offender for whom a short term of imprisonment is a sufficient shock, without any suspension, that would be enough. Sometimes 14 or 28 days may suffice . . . In that case that should be the order of the court, without any partial suspension at all. The imposition of a very short term will also make possible the ordering of a fine or a compensation order in addition, when such a course is appropriate.

If imprisonment is necessary, and if a very short sentence is not enough, and if it is not appropriate to suspend the sentence altogether, then partial suspension should be considered. Great care must be taken to ensure that the power is not used in a way which may serve to increase the length of sentence. It is not possible satisfactorily to forecast the precise way in which the provisions of s 47 might be used. In general the type of case that we have in mind is where the gravity of the offence is such that at least six months' imprisonment is merited, but when there are mitigating circumstances which point towards a measure of leniency not sufficient to warrant total suspension. Examples are always dangerous, but we venture very tentatively to suggest a few: first of all, some serious "one-off" acts of violence which are usually met with immediate terms of imprisonment; some cases of burglary which at present warrant 18 months' or two years' imprisonment, where the offender is suitably qualified in terms of his record; some cases of fraud on public departments or some credit card frauds, where a short immediate sentence would be insufficient; some cases of handling involving medium-range sums of money; some thefts involving breach of trust; some cases of stealing from employers. All these are examples of cases where it may be possible to suspend part of the sentence without harm to the public and with benefit to the prisoner.

We would like to echo the words of the Home Office Advisory Council on the Penal System in their *Sentences of Imprisonment; a review of maximum penalties* (1978) para 282:

". . . we view the partially suspended sentence as a legitimate means of exploiting one of the few reliable pieces of criminological knowledge that many offenders sent to prison for the first time do not subsequently re-offend. We see it not as a means of administering a 'short, sharp shock', nor as a substitute for a wholly suspended sentence, but as especially applicable to serious first offenders or first-time prisoners who are bound to have to serve some time in prison, but who may well be effectively deterred by eventually serving only a small part of even the minimum sentence appropriate to the offence. This, in our view, must be its principal role."

We would like to add another type of offender: prisoners whose last term of imprisonment was some considerable time ago. We think that the power can be used on occasions where something more than a short sentence of immediate imprisonment is required to mark public disapproval and as a deterrent to others, but where the circumstances of the particular offender are such that some short term of immediate imprisonment, coupled with the threat involved in the suspension of the remainder, is enough to punish him for what he has done and to deter him in the future.'

It should be noted that:

(a) it is undesirable for the court to pass an immediate sentence on one count and a consecutive sentence partly suspended on another count[16].

16 *R v McCarthy* [1983] Crim LR 201. The court is entitled to treat the consecutive sentences as one term by virtue of s 57(2) of the Powers of Criminal Courts Act 1973 and Criminal Justice Act 1982 Sch 14.

The correct course is to treat the consecutive terms as a single term and provide that part of that aggregate term is to be suspended;

(b) the court cannot make a probation order at the same time that it is passing a partly suspended sentence for some other offence[17]. There is also no power to provide that an offender shall be under supervision during the period of suspension.

EXTENDED SENTENCES

Where the court is dealing with a particularly grave crime the offence itself will be the paramount factor in determining the appropriate sentence. The table set out earlier in this chapter shows that the court generally has power to impose very substantial terms of imprisonment in such circumstances.

In other cases, however, the length of the sentence will depend on both the nature of the offence and the offender's previous record. In some such cases the record will be the paramount factor because it will indicate that the court is dealing with a persistent offender – a person who habitually commits crime (sometimes of a relatively minor nature), and who does not appear to be deterred by the sentences already passed upon him. The law makes special provisions for such recidivists by:

(1) permitting the court to sentence them to a term which exceeds the statutory maximum for the offence (e g a sentence of five years might be imposed on an habitual burglar on a charge of going equipped for theft which would normally only carry a maximum sentence of three years);

(2) enabling the Secretary of State to direct that they should be on licence and subject to recall for the whole length of their sentence (i e that even after the date when they would otherwise have been released on remission under supervision they are liable to be brought back to prison).

In order to achieve either, or both of these results, the court, in passing sentence, must certify that it is for an extended term within s 25 of the Powers of Criminal Courts Act 1973. Such a certificate may be issued if:

(1) the accused has now been convicted of an offence punishable with imprisonment for two years or more;

(2) he is a persistent offender as defined in s 28[18];

(3) it is expedient to protect the public from him for a substantial period[19].

---

17 Criminal Law Act 1977 Sch 9 para 1.
18 Section 28(3) sets out the relevant condition. Section 28(2) enables a sentence to be extended to ten years where the statutory maximum is less than ten years and to not more than five years if the maximum is less than five years.
19 The theory behind such sentences is discussed in *DPP v Ottewell* [1970] AC 642, [1968] 3 All ER 153. The point to note is that an extended sentence may be for a term less than the statutory maximum but greater than would be normal for the offence but for the offender's record.

The use of this provision has declined rapidly since its introduction and it would seem that there should be a more flexible system of securing supervision of recidivists after their release from custody.

Chapter 13

Non-custodial sentences upon adults

PROBATION

(a) The power to make an order
Where a court is of opinion that an offender aged 17 or over does not merit a
sentence of imprisonment and yet is in need of continuing support and
assistance if he is to re-establish himself as a law-abiding member of the
community, that court may, instead of sentencing him, order that he should
be placed on probation for a fixed period during which he will be supervised
by an experienced social worker.

The power to make a probation order is provided by s 2 of the Powers of
Criminal Courts Act 1973. The procedure when the court is minded to
make such an order is as follows:

(1) The court explains to the offender:
    (a) his obligations under the proposed order including any special
        conditions which will be attached to it; and
    (b) that he is liable to be sentenced for his present offence if he fails to
        comply with the terms of the order or commits a further offence.
(2) The offender must specifically agree to the order being made.
(3) The court then makes the order *instead* of passing sentence. The court
    must specify the period of the order which must not be less than six
    months and not exceed three years[1].
(4) Where the court is not the magistrates' court for the area in which the
    offender resides, a copy of the order is sent to that court which then
    becomes the supervising court.

(b) Conditions attached to the order
The court has a general power under s 2(3) to require the probationer to
comply with *such requirements as (it) . . . considers necessary for securing the good
conduct of the offender or for preventing a repetition by him of the same offence or the
commission of other offences*[2]. Under this provision, the court commonly
requires the probationer to be of good behaviour and lead an industrious

---

1 Note: Criminal Law Act 1977 s 57, enables the Home Secretary to amend the statutory
   periods set out in the Powers of Criminal Courts Act 1973.
2 Although the court has no power to make a condition of a probation order requiring the
   defendant to compensate his victim, in effect this can be achieved by making an order
   under s 35 of the Powers of Criminal Courts Act 1973 at the same time as the probation
   order. See p 252 below.

life, to notify the probation officer of any change of address, to keep in touch with the probation officer in accordance with such instructions as he may from time to time give and, if the officer so requires it, to receive visits from him at the probationer's home. In addition to these general conditions, the court, in appropriate cases, may order:

(1) That the probationer should reside at a *specified hostel* or home or institution[3]. The probationer is not in custody and will be free to go out to work every day and to leave the hostel in the evenings and at weekends for recreation:

> 'They are suitable for offenders who have a number of previous convictions, including some who have served periods in custody. Social and emotional inadequacy is likely to be a common factor among these offenders, who will also include some limited and irresponsible people who, by reason of their background, are likely to be socially disorganised and to lack community and family support. In many instances offenders will be without home ties or permanent roots in any particular place, and in such cases an important aspect of a hostel's rehabilitation programme will be the recognition and fostering of any ties, however tenuous, which may be developed. Hostel placements, however, are unlikely to be suitable for the most serious offenders or those who by reason of their personal and emotional disturbances or their addiction to alcohol or drugs need a degree of care or containment which it is not possible to provide in a hostel[4].'

(2) That the probationer should attend a *day training centre*[5]. These centres are being established under the provisions of s 4 of the Powers of Criminal Courts Act 1973 and are intended to provide short-term intensive training for socially inadequate offenders – those with 'fragmented work records, ill-health, broken or difficult family situations'. The overriding aim of the centres will be 'to foster self-confidence and reduce feelings of personal and social inadequacy' by personal counselling, group discussions and teaching simple social skills, such as how to make a job application or how to budget. The centres will *not* teach vocational skills. The maximum attendance will be for 60 days, so that the centre will provide an initial period of intensive training and personal reassessment at the commencement of the offender's probation.

(3) That the probationer should receive *psychiatric treatment*[6]. This form of order is discussed later under the general topic of mentally sick offenders.

(c) Enforcement of probation orders

A probationer may be in breach of a probation order in two ways:

(1) by failing to comply with one of the requirements of the order; or
(2) by committing a further offence.

Where the breach complained of is failure to comply with a requirement of the order, the probationer is brought before the supervising magistrates'

---

3 Powers of Criminal Courts Act 1973 s 3(5).
4 *The Sentence of the Court* (HMSO, 1986) para 6.9.
5 Centres in Inner London (Camberwell), Merseyside, Sheffield and Pontypridd were originally set up in 1973 on an experimental basis. There are now 60 approved day centres.
6 Powers of Criminal Courts Act 1973 s 3.

court which must first determine whether there has been a breach of the order. If a breach is found to have occurred the magistrates may:

(1) fine him up to £400[7];
(2) if he is under 21, make an attendance centre order;
(3) make a community service order;

in which cases the probation order continues.

(4) if the probation order was made by a magistrates' court, discharge the order and sentence him for the original offence;
(5) if the order was made by the Crown Court, commit him to the appropriate sitting of the court. The Crown Court may then act as in (1) or (3) above, *or* discharge the order and sentence him for the original offence[8].

If the probationer has committed a further offence, he may (in addition to whatever sentence he receives for that offence), be sentenced for the original offence so that the probation order is terminated. Alternatively, the court, instead of passing sentence for the original offence, may permit the probation order to continue[9].

(d) Discharge and variation of probation orders

During the currency of a probation order, the terms of the order may be varied or a conditional discharge may be substituted for the order by either the supervising court or the court which made the order. The original court may also, on application, discharge the order. Such a course is appropriate where it has become clear during the period of probation that the probationer has responded so well that it is appropriate to terminate the order.

CONDITIONAL DISCHARGE AND BIND-OVER

By s 7(1) of the Powers of Criminal Courts Act 1973, any court may, instead of sentencing an offender for an offence, make an order discharging him subject to the condition that he commits no offence during a specified period not exceeding three years. If the offender should commit a further offence during the relevant period, he is liable to be punished, both for that further offence, and for the original matter. An order of conditional discharge differs from a probation order in that the offender is not subject to any supervision during the period in question. It differs from a suspended sentence in that there is no predetermined penalty for the original offence which will come into force if there is a further conviction.

Since the Justices of the Peace Act 1361, magistrates have had power to require that any person appearing before them (even as a complainant or a witness) should enter into a recognizance, with or without sureties, to keep the peace and be of good behaviour. The power is commonly used to deal expeditiously with cross-assault summonses issued by neighbours who have

---

7 See ibid s 6(3).
8 Ibid s 6(6).
9 Ibid s 8. Note – where the order was originally imposed by a magistrates' court, and the probationer is subsequently convicted by some other magistrates' court, that court may deal with him for the original offence with the consent of the original court, or of the supervising court. Where the order was originally imposed by the Crown Court and he is subsequently convicted by a magistrates' court that court is bound to commit him to the Crown Court for the breach of probation.

fallen out with each other. In these cases, the bind-over occurs without anyone having been convicted.

The same power can also be employed by magistrates or the Crown Court in dealing with convicted persons. The effect of the order is that the offender stands to forfeit the stated recognizance if he fails to be of good behaviour, or to keep the peace, during the period of the bind-over. It is not necessary to prove the commission of a further offence to establish a breach of the order. Appeal will lie to the Crown Court from any order of a magistrates' court requiring a person to be bound over[10].

COMMUNITY SERVICE ORDERS

(a) The power to make the order
Section 14 of the Powers of Criminal Courts Act 1973 enables the courts to order that offenders who have attained 16 years of age should, instead of being dealt with in any other way[11], perform specific unpaid work of benefit to the community for a stated number of hours (not less than 40 nor more than 240[12]) over a period of 12 months. The following conditions must be satisfied before such an order can be made:

(1) arrangements must exist in the area where he lives for persons to perform such work;
(2) the court must have obtained a report confirming his suitability to be placed under such an order[13];
(3) the court must explain to him the purpose and effect of the order and its powers if he fails to comply with the order;
(4) the offender must agree to the making of the order.

The order is supervised by the magistrates' court for the area in which the offender lives and by a probation officer for that area.

Community service orders were introduced with the primary purpose of producing a constructive alternative for those offenders who would otherwise have received a short custodial sentence. But the power is not confined to the case where the court would otherwise impose imprisonment and might, for example, be appropriate for offenders whose offences show a certain degree of selfish disregard for the community without causing substantial injury[14]. What is essential, however, in every case, is that the offender's situation is sufficiently stable to enable him to maintain a

10 Magistrates' Courts (Appeal from Binding Over Orders) Act 1956.
11 Therefore, the court cannot make a probation order or fine the offender for the offence as well as imposing a community service order for *that* offence. The court may, however, order the offender to pay compensation or make restitution at the same time as it makes the order. The court may fine the offender or make a probation order in respect of some other offence but it must not impose a suspended sentence: *R v Starie* (1979) 69 Cr App Rep 239, [1979] Crim LR 731.
12 In the case of an offender under 17, the maximum number of hours is 120.
13 If the court adjourns sentence specifically with a view to obtaining a report as to the offender's fitness for a community service order, it is bound to impose that order if the report is favourable: see *R v Millwood* [1982] Crim LR 832. If it, therefore, wishes to keep its options open, it must clearly state that the report is being obtained on a 'without prejudice' basis.
14 When the offence is one which would not have involved immediate imprisonment, a short period of community service is appropriate; where a custodial sentence of about 9–12 months would have been appropriate, the correct period of community service might be about 190 hours: see *R v Lawrence* [1982] Crim LR 377.

commitment to complete the order. We set out below a chart showing the main offences in respect of which community service orders were made in 1983[15]:

	Crown Court	*Magistrates' courts*
Theft and handling	3,151	11,313
Burglary	2,672	5,273
Violence	858	1,883
Fraud	456	1,421
Motoring offences	354	2,336

(b) The nature of the order

While the sort of work done varies in different parts of the country the general picture is as follows:

> 'All work is unpaid and of a sort normally undertaken by voluntary effort; some tasks involve offenders working alongside volunteers. The extent to which tasks involve contact with beneficiaries varies widely: helping in outdoor conservation projects, building adventure playgrounds, repairing toys for children in need, painting and decorating houses and flats for the elderly and handicapped are examples of tasks at one end of the spectrum. At the other are tasks which involve close personal contact such as swimming coaching for handicapped children, visiting and helping the elderly and helping at disabled people's sports clubs. Should an offender have particular skills or aptitudes it may well be possible for these to be used[16].'

(c) Breach of order and further offences

If the offender fails to comply with the requirements of the order, he may be brought before the supervising court, which may:

(1) fine him up to £400 and direct that the order continue;
(2) if the order was imposed by a magistrates' court, revoke the order and punish him for the original offence;
(3) if the order was imposed by the Crown Court, commit him to that court which can then act as in (1) or (2) above[17].

The commission of a further offence during the currency of a community service order does not automatically lead to the termination of the order, but:

(1) if he is convicted by a magistrates' court, that court may only revoke the community service order if it is imposing a custodial sentence for the new offence. The magistrates, however, cannot impose any sentence for the original offence. If the community service order was imposed by the Crown Court, the magistrates must commit the offender to the Crown Court, but that court also cannot sentence for the original offence;
(2) if he is convicted by the Crown Court, that court may revoke the order and sentence him for the original offence[18].

15 Reproduced from *The Sentence of the Court.*
16 Ibid para 7.14.
17 Powers of Criminal Courts Act 1973 s 16.
18 Ibid s 17.

FINES

The most common form of sentence imposed by the courts on offenders is a fine. So far as the Crown Court is concerned, the maximum fine which can be imposed is usually specified in the statute creating the offence. In the magistrates' courts the position is:

(a) the maximum for offences triable either way is £2000[19];
(b) the maximum for a summary offence is determined by reference to a standard scale. The current maximum fines on the scale are: level 1, £50; level 2, £100; level 3, £400; level 4, £1000 and level 5, £2000[20].

The correct approach for the court in determining the amount of a fine is to decide first what is the appropriate penalty to mark the gravity of the offence (and to take into account any profit the offender may have made from the offence). The court is then bound to consider the means of the offender[1]; save in exceptional circumstances, the fine should not exceed the sum he could pay over a period of 12 months[2]. If the offender could not afford to pay the appropriate penalty, then the fine should be reduced[3]. The court cannot send a person to prison for an offence which would normally be dealt with by a fine because he has not the means to pay[4].

It follows from the principles set out above that no one can be required to pay a fine unless:

(1) he appears to have the means to pay at once; or
(2) it seems that he is unlikely to remain in the United Kingdom; or
(3) the court proposes to pass an immediate sentence for some other offence or he is serving such a sentence[5].

In these cases, the offender may be committed to prison straight away for failure to pay the fine or the court may issue a suspended warrant giving a limited time to pay. In all other cases, the court must give him a stated period in which to pay. The responsibility for the collection of fines in these circumstances rests exclusively with the magistrates' courts. This means that once the Crown Court has imposed a fine, and stated the period for payment (and directed, as it must do under s 31(2) of the Powers of Criminal Courts Act 1973, the length of imprisonment for default) the matter is then remitted to the magistrates' court for the area in which the offender resides.

Where the offender fails to pay his fine in the period permitted by the court, he will be summoned to attend a *means enquiry* at which the court will consider his income and capital, and his necessary expenses, and may then make one of the following orders:

(1) *Money payment supervision order* (Magistrates' Courts Act 1980 s 88): under this order a probation officer is directed to supervise the payment of the fine by the offender.

19 Magistrates' Courts Act 1980 s 32(1).
20 Criminal Justice Act 1982 s 37(1).
 1 Magistrates' Courts Act 1980 s 35.
 2 *R v Knight* (1980) 2 Cr App Rep (S) 82, CA.
 3 See *R v Ashmore* [1974] Crim LR 375 and commentary by Mr David Thomas.
 4 *R v Reeves* (1972) 56 Cr App Rep 366.
 5 Powers of Criminal Courts Act 1973 s 31(3).

(2) *Attachment of earnings order* (Attachment of Earnings Act 1971 s 1(3)): this enables the court to direct that a weekly sum should be stopped out of the offender's wages by his employer and remitted directly to the court.

(3) *Committal warrant* (Magistrates' Courts Act 1980 s 76): if the court is of opinion that he has the means to pay, or that other means of enforcement are impracticable because of the offender's wilful refusal or culpable neglect to pay the fine, it may commit the offender to prison[6].

(4) *Suspended warrant* (Magistrates' Courts Act 1980 s 77): the court may, in the circumstances where it could commit to prison, instead suspend the warrant so long as the offender complies with specified conditions as to payment.

(5) Make a *community service order* instead of committing him to prison in the circumstances specified in (3) above (Criminal Justice Act 1972 s 49 – this provision has not yet been brought into force)[7].

Where a means enquiry is held the court may feel that the appropriate course is to remit the whole, or part of the fine, because of the offender's changed financial position as revealed upon such enquiry[8]. Where the fine was originally imposed by the Crown Court the consent of that court is required before a remission can be made[9].

DEFERRED SENTENCE

By s 1 of the Powers of Criminal Courts Act 1973, both the Crown Court and the magistrates' court may, with the consent of the offender, defer passing sentence for a period of not more than six months. This power is intended to give the offender a chance to show the court that his promises of reformation are realistic and capable of fulfilment. The Court of Appeal has given the following guidance as to how the courts should approach the power to defer sentences:

'The power is not to be used as an easy way out for a court which is unable to make up its mind about the correct sentence. Experience has shown that great care should be exercised by the court when using this power. . .

The court should make it clear to the defendant what the particular purposes are which the court has in mind under s 1(1) of the Act and what conduct is expected of him during deferment. . . It is essential that the deferring court should make a careful note of the purposes for which the sentence is being deferred and what steps, if any, it expects the defendant to take during the period

---

6 The maximum periods which may be imposed for default are as follows:

An amount not exceeding £50	7 days
£51–100	14 days
£101–400	30 days
£401–1000	60 days
£1001–2000	90 days
£2001–5000	6 months
£5001–10,000	9 months
Over £10,000	12 months

See Powers of Criminal Courts Act 1973 s 31(3A).
7 The court has also, in theory, the power to levy distress on the offender's goods or take proceedings in the civil courts for recovery of the fine.
8 Magistrates' Courts Act 1980 s 85.
9 Powers of Criminal Courts Act 1973 s 32(4).

of deferment. Ideally the defendant himself should be given notice in writing of what he is expected to do or refrain from doing, so that there can be no doubt in his mind what is expected of him.

Thus the task of the court which comes to deal with the offender at the expiration of the period of deferment is as follows:

First the purpose of the deferment and any requirement imposed by the deferring court must be ascertained. Secondly, the court must determine if the defendant has substantially conformed or attempted to conform with the proper expectations of the deferring court, whether with regard to finding a job or as the case may be. If he has, then the defendant may legitimately expect that an immediate custodial sentence will not be imposed. If he has not, then the court should be careful to state with precision in what respects he has failed.

If the court does not set out its reasons in this way, there is a danger, particularly where the sentencing court is differently constituted from the deferring court, that it may appear that the former is disregarding the deferment and is saying in effect that the sentence should never have been deferred and that the defendant should have been sentenced to immediate imprisonment by the latter'[10].

When the offender subsequently appears for sentence, the court (which should if at all possible comprise the same judge or magistrates as ordered deferment) should not impose a custodial sentence unless his conduct since his last appearance has been unsatisfactory[11]. The advocate who appears at the initial hearing should regard himself as bound, if it is at all possible to do so, to appear at the subsequent hearing[12].

ABSOLUTE DISCHARGE

Where an offender is convicted by a court which is of the opinion that he should receive no penalty for the offence, that court may make an order discharging him absolutely[13]. Such an order is made when the accused is technically in breach of the law but there is no blameworthiness attached to his acts.

ANCILLARY ORDERS

Compensation orders
Section 35 of the Powers of Criminal Courts Act 1973 provides that:

'a court by or before which a person is convicted of an offence, instead of or in addition to dealing with him in any other way, may, on application or otherwise, make an order . . . requiring him to pay compensation for any personal injury, loss or damage resulting from that offence or any other offence which is taken into consideration by the court in determining sentence.'

10 Per Lord Lane CJ in *R v George* [1984] 3 All ER 13, 79 Cr App Rep 26.
11 *R v Gilby* [1975] 2 All ER 743, [1975] 1 WLR 924. And note that if after deferment the offender is convicted of some other offence, the convicting court can deal with him for the matter for which sentence was already deferred or (in the case of a magistrates' court convicting an offender upon whom sentence was deferred by the Crown Court) commit him to the original court to be dealt with at once (s 4 as amended by Criminal Law Act 1977 Sch 12).
12 *R v Ryan* [1976] Crim LR 508.
13 Powers of Criminal Courts Act 1973 s 7.

The power of the Crown Court to order compensation is unlimited; the power of the magistrates' court is limited to £2000[14]. Such an order might be appropriate in many different types of case, for example where property has been stolen and not recovered, where a person suffers injury in an assault, where property is deliberately damaged, where a car which has been taken without authority is damaged. The power, however, is not to be exercised as a substitute for punishment, nor is it to be employed where there is any substantial question about the accused's liability to compensate a particular claimant or where it would seem he lacks the means to do so:

'Compensation orders were not introduced into our law to enable the convicted to buy themselves out of the penalties of crime, but as a convenient and rapid means of avoiding the expense of resorting to civil litigation where the criminal clearly has means which would enable the compensation to be paid. . . Compensation orders should certainly not be used where there is any doubt as to liability to compensate, nor should they be used when there is any real doubt as to whether the convicted man can find compensation[15].'

It would appear that before making a compensation order the court has to consider the following points:

(1) Is it clearly established that the offender is, by reason of the facts of the offence, liable to compensate somebody? Where he disputes this issue, the court must not make an order unless the issue has been resolved by the evidence leading to his conviction.

Example. K pleaded guilty to burglary of a dwelling house. In mitigation his counsel made it clear that although K admitted stealing certain property from the house, he denied he had stolen certain rings which it was alleged were missing. The Court of Appeal held that the Crown Court was wrong to make a compensation order in respect of the rings. Per Lord Widgery CJ: 'where in the course of proceedings the accused, whether by himself or through his counsel, raises the issue that the goods were not stolen at all, the court should not consider making a compensation order unless an application in that behalf is made, presumably on behalf of the victim, and the applicant is prepared to show as a matter of fact on evidence that the goods were in fact the subject of the theft. Even then the matter is discretionary and the court should hesitate to embark on any complicated investigation of this kind even at the suit of an applicant making a positive application. But in the absence of a specific application, when an issue of fact of this sort is raised we think that the court should refuse in its discretion to make a compensation order, leaving the victim with his or her civil remedy[16].'

(2) Assuming liability to compensate is clearly established, can the court make a fair assessment of compensation? Section 35(1A) provides that:

'Compensation . . . shall be of such amount as the court considers appropriate, having regard to any evidence and to any representations that are made by or on behalf of the accused or the prosecutor.'

---

14 Magistrates' Courts Act 1980 s 40: the limit is £2000 for each offence of which the offender has been convicted: the sum awarded in respect of offences taken into consideration cannot exceed the aggregate amount for the offences of which he has been convicted less the amount awarded in respect of each of those particular offences.
15 Per Scarman LJ in *R v Inwood* (1974) 60 Cr App Rep 70.
16 *R v Kneeshaw* [1975] QB 57, [1974] 1 All ER 896.

It is submitted that although the amount of compensation does not have to be proved by strict evidence, if there is a real issue, the court should either make no order or limit its order to a sum which could not be disputed. The victim will, of course, be entitled to claim the full amount of his loss in civil proceedings.

(3) Is a compensation order appropriate in view of the means of the offender and any other punishment which is being imposed? The court is obliged by s 35(4) to have regard to the offender's means: the order should be one which he can clearly discharge over a reasonable period[17] (in practice, two years is accepted as the upper limit). In particular, the court must be alive to the possibility that an order which the accused might have difficulty in discharging could lead him to commit other offences[18].

A compensation order may be made instead of, or in addition to, any other punishment – thus, for example, an order can be made in addition to a fine or at the same time as a probation order. When the order is made together with a fine, the court should determine an overall sum which the offender can properly pay and then should give preference to the compensation order – i e the fine may have to be reduced to ensure the overall sum is within his means[19].

It should be noted that the courts have a separate power under s 28 of the Theft Act 1968 to make orders for restitution by the delivery up of stolen goods or other goods bought with the proceeds of such goods or for compensation out of any money taken from the offender on his arrest. It must, however, be clear beyond dispute that the property in question has been stolen from the applicant, or represents the proceeds of such a theft[20].

Forfeiture orders

Where an offender is convicted at the Crown Court or at a magistrates' court of an offence punishable on indictment with two years' imprisonment or more, the court may make an order forfeiting any property *which has been lawfully seized from him or was in his possession or under his control at the time of his arrest* if it is established that the property in question:

'(a) has been used for the purpose of committing or facilitating the commission of any offence; or
 (b) was intended by him to be used for that purpose[1].'

Example. L pleaded guilty to the offence under s 22 of the Theft Act 1968 of undertaking or assisting in the removal of stolen property. He had used his car to transport stolen goods at the request of the thieves. The Court of Appeal held that a forfeiture order was properly made in respect of the car[2].

Various enactments also provide for forfeiture in respect of specific offences, e g:

(1) Offensive weapons – Prevention of Crime Act 1953 s 1(2).

---

17 See *R v Daly* [1974] 1 All ER 290, [1974] 1 WLR 133.
18 See *R v Oddy* [1974] 2 All ER 666, [1974] 1 WLR 1212.
19 Powers of Criminal Courts Act 1973 s 1(4A).
20 See *R v Ferguson* [1970] 2 All ER 820, 54 Cr App Rep 410 and *R v Thibeault* (1983) 76 Cr App Rep 201.
 1 Powers of Criminal Courts Act 1973 s 43.
 2 *R v Lidster* [1976] Crim LR 80.

(2) Firearms – Firearms Act 1968 s 52.
(3) Drugs – Misuse of Drugs Act 1971 s 27.
(4) Obscene articles – Obscene Publications Act 1959 s 3.
(5) Customs offences – Customs and Excise Management Act 1979 s 49 (in the case of illegal importation of prohibited drugs, the Customs seize the property in question under the statutory powers and, in consequence, there is no need for the court to make forfeiture orders).[2a]

Disqualification from driving
The Crown Court (but *not* a magistrates' court) may disqualify an offender from driving where a motor vehicle was used (by the person convicted or by anyone else) for the purpose of committing, or facilitating the commission, of an offence[3]. This power is, of course, quite separate from the power to disqualify for road traffic offences (as to which see p 257 below). The disqualification may be for such period as the court thinks appropriate, but where the court is passing an immediate sentence of imprisonment it should not normally impose disqualification which will continue after the offender's release if this would affect his ability to obtain employment[4].

Deportation
Section 3(6) of the Immigration Act 1971 provides that:

'a person who is not a British citizen shall . . . be liable to deportation from the United Kingdom if, after he has attained the age of 17, he is convicted of an offence for which he is punishable with imprisonment and on his conviction is recommended by a court empowered by this Act to do so[5].'

Both the Crown Court and magistrates' courts have the power to make such a recommendation: however, before it can be made, the defendant must (not less than seven days previously) have been served with a notice explaining his liability to deportation. The following guidelines have been laid down as to when a recommendation for deportation is appropriate:

'First, the court must consider whether the accused's continued presence in the United Kingdom is to its detriment. This country has no use for criminals of other nationalities, particularly if they have committed serious crimes or have long criminal records. That is self-evident. The more serious the crime and the longer the record the more obvious it is that there should be an order recommending deportation. On the other hand, a minor offence would not merit an order recommending deportation. In the Greater London area, for example, shoplifting is an offence which is frequently committed by visitors to this country. Normally an arrest for shoplifting followed by conviction, even if there were more than one offence being dealt with, would not merit a recommendation for deportation. But a series of shoplifting offences on different occasions may justify a recommendation for deportation. Even a first offence of shoplifting might merit a recommendation if the offender were a member of a gang carrying out a planned raid on a departmental store.
    Secondly, the courts are not concerned with the political systems which operate

2a Note: under the Drug Trafficking Offences Act 1986 the Crown Court is required to determine whether a person convicted of drug trafficking has made any benefit from the offence and must order him to pay that amount before passing any other sentence.
3 Powers of Criminal Courts Act 1973 s 43.
4 *R v Wright* (1979) 1 Cr App Rep (S) 82.
5 Note: Commonwealth citizens and citizens of the Republic of Ireland who (a) were resident in this country on 1 January 1973 and (b) have been ordinarily resident here for five years preceding conviction, are exempt from deportation: Immigration Act 1971 s 7 and Pakistan Act 1973 Sch 3.

in other countries. They may be harsh; they may be soft; they may be oppressive; they may be the quintessence of democracy. The court has no knowledge of those matters over and above that which is common knowledge; and that may be wrong. In our judgment it would be undesirable for this court or any other court to express views about regimes which exist outside the United Kingdom of Great Britain and Northern Ireland. It is for the Home Secretary to decide in each case whether an offender's return to his country of origin would have consequences which would make his compulsory return unduly harsh. The Home Secretary has opportunities of informing himself about what is happening in other countries which the courts do not have. . .

The next matter to which we invite attention by way of guidelines is the effect that an order recommending deportation will have upon others who are not before the court and who are innocent persons. This court and all other courts would have no wish to break up families or impose hardship on innocent people. The case of Fernandez illustrates this very clearly indeed. Mrs Fernandez is an admirable person, a good wife and mother, and a credit to herself and someone whom most of us would want to have in this country. As we have already indicated, if her husband is deported she will have a heartrending choice to make: whether she should go with her husband or leave him and look after the interests of the children. That is the kind of situation which should be considered very carefully before a recommendation for deportation is made[6].'

The Secretary of State does not have to follow the court's recommendations:

'In coming to a decision on whether to deport the Home Secretary considers: the nature of the offence; the extent of the offender's criminal record; the length of the offender's stay in the UK and the strength of the offender's connections with it; the offender's age, personal history and domestic circumstances; any compassionate considerations and any representations made by or on behalf of the offender. Deportation of a first offender is unlikely unless the offence is serious, a number of other offences are being taken into consideration or the offence is under the Immigration Act 1971[7].'

Criminal bankruptcy

Where persons can be shown to have suffered loss in excess of £15,000 as a result of the offence in question, the Crown Court may make a criminal bankruptcy order under s 39 of the Powers of Criminal Courts Act 1973. The effect of the order is that the offender is treated for the purposes of s 119 of the Insolvency Act 1985 as being a person who can be declared bankrupt by the Bankruptcy Court. The Director of Public Prosecutions will file a petition for the offender to be adjudicated bankrupt and his property will be seized for the benefit of the persons who have suffered loss as a result of the offence.

ROAD TRAFFIC CASES

Where an offender is convicted of a road traffic offence the court will normally impose a *fine* and order his licence to be endorsed with a number of *penalty points*; in some cases, the court will have to impose, or may impose, *disqualification*.

6 Per Lawton LJ in *R v Nazari* [1980] 3 All ER 880, 71 Cr App Rep 87. Note where the offender comes from an EEC country there must be 'a genuine and sufficiently serious threat to the requirements of public policy affecting one of the fundamental interests of society': see *R v Secretary of State for Home Affairs, ex p Santillo* [1981] 2 All ER 897 at 917.

7 *The Sentence of the Court* para 14.13. And see Statement of Changes in Immigration Rules 1983 paras 148–170.

The fine

The Magistrates' Association has produced a table showing suggested penalties for different traffic offences. The aim is to achieve a consistent approach to the level of fines throughout the country. The preface to the table states:

> 'The list provides a suggested figure which the courts might wish to increase or decrease in their discussion as to the proper penalty in each case. The responsibility for the sentence is that of the bench in each particular case and the penalty in each case must be judicially assessed in accordance with the circumstances of the particular offence and of the offender.'

In practice, the advocate in any road traffic case has to be aware of the suggested penalty in the table because the likelihood is that this will be the starting point of the court in determining the fine; for that reason we have reproduced the 1985 table as an appendix to the book (see p 349 below).

Penalty points

Ordinarily, where a person is convicted of a road traffic offence the court is bound to order that there should be endorsed on his licence particulars of the conviction and of the number of penalty points in respect of the offence[8].

> *Example.* D is convicted of careless driving under s 3 of the Road Traffic Act 1972. This is the first offence. The magistrates are likely to impose a fine in the region of £60 (see table p 350 below) and, in addition, will order his licence to be endorsed with between 2–5 penalty points, depending on the seriousness of the offence.

Where, as often happens, the offender is convicted of more than one offence (eg careless driving and no insurance) committed on the same occasion the maximum number of penalty points is the highest number which can be awarded for one of these offences:

> *Example.* Careless driving – 2–5 points; no insurance – 4–8 points; the maximum which can be imposed is 8 points.

Note the appropriate number of penalty points in any given case can be seen from the table (p 349 below). In very rare cases the court may be persuaded that there are *special reasons*[9] for not ordering penalty points to be endorsed on the licence. A *special reason* is a mitigating factor relating to the particular circumstances of the offence itself (eg a sudden emergency forcing a person to drive while uninsured); but circumstances relating to the offender (eg he would lose his job if unable to drive) can never be *special reasons*[10]. The defendant must give evidence to substantiate the alleged *special reason*.

Disqualification

There are three different cases where the court has to consider disqualification in the context of a road traffic offence:

(1) Obligatory disqualification. The court is obliged in certain cases to impose disqualification for at least 12 months. Within this category are included offences of causing death by reckless driving, drunken driving or driving

8 Road Traffic Act 1972 s 101; Transport Act 1981 s 19(1).
9 Road Traffic Act 1972 s 101(2).
10 See, eg, *Police Prosecutor v Humphreys* [1970] Crim LR 234: solicitor's clerk exceeding speed limit to get to court in time to instruct counsel; held – a special reason.

with excess alcohol and failing to provide a specimen of breath, blood, or urine[11]. The only circumstances in which the court can reduce the period of disqualification or make no order is where the offender shows by sworn evidence *special reasons*, ie mitigating factors relating to the offence itself in the sense described above.

(ii) Discretionary disqualification. In many other cases (for example, careless driving, failing to stop or report an accident, driving while disqualified or uninsured), the court has the power to order disqualification if it feels it appropriate on the facts of the particular case. In practice, magistrates' courts rarely exercise this power unless there is something particularly heinous in the circumstances of the offence or there has been a deliberate contravention of the law. Where the court is considering discretionary disqualification, the advocate can advance any mitigating factors, ie he is *not* confined to advancing 'special reasons'. It would, therefore, be perfectly proper to put forward an argument that the offender's previous record in the context of his average mileage in any year indicates that he is generally a careful driver or that he needs his licence for his job.

(iii) Penalty point disqualification. If an offender has, as a result of offences committed within a three-year period, accumulated a total of 12 penalty points or more he will be liable to a minimum period of disqualification of six months[12]. (If he has been disqualified within the three years before the date on which the latest offence was committed, the minimum period of further disqualification is 12 months; if he has been disqualified twice during the three-year period, the minimum is two years.) The court may reduce the period of disqualification or order no disqualification if there are *mitigating circumstances*[13]. Such grounds are wider than those which can amount to *special reasons*; thus the court is not confined to looking at the circumstances of the offence, but is entitled to consider such matters as exceptional hardship to the offender, eg if he were to lose his job because he was unable to drive. However, the rule is still that disqualification should be the ordinary result of accumulating 12 penalty points and it is expressly provided the following are not deemed to be mitigating circumstances:

'(a) any circumstances that are alleged to make the offence or any of the offences not a serious one;
(b) hardship, other than exceptional hardship; or
(c) any circumstances which, within the three years immediately preceding the conviction, have been taken into account under (the penalty point system) in ordering the offender to be disqualified for a shorter period or not ordering him to be disqualified[14].'

A penalty point disqualification cannot be consecutive to any other order of disqualification; in effect, the court imposes a single term, taking into account all the offences, in deciding how long it should be. It should be

11 The other offences carrying obligatory disqualification are: (i) manslaughter by the driver of a motor vehicle, and (ii) reckless driving committed within three years of a similar offence or an offence of causing death by reckless driving; (iii) motor racing on the highway.
12 Transport Act 1981 s 19.
13 Ibid s 19(2). The disqualification is mandatory 'unless the court is satisfied having regard to all the circumstances . . . that there are grounds for mitigating the normal consequences of the conviction'.
14 Ibid s 19(6).

noted that once the disqualification is imposed for any reason the offender's record is 'wiped clean' – ie when his licence is returned all penalty points will have been removed.

The courts have the power to remove orders for disqualification over two years in length after the expiry of part of the period whether the disqualification was mandatory or discretionary[15]. Where an offender who has been disqualified by a magistrates' court gives notice of appeal to the Crown Court, application can be made to the magistrates to suspend their order pending the appeal[16]. This course is worth taking, for example, where the magistrates' court in a penalty points case rejects a plea based on hardship or makes an order for a reduced period of disqualification.

15 Road Traffic Act 1972 s 95. The relevant periods after which an application can be made are:
   if disqualification is for 10 years – 5 years
   if disqualification is for 4 years or more but less than 10 – half the period
   if disqualification is for less than 4 years – 2 years.
16 Road Traffic Act 1972 s 94(1); if suspension is refused the applicant can make a fresh application at once to the Crown Court: s 94A.

Chapter 14

Young people in trouble

DETENTION

We have already seen that no person under the age of 21 can in any circumstances be sent to prison[1]. A young person convicted on indictment of a crime so grave that an adult could be sent to prison for 14 years (or a child convicted of manslaughter or attempted murder) *may* be sentenced to *detention* for a specified period[2]. The Home Secretary has power to release him on licence. Where a child or young person under 18 is convicted of murder he *must* be detained during Her Majesty's pleasure[3].

YOUTH CUSTODY

Offenders aged not less than 15 and not more than 20 may be sentenced by the Crown Court or a magistrates' court to a term of youth custody[4]. The sentence will normally be served at a 'youth custody centre' (often the former borstal institutions but with a different regime). The sentence cannot normally be imposed if the court wishes the offender to serve a term up to four months (in that case a detention centre order must be made – see below). The maximum term for offenders under 17 is 12 months' youth custody; for older offenders[5] the maximum is determined by the statutory provision creating the offence (but subject to the usual six months maximum for any one offence when a custodial sentence is imposed by a magistrates' court[6]). It is particularly important that young offenders should not be subjected to custodial sentences unless every other alternative has been considered and rejected; for this reason, the law places the following restrictions on the availability of such a sentence:

(i)   the court must be of opinion that one of the following conditions is satisfied:
 (a) it appears that the offender is unable or unwilling to respond to non-custodial penalties; or

---

1 Powers of Criminal Courts Act 1973 s 19(1).
2 Children and Young Persons Act 1933 s 53(2).
3 Ibid s 53(1).
4 Criminal Justice Act 1982 s 6(1).
5 Note: if he reaches 21 while serving a sentence of youth custody, the Home Secretary may direct that he serves the remainder of the term in an adult prison: see s 13.
6 Magistrates' Courts Act 1980 s 31.

  (b) a custodial sentence is necessary for the protection of the public; or

  (c) the offence is so serious that a non-custodial sentence cannot be justified[7];

(ii) a social enquiry report has been obtained[8];

(iii) the defendant is legally represented[9].

The regime to which the young offender will be subjected has been described as follows:

'Youth custody centres are divided into open, closed and long-term establishments, and the allocation of youth custody inmates takes account of this, and also of the specialist, medical, psychiatric and educational facilities at certain establishments. Youth custody centres aim to provide inmates with flexible but coherent programmes consisting of . . . activities such as work, education, physical education, vocational and other training and community service. Preparation of inmates for release is carried out in co-operation with the services responsible for supervision[10].'

The offender is eligible for release on parole after he has served six months (or one-third of his sentence if that is greater)[11]; whether or not he is released on licence, he will receive one-third remission of sentence for good behaviour[12]. All offenders are subject to statutory supervision after release; if he has been released on parole he is liable to recall for failing to comply with the requirements of the supervising officer; if he has not been given parole, he is liable to a fine or up to 30 days' custody[13].

DETENTION CENTRES

Both the Crown Court and magistrates' courts may commit male offenders over 14 and under 21 to a *detention centre* for a period not less than 21 days and not exceeding four months[14]. The restrictions discussed above concerning sentencing of young offenders to custodial regimes apply (ie the court must be satisfied there is no alternative, it must have obtained a social enquiry report and the young offender must be legally represented). The idea of a detention centre is that the offender should be subjected for a short period to a system of rigorous discipline, not unlike the initial period of induction into the armed services:

---

7 Criminal Justice Act 1982 s 1(4).
8 Ibid s 2. The court may direct that it is unnecessary to obtain a report: if magistrates so decide they must state their reasons.
9 Ibid s 3. The restriction does not apply when the offender has refused an offer of legal aid or is ineligible because of his means.
10 *The Sentence of the Court* para 10.8.
11 Criminal Justice Act 1982 Sch 14.
12 Time spent in custody prior to sentence counts in determining the term actually to be served.
13 Criminal Justice Act 1982 s 15(11).
14 Criminal Justice Act 1982 s 4. Note: the detention centre order should not be made in the absence of special circumstances in respect of a young offender who has already served a term of youth custody; there is, however, no restriction on imposing a second term in a detention centre on a young offender (s 4(5)). If the court is dealing with an offender who is already in a detention centre for some other offence, it may make a further detention centre order (but the maximum aggregate term served under both orders must not be more than four months) or it may pass a youth custody sentence for a greater term: see s 5(2) and (5).

'Since 6 March 1985 all detention centres in England and Wales have operated a consistent regime featuring a brisk initial two-week programme, a structured grade system incorporating incentives to effort and good conduct; and a disciplined daily routine including such activities as parades and inspections, work, education and physical training[15].'

The offender automatically receives remission of one-third of his sentence (which is only forfeited in the case of bad behaviour). Time spent in custody before sentence counts towards the sentence. On release the offender is subject to three months' supervision; failure to comply with the requirements of supervision can result in his being brought before a magistrates' court and being fined up to £200 or ordered to serve up to 30 days in custody.

CARE ORDERS

The Children and Young Persons Act 1969 empowers any court dealing with a child or young person (ie a person under 17) in trouble (whether or not through any fault of his own) to commit that child or young person into the care of the local authority who thereupon assume parental rights and responsibilities over them. We have already seen that such an order may be made:

(1) as a result of *care* proceedings (which in only some cases will involve a finding of criminality)[16];
(2) as a result of a finding of guilt in *criminal* proceedings[17].

In both proceedings the *care order* involves, in practice, a decision by the juvenile court that the child is in need of care and control which he is unlikely to receive unless such an order is made. The local authority is bound to review the order every six months, and the child's parents have power to require the authority to justify the continuation in force of the order by applying to the juvenile court to discharge it[18].

The Act contemplates that the local authority should have a wide discretion as to the appropriate form of treatment for the individual offenders. Some children will remain at home with one or other parent. Many will go to *community homes* at which they will receive full-time education (or go out to school) and at the same time live in a more secure environment than at home. Other children will be boarded out at *foster-homes* where they will live in a family environment. In every case, the regime to which the child or young person is subjected should not be punitive. The only relevance of the finding of criminality is that it indicates misfortune and the need for the child or young person to grow up in a better environment.

Where a juvenile who is already subject to a care order commits an offence the court may add a *charge and control condition*[19] to the existing care order. The effect of such a condition is that he is removed from the home at

15 *The Sentence of the Court* (HMSO, 1986) para 10.4
16 Children and Young Persons Act 1969 s 1(3).
17 Ibid s 7(7)(a). Note that in a criminal case the court must be of opinion that a care order is appropriate because of the seriousness of the offence *and* that the juvenile is in need of care and control which he is unlikely to receive unless the court makes a care order. Note also that generally the juvenile must be legally represented before an order is made (s 7A).
18 Ibid s 21(2).
19 Ibid s 20A.

which he has been living (usually with one or other parent) and lives at a community home (or with foster parents) for a period of not more than six months. In exceptional cases the court may direct that the local authority may allow the child to live with one parent but not the other.

SUPERVISION ORDERS

Section 7(7) of the Children and Young Persons Act 1969 enables the court to place a child or young person under the supervision of a child-care officer. The theory behind such an order is similar to probation, ie that a trained social worker should assume a general responsibility for seeing that the child keeps out of trouble and develops into a happy member of the community. The order differs from probation in that the consent of the child is not required before it can be made, a breach of a requirement of the order does not in itself render the offender liable to punishment for the initial offence[20] and the supervising officer is normally a member of the local social services department rather than the probation service.

The supervision order may include the following requirements:

(1) that the supervised person *resides* with an individual named in the order (eg with his elder brother or an aunt)[1];
(2) that he should be subject to a curfew, ie remain indoors at a specified address for a period of up to 30 days between a specified time after 6 pm and 6 am. This is called a *night restriction order*. He may only go out when accompanied by his parents, guardians, supervising officer or someone specified in the order[2]. The days when the order is effective need not be consecutive, so the order may apply only to weekends but must not extend over a longer period than 90 days;
(3) that he must not take part in specified activities (eg attendance at football matches) either on specified days or throughout the order[3];
(4) that the offender should receive *intermediate treatment* (ie character training away from home) for a limited period under the direction of the supervising officer[4],
(5) that the offender should receive either in-patient or out-patient treatment for *psychiatric* disorder[5].

ATTENDANCE CENTRES

Section 16 of the Criminal Justice Act 1982 enables the Crown Court, a magistrates' court or juvenile court to order an offender[6] under the age of 21 to attend for a specified number of hours spread over a number of weeks at a centre for character training. The court will normally specify a period of up to 12 hours in aggregate, although longer periods (up to 24 hours if under 17 and up to 36 hours for offenders over 17) may be imposed if the court feels

20 Except where the young person subject to the order has attained 18: see s 15(4). But breach of the order will result in review before the court which may then make a care order: s 16.
1 Children and Young Persons Act 1969 s 12(1).
2 Ibid s 12(3C).
3 Ibid s 12(3C).
4 Ibid s 12(2).
5 Ibid s 12(4) and (5).
6 An order may be made in respect of an offender who is in breach of a probation or supervision order or has failed to pay a fine or compensation.

the normal period would be inadequate. The offender must not have already undergone any form of custodial sentence. These centres are usually run by police officers on Saturday afternoons, and typically involve the offender in a period of physical training followed by craftwork or hobbies or lectures on social matters. They have been used, for example, against otherwise law-abiding youngsters who engage in football hooliganism at weekends. It is desirable that magistrates making such an order in the case of a boy under 17 should stress the importance of one of his parents accompanying him the first time he attends the centre. It has been found that a preliminary discussion with the boy's parents can make a considerable difference to the efficacy of the order. If the offender fails to attend the centre or breaks the attendance centre rules he will be brought before the local magistrates' court which may sentence him for the original offence (or commit to the Crown Court).

MINOR PENALTIES

The courts also have the following powers in dealing with offenders who have not attained 17 years of age:

(1) *Fine*: £100 maximum if under 14; £400 maximum if under 17[7]. Since a child will normally be unable to pay a fine, the court must direct that the fine (and any compensation order or order for costs) be paid by his parents[8].
(2) *Binding over child or young person or his parents*: the court may bind over the offender's parents to take proper care of him and exercise proper control over him. This power can only be exercised with the parent's consent but this would usually be forthcoming because, if the parent was not prepared to enter into such an undertaking, the court would have to consider bringing in the local child-care service.
(3) *Conditional and absolute discharge*.
(4) *Disqualification from driving*.
(5) *Orders for compensation and restitution* (see p 252).

It should be remembered that many juvenile offenders are never brought to court because the police are prepared, providing they admit their guilt, to caution them.

7 Magistrates' Courts Act 1980 s 36.
8 Children and Young Persons Act 1933 s 55. This does not apply where it would be unreasonable to make an order for payment by the parent in the circumstances of the case.

Chapter 15

Mentally ill offenders

Both the Crown Court and magistrates' courts have the power under s 37 of the Mental Health Act 1983, to order the compulsory admission of a convicted offender[1] to a mental hospital[2]. Before such an order can be made four conditions must be satisfied:

(1) Two doctors (one an approved psychiatrist) must certify to the court that the offender is suffering from mental illness, psychopathic disorder or severe mental impairment to a degree as warrants his detention.

(2) That detention for medical treatment is appropriate (and in the case of psychopathic disorders or mental impairment, that such treatment is likely to alleviate or prevent a deterioration of his condition).

(3) A hospital must be willing to admit the offender within 28 days.

(4) The court must be of opinion that such an order is the most suitable method of disposing of the case.

The effect of the order is that the offender may be taken to a mental hospital and detained there until discharged either by the hospital authorities or by the Mental Health Review Tribunal. It should be noted that it sometimes happens that the court is faced with the situation where no hospital is prepared to admit the offender; in such a case the court can require the appropriate regional health authority to provide information about suitable hospitals; it cannot however compel the authority to find a suitable place.

Where the offender is dangerous or violent, the order may direct that he be detained at a *special hospital* (Broadmoor, Rampton or Moss Side). In such a case a *restriction order*, under s 41 of the Act, should always be made. The effect of such an order is that the hospital order lasts at least for the duration of the restriction order (which may be without limit of time) and

---

1 Or a person who has not pleaded at a magistrates' court, if that court is of opinion that he did the act or omission charged (s 37(3)).

2 Alternatively, the court can make a *guardianship order* which has the effect of placing the offender under the guardianship of the local social services department; that authority is vested with all the powers over the offender which would be exercisable by a father over a child of less than 14 years of age. Note also the power of the court under s 38 of the Mental Health Act 1983 to make an interim order lasting initially for up to 12 weeks (but by extensions to six months) after which the court can review the situation.

the patient can only be discharged, transferred to another hospital or granted leave of absence with the approval of the Home Secretary. The patient will initially be discharged under conditions as to residence and supervision. A *restriction* order can only be made by the Crown Court, so that if magistrates feel that such an order is appropriate, they must commit the offender to the Crown Court for that purpose.

Where an offender is found by a jury to be unfit to plead, or not guilty by reason of insanity, the court must order that he be admitted to such hospital as the Home Secretary directs[3]. If the offender is thought to be dangerous he will be detained at a *special* hospital; otherwise he will be admitted to a psychiatric hospital in his home area. In either event he will be detained as if he had been admitted under a hospital order with a restriction order without limitation of time. In rare cases, a person found unfit to plead may, on his recovery, be remitted for trial.

PROBATION WITH CONDITION OF TREATMENT

Section 3 of the Powers of Criminal Courts Act 1973 enables any court to include in a probation order a requirement that the offender shall submit for a specified period of not more than 12 months from the date of the order to treatment with a view to the improvement of his mental condition. The requirement can only be made upon the oral or written evidence of a qualified doctor[4]. Obviously, the order would not be made where a hospital order would be appropriate, but it should be noted that the probationer may nevertheless be required to submit to in-patient as well as non-residential treatment.

TREATMENT DURING CUSTODIAL SENTENCES

The Home Secretary has power under s 47 of the Mental Health Act 1983 to order the transfer of persons from prison to mental hospitals in circumstances where they are suffering from mental disorder within the meaning of the Act. There are, however, many other people in prison who, although by no means falling within the Act, could benefit from psychiatric treatment. The principal exception to this is *Grendon Underwood*, which is a maximum security prison dealing exclusively with offenders suffering from personality orders who need psychiatric help. The regime is based on a high degree of personal freedom within the confines of the prison and a low staff/prisoner ratio. At the present time *Grendon* and the psychiatric centres at a few prisons must be considered exceptional and can only benefit a very small proportion of the prison population. It is of note that the Committee on Mentally Abnormal Offenders which reported in 1975 commented on the misconception entertained by many courts that a mentally disturbed offender will receive treatment in prison:

'. . . it is undesirable to convey to the offender the impression that medical treatment will certainly be given to him in prison. This may lead to the erroneous

3 Criminal Procedure (Insanity) Act 1964 s 5(1)(a), (c).
4 Ie approved under the Mental Health Act 1959 s 28.

assumption on his part that the sentence is being imposed for the express purpose of enabling him to receive medical treatment that will "cure" his criminal behaviour. If, as frequently happens, it turns out that he does not receive medical treatment . . . the offender may feel that he has a grievance against the authorities and that if he offends again it is not his fault[5].'

5 Cmnd 6244 para 13.12 (HMSO, 1975).

Statutes

Statutes

MAGISTRATES' COURTS ACT 1980

Criminal Jurisdiction and Procedure: Committal Proceedings

6. Discharge or committal for trial

(1) Subject to the provisions of this and any other Act relating to the summary trial of indictable offences, if a magistrates' court inquiring into an offence as examining justices is of opinion, on consideration of the evidence and of any statement of the accused, that there is sufficient evidence to put the accused on trial by jury for any indictable offence, the court shall commit him for trial; and, if it is not of that opinion, it shall, if he is in custody for no other cause than the offence under inquiry, discharge him.

(2) A magistrates' court inquiring into an offence as examining justices may, if satisfied that all the evidence before the court (whether for the prosecution or the defence) consists of written statements tendered to the court under section 102 below, with or without exhibits, commit the accused for trial for the offence without consideration or the contents of those statements, unless:

(a) the accused or one of the accused [has no solicitor acting for him in the case (whether present in court or not)];

(b) counsel or a solicitor for the accused or one of the accused, as the case may be, has requested the court to consider a submission that the statements disclose insufficient evidence to put that accused on trial by jury for the offence;

and subsection (1) above shall not apply to a committal for trial under this subsection.

(3) Subject to section 4 of the Bail Act 1976 and section 41 below, the court may commit a person for trial:

(a) in custody, that is to say, by committing him to custody there to be safely kept until delivered in due course of law, or

(b) on bail in accordance with the Bail Act 1976, that is to say, by directing him to appear before the Crown Court for trial;

and where his release on bail is conditional on his providing one or more surety or sureties and, in accordance with section 8(3) of the Bail Act 1976, the court fixes the amount in which the surety is to be bound with a view to his entering into his recognizance subsequently in accordance with subsections (4) and (5) or (6) of that section the court shall in the meantime commit the accused to custody in accordance with paragraph (a) of this subsection.

(4) Where the court has committed a person to custody in accordance with paragraph (a) of subsection (3) above, then, if that person is in custody for no other cause, the court may, at any time before his first appearance before the Crown Court, grant him bail in accordance with the Bail Act 1976 subject to a duty to appear before the Crown Court for trial.

(5) Where a magistrates' court acting as examining justices commits any person for trial or determines to discharge him, the clerk of the court shall, on the day on which the committal proceedings are concluded or the next day, cause to be displayed in a part of the court house to which the public have access a notice –

(a) in either case giving that person's name, address, and age (if known);

(b) in a case where the court so commits him, stating the charge or charges on which he is committed and the court to which he is committed;

(c) in a case where the court determines to discharge him, describing the offence charged and stating that it has so determined;

but this subsection shall have effect subject to section 4 and 6 of the Sexual Offences (Amendment) Act 1976 (anonymity of complainant and accused in rape etc. cases).

(6) A notice displayed in pursuance of subsection (5) above shall not contain the name or address of any person under the age of 17 unless the justices in question have stated that in their opinion he would be mentioned in the notice apart from the preceding provisions of this subsection and should be mentioned in it for the purpose of avoiding injustice to him.

8. Restrictions on reports of committal proceedings

(1) Except as provided by subsections (2), (3) and (8) below, it shall not be lawful to publish in Great Britain a written report, or to broadcast [or include in a cable programme] in Great Britain a report, of any committal proceedings in England and Wales containing any matter other than that permitted by subsection (4) below.

(2) [Subject to subsection (2A) below] a magistrates' court shall, on an application for the purpose made with reference to any committal proceedings by the accused or one of the accused, as the case may be, order that subsection (1) above shall not apply to reports of those proceedings.

[(2A) Where in the case of two or more accused one of them objects to the making of an order under subsection (2) above, the court shall make the order if, and only if, it is satisfied, after hearing the representations of the accused, that it is in the interests of justice to do so.

(2B) An order under subsection (2) above shall not apply to reports of proceedings under subsection (2A) above, but any decision of the court to make or not to make such an order may be contained in reports published [broadcast or included in a cable programme] before the time authorised by subsection (3) below.]

(3) It shall not be unlawful under this section to publish [broadcast or include in a cable programme] a report of committal proceedings containing any matter other than that permitted by subsection (4) below:

(a) where the magistrates' court determines not to commit the accused, or determines to commit none of the accused, for trial, after it so determines;

(b) where the court commits the accused or any of the accused for trial, after the conclusion of his trial or, as the case may be, the trial of the last to be tried;

and where at any time during the inquiry the court proceeds to try summarily the case of one or more of the accused under section 25(3) or (7) below, while committing the other accused or one or more of the other accused for trial, it shall not be unlawful under this section to publish [broadcast or include in a cable programme] as part of a report of the summary trial, after the court determines to proceed as aforesaid, a report of so much of the committal proceedings containing any such matter as takes place before the determination.

(4) The following matters may be contained in a report of committal proceedings published [broadcast or included in a cable programme] without an order under subsection (2) above before the time authorised by subsection (3) above, that is to say:

(a) the identity of the court and the names of the examining justices;

(b) the names, addresses and occupations of the parties and witnesses and the ages of the accused and witnesses;

(*c*) the offence or offences, or a summary of them, with which the accused is or are charged;

(*d*) the names of counsel and solicitors engaged in the proceedings;

(*e*) any decision of the court to commit the accused or any of the accused for trial, and any decision of the court on the disposal of the case of any accused not committed;

(*f*) where the court commits the accused or any of the accused for trial, the charge or charges, or a summary of them, on which he is committed and the court to which he is committed;

(*g*) where the committal proceedings are adjourned, the date and place to which they are adjourned;

(*h*) any arrangements as to bail on committal or adjournment;

(*i*) whether legal aid was granted to the accused or any of the accused.

(5) If a report is published [broadcast or included in a cable programme] in contravention of this section, the following persons, that is to say:

(*a*) in the case of a publication of a written report as part of a newspaper or periodical, any proprietor, editor or publisher of the newspaper or periodical;

(*b*) in the case of a publication of a written report otherwise than as part of a newspaper or periodical, the person who publishes it;

(*c*) in the case of a broadcast of a report, any body corporate which transmits or provides the programme in which the report is broadcast and any person having functions in relation to the programme corresponding to those of the editor of a newspaper or periodical,

[(*d*) in the case of an inclusion of a report in a cable programme, any body corporate which sends or provides the programme and any person having functions in relation to the programme corresponding to those of an editor of a newspaper,]

shall be liable to summary conviction to a fine not exceeding [level 5 on the standard scale].

(6) Proceedings for an offence under this section shall not, in England and Wales, be instituted otherwise than by or with the consent of the Attorney-General.

(7) Subsection (1) above shall be in addition to, and not in derogation from, the provisions of any other enactment with respect to the publication of reports and proceedings of magistrates' and other courts.

(8) For the purposes of this section committal proceedings shall, in relation to an information charging an indictable offence, be deemed to include any proceedings in the magistrates' court before the court proceeds to inquire into the information as examining justices; but where a magistrates' court which has begun to try an information summarily discontinues the summary trial in pursuance of section 25(2) or (6) below and proceeds to inquire into the information as examining justices, that circumstance shall not make it unlawful under this section for a report of any proceedings on the information which was published [broadcast or included in a cable programme] before the court determined to proceed as aforesaid to have been so published or broadcast.

(9) . . .

(10) In this section:

'broadcast' means broadcast by wireless telegraphy sounds or visual images intended for general reception;

['cable programme' means a programme included in a cable programme service;]

'publish', in relation to a report, means publish the report, either by itself or as part of a newspaper or periodical, for distribution to the public.

CRIMINAL JURISDICTION AND PROCEDURE: SUMMARY TRIAL OF INFORMATION

11. Non-appearance of accused; general provisions

(1) Subject to the provisions of this Act, where at the time and place appointed for

the trial or adjourned trial of an information the prosecutor appears but the accused does not, the court may proceed in his absence.

(2) Where a summons has been issued, the court shall not begin to try the information in the absence of the accused unless either it is proved to the satisfaction of the court, on oath or in such other manner as may be prescribed, that the summons was served on the accused within what appears to the court to be a reasonable time before the trial or adjourned trial or the accused has appeared on a previous occasion to answer to the information.

(3) A magistrates' court shall not in a person's absence sentence him to imprisonment or detention in a detention centre or make an order under section 23 of the Powers of Criminal Courts Act 1973 that a suspended sentence passed on him shall take effect.

(4) A magistrates' court shall not in a person's absence impose any disqualification on him, except on resumption of the hearing after an adjournment under section 10(3) above; and where a trial is adjourned in pursuance of this subsection the notice required by section 10(2) above shall include notice of the reason for the adjournment.

12. Non-appearance of accused: plea of guilty

(1) Subject to subsection (7) below, this section shall apply where a summons has been issued requiring a person to appear before a magistrates' court, other than a juvenile court, to answer to an information for a summary offence, not being an offence for which the accused is liable to be sentenced to be imprisoned for a term exceeding 3 months, and the clerk of the court is notified by or on behalf of the prosecutor that the following documents have been served upon the accused with the summons, that is to say:

(a) a notice containing such statement of the effect of this section as may be prescribed; and

(b) a concise statement in the prescribed form of such facts relating to the charge as will be placed before the court by or on behalf of the prosecutor if the accused pleads guilty without appearing before the court.

(2) Subject to subsections (3) to (5) below, where the clerk of the court receives a notification in writing purporting to be given by the accused or by a solicitor acting on his behalf that the accused desires to plead guilty without appearing before the court, the clerk of the court shall inform the prosecutor of the receipt of the notification and if at the time and place appointed for the trial or adjourned trial of the information the accused does not appear and it is proved to the satisfaction of the court, on oath or in such other manner as may be prescribed, that the notice and statement of facts referred to in subsection (1) above have been served upon the accused with the summons, then:

(a) subject to section 11(3) and (4) above, the court may proceed to hear and dispose of the case in the absence of the accused, whether or not the prosecutor is also absent, in like manner as if both parties had appeared and the accused had pleaded guilty; or

(b) if the court decides not to proceed as aforesaid, the court shall adjourn or further adjourn the trial for the purpose of dealing with the information as if the notification aforesaid had not been given.

(3) If at any time before the hearing the clerk of the court receives an intimation in writing purporting to be given by or on behalf of the accused that he wishes to withdraw the notification aforesaid, the clerk of the court shall inform the prosecutor thereof and the court shall deal with the information as if this section had not been passed.

(4) Before accepting the plea of guilty and convicting the accused in his absence under subsection (2) above, the court shall cause the notification and statement of facts aforesaid, including any submission received with the notification which the accused wishes to be brought to the attention of the court with a view to mitigation of sentence, to be read out before the court [by the clerk of the court].

(5) If the court proceeds under subsection (2) above to hear and dispose of the case in the absence of the accused, the court shall not permit any statement to be made by or on behalf of the prosecutor with respect to any facts relating to the offence charged other than the statement of facts aforesaid except on a resumption of the trial after an adjournment under section 10(3) above.

(6) In relation to an adjournment by reason of the requirements of paragraph (b) of subsection (2) above or to an adjournment on the occasion of the accused's conviction in his absence under that subsection, the notice required by section 10(2) above shall include notice of the reason for the adjournment.

(7) The Secretary of State may by order made by statutory instrument provide that this section shall not apply in relation to such offences (in addition to an offence for which the accused is liable to be sentenced to be imprisoned for a term exceeding 3 months) as may be specified in the order, and any order under this subsection –

(*a*) may vary or revoke any previous order thereunder; and

(*b*) shall not be made unless a draft thereof has been approved by resolution of each House of Parliament.

(8) Any such notice of statement as is mentioned in subsection (1) above may be served in Scotland with a summons which is so served under the Summary Jurisdiction (Process) Act 1881.

(9) Where the clerk of the court has received such a notification as is mentioned in subsection (2) above but the accused nevertheless appears before the court at the time and place appointed for the trial or adjourned trial the court may, if the accused consents, proceed under this section as if he were absent.]

CRIMINAL JURISDICTION AND PROCEDURE: OFFENCES TRIABLE ON INDICTMENT OR SUMMARILY

17. Certain offences triable either way

(1) The offences listed in Schedule 1 to this Act shall be triable either way.

(2) Subsection (1) above is without prejudice to any other enactment by virtue of which any offence is triable either way.

18. Initial procedure on information against adult for offence triable either way

(1) Sections 19 to 23 below shall have effect where a person who has attained the age of 17 appears or is brought before a magistrates' court on an information charging him with an offence triable either way.

(2) Without prejudice to section 11(1) above, everything that the court is required to do under sections 19 to 22 below must be done before any evidence is called and, subject to subsection (3) below and section 23 below, with the accused present in court.

(3) The court may proceed in the absence of the accused in accordance with such of the provisions of sections 19 to 22 below as are applicable in the circumstances if the court considers that by reason of his disorderly conduct before the court it is not practicable for the proceedings to be conducted in his presence; and subsections (3) to (5) of section 23 below, so far as applicable, shall have effect in relation to proceedings conducted in the absence of the accused by virtue of this subsection (references in those subsections to the person representing the accused being for this purpose read as reference to the person, if any, representing him).

(4) A magistrates' court proceeding under sections 19 to 23 below may adjourn the proceedings at any time, and on doing so on any occasion when the accused is present may remand the accused, and shall remand him if –

(*a*) on the occasion on which he first appeared, or was brought, before the court to answer to the information he was in custody or, having been released on bail, surrendered to the custody of the court; or

(*b*) he has been remanded at any time in the course of proceedings on the information;

and where the court remands the accused, the time fixed for the resumption of the proceedings shall be that at which he is required to appear or be brought before the court in pursuance of the remand [or would be required to be brought before the court but for section 128(3A) below].

(5) The functions of a magistrates' court under sections 19 to 23 below may be discharged by a single justice, but the foregoing provision shall not be taken to authorise the summary trial of an information by a magistrates' court composed of less than two justices.

19. Court to begin by considering which mode of trial appears more suitable
(1) The court shall consider whether, having regard to the matters mentioned in subsection (3) below and any representations made by the prosecutor or the accused, the offence appears to the court more suitable for summary trial or for trial on indictment.

(2) Before so considering, the court –

(*a*) shall cause the charge to be written down, if this has not already been done, and read to the accused; and

(*b*) shall afford first the prosecutor and then the accused an opportunity to make representations as to which mode of trial would be more suitable.

(3) The matters to which the court is to have regard under subsection (1) above are the nature of the case; whether the circumstances make the offence one of serious character; whether the punishment which a magistrates' court would have power to inflict for it would be adequate; and any other circumstances which appear to the court to make it more suitable for the offence to be tried in one way rather than the other.

(4) If the prosecution is being carried on by the Attorney General, the Solicitor General or the Director of Public Prosecutions and he applies for the offence to be tried on indictment, the preceding provisions of this section and sections 20 and 21 below shall not apply, and the court shall proceed to inquire into the information as examining justices.

[(5) The power of the Director of Public Prosecutions under subsection (4) above to apply for an offence to be tried on indictment shall not be exercised except with the consent of the Attorney General.]

20. Procedure where summary trial appears more suitable
(1) If, where the court has considered as required by section 19(1) above, it appears to the court that the offence is more suitable for summary trial, the following provisions of this section shall apply (unless excluded by section 23 below).

(2) The court shall explain to the accused in ordinary language:

(*a*) that it appears to the court more suitable for him to be tried summarily for the offence, and that he can either consent to be so tried or, if he wishes, be tried by a jury; and

(*b*) that if he is tried summarily and is convicted by the court, he may be committed for sentence to the Crown Court under section 38 below if the convicting court, on obtaining information about his character and antecedents, is of opinion that they are such that greater punishment should be inflicted than the convincing court has power to inflict for the offence.

(3) After explaining to the accused as provided by subsection (2) above the court shall ask him whether he consents to be tried summarily or wishes to be tried by a jury, and –

(*a*) if he consents to be tried summarily, shall proceed to the summary trial of the information;

(*b*) if he does not so consent, shall proceed to inquire into the information as examining justices.

21. Procedure where triable on indictment appears more suitable
If, where the court has considered as required by section 19(1) above, it appears to the court that the offence is more suitable for trial on indictment, the court shall tell

the accused that the court has decided that it is more suitable for him to be tried for the offence by a jury, and shall proceed to inquire into the information as examining justices.

22. Certain offences triable either way to be tried summarily if value involved is small

(1) If the offence charged by the information is one of those mentioned in the first column of Schedule 2 to this Act (in this section referred to as 'scheduled offences') then, subject to subsection (7) below, the court shall, before proceeding in accordance with section 19 above, consider whether, having regard to any representations made by the prosecutor or the accused, the value involved (as defined in subsection (10) below) appears to the court to exceed the relevant sum.

For the purposes of this section the relevant sum is [£400].

(2) If, where subsection (1) above applies, it appears to the court clear that, for the offence charged, the value involved does not exceed the relevant sum, the court shall proceed as if the offence were triable only summarily, and sections 19 to 21 above shall not apply.

(3) If, where subsection (1) above applies, it appears to the court clear that, for the offence charged, the value involved exceeds the relevant sum, the court shall thereupon proceed in accordance with section 19 above in the ordinary way without further regard to the provisions of this section.

(4) If, where subsection (1) above applies, it appears to the court for any reason no clear whether, for the offence charged, the value involved does or does not exceed the relevant sum, the provisions of subsections (5) and (6) below shall apply.

(5) The court shall cause the charge to be written down, if this has not already been done, and read to the accused, and shall explain to him in ordinary language –
  (a) that he can, if he wishes, consent to be tried summarily for the offence and that if he consents to be so tried, he will definitely be tried in that way; and
  (b) that if he is tried summarily and is convicted by the court, his liability to imprisonment or a fine will be limited as provided in section 33 below.

(6) After explaining to the accused as provided by subsection (5) above the court shall ask him whether he consents to be tried summarily and:
  (a) if he so consents, shall proceed in accordance with subsection (2) above as if that subsection applied;
  (b) if he does not so consent, shall proceed in accordance with subsection (3) above as if that subsection applied.

(7) Subsection (1) above shall not apply where the offence charged –
  (a) is one of two or more offences with which the accused is charged on the same occasion and which appear to the court to constitute or form part of a series of two or more offences of the same or a similar character; or
  (b) consists in the indictment to commit two or more scheduled offences.

(8) Where a person is convicted by a magistrates' court of a scheduled offence, it shall not be open to him to appeal to the Crown Court against the conviction on the ground that the convicting court's decision as to the value involved was mistaken.

(9) If, where subsection (1) above applies, the offence charged is one with which the accused is charged jointly with a person who has not attained the age of 17, the reference in that subsection to any representations made by the accused shall be read as including any representations made by the person under 17.

(10) In this section 'the value involved', in relating to any scheduled offence, means the value indicated in the second column of Schedule 2 to this Act, measured as indicated in the third column of that Schedule; and in that Schedule 'the material time' means the time of the alleged offence.

23. Power of court, with consent of legally represented accused, to proceed in his absence

(1) Where:
  (a) the accused is represented by counsel or a solicitor who in his absence

signifies to the court the accused's consent to the proceedings for determining how he is to be tried for the offence being conducted in his absence; and

(b) the court is safisfied that there is good reason for proceeding in the absence of the accused,

the following provisions of this section shall apply.

(2) Subject to the following provisions of this section, the court may proceed in the absence of the accused in accordance with such of the provisions of sections 19 to 22 above as are applicable in the circumstances.

(3) If, in a case where subsection (1) of section 22 above applies, it appears to the court as mentioned in subsection (4) of that section, subsections (5) and (6) of that section shall not apply and the court –

(a) if the accused's consent to be tried summarily has been or is signified by the person representing him, shall proceed in accordance with subsection (2) of that section as if that subsection applied; or

(b) if that consent has not been and is not so signified, shall proceed in accordance with subsection (3) of that section as if that subsection applied.

(4) If, where the court has considered as required by section 19(1) above, it appears to the court that the offence is more suitable for summary trial then –

(a) if the accused's consent to be tried summarily has been or is signified by the person representing him, section 20 above shall not apply, and the court shall proceed to the summary trial of the information; or

(b) if that consent has not been and is not so signified, section 20 above shall not apply and the court shall proceed to inquire into the information as examining justices and may adjourn the hearing without remanding the accused.

(5) If, where the court has considered as required by section 19(1) above, it appears to the court that the offence is more suitable for trial on indictment, section 21 above shall not apply, and the court shall proceed to inquire into the information as examining justices and may adjourn the hearing without remanding the accused.

24. Summary trial of information against child or young person for indictable offence

(1) Where a person under the age of 17 appears or is brought before a magistrates' court on an information charging him with an indictable offence other than homicide, he shall be tried summarily unless –

(a) he has attained the age of 14 and the offence is such as is mentioned in subsection (2) of section 53 of the Children and Young Persons Act 1933 (under which young persons convicted on indictment of certain grave crimes may be sentenced to be detained for long periods) and the court considers that if he is found guilty of the offence it ought to be possible to sentence him in pursuance of that subsection; or

(b) he is charged jointly with a person who has attained the age of 17 and the court consider it necessary in the interests of justice to commit them both for trial;

and accordingly in a case falling within paragraph (a) or (b) of this subsection the court shall commit the accused for trial if either it is of opinion that there is sufficient evidence to put him on trial or it has power under section 6(2) above so to commit him without consideration of the evidence.

(2) Where, in a case falling within subsection (1)(b) above, a magistrates' court commits a person under the age of 17 for trial for an offence with which he is charged jointly with a person who has attained that age, the court may also commit him for trial for any other indictable offence with which he is charged at the same time (whether jointly with the person who has attained that age or not) if that other offence arises out of circumstances which are the same as or connected with those giving rise to the first-mentioned offence.

(3) If on trying a person summarily in pursuance of subsection (1) above the court finds him guilty, it may impose a fine of an amount not exceeding [£400] or may exercise the same powers as it could have exercised if he had been found guilty

of an offence for which, but for section [1(1) of the Criminal Justice Act 1982, it could have sentenced him to imprisonment for a term not exceeding –

(a) the maximum term of imprisonment for the offence on conviction on indictment; or

(b) six months,

whichever is the less.]

(4) In relation to a person under the age of 14 subsection (3) above shall have effect as if for the words '[£400]' there were substituted the words '[£100]'; but this subsection shall cease to have effect on the coming into force of section 4 of the Children and Young Persons Act 1969 (which prohibits criminal proceedings against children).

25. Power to change from summary trial to committal proceedings, and vice versa

(1) Subsections (2) to (4) below shall have effect where a person who has attained the age of 17 appears or is brought before a magistrates' court on an information charging him with an offence triable either way.

(2) Where the court has (otherwise than in pursuance of section 22(2) above) begun to try the information summarily, the court may, at any time before the conclusion of the evidence for the prosecution, discontinue the summary trial and proceed to inquire into the information as examining justices and, on doing so, may adjourn the hearing without remanding the accused.

(3) Where the court has begun to inquire into the information as examining justices, then, if at any time during the inquiry it appears to the court, having regard to any representations made in the presence of the accused by the prosecutor, or made by the accused, and to the nature of the case, that the offence is after all more suitable for summary trial, the court may, after doing as provided in subsection (4) below, ask the accused whether he consents to be tried summarily and, if he so consents, may [subject to subsection (3A) below] proceed to try the information summarily; but if the prosecution is being carried on by the Attorney General, the Solicitor General or the Director of Public Prosecutions, the court shall not act under this subsection without his consent.

(4) Before asking the accused under subsection (3) above whether he consents to be tried summarily, the court shall in ordinary language –

(a) explain to him that it appears to the court more suitable for him to be tried summarily for the offence, but that this can only be done if he consents to be so tried; and

(b) unless, it has already done so, explain to him, as provided in section 20(2)(b) above, about the court's power to commit to the Crown Court for sentence.

(5) Where a person under the age of 17 appears or is brought before a magistrates' court on an information charging him with an indictable offence other than homicide, and the court:

(a) has begun to try the information summarily on the footing that the case does not fall within paragraph (a) or (b) of section 24(1) above and must therefore be tried summarily, as required by the said section 24(1); or

(b) has begun to inquire into the case as examining justices on the footing that the case does not fall,

subsection (6) or (7) below, as the case may be, shall have effect.

(6) If, in a case falling within subsection (5)(a) above, it appears to the court at any time before the conclusion of the evidence for the prosecution that the case is after all one which under the said section 24(1) ought not to be tried summarily, the court may discontinue the summary trial and proceed to inquire into the information as examining justices and, on doing so, may adjourn the hearing without remanding the accused.

(7) If, in a case falling within subsection (5)(b) above, it appears to the court at any time during the inquiry that the case is after all one which under the said section 24(1) ought to be tried summarily, the court may proceed to try the information summarily.

37. Committal to Crown Court with a view to Youth Custody

[(1) Where a person who is not less than 15 nor more than 16 years old is convicted by a magistrates' court of an offence punishable on conviction on indictment with a term of imprisonment exceeding six months, then, if the court is of opinion that he should be sentenced to a greater term of youth custody than it has power to impose, the court may commit him in custody or in bail to the Crown Court for sentence.

(1A) If by virtue of an order made under section 14 of the Criminal Justice Act 1982, the term specified in section 7(5) of that Act as the usual term of youth custody is increased to a term exceeding six months, subsection (1) above shall have effect, for so long as the term so specified exceeds six months, as if after the word 'opinion' there were inserted the following words:

'(a) that a youth custody sentence should be passed on him but that it has no power to do so; or

(b)'.]

(2) A person committed in custody under section (1) above shall be committed:

(a) if the court has been notified by the Secretary of State that a remand centre is available for the reception, from that court, of persons of the class or description of the person committed, to a remand centre;

(b) if the court has not been so notified, to a prison.

38. Committal for sentence on summary trial of offence triable either way

Where the summary trial of an offence triable either way (not being an offence as regards which this section is excluded by section 33 above) a person who is not less than 17 years old is convicted of the offence, then, if on obtaining information about his character and antecedents the court is of opinion that they are such that greater punishment should be inflicted for the offence than the court has power to inflict, the court may, in accordance with section 56 of the Criminal Justice Act 1967, commit him in custody or on bail to the Crown Court for sentence in accordance with the provisions of section 42 of the Powers of Criminal Courts Act 1973.

39. Cases where magistrates' court may remit offender to another such court for sentence

(1) Where a person who has attained the age of 17 ('the offender') has been convicted by a magistrates' court ('the convicting court') of an offence to which this section applies ('the instant offence') and:

(a) it appears to the convicting court that some other magistrates' court ('the other court') has convicted him of another such offence in respect of which the other court has neither passed sentence on him nor committed him to the Crown Court for sentence nor dealt with him in any other way; and

(b) the other court consents to his being remitted under this section to the other court,

the convicting court may remit him to the other court to be dealt with in respect of the instant offence by the other court instead of by the convicting court.

(2) The offender, if remitted under this section, shall have no right of appeal against the order of remission.

(3) Where the convicting court remits the offender to the other court under this section, it shall adjourn the trial of the information charging him with the instant offence, and:

(a) section 128 below and all other enactments (whenever passed) relating to remand or the granting of bail in criminal proceedings shall have effect in relation to the convicting court's power or duty to remand the offender on that adjournment as if any reference to the court to or before which the person remanded is to be brought or appear after remand where a reference to the court to which he is being remitted; and

(b) subject to subsection (4) below, the other court may deal with the case in any way in which it would have power to deal with it (including, where applicable, the remission of the offender under this section to another magistrates' court in respect of the instant offence) if all proceedings relating to that offence which took place before the convicting court had taken place before the other court.

(4) Nothing in this section shall preclude the convicting court from making any order which it has power to make under section 28 of the Theft Act 1968 (orders for restitution) by virtue of the offender's conviction of the instant offence.

(5) Where the convicting court has remitted the offender under this section to the other court, the other court may remit him back to the convicting court; and the provisions of subsection (3) above (so far as applicable) shall apply with the necessary modifications in relation to any remission under this subsection.

(6) This section applies to:

(*a*) any offence punishable with imprisonment; and

(*b*) any offence in respect of which the convicting court has a power or duty to order the offender to be disqualified under section 93 of the Road Traffic Act 1972 (disqualification for certain motor offences);

and in this section 'conviction' includes a finding under section 30(1) above that the person in question did the act or made the omission charged, and 'convicted' shall be construed accordingly.

BAIL ACT 1976

INCIDENTS OF BAIL IN CRIMINAL PROCEEDINGS

3. General provisions

(1) A person granted bail in criminal proceedings shall be under a duty to surrender to custody, and that duty is enforceable in accordance with section 6 of this Act.

(2) No recognizance for his surrender to custody shall be taken from him.

(3) Except as provided by this section:

(*a*) no security for his surrender to custody shall be taken from him,

(*b*) he shall not be required to provide a surety or sureties for his surrender to custody, and

(*c*) no other requirement shall be imposed on him as a condition of bail.

(4) He may be required, before release on bail, to provide a surety or sureties to secure his surrender to custody.

(5) If it appears that he is unlikely to remain in Great Britain until the time appointed for him to surrender to custody, he may be required, before release on bail, to give security for his surrender to custody.

The security may be given by him or on his behalf.

(6) He may be required (but only by a court) to comply, before release on bail or later, with such requirements as appear to the court to be necessary to secure that:

(*a*) he surrenders to custody,

(*b*) he does not commit an offence while on bail,

(*c*) he does not interfere with witnesses or otherwise obstruct the course of justice whether in relation to himself or any other person,

(*d*) he makes himself available for the purposes of enabling enquiries or a report to be made to assist the court in dealing with him for the offence.

[(6A) In the case of a person accused of murder the court granting bail shall, unless it considers that satisfactory reports on his mental condition have already been obtained, impose as conditions of bail:

(*a*) a requirement that the accused shall undergo examination by two medical practitioners for the purpose of enabling such reports to be prepared; and

(*b*) a requirement that he shall for that purpose attend such an institution or place as the court directs and comply with any other directions which may be given to him for that purpose by either of those practitioners.

(6B) Of the medical practitioners referred to in subsection (6A) above at least one shall be a practitioner approved for the purposes of [section 12 of the Mental Health Act 1983.]]

(7) If a parent or guardian of a child or young person consents to be surety for the child or young person for the purposes of this subsection, the parent or guardian may be required to secure that the child or young person complies with any requirement imposed on him by virtue of [subsection (6) or (6A) above]

  (a) no requirement shall be imposed on the parent or the guardian of a young person by virtue of this subsection where it appears that the young person will attain the age of seventeen before the time to be appointed for him to surrender to custody; and

  (b) the parent or guardian shall not be required to secure compliance with any requirement to which his consent does not extend and shall not, in respect of those requirements to which his consent does extend, be bound in a sum greater than £50.

(8) Where a court has granted bail in criminal proceedings [that court or, where that court has committed a person on bail to the Crown Court for trial or to be sentenced or otherwise dealt with, that court or the Crown Court may] on application:

  (a) by or on behalf of the person to whom [bail was] granted, or

  (b) by the prosecutor or a constable.

vary the conditions of bail or impose conditions in respect of bail which it [has been] granted unconditionally.

(9) This section is subject to [sub-section (2) of section 30 of the Magistrates' Courts Act 1980] (conditions of bail on remand for medical examination).

BAIL FOR ACCUSED PERSONS AND OTHERS

4. General right to bail of accused persons and others

(1) A person to whom this section applies shall be granted bail except as provided in Schedule 1 to this Act.

(2) This section applies to a person who is accused of an offence when:

  (a) he appears or is brought before a magistrates' court or the Crown Court in the course of or in connection with proceedings for the offence, or

  (b) he applies to a court for bail in connection with the proceedings.

This subsection does not apply as respects proceedings on or after a person's conviction of the offence or proceedings against a fugitive offender for the offence.

(3) This section also applies to a person who, having been convicted of an offence, appears or is brought before a magistrates' court to be dealt with under section 6 or section 16 of the Powers of Criminal Courts Act 1973 (breach of requirement of probation or community service order).

(4) This section also applies to a person who has been convicted of an offence and whose case is adjourned by the court for the purpose of enabling inquiries or a report to be made to assist the court in dealing with him for the offence.

(5) Schedule 1 to this Act also has effect as respects conditions of bail for a person to whom this section applies.

(6) In Schedule 1 to this Act 'the defendant' means a person to whom this section applies and any reference to a defendant whose case is adjourned for inquiries or a report is a reference to a person to whom this section applies by virtue of subsection (4) above.

(7) This section is subject to [section 41 of the Magistrates' Courts Act 1980] (restriction of bail by magistrates court in cases of treason).

SUPPLEMENTARY

5. Supplementary provisions about decisions on bail

(1) Subject to subsection (2) below, where:

  (a) a court or constable grants bail in criminal proceedings, or (*b*) a court withholds bail in criminal proceedings from a person to whom section 4 of this Act applies, or

(*c*) a court, officer of a court or constable appoints a time or place or a court or officer of a court appoints a different time or place for a person granted bail in criminal proceedings to surrender to custody, or

(*d*) a court varies any conditions of bail or imposes conditions in respect of bail in criminal proceedings.

that court, officer or constable shall make a record of the decision in the prescribed manner and containing the prescribed particulars and, if requested to do so by the person in relation to whom the decision was taken, shall cause him to be given a copy of the record of the decision as soon as practicable after the record is made.

(2) Where bail in criminal proceedings is granted by endorsing a warrant of arrest for bail the constable who releases on bail the person arrested shall make the record required by subsection (1) above instead of the judge or justice who issued the warrant.

(3) Where a magistrates' court or the Crown Court:

(*a*) withholds bail in criminal proceedings, or

(*b*) imposes conditions in granting bail in criminal proceedings, or

(*c*) varies any conditions of bail or imposes conditions in respect of bail in criminal proceedings.

and does so in relation to a person to whom section 4 of this Act applies, then the court shall, with a view to enabling him to consider making an application in the matter to another court, give reasons for withholding bail or for imposing or varying the conditions.

(4) A court which is by virtue of subsection (3) above required to give reasons for its decision shall include a note of those reasons in the record of its decision and shall (except in a case where, by virtue of subsection (5) below, this need not be done) give a copy of that note to the person in relation to whom the decision was taken.

(5) The Crown Court need not give a copy of the note of the reasons for its decision to the person in relation to whom the decision was taken where that person is represented by counsel or a solicitor unless his counsel or solicitor requests the court to do so.

(6) Where a magistrates' court withholds bail in criminal proceedings from a person who is not represented by counsel or a solicitor, the court shall:

(*a*) if it is committing him for trial to the Crown Court, inform him that he may apply to the High Court or to the Crown Court to be granted bail:

(*b*) in any other case, inform him that he may apply to the High Court for that purpose.

(7) Where a person has given security in pursuance of section 3(5) above, and a court is satisfied that he failed to surrender to custody then, unless it appears that he had reasonable cause for his failure, the court may order the forefeiture of the security.

(8) If a court orders the forefeiture of a security under subsection (7) above, the court may declare that the forfeiture extends to such amount less than the full value of the security as it thinks fit to order.

[(8A) An order under subsection (7) above shall, unless previously revoked, take effect at the end of twenty-one days beginning with the day on which it is made.

(8B) A court which has ordered the forfeiture of a security under subsection (7) above may, if satisfied on an application made by or on behalf of the person who gave it that he did after all have reasonable cause for his failure to surrender to custody, by order remit the forfeiture or declare that it extends to such amount less than the full value of the security as it thinks fit to order.

(8C) An application under subsection (8B) above may be made before or after the order for forfeiture has taken effect, but shall not be entertained unless the court is satisfied that the prosecution was given reasonable notice of the applicant's intention to make it.]

(9) A security which has been ordered to be forfeited by a court under subsection

(7) above shall, to the extent of the forfeiture:
  (*a*) if it consists of money, be accounted for and paid in the same manner as a fine imposed by that court would be;
  (*b*) if it does not consist of money, be enforced by such magistrates' court as may be specified in the order.
  [(9A) Where an order is made under subsection (8B) above after the order for forfeiture of the security in question has taken effect, any money which would have fallen to be repaid or paid over to the person who gave the security if the order under subsection (8B) has been made before the order for forfeiture took effect shall be repaid or paid over to him.]
  (10) In this section 'prescribed' means, in relation to the decision of a court or an officer of a court, prescribed by Supreme Court rules, Courts-Martial Appeal rules, Crown Court rules or magistrates' courts rules, as the case requires or, in relation to a decision of a constable, prescribed by direction of the Secretary of State.

8. Bail with sureties

(1) This section applies where a person is granted bail in criminal proceedings on condition that he provides one or more surety or sureties for the purposes of securing that he surrenders to custody.
  (2) In considering the suitability for that purpose of a proposed surety, regard may be had (amongst other things) to:
  (*a*) the surety's financial resources;
  (*b*) his character and any previous convictions of his; and
  (*c*) his proximity (whether in point of kinship, place or residence or otherwise) to the person for whom he is to be surety.
  (3) Where a court grants a person bail in criminal proceedings on such a condition but is unable to release him because no surety or no suitable surety is available, the court shall fix the amount in which the surety is to be bound and subsections (4) and (5) below, or in a case where the proposed surety resides in Scotland subsection (6) below, shall apply for the purpose of enabling the recognizance of the surety to be entered into subsequently.
  (4) Where this subsection applies the recognizance of the surety may be entered into before such of the following persons or descriptions of persons as the court may by order specify or, if it makes no such order, before any of the following persons, that is to say:
  (*a*) where the decision is taken by a magistrates' court, before a justice of the peace, a justices' clerk or a police officer who either is of the rank of inspector or above or is in charge of a police station or, if magistrates' courts rules so provide, by a person of such other description as is specified in the rules;
  (*b*) where the decision is taken by the Crown Court, before any of the persons specified in paragraph (*a*) above or, if Crown Court rules so provide, by a person of such other description as is specified in the rules;
  (*c*) where the decision is taken by the High Court or the Court of Appeal, before any of the persons specified in paragraph (*a*) above or, if Supreme Court rules so provide, by a person of such other description as is specified in the rules;
  (*d*) where the decision is taken by the Courts-Martial Appeal Court, before any of the persons specified in paragraph (*a*) above or, if Courts-Martial Appeal rules so provide, by a person of such other description as is specified in the rules;
and Supreme Court rules, Crown Court rules, Courts-Martial Appeal rules or magistrates' courts rules may also prescribe the manner in which a recognizance which is to be entered into before such a person is to be entered into and the persons by whom and the manner in which the recognizance may be enforced.
  (5) Where a surety seeks to enter into his recognizance before any person in accordance with subsection (4) above that person declines to take his recognizance because he is not satisfied of the surety's suitability, the surety may apply to:
  (*a*) the court which fixed the amount of the recognizance in which the surety was to be bound, or

(*b*) a magistrates' court for the petty sessions area in which he resides,
for that court to take his recognizance and that court shall, if satisfied of his
suitability, take his recognizance.

(6) Where this subsection applies, the court, if satisfied of the suitability of the
proposed surety, may direct that arrangements be made for the recognizance of the
surety to be entered into in Scotland before any constable, within the meaning of the
Police (Scotland) Act 1967, having charge at any police office or station in like
manner as the recognizance would be entered into in England or Wales.

(7) Where, in pursuance of subsection (4) or (6) above, a recognizance is entered
into otherwise than before the court that fixed the amount of the recognizance, the
same consequences shall follow as if it had been entered into before that court.

SCHEDULE 1

PERSONS ENTITLED TO BAIL: SUPPLEMENTARY PROVISIONS

PART I

DEFENDANTS ACCUSED OR CONVICTED OF IMPRISONABLE OFFENCES

Defendants to whom Part I applies
1. Where the offence of one of the offences of which the defendant is accused or convicted in
the proceedings is punishable with imprisonment the following provisions of this Part of this
Schedule apply.

Exceptions to right to bail
2. The defendant need not be granted bail if the court is satisfied that there are substantial
grounds for believing that the defendant, if released on bail (whether subject to conditions or
not) would:
(*a*) fail to surrender to custody, or
(*b*) commit an offence while on bail, or
(*c*) interfere with witnesses or otherwise obstruct the course of justice, whether in relation to
himself or any other person

3. The defendant need not be granted bail if the court is satisfied that the defendant should
be kept in custody for his own protection or, if he is a child or young person, for his own welfare.

4. The defendant need not be granted bail if he is in custody in pursuance of the sentence of
a court or of any authority acting under any of the Services Acts.

5. The defendant need not be granted bail where the court is satisfied that it has not been
practicable to obtain sufficient information for the purpose of taking the decisions required by
this Part of this Schedule for want of time since the institution of the proceedings against him.

6. The defendant need not be granted bail if, having been released on bail in or in
connection with the proceedings for the offence, he has been arrested in pursuance of section 7
of this Act.

Exception applicable only to defendant whose case is adjourned for inquiries or a report
7. Where his case is adjourned for inquiries or a report, the defendant need not be granted
bail if it appears to the court that it would be impracticable to complete the inquiries or make
the report without keeping the defendant in custody.

Restriction of conditions of bail
8.(1) Subject to sub-paragraph (3) below, where the defendant is granted bail, no
conditions shall be imposed under subsections (4) to (7) of section 3 of this Act unless it
appears to the court that it is necessary to do so for the purpose of preventing the occurrence of
any of the events mentioned in paragraph 2 of this Part of this Schedule or, in the case of a
condition under subsection (6)(*d*) of that section, that it is necessary to impose it to enable
inquiries or a report to be made into the defendant's physical or mental condition.
(2) Sub-paragraph (1) above also applies to any application to the court to vary the
conditions of bail or to impose conditions in respect of bail which has been granted unconditionally.
(3) The restriction imposed by sub-paragraph (1) above shall not [apply to the conditions
required to be imposed under section 3(6A) of this Act or] operate to override the direction in

[section 30(2) of the Magistrates' Courts Act 1980] to a magistrates' court to impose conditions of bail under section 3(6)(d) of this Act of the description specified in [the said section 30(2)] in the circumstances so specified.

Decisions under paragraph 2

9. In taking the decisions required by paragraph 2 of this Part of this Schedule, the court shall have regard to such of the following considerations as appear to it to be relevant, that is to say:

    (*a*) the nature and seriousness of the offence or default (and the probable method of dealing with the defendant for it),

    (*b*) the character, antecedents, associations and community ties of the defendant,

    (*c*) the defendants' record as respect the fulfilment of his obligations under previous grants of bail in criminal proceedings,

    (*d*) except in the case of a defendant whose case is adjourned for inquiries or a report, the strength of the evidence of his having committed the offence or having defaulted,

as well as to any others which appears to be relevant.

POWERS OF CRIMINAL COURTS ACT 1973

Powers of Courts to Deal with Offenders: Preliminary

1. Deferment of sentence

(1) Subject to the provisions of this section, the Crown Court or a magistrates' court may defer passing sentence on an offender for the purpose of enabling the court [or any other court to which it falls to deal with him to have regard, in dealing with him], to his conduct after conviction (including, where appropriate, the making by him of reparation for his offence) or to any change in his circumstances.

(2) Any deferment under this section shall be until such date as may be specified by the court, not being more than six months after the date [on which the deferment is announced by the court]; and [subject to subsection (8A) below,] where the passing of sentence has been deferred under this section it shall not be further deferred thereunder.

(3) The power conferred by this section shall be exercisable only if the offender consents and the court is satisfied, having regard to the nature of the offence and the character and circumstances of the offender, that it would be in the interests of justice to exercise the power.

(4) A court which under this section has deferred passing sentence on an offender may [deal with] him before the expiration of the period of deferment if during that period he is convicted in Great Britain of any offence.

[(4A) If an offender on whom a court has under this section deferred passing sentence in respect of one or more offences is during the period of deferment convicted in England or Wales of any offence ('the subsequent offence'), then, without prejudice to subsection (4) above, the court which (whether during that period or not) passes sentence on him for the subsequent offence may also, if this has not already been done, [deal with] him for the first-mentioned offence or offences:

    Provided that:

    (*a*) the power conferred by this subsection shall not be exercised by a magistrates' court if the court which deferred passing sentence was the Crown Court; and

    (*b*) the Crown Court, in exercising that power in a case in which the court which deferred passing sentence was a magistrates' court, shall not pass any sentence which could not have been passed by a magistrates' court in exercising it.]

(5) Where a court which under this section has deferred passing sentence on an offender proposes to [deal with] him, whether on the date originally specified by the court or by virtue of subsection (4) above before that date, [or where the offender does not appear on the date specified, the court] may issue a summons requiring him to appear before the court, or may issue a warrant for his arrest.

[(6) It is hereby declared that in deferring the passing of sentence under this section a magistrates' court is to be regarded as exercising the power of adjourning the trial which is conferred by [section 10(1) of the Magistrates' Courts Act 1980] and that accordingly [sections 11(1) and 13(1), (2) and (5) of that Act] (non-appearance of the accused) [apply] (without prejudice to subsection (5) above) if the offender does not appear on the date specified in pursuance of subsection (2) above.]

[(6A) Notwithstanding any enactment, a court which under this section defers passing sentence on an offender shall not on the same occasion remand him.]

(7) Nothing in this section shall affect the power of the Crown Court to bind over an offender to come up for judgement when called upon or the power of any court to defer passing sentence for any purpose for which it may lawfully do so apart from this section.

[(8) The power of a court under this section to deal with an offender in a case where the passing of sentence has been deferred thereunder:

(a) includes power to deal with him in any way in which the court which deferred passing sentence could have dealt with him; and

(b) without prejudice to the generality of the foregoing, in the case of a magistrates' court, includes the power conferred by section 37 or 38 of the Magistrates' Courts Act 1980 to commit him to the Crown Court for sentence.]

[(8A) Where, in a case where the passing of sentence on an offender in respect of one or more offences has been deferred under this section, a magistrates' court deals with him by committing him to the Crown Court under section 37 or 38 of the Act of 1980, the power of the Crown Court to deal with him includes the same power to defer passing sentence on him as if he had just been convicted of the offence or offences on indictment before the court.]

POWERS OF COURTS TO DEAL WITH OFFENDERS: PROBATION AND DISCHARGE

2. Probation

(1) Where a court by or before which a person of or over seventeen years of age is convicted of an offence (not being an offence the sentence for which is fixed by law) is of opinion that having regard to the circumstances, including the nature of the offence and the character of the offender, it is expedient to do so, the court may, instead of sentencing him, make a probation order, that is to say, an order requiring him to be under the supervision of a probation officer for a period to be specified in the order of [not less than six months] nor more than three years.

For the purposes of this subsection the age of a person shall be deemed to be that which it appears to the court to be after considering any available evidence.

(2) A probation order shall name the petty sessions area in which the offender resides or will reside; and the offender shall (subject to the provisions of Schedule 1 to this Act relating to probationers who change their residence) be required to be under the supervision of a probation officer appointed for or assigned to that area.

In this Act 'supervising court' means, in relation to a probation order, a magistrates' court acting for the petty sessions area for the time being named in the order.

(3) Subject to the provisions of subsection (4) below and sections 3 and 4 [, 4A and 4B] of this Act a probation order may in addition require the offender to comply during the whole or any part of the probation period with such requirements as the court, having regard to the circumstances of the case, considers necessary for securing the good conduct of the offender or for preventing a repetition by him of the same offence or the commission of other offences.

(4) Without prejudice to the power of the court under section 35 of this Act to make a compensation order, the payment of sums by way of damages for injury or compensation for loss shall not be included among the requirements of a probation order.

(5) Without prejudice to the generality of subsection (3) above, a probation order may include requirements relating to the residence of the offender, but:

(*a*) before making an order containing any such requirements, the court shall consider the home surroundings of the offender: and

[(*b*) where the order requires the offender to reside in an approved probation hostel or any other institution, the period for which he is so required to reside shall be specified in the order.]

(6) Before making a probation order, the court shall explain to the offender in ordinary language the effect of the order (including any additional requirements proposed to be inserted therein . . .) and that if he fails to comply with it or commits another offence he will be liable to be sentenced for the original offence; and the court shall not make the order unless he expresses his willingness to comply with its requirements.

(7) The court by which a probation order is made shall forthwith give copies of the order to a probation officer assigned to the court, and he shall give a copy to the offender, to the probation officer responsible for the supervision of the offender and to the person in charge of any institution in which the probationer is required by the order to reside; and the court shall, except where it is itself the supervising court, send to the clerk to the justices for the petty sessions area named in the order a copy of the order, together with such documents and information relating to the case as it considers likely to be of assistance to the supervising court.

(8) . . .

[(9) The Secretary of State may by order direct that subsection (1) above shall be amended by substituting , for the minimum or maximum period specified in that subsection as originally enacted or as previously amended under this subsection, such period as may be specified in the order.

(10) An order under subsection (9) above may make in paragraph 3(2)(a) of Schedule 1 to this Act any amendment which the Secretary of State thinks necessary in consequence of any substitution made by the order.]

3. Probation orders requiring treatment for mental condition

(1) Where the court is satisfied, on the evidence of a duly qualified medical practitioner approved for the purposes of [section 12 of the Mental Health Act 1983], that the mental condition of an offender is such as requires and may be susceptible to treatment but is not such as to warrant his detention in pursuance of a hospital order under [Part III of that Act], the court may, if it makes a probation order, include in it a requirement that the offender shall submit, during the whole of the probation period or during such part of that period as may be specified in the order, to treatment by or under the direction of a duly qualified medical practitioner with a view to the improvement of the offender's mental condition.

(2) The treatment required by any such order shall be such one of the following kinds of treatment as may be specified in the order, that is to say:

(*a*) treatment as a resident patient in a [hospital within the meaning of the Mental Health Act 1983 or mental nursing home within the meaning of the Nursing Homes Act 1975], not being a special hospital within the meaning of [the National Health Service Act 1977];

(*b*) treatment as a non-resident patient at such institution or place as may be specified in the order; or

(*c*) treatment by or under the direction of such duly qualified medical practitioner as may be specified in the order;

but the nature of the treatment shall not be specified in the order except as mentioned in paragraph (a), (b) or (c) above.

(3) A court shall not by virtue of this section include in a probation order a requirement that an offender shall submit to treatment for his mental condition unless it is satisfied that arrangements have been made for the treatment intended to be specified in the order (including arrangements for the reception of the offender where he is to be required to submit to treatment as a resident patient).

(4) While the probationer is under treatment as a resident patient in pursuance of a requirement of the probation order, the probation officer responsible for his

supervision shall carry out the supervision of such extent only as may be necessary for the purpose of the discharge or amendment of the order.

(5) Where the medical practitioner by whom or under whose direction a probationer is being treated for his mental condition in pursuance of a probation order is of opinion that part of the treatment can be better or more conveniently given in or at an institution or place not specified in the order, being an institution or place in or at which the treatment of the probationer will be given by or under the direction of a duly qualified medical practitioner, he may, with the consent of the probationer, make arrangements for him to be treated accordingly; and the arrangements may provide for the probationer to receive part of his treatment as a resident patient in an institution or place notwithstanding that the institution or place is not one which could have been specified for that purpose in the probation order.

(6) Where any such arrangements as are mentioned in subsection (5) above are made for the treatment of a probationer:

(a) the medical practitioner by whom the arrangements are made shall give notice in writing to the probation officer responsible for the supervision of the probationer, specifying the institution or place in or at which the treatment is to be carried out; and

(b) the treatment provided for by the arrangements shall be deemed to be treatment to which he is required to submit in pursuance of the probation order.

(7) [Subsections (2) and (3) of section 54 of the Mental Health Act 1983] shall have effect with respect to proof for the purposes of subsection (1) above of an offender's mental condition as they have effect with respect to proof of an offender's mental condition for the purposes of [section 37(2)(a)] of that Act.

(8) The provisions of this section shall apply in relation to a probation order made or amended by virtue of section 10 of this Act only so far as indicated in subsection (3) of that section, and except as provided by this section or section 10 a court shall not include in a probation order a requirement that the probationer shall submit to treatment for his mental condition.

6. Breach of requirement of probation order

(1) If at any time during the probation period it appears on information to a justice of the peace on whom jurisdiction is conferred by subsection (2) below that the probationer has failed to comply with any of the requirements of the order, the justice may issue a summons requiring the probationer to appear at the place and time specified therein, or may, if the information is in writing and on oath, issued a warrant for his arrest.

(2) The following justices shall have jurisdiction for the purposes of subsection (1) above, that is to say:

(a) if the probation order was made by a magistrates' court, any justice acting for the petty sessions area for which that court or the supervising court acts;

(b) in any other case, any justice acting for the petty sessions area for which the supervising court acts;

and any summons or warrant issued under this section shall direct the probationer to appear or be brought before a magistrates' court acting for the petty sessions area for which the justice issuing the summons or warrant acts.

(3) If it is proved to the satisfaction of the magistrates' court before which a probationer appears or is brought under this section that the probationer has failed to comply with any of the requirements of the probation order, then, subject to the following provisions of this subsection, that court may deal with him in respect of the failure in any one of the following ways, that is to say:

(a) it may impose on him a fine not exceeding [£400];

(b) subject to subsection (10) below, it may make a community service order in respect of him;

(c) in a case to which section [17 of the Criminal Justice Act 1982] applies, it may make an order under that section requiring him to attend at an attendance centre; or (*d*) where the probation order was made by a magistrates' court, it may deal with him for the offence in respect of which the probation order was made, in any manner in which it could deal with him if it had just convicted him of that offence.

(4) Where the probation order was made by the Crown Court, and a magistrates' court has power to deal with the probationer under subsection (3)(a), (b) or (c) above in respect of a failure to comply with any of the requirements of the order, the magistrates' court may instead commit him to custody or release him on bail until he can be brought or appear before the Crown Court.

(5) A magistrates' court which deals with a probationer's case under subsection (4) above shall send to the Crown Court a certificate signed by a justice of the peace, certifying that the probationer has failed to comply with such of the requirements of the probation order as may be specified in the certificate, together with such other particulars of the case as may be desirable; and a certificate purporting to be so signed shall be admissible as evidence of the failure before the Crown Court.

(6) Where by virtue of subsection (4) above the probationer is brought or appears before the Crown Court, and it is proved to the satisfaction of the court that he has failed to comply with any of the requirements of the probation order, the court may deal with him in respect of the failure in any one of the following ways, that is to say:

(*a*) it may impose on him a fine not exceeding [£400];
(*b*) subject to subsection (10) below, it may make a community service order in respect of him; or
(*c*) it may deal with him for the offence in respect of which the probation order was made in any manner in which it could deal with him if he had just been convicted before the Crown Court of that offence.

(7) A probationer who is required by the probation order to submit to treatment for his mental condition shall not be treated for the purposes of this section as having failed to comply with that requirement on the ground only that he has refused to undergo any surgical, electrical or other treatment if, in the opinion of the court, his refusal was reasonable having regard to all the circumstances; and without prejudice to the provisions of section 8 of this Act, a probationer who is convicted of an offence committed during the probation period shall not on that account be liable to be dealt with under this section in respect of a failure to comply with any requirement of the probation order.

(8) Any exercise by a court of its powers under subsection (3)(a), (b) or (c) or (6)(a) or (b) above shall be without prejudice to the continuance of the probation order.

(9) A fine imposed under sub-section (3)(a) above in respect of a failure to comply with the requirements of a probation order shall be deemed for the purposes of any enactment to be a sum adjudged to be paid by a conviction.

(10) Section 14(2) of this Act and, so far as applicable, the other provisions of this Act relating to community service orders shall have effect in relation to a community service order under this section as they have effect in relation to a community service order in respect of an offender, but as if the power conferred by sections 16 and 17 of this Act to deal with the offender for the offence in respect of which the community service order was made were a power to deal with the probationer for the failure to comply with the requirements of the probation order in respect of which the community service order was made.

7. Absolute and conditional discharge

(1) Where a court by or before which a person is convicted of an offence (not being an offence the sentence for which is fixed by law) is of opinion, having regard to the circumstances including the nature of the offence and the character of the offender, that it is inexpedient to inflict punishment and that a probation order is not appropriate, the court may make an order discharging him absolutely, or, if the court thinks fit, discharging him subject to the condition that he commits no offence

during such period, not exceeding three years from the date of the order, as may be specified therein.

(2) An order discharging a person subject to such a condition is in this Act referred to as 'an order for conditional discharge', and the period specified in any such order (subject to section 8(1) of this Act) as 'the period of conditional discharge'.

(3) Before making an order for conditional discharge the court shall explain to the offender in ordinary language that if he commits another offence during the period of conditional discharge he will be liable to be sentenced for the original offence.

(4) Where, under the following provisions of this Part of this Act, a person conditionally discharged under this section is sentenced for the offence in respect of which the order for conditional discharge was made, that order shall cease to have effect.

[(5) The Secretary of State may by order direct that subsection (1) above shall be amended by substituting, for the maximum period specified in that subsection as originally enacted or as previously amended under this subsection, such period as may be specified in the order.]

8. Commission of further offence by probationer or person conditionally discharged

(1) If it appears to the Crown Court, where that court has jurisdiction in accordance with subsection (2) below, or to a justice of the peace having jurisdiction in accordance with that subsection, that a person in whose case a probation order or an order for conditional discharge has been made has been convicted by a court in any part of Great Britain of an offence committed during the relevant period, and has been dealt with in respect of that offence, that court or justice may, subject to subsection (3) below, issue a summons requiring that person to appear at the place and time specified therein or a warrant for his arrest.

In this section 'the relevant period' means, in relation to a probation order, the probation period, and in relation to an order for conditional discharge, the period of conditional discharge.

(2) Jurisdiction for the purposes of subsection (1) above may be exercised:

(*a*) if the probation order or order for conditional discharge was made by the Crown Court, by that court;

(*b*) if the order was made by a magistrates' court, by a justice acting for the petty sessions area for which that court acts;

(*c*) in the case of a probation order, by whatever court it was made, by a justice acting for the petty sessions area for which the supervising court acts.

(3) A justice of the peace shall not issue a summons under this section except on information and shall not issue a warrant under this section except on information in writing and on oath.

(4) Subject to subsection (5) below, a summons or warrant issued under this section shall direct the person to whom it relates to appear or to be brought before the court by which the probation order or the order for conditional discharge was made.

(5) In the case of a probation order made by a magistrates' court, a summons or warrant issued by a justice acting for the petty sessions area for which the supervising court acts may specify the supervising court instead of the court which made the order.

(6) If a person in whose case a probation order or an order for conditional discharge has been made by the Crown Court is convicted by a magistrates' court of an offence committed during the relevant period, the magistrates' court may commit him to custody or release him on bail until he can be brought or appear before the Crown Court; and if it does so the magistrates' court shall send to the Crown Court a copy of the minute or memorandum of the conviction entered in the register, signed by the clerk of the court by whom the register is kept.

(7) Where it is proved to the satisfaction of the court by which a probation order or an order for conditional discharge was made, or to the satisfaction of that court or the supervising court in the case of a probation order made by a magistrates' court, that the person in whose case the order was made has been convicted of an offence committed during the relevant period, the court may deal with him, for the offence for which the order was made, in any manner in which it could deal with him if he had just been convicted by or before that court of that offence.

(8) If a person in whose case a probation order or an order for conditional discharge has been made by a magistrates' court is convicted before the Crown Court of an offence committed during the relevant period, or is dealt with by the Crown Court for any such offence in respect of which he was committed for sentence to the Crown Court, the Crown Court may deal with him, for the offence for which the order was made, in any manner in which the magistrates' court could deal with him if it had just convicted him of that offence.

(9) If a person in whose case a probation order or an order for conditional discharge has been made by a magistrates' court is convicted by another magistrates' court of any offence committed during the relevant period, that court may, with the consent of the court which made the order or, in the case of a probation order, with the consent of that court or of the supervising court, deal with him, for the offence for which the order was made, in any manner in which the court could deal with him if it had just convicted him of that offence.

POWERS OF COURTS TO DEAL WITH OFFENDERS: COMMUNITY SERVICE ORDERS

14. Community service orders in respect of convicted persons
(1) Where a person of or over [sixteen] years of age is convicted of an offence punishable with imprisonment, the court by or before which he is convicted may, instead of dealing with him in any other way (but subject to subsection (2) below) make an order (in this Act referred to as 'a community service order') requiring him to perform unpaid work in accordance with the subsequent provisions of this Act . . .

The reference in this subsection to an offence punishable with imprisonment shall be construed without regard to any prohibition or restriction imposed by or under any enactment on the imprisonment of young offenders.

[(1A) The number of hours which a person may be required to work under a community service order shall be specified in the order and shall be in the aggregate:
(*a*) not less than 40; and
(*b*) not more:
    (i) in the case of an offender aged sixteen, than 120; and
    (ii) in other cases, than 240.]

[(2) A court shall not make a community service order in respect of any offender unless the offender consents and after considering a report by a probation officer or by a social worker of a local authority social services department about the offender and his circumstances and, if the court thinks it necessary, hearing a probation officer or a social worker of a local authority social services department, the court is satisfied that the offender is a suitable person to perform work under such an order.]

[(2A) Subject to sections 17A and 17B below:
(*a*) a court shall not make a community service order in respect of any offender who is of or over seventeen years of age unless the court is satisfied that provision for him to perform work under such an order can be made under the arrangements for persons to perform work under such orders which exist in the petty sessions area in which he resides or will reside; and
(*b*) a court shall not make a community service order in respect of an offender who is under seventeen years of age unless:
    (i) it has been notified by the Secretary of State that arrangements exist for per-

sons of the offender's age who reside in the petty sessions area in which the
offender resides or will reside to perform work under such orders; and

(ii) it is satisfied that provision can be made under the arrangements for him
to do so.]

(3) Where a court makes community service orders in respect of two or more
offences of which the offender has been convicted by or before the court, the court
may direct that the hours of work specified in any of those orders shall be concurrent
with or additional to those specified in any other of those orders, but so that the total
number of hours which are not concurrent shall not exceed the maximum [specified
in paragraph (b)(i) or (ii) of subsection (1A) above].

(4) A community service order shall specify the petty sessions areas in which the
offender resides or will reside; and the functions conferred by the subsequent
provisions of this Act in the relevant officer shall be discharged by a probation officer
appointed for or assigned to the area for the time being specified in the order
,whether under this subsection or by virtue of section 17(5) of this Act), or by a
person appointed for the purposes of those provisions by the [probation committee]
for that area.

(5) Before making a community service order the court shall explain to the
offender in ordinary language:

(a) the purpose and effect of the order (and in particular the requirements of the
order as specified in section 15 of this Act);

(b) the consequences which may follow under section 16 if he fails to comply with
any of those requirements; and

(c) that the court has under section 17 the power to review the order on the
application either of the offender or of a probation officer.

(6) The court by which a community service order is made shall forthwith give
copies of the order to a probation officer assigned to the court and he shall give a
copy to the offender and to the relevant officer; and the court shall, except where it is
itself a magistrates' court acting for the petty sessions area specified in the order,
send to the clerk to the justices for the petty sessions aera specified in the order a
copy of the order, together with such documents and information relating to the case
as it considers likely to be of assistance to a court acting for that area in exercising its
functions in relation to the order.

(7) The Secretary of State may by order direct that [subsection (1A) above shall
be amended by substituting for the maximum number of hours for the time being
specified in paragraph (b)(i) or (ii) of that subsection], such number of hours as
may be specified in the order.

(8) Nothing in subsection (1) above shall be construed as preventing a court
which makes a community service order in respect of any offence from making an
order for costs against, or imposing any disqualification on, the offender or from
making in respect of the offence an order under section 35, 39, 43 or 44 of this Act, or
under section 28 of the Theft Act 1968.

15. Obligations of persons subject to community service order

(1) An offender in respect of whom a community service order is in force shall:

(a) report to the relevant officer and subsequently from time to time notify him of
any change of address; and

(b) perform for the number of hours specified in the order such work at such times
as he may be instructed by the relevant officer.

(2) Subject to section 17(1) of this Act, the work required to be performed under
a community service order shall be performed during the period of twelve months
beginning with the date of the order [; but unless revoked, the order shall remain in
force until the offender has worked under it for the number of hours specified in it.]

(3) The instructions given by the relevant officer under this section shall, so far as
practicable, be such as to avoid any conflict with the offender's religious beliefs and
any interference with the times, if any, at which he normally works or attends a
school or other educational establishment.

16. Breach of requirements of community service order

(1) If at any time while a community service order is in force in respect of an offender it appears on information to a justice of the peace acting for the petty sessions area for the time being specified in the order that the offender has failed to comply with any of the requirements of section 15 of this Act (including any failure satisfactorily to perform the work which he has been instructed to do), the justice may issue a summons requiring the offender to appear at the place and time specified therein, or may, if the information is in writing and on oath, issue a warrant for his arrest.

(2) Any summons or warrant issued under this section shall direct the offender to appear or be brought before a magistrates' court acting for the petty sessions area for the time being specified in the community service order.

(3) If it is proved to the satisfaction of the magistrates' court before which an offender appears or is brought under this section that he has failed without reasonable excuse to comply with any of the requirements of section 15 the court may, without prejudice to the continuance of the order, impose on him a fine not exceeding [£400] or may:

(a) if the community service order was made by a magistrates' court, revoke the order and deal with the offender, for the offence in respect of which the order was made, in any manner in which he could have been dealt with for that offence by the court which made the order if the order had not been made;

(b) if the order was made by the Crown Court, commit him to custody or release him on bail until he can be brought or appear before the Crown Court.

(4) A magistrates' court which deals with an offender's case under subsection (3)(b) above shall send to the Crown Court a certificate signed by a justice of the peace certifying that the offender has failed to comply with the requirements of section 15 in the respect specified in the certificate, together with such other particulars of the case as may be desirable; and a certificate purporting to be so signed shall be admissible as evidence of the failure before the Crown Court.

(5) Where by virtue of subsection (3)(b) above the offender is brought or appears before the Crown Court and it is proved to the satisfaction of the court that he has failed to comply with any of the requirements of section 15, that court may either:

(a) without prejudice to the continuance of the order, impose on him a fine not exceeding [£400]; or

(b) revoke the order and deal with him, for the offence in respect of which the order was made, in any manner in which he could have been dealt with for that offence by the court which made the order if the order had not been made.

(6) A person sentenced under subsection (3)(a) above for an offence may appeal to the Crown Court against the sentence.

(7) In proceedings before the Crown Court under this section any question whether the offender has failed to comply with the requirements of section 15 shall be determined by the court and not by the verdict of a jury.

(8) A fine imposed under this section shall be deemed for the purposes of any enactment to be a sum adjudged to be paid by a conviction.

17. Amendment and revocation of community service orders, and substitution of other sentences

(1) Where a community service order is in force in respect of any offender and, on the application of the offender or the relevant officer, it appears to a magistrates' court acting for the petty sessions area for the time being specified in the order that it would be in the interests of justice to do so having regard to circumstances which have arisen since the order was made, the court may extend, in relation to the order, the period of twelve months specified in section 15(2) of this Act.

(2) Where such an order is in force and on any such application it appears to a magistrates' court acting for the petty sessions area so specified that, having regard to such circumstances, it would be in the interests of justice that the order should be revoked or that the offender should be dealt with in some other manner for the offence in respect of which the order was made, the court may:

(*a*) if the order was made by a magistrates' court, revoke the order or revoke it and deal with the offender for that offence in any manner in which he could have been dealt with for that offence by the court which made the order if the order had not been made;

(*b*) if the order was made by the Crown Court, commit him to custody or release him on bail until he can be brought or appear before the Crown Court;

and where the court deals with his case under paragraph (b) above it shall send to the Crown Court such particulars of the case as may be desirable.

[(3) Where an offender in respect of whom such an order is in force:

(*a*) is convicted of an offence before the Crown Court; or

(*b*) is committed by a magistrates' court to the Crown Court for sentence and is brought or appears before the Crown Court; or

(*c*) by virtue of subsection (2)(b) above is brought or appears before the Crown Court,

and it appears to the Crown Court to be in the interests of justice to do so, having regard to circumstances which have arisen since the order was made, the Crown Court may revoke the order or revoke the order and deal with the offender, for the offence in respect of which the order was made, in any manner in which he could have been dealt with for that offence by the court which made the order if the order had not been made.]

(4) A person sentenced under subsection (2)(a) above for an offence may appeal to the Crown Court against the sentence:

[(4A) Where:

(*a*) an offender in respect of whom a community service order is in force is convicted of an offence before a magistrates' court other than a magistrates' court acting for the petty sessions area for the time being specified in the order; and

(*b*) the court imposes a custodial sentence on him; and

(*c*) it appears to the court, on the application of the offender or the relevant officer, that it would be in the interests of justice to do so having regard to circumstances which have arisen since the order was made,

the court may:

(i) if the order was made by a magistrates' court, revoke it; and

(ii) if the order was made by the Crown Court, commit him in custody or release him on bail until he can be brought or appear before the Crown Court;

and where the court deals with his case under subparagraph (ii) above, it shall send to the Crown Court such particulars of the case as may be desirable.

(4B) Where by virtue of subsection (4A)(c)(ii) above the offender is brought or appears before the Crown Court and it appears to the Crown Court to be in the interests of justice to do so, having regard to circumstances which have arisen since the order was made, the Crown Court may revoke the order.]

[(5) If:

(*a*) a magistrates' court acting for the petty sessions area for the time being specified in a community service order is satisfied that the offender proposes to change, or has changed, his residence from that petty sessions area to another petty sessions area; and

(*b*) the conditions specified in subsection (5A) below are satisfied,

the court may, and on the application of the relevant officer shall, amend the order by substituting the other petty sessions area for the area specified in the order.]

[(5A) The conditions referred to in subsection (5) above are:

(*a*) if the offender is of or over 17 years of age, that it appears to the court that provision can be made for him to perform work under the community service order under the arrangements which exist for persons who reside in the other petty sessions area to perform work under such orders; and

(*b*) if the offender is under 17 years of age:

(i) that the court has been notified by the Secretary of State that arrangements exist for persons of his age who reside in the other petty sessions area to perform work under such orders; and

(ii) it appears to the court that provision can be made under the arrangements for him to do so.]

(6) Where a community service order is amended by a court under subsection (5) above the court shall send to the clerk to the justices for the new area specified in the order a copy of the order, together with such documents and information relating to the case as it considers likely to be of assistance to a court acting for that area in exercising its functions in relation to the order.

(7) Where a magistrates' court proposes to exercise its powers under subsection (1) or (2) above otherwise than on the application of the offender it shall summon him to appear before the court and, if he does not appear in answer to the summons, may issue a warrant for his arrest.

POWERS OF COURTS TO DEAL WITH OFFENDERS: IMPRISONMENT, BORSTAL TRAINING AND DETENTION: GENERAL PROVISIONS

20. Restriction on imposing sentence of imprisonment on persons who have not previously served prison sentences

(1) No court shall pass a sentence of imprisonment on a person of or over twenty-one years of age on whom such a sentence has not previously been passed by a court in any part of the United Kingdom unless the court is of opinion that no other method of dealing with him is appropriate; and for the purpose of determining whether any other method of dealing with any such person is appropriate the court shall obtain and consider information about the circumstances, and shall take into account any information before the court which is relevant to his character and his physical and mental condition.

(2) Where a magistrates' court passes a sentence of imprisonment on any such person as is mentioned in subsection (1) above, the court shall state the reason for its opinion that no other method of dealing with him is appropriate, and cause that reason to be specified in the warrant of commitment and to be entered in the register.

(3) For the purposes of this section:

(*a*) a previous sentence of imprisonment which has been suspended and which has not taken effect under section 23 of this Act or under section 19 of the Treatment of Offenders Act (Northern Ireland) 1968 shall be disregarded; and

(*b*) 'sentence of imprisonment' does not include a committal or attachment for contempt of court.

(4) Subsection (1) above does not affect the power of a court to pass sentence on any person for an offence the sentence for which is fixed by law.

[(5) For the purposes of this section the age of a person shall be deemed to be that which it appears to the court to be after considering any available evidence.]

20A. Social inquiry report for purposes of s 20

[(1) Subject to subsection (2) below, the court shall in every case obtain a social inquiry report for the purpose of determining under section 20(1) above whether there is any appropriate method of dealing with an offender other than imprisonment.

(2) Subsection (1) above does not apply if, in the circumstances of the case, the court is of the opinion that it is unnecessary to obtain a social inquiry report.

(3) Where a magistrates' court passes a sentence of imprisonment on a person of or over 21 years of age on whom such a sentence has not previously been passed by a court in any part of the United Kingdom without obtaining a social inquiry report, it shall state in open court the reason for its opinion that it was unnecessary to obtain such a report.

(4) A magistrates' court shall cause a reason stated under subsection (3) above to be specified in the warrant of commitment and to be entered in the register.

(5) No sentence shall be invalidated by the failure of a court to comply with

subsection (1) above, but any other court on appeal from that court shall obtain a social inquiry report if none was obtained by the court below, unless it is of the opinion that in the circumstances of the case it is unnecessary to do so.

(6) In determining whether it should deal with the appellant otherwise than by passing a sentence of imprisonment on him the court hearing the appeal shall consider any social inquiry report obtained by it or by the court below.

(7) In this section 'social inquiry report' means a report about a person and his circumstances made by a probation officer.]

21. Restriction on imposing sentences of imprisonment Youth Custody on persons not legally represented.

(1) A magistrates' court on summary conviction or the Crown Court on committal for sentence or on conviction on indictment shall not pass a sentence of imprisonment, . . . on a person who is not legally represented in that court and has not been previously sentenced to that punishment by a court in any part of the United Kingdom, unless either:

> (*a*) he applied for legal aid and the application was refused on the ground that it did not appear his means were such that he required assistance; or
>
> (*b*) having been informed of his right to apply for legal aid and had the opportunity to do so, he refused or failed to apply.

(2) For the purposes of this section a person is to be treated as legally represented in a court if, but only if, he has the assistance of counsel or a solicitor to represent him in the proceedings in that court at some time after he is found guilty and before he is sentenced, and in subsection (1)(a) and (b) above 'legal aid' means legal aid for the purposes of proceedings in that court, whether the whole proceedings or the proceedings on or in relation to sentence; but in the case of a person committed to the Crown Court for sentence or trial, it is immaterial whether he applied for legal aid in the Crown Court to, or was informed of his right to apply by, that court or the court which committed him.

(3) For the purposes of this section:

> (*a*) a previous sentence of imprisonment which has been suspended and which has not taken effect under section 23 of this Act under section 19 of the Treatment of Offenders Act (Northern Ireland) 1968 shall be disregarded;
>
> (*b*) 'sentence of imprisonment' does not include a committal or attachment for contempt of court.

POWERS OF COURTS TO DEAL WITH OFFENDERS: SUSPENDED SENTENCES OF IMPRISONMENT

22. Suspended sentences of imprisonment

(1) Subject to subsection (2) below, a court which passes a sentence of imprisonment for a term of not more than two years for an offence may order that the sentence shall not take effect unless, during a period specified in the order, being not less than one year or more than two years from the date of the order, the offender commits in Great Britain another offence punishable with imprisonment and thereafter a court having power to do so orders under section 23 of this Act that the original sentence shall take effect; and in this Part of this Act 'operational period', in relation to a suspended sentence, means the period so specified.

(2) A court shall not deal with an offender by means of a suspended sentence unless the case appears to the court to be one in which a sentence of imprisonment would have been appropriate in the absence of any power to suspend such a sentence by an order under subsection (1) above.

(3) A court which passes a suspended sentence on any person for an offence shall not make a probation order in his case in respect of another ofence of which he is convicted by or before the court or for which he is dealt with by the court.

(4) On passing a suspended sentence the court shall explain to the offender in

ordinary language his liability under section 23 of this Act if during the operational period he commits an offence punishable with imprisonment.

(5) Where a court has passed a suspended sentence on any person, and that person is subsequently sentenced to Borstal training, he shall cease to be liable to be dealt with in respect of the suspended sentence unless the subsequent sentence or any conviction or finding on which it was passed is quashed on appeal.

(6) Subject to any provision to the contrary contained in the Criminal Justice Act 1967, this Act or any enactment passed or instrument made under any enactment after 31st December 1967:

    (*a*) a suspended sentence which has not taken effect under section 23 of this Act shall be treated as a sentence of imprisonment for the purposes of all enactments and instruments made under enactments except any enactment or instrument which provides for disqualification for or loss or office, or forfeiture of pensions, of persons sentenced to imprisonment; and

    (*b*) where a suspended sentence has taken effect under that section, the offender shall be treated for the purposes of the enactments and instruments excepted by paragraph (a) above as having been convicted on the ordinary date on which the period allowed for making an appeal against an order under that section expires or, if such an appeal is made, the date on which it is finally disposed of or abandoned or fails for non-prosecution.

23. Power of court on conviction of further offence to deal with suspended sentence

(1) Where an offender is convicted of an offence punishable with imprisonment committed during the operational period of a suspended sentence and either he is so convicted by or before a court having power under section 24 of this Act to deal with him in respect of the suspended sentence or he subsequently appears or is brought before such a court, then, unless the sentence has already taken effect, that court shall consider his case and deal with him by one of the following methods:

    (*a*) the court may order that the suspended sentence shall take effect with the original term unaltered;

    (*b*) it may order that the sentence shall take effect with the substitution of a lesser term for the original term;

    (*c*) it may be order vary the original order under section 22(1) of this Act by substituting for the period specified therein a period expiring not later than two years from the date of the variation; or

    (*d*) it may make no order with respect to the suspended sentence;

and a court shall make an order under paragraph (a) of this subsection unless the court is of opinion that it would be unjust to do so in view of all the circumstances . . . including the facts of the subsequent offence, and where it is of that opinion the court shall state its reasons.

(2) Where a court orders that a suspended sentence shall take effect, with or without any variation of the original term, the court may order that that sentence shall take effect immediately or that the term thereof shall commence on the expiration of another term of imprisonment passed on the offender by that or another court.

(3)–(5) . . .

(6) In proceedings for dealing with an offender in respect of a suspended sentence which take place before the Crown Court any question whether the offender has been convicted of an offence punishable with imprisonment committed during the operational period of the suspended sentence shall be determined by the court and not by the verdict of a jury.

(7) Where a court deals with an offender under this section in respect of a suspended sentence the appropriate officer of the court shall notify the appropriate officer of the court which passed the sentence of the method adopted.

(8) Where on consideration of the case of an offender a court makes no order with respect to a suspended sentence, the appropriate officer of the court shall record that fact.

(9) For the purposes of any enactment conferring rights of appeal in criminal cases any order made by a court with respect to a suspended sentence shall be treated as a sentence passed on the offender by that court for the offence for which the suspended sentence was passed.

24. Court by which suspended sentence may be dealt with.

(1) An offender may be dealt with in respect of a suspended sentence by the Crown Court or, where the sentence was passed by a magistrates' court, by any magistrates' court before which he appears or is brought.

(2) Where an offender is convicted by a magistrates' court of an offence punishable with imprisonment and the court is satisfied that the offence was committed during the operational period of a suspended sentence passed by the Crown Court:

(a) the court may, if it thinks fit, commit him in custody or on bail to the Crown Court; and

(b) if it does not, shall give written notice of the conviction to the appropriate officer of the Crown Court.

(3) For the purposes of this section and of section 25 of this Act a suspended sentence passed on an offender on appeal shall be treated as having been passed by the court by which he was orginally sentenced.

25. Procedure where court convicting of further offence does not deal with suspended sentence.

(1) If it appears to the Crown Court, where that court has jurisdiction in accordance with subsection (2) below, or to a justice of the peace having jurisdiction in accordance with that subsection, that an offender has been convicted in Great Britain of an offence punishable with imprisonment committed during the operational period of a suspended sentence and that he has not been dealt with in respect of the suspended sentence, that court or justice may, subject to the following provisions of this section, issue a summons requiring the offender to appear at the place and time specified therein, or a warrant for his arrest.

(2) Jurisdiction for the purposes of subsection (1) above may be exercised:

(a) if the suspended sentence was passed by the Crown Court, by that court;

(b) if it was passed by a magistrates' court, by a justice acting for the area for which that court acted.

(3) Where an offender is convicted by a court in Scotland of an offence punishable with imprisonment and the court is informed that the offence was committed during the operational period of a suspended sentence passed in England or Wales, the court shall give written notice of the conviction to the appropriate officer of the court by which the suspended sentence was passed.

(4) Unless he is acting in consequence of a notice under subsection (3) above, a justice of the peace shall not issue a summons under this section except on information, and shall not issue a warrant under this section except on information in writing and on oath.

(5) A summons or warrant issued under this section shall direct the offender to appear or to be brought before the court by which the suspended sentence was passed.

26. Suspended sentence supervision orders.

(1) Where a court passes on an offender a suspended sentence for a term of more than six months for a single offence, the court may make a suspended sentence supervision order (in this Act referred to as 'a supervision order') placing the offender under the supervision of a supervising officer for a period specified in the order, being a period not exceeding the operational period of the suspended sentence.

(2) The Secretary of State may by order:

(a) direct that subsection (1) above be amended by substituting, for the number of months specified in the subsection as originally enacted or as previously amended under this paragraph, such other number (not more than six) as the order may specify; or

(b) make in that subsection the repeals necessary to enable a court to make a supervision order thereunder in the case of any suspended sentence, whatever the length of the term.

(3) A supervision order shall specify the petty sessions area in which the offender resides or will reside; and the supervising officer shall be a probation officer appointed for or assigned to the area for the time being specified in the order (whether under this subsection or by virtue of subsection (6) below).

(4) An offender in respect of whom a supervision order is in force shall keep in touch with the supervising officer in accordance with such instructions as he may from time to time be given by that officer and shall notify him of any change of address.

(5) The court by which a supervision order is made shall forthwith give copies of the order to a probation officer assigned to the court, and he shall give a copy to the offender and the supervising officer; and the court shall, except where it is itself a magistrates' court acting for the petty sessions area specified in the order, send to the clerk to the justices for the petty sessions area specified in the order a copy of the order, together with such documents and information relating to the case as it considers likely to be of assistance to a court acting for that area in exercising its functions in relation to the order.

(6) If a magistrates' court acting for the petty sessions area for the time being specified in a supervision order is satisfied that the offender proposes to change, or has changed, his residence from that petty sessions area to another petty sessions area, the court may, and on the application of the supervising officer shall, amend the order by substituting the other petty sessions area for the area specified in the order.

(7) Where a supervision order is amended by a court under subsection (6) above the court shall send to the clerk to the justices for the new area specified in the order a copy of the order, together with such documents and information relating to the case as it considers likely to be of assistance to a court acting for that area in exercising its functions in relation to the order.

(8) A supervision order shall cease to have effect if before the end of the period specified in it:

(a) a court orders under section 23 of this Act that a suspended sentence passed in the proceedings in which the order was made shall have effect; or

(b) the order is discharged or replaced under the subsequent provisions of this section.

(9) A supervision order may be discharged, on the application of the supervising officer or the offender:

(a) If it was made by the Crown Court and includes a direction reserving the power of discharging it to that court, by the Crown Court;

(b) in any other case by a magistrates' court acting for the petty sessions area for the time being specified in the order.

(10) Where under section 23 of this Act a court deals with an offender in respect of a suspended sentence by varying the operational period of the sentence or by making no order with respect to the sentence, the court may make a supervision order in respect of the offender:

(a) in place of any such order made when the suspended sentence was passed; or

(b) if the court which passed the sentence could have made such an order but did not do so; or

(c) if that court could not then have made such an order but would have had power to do so if subsection (1) above had then had effect as it has effect at the time when the offender is dealt with under section 23.

(11) On making a supervision order the court shall in ordinary language explain its effect to the offender.

27. Breach of requirement of suspended sentence supervision order.

(1) If at any time while a supervision order is in force in respect of an offender it

appears on information to a justice of the peace acting for the petty sessions area for the time being specified in the order that the offender has failed to comply with any of the requirements of section 26(4) of this Act, the justice may issue a summons requiring the offender to appear at the place and time specified therein, or may, if the information is in writing and on oath, issue a warrant for his arrest.

(2) Any summons or warrant issued under this section shall direct the offender to appear or be brought before a magistrates' court acting for the petty sessions area for the time being specified in the supervision order.

(3) If it is proved to the satisfaction of the court before which an offender appears or is brought under this section that he has failed without reasonable cause to comply with any of the requirements of section 26(4) the court may, without prejudice to the continuance of the order, impose on him a fine not exceeding [£400].

(4) A fine imposed under this section shall be deemed for the purposes of any enactment to be a sum adjudged to be paid by a conviction.

POWERS OF COURTS TO DEAL WITH OFFENDERS: COMPENSATION ORDERS

35. Compensation orders against convicted persons.
[(1) Subject to the provisions of this Part of this Act and to section 40 of the Magistrates' Courts Act 1980 (which imposes a monetary limit on the powers of a magistrates' court under this section), a court by or before which a person is convicted of an offence, instead of or in addition to dealing with him in any other way, may, on application or otherwise, make an order (in this Act referred to as 'a compensation order') requiring him to pay compensation for any personal injury, loss or damage resulting from that offence or any other offence which is taken into consideration by the court in determining sentence.]

[(1A) Compensation under subsection (1) above shall be of such amount as the court considers appropriate, having regard to any evidence and to any representations that are made by or on behalf of the accused or the prosecutor.]

(2) In the case of an offence under the Theft Act 1968, where the property in question is recovered, any damage to the property occurring while it was out of the owner's possession shall be treated for the purposes of subsection (1) above as having resulted from the offence, however and by whomsoever the damage was caused.

(3) No compensation order shall be made in respect of loss suffered by the dependents of a person in consequence of his death, and no such order shall be made in respect of injury, loss or damage due to an accident arising out of the presence of a motor vehicle on a road, except such damage as is treated by subsection (2) above as resulting from an offence under the Theft Act 1968.

(4) In determining whether to make a compensation order against any person, and in determining the amount to be paid by any person under such an order, the court shall have regard to his means so far as they appear or are known to the court.

[(4A) Where the court considers:
(a) that it would be appropriate both to impose a fine and to make a compensation order; but
(b) that the offender has insufficient means to pay both an appropriate fine and appropriate compensation,
the court shall give preference to compensation (though it may impose a fine as well).]

(5) . . .

POWERS OF COURTS TO DEAL WITH OFFENDERS: MISCELLANEOUS POWERS

43. Power to deprive offender of property used, or intended for use, for purposes of crime.
(1) Where a person is convicted of an offence punishable on indictment with imprisonment for a term of two years or more and the court by or before which he is

convicted is satisfied that any property which was in his possession or under his control at the time of his apprehension:

(*a*) has been used for the purposes of committing, or facilitating the commission of, any offence; or

(*b*) was intended by him to be used for that purpose;

the court may make an order under this section in respect of that property.

(2) Facilitating the commission of an offence shall be taken for the purposes of this section and section 44 of this Act to include the taking of any steps after it has been committed for the purpose of disposing of any property to which it relates or of avoiding apprehension or detection, and references in this or that section to an offence punishable with imprisonment shall be construed without regard to any prohibition or restriction imposed by or under any enactment on the imprisonment of young offenders.

(3) An order under this section shall operate to deprive the offender of his rights, if any, in the property to which it relates, and the property shall (if not already in their possession) be taken into the possession of the police.

(4) The Police (Property) Act 1897 shall apply, with the following modifications, to property which is in the possession of the police by virtue of this section:

(*a*) no application shall be made under section 1(1) of that Act by any claimant of the property after the expiration of six months from the date on which the order in respect of the property was made under this section; and

(*b*) no such application shall succeed unless the claimant satisfies the court either that he had not consented to the offender having possession of the property or that he did not know, and had no reason to suspect, that the property was likely to be used for the purpose mentioned in subsection (1) above.

(5) In relation to property which is in the possession of the police by virtue of this section, the power to make regulations under section 2(1) of the Police (Property) Act 1897 (disposal of property in cases where the owner of the property has not been ascertained and no order of a competent court has been made with respect thereto) shall include power to make regulations for disposal in cases where no application by a claimant of the property has been made within the period specified in subsection (4)(a) above or no such application has succeeded.

44. Driving disqualification where vehicle used for purpose of crime.

(1) This section applies where a person is convicted before the Crown Court of an offence punishable on indictment with imprisonment for a term of two years or more or, having been convicted by a magistrates' court of such an offence, is committed under [section 38 of the Magistrates' Courts Act 1980] to the Crown Court for sentence.

(2) If in a case to which this section applies the Crown Court is satisfied that a motor vehicle was used (by the person convicted or by anyone else) for the purpose of committing, or facilitating the commission of, the offence in question (within the meaning of section 43 of this Act), the court may order the person convicted to be disqualified, for such period as the court thinks fit, for holding or obtaining a licence to drive a motor vehicle granted under Part III of the Road Traffic Act 1972.

(3) A court which makes an order under this section disqualifying a person for holding or obtaining any such licence as is mentioned in subsection (2) above shall require him to produce any such licence held by him; and:

(*a*) if he does not produce the licence as required he shall be guilty of an offence under section 101(4) of the Road Traffic Act 1972 (failure to produce licence for endorsement); and

(*b*) if he applies under section 95 of that Act for the disqualification to be removed and the court so orders, subsection (4) of that section shall not have effect so as to require particulars of the order to be endorsed on the licence, but the court shall send notice of the order to the Secretary of State and section 105(5) of that Act (procedure for sending notice to Secretary of State) shall apply to the notice.

POLICE AND CRIMINAL EVIDENCE ACT 1984

QUESTIONING AND TREATMENT OF PERSONS BY POLICE

56. Right to have someone informed when arrested.

(1) Where a person has been arrested and is being held in custody in a police station or other premises, he shall be entitled, if he so requests, to have one friend or relative or other person who is known to him or who is likely to take an interest in his welfare told, as soon as is practicable except to the extent that delay is permitted by this section, that he has been arrested and is being detained there.

(2) Delay is only permitted:

(a) in the case of a person who is in police detention for a serious arrestable offence; and

(b) if an officer of at least the rank of superintendent authorises it.

(3) In any case the person in custody must be permitted to exercise the right conferred by subsection (1) above within 36 hours from the relevant time, as defined in section 41(2) above.

(4) An officer may give an authorisation under subsection (2) above orally or in writing but, if he gives it orally, he shall confirm it in writing as soon as is practicable.

(5) [Subject to sub-section (5A) below] An officer may only authorise delay where he has reasonable grounds for believing that telling the named person of the arrest:

(a) will lead to interference with or harm to evidence connected with a serious arrestable offence or interference with or physical injury to other persons; or

(b) will lead to the alerting of other persons suspected of having committed such an offence but not yet arrested for it; or

(c) will hinder the recovery of any property obtained as a result of such an offence.

[(5A) An officer may also authorise delay where the serious arrestable offence is a drug trafficking offence and the officer has reasonable grounds for believing:

(a) that the detained person has benefited from drug trafficking, and

(b) that the recovery of the value of that person's proceeds of drug trafficking will be hindered by telling the named person of the arrest.]

(6) If a delay is authorised:

(a) the detained person shall be told the reason for it; and

(b) the reason shall be noted on his custody record.

(7) The duties imposed by subsection (6) above shall be performed as soon as is practicable.

(8) The rights conferred by this section on a person detained at a police station or other premises are exercisable whenever he is transferred from one place to another; and this section applies to each subsequent occasion on which they are exercisable as it applies to the first such occasion.

(9) There may be no further delay in permitting the exercise of the right conferred by subsection (1) above once the reason for authorising delay ceases to subsist.

(10) In the foregoing provisions of this section references to a person who has been arrested include references to a person who has been detained under the terrorism provisions and 'arrest' includes detention under those provisions.

(11) In its application to person who has been arrested or detained under the terrorism provisions:

(a) subsection (2)(a) above shall have effect as if for the words 'for a serious arrestable offence' there were substituted the words 'under the terrorism provisions';

(b) subection (3) above shall have effect as if for the words from 'within' onwards there were substituted the words 'before the end of the period beyond which he may no longer be detained without the authority of the Secretary of State'; and

(c) subsection (5) above shall have effect as if at the end there were added 'or

(d) will lead to interference with the gathering of information about the commission, preparation or instigation of acts of terrorism; or

(e) by alerting any person, will make it more difficult:

    (i) to prevent an act of terrorism; or

    (ii) to secure the apprehension, prosecution or conviction of any person in connection with the commission, preparation or instigation of an act of terrorism.'.

57. Additional rights of children and young persons.

The following subsections shall be substituted for section 34(2) of the Children and Young Persons Act 1933:

'(2) Where a child or young person is in police detention such steps as are practicable shall be taken to ascertain the identity of a person responsible for his welfare.

(3) If it is practicable to ascertain the identify of a person responsible for the welfare of a child or young person, that person shall be informed, unless it is not practicable to do so:

(a) that the child or young person has been arrested;

(b) why he has been arrested; and

(c) where he is being detained.

(4) Where information falls to be given under subsection (3) above, it shall be given as soon as it is practicable to do so.

(5) For the purposes of this section the persons who may be responsible for the welfare of a child or young person are:

(a) his parent or guardian; or

(b) any other person who has for the time being assumed responsibility for his welfare.

(6) If it is practicable to give a person responsible for the welfare of the child or young person the information required by subsection (3) above, that person shall be given it as soon as it is practicable to do so.

(7) If it appears that at the time of his arrest a supervision order, as defined in section 11 of the Children and Young Persons Act 1969, is in force in respect of him, the person responsible for his supervision shall also be informed as described in subsection (3) above as soon as it is reasonably practicable to do so.

(8) The reference to a parent or guardian in subsection (5) above is;

(a) in the case of a child or young person in the care of a local authority, a reference to that authority; and

(b) in the case of a child or young person in the care of a voluntary organisation in which parental rights and duties with respect to him are vested by virtue of a resolution under section 64(1) of the Child Care Act 1980, a reference to that organisation.

(9) The rights conferred on a child or young person by subsections (2) to (8) above are in addition to his rights under section 56 of the Police and Criminal Evidence Act 1984.

(10) The reference in subsection (2) above to a child or young person who is in police detention includes a reference to a child or young person who has been detained under the terrorism provisions; and in subsection (3) above 'arrest' includes such detention.

(11) In subsection (10) above 'the terrorism provisions' has the meaning assigned to it by section 65 of the Police and Criminal Evidence Act 1984.'.

58. Access to legal advice.

(1) A person arrested and held in custody in a police station or other premises shall be entitled, if he so requests, to consult a solicitor privately at any time.

(2) Subject to subsection (3) below, a request under subsection (1) above and the time at which it was made shall be recorded in the custody record.

(3) Such a request need not be recorded in the custody record of a person who makes it at a time while he is at a court after being charged with an offence.

(4) If a person makes such a request, he must be permitted to consult a solicitor as soon as is practicable except to the extent that delay is permitted by this section.

(5) In any case he must be permitted to consult a solicitor within 36 hours from the relevant time, as defined in section 41(2) above.

(6) Delay in compliance with a request is only permitted:

(*a*) in the case of a person who is in police detention for a serious arrestable offence; and

(*b*) if an officer of at least the rank of superintendent authorises it.

(7) An officer may give an authorisation under subsection (6) above orally or in writing but, if he gives it orally, he shall confirm it in writing as soon as is practicable.

(8) [Subject to sub-section (8A) below] An officer may only authorise delay where he has reasonable grounds for believing that the exercise of the right conferred by subsection (1) above at the time when the person detained desires to exercise it:

(*a*) will lead to interference with or harm to evidence connected with a serious arrestable offence or interference with or physical injury to other persons; or

(*b*) will lead to the alerting of other persons suspected of having committed such an offence but not yet arrested for it; or

(*c*) will hinder the recovery of any property obtained as a result of such an offence.

[(8A) An officer may also authorise delay where the serious arrestable offence is a drug trafficking offence and the officer has reasonable grounds for believing:

(*a*) that the detained person has benefited from drug trafficking, and

(*b*) that the recovery of the value of that person's proceeds of drug trafficking will be hindered by the exercise of the right conferred by subsection (1) above.]

(9) If delay is authorised:

(*a*) the detained person should be told the reason for it; and

(*b*) the reason shall be noted on his custody record.

(10) The duties imposed by subsection (9) above shall be performed as soon as is practicable.

(11) There may be no further delay in permitting the exercise of the right conferred by subsection (1) above once the reason for authorising delay ceases to subsist.

(12) The reference in subsection (1) above to a person arrested includes a reference to a person who has been detained under the terrorism provisions.

(13) In the application of this section to a person who has been arrested or detained under the terrorism provisions:

(*a*) subsection (5) above shall have effect as if for the words from 'within' onwards there were substituted the words 'before the end of the period beyond which he may no longer be detained without the authority of the Secretary of State';

(*b*) subsection (6)(a) above shall have effect as if for the words 'for a serious arrestable offence' there were substituted the words 'under the terrorism provisions'; and

(*c*) subsection (8) above shall have effect as if at the end there were added 'or

(*d*) will lead to interference with the gathering of information about the commission, preparation or instigation of acts of terrorism; or

(*e*) by alerting any person, will make it more difficult:

(i) to prevent an act of terrorism; or

(ii) to secure the apprehension, prosecution or conviction of any person in connection with the commission, preparation or instigation of an act of terrorism.'.

(14) If an officer of appropriate rank has reasonable grounds for believing that, unless he gives a direction under subsection (15) below, the exercise by a person

arrested or detained under the terrorism provisions of the right conferred by subsection (1) above will have any of the consequences specified in subsection (8) above (as it has effect by virtue of subsection (13) above), he may give a direction under that subsection.

(15) A direction under this subsection is a direction that a person desiring to exercise the right conferred by subsection (1) above may only consult a solicitor in the sight and hearing of a qualified officer of the uniformed branch of the force of which the officer giving the direction is a member.

(16) An officer is qualified for the purpose of subsection (15) above if:

(a) he is of at least the rank of inspector; and

(b) in the opinion of the officer giving the direction he has no connection with the case.

(17) An officer is of appropriate rank to give a direction under subsection (15) above if he is of at least the rank of Commander or Assistant Chief Constable.

(18) A direction under subsection (15) above shall cease to have effect once the reason for giving it ceases to subsist.

CODES OF PRACTICE – GENERAL

66. Codes of practice.

The Secretary of State shall issue codes of practice in connection with:

(a) the exercise by police officers of statutory powers:

(i) to search a person without first arresting him; or

(ii) to search a vehicle without making an arrest;

(b) the detention, treatment, questioning and identification of persons by police officers;

(c) searches of premises by police officers; and

(d) the seizure of property found by police officers on persons or premises.

67. Codes of practice – supplementary.

(1) When the Secretary of State proposes to issue a code of practice to which this section applies, he shall prepare and publish a draft of that code, shall consider any representations made to him about the draft and may modify the draft accordingly.

(2) This section applies to a code of practice under section 60 or 66 above.

(3) The Secretary of State shall lay before both Houses of Parliament a draft of any code of practice prepared by him under this section.

(4) When the Secretary of State has laid the draft of a code before Parliament, he may bring the code into operation by order made by statutory instrument.

(5) No order under subsection (4) above shall have effect until approved by a resolution of each House of Parliament.

(6) An order bringing a code of practice into operation may contain such transitional provisions or savings as appear to the Secretary of State to be necessary or expedient in connection with the code of practice thereby brought into operation.

(7) The Secretary of State may from time to time revise the whole or any part of a code of practice to which this section applies and issue that revised code; and the foregoing provisions of this section shall apply (with appropriate modifications) to such a revised code as they apply to the first issue of a code.

(8) A police officer shall be liable to disciplinary proceedings for a failure to comply with any provisions of such a code, unless such proceedings are precluded by section 104 below.

(9) Persons other than police officers who are charged with the duty of investigating offences or charging offenders shall in the discharge of that duty have regard to any relevant provisions of such a code.

(10) A failure on the part:

(a) of a police office to comply with any provision of such a code; or

(b) of any person other than a police officer who is charged with the duty of

investigating offences or charging offenders to have regard to any relevant provision of such a code in the discharge of that duty,
shall not of itself render him liable to any criminal or civil proceedings.

(11) In all criminal and civil proceedings any such code shall be admissible in evidence; and if any provision of such a code appears to the court or tribunal conducting the proceedings to be relevant to any question arising in the proceedings it shall be taken into account in determining that question.

(12) In this section 'criminal proceedings' includes:

(*a*) proceedings in the United Kingdom or elsewhere before a court-martial constituted under the Army Act 1955, the Air Force Act 1955 or the Naval Discipline Act 1957 or a disciplinary court constituted under section 50 of the said Act of 1957:

(*b*) proceedings before the Courts-Martial Appeal Court; and

(*c*) proceedings before a Standing Civilian Court.

EVIDENCE IN CRIMINAL PROCEEDINGS – GENERAL: CONVICTIONS AND ACQUITTALS

73. Proof of convictions and acquittals.

(1) Where in any proceedings the fact that a person has in the United Kingdom been convicted or acquitted of an offence otherwise than by a Service court is admissible in evidence, it may be proved by producing a certificate of conviction or, as the case may be, of acquittal relating to that offence, and proving that the person named in the certificate as having been convicted or acquitted of the offence is the person whose conviction or acquittal of the offence is to be proved.

(2) For the purposes of this section a certificate of conviction or of acquittal:

(*a*) shall, as regards a conviction or acquittal on indictment, consist of a certificate, signed by the clerk of the court where the conviction or acquittal took place, giving the substance and effect (omitting the formal parts) of the indictment and of the conviction or acquittal; and

(*b*) shall, as regards a conviction or acquittal on a summary trial, consist of a copy of the conviction or of the dismissal of the information, signed by the clerk of the court where the conviction or acquittal took place or by the clerk of the court, if any, to which a memorandum of the conviction or acquittal was sent;

and a document purporting to be a duly signed certificate of conviction or acquittal under this section shall be taken to be such a certificate unless the contrary is proved.

(3) References in this section to the clerk of a court include references to his deputy and to any other person having the custody of the court record.

(4) The method of proving a conviction or acquittal authorised by this section shall be in addition to and not to the exclusion of any other authorised manner of proving a conviction or acquittal.

74. Conviction as evidence of commission of offence.

(1) In any proceedings the fact that a person other than the accused has been convicted of an offence by or before any court in the United Kingdom or by a Service court outside the United Kingdom shall be admissible in evidence for the purpose of proving, where to do so is relevant to any issue in those proceedings, that that person committed that offence, whether or not any other evidence of his having committed that offence is given.

(2) In any proceedings in which by virtue of this section a person other than the accused is proved to have been convicted of an offence by or before any court in the United Kingdom or by a Service court outside the United Kingdom, he shall be taken to have committed that offence unless the contrary is proved.

(3) In any proceedings where evidence is admissible of the fact that the accused has committed an offence, in so far as that evidence is relevant to any matter in issue in the proceedings for a reason other than a tendency to show in the accused a

disposition to commit the kind of offence with which he is charged, if the accused is proved to have been convicted of the offence:
(a) by or before any court in the United Kingdom; or
(b) by a Service court outside the United Kingdom,
he shall be taken to have committed that offence unless the contrary is proved.
(4) Nothing in this section shall prejudice:
(a) the admissibility in evidence of any conviction which would be admissible apart from this section; or
(b) the operation of any enactment whereby a conviction or a finding of fact in any proceedings is for the purposes of any other proceedings made conclusive evidence of any fact.

75. Provisions supplementary to section 74.

(1) Where evidence that a person has been convicted of an offence is admissible by virtue of section 74 above, then without prejudice to the reception of any other admissible evidence for the purpose of identifying the facts on which the conviction was based:
(a) the contents of any document which is admissible as evidence or the conviction; and
(b) the contents of the information, complaint, indictment or charge-sheet on which the person in question was convicted,
shall be admissible in evidence for that purpose.
(2) Where in any proceedings the contents of any document are admissible in evidence by virtue of subsection (1) above, a copy of that document, or of the material part of it, purporting to be certified or otherwise authenticated by or on behalf of the court or authority having custody of that document shall be admissible in evidence and shall be taken to be a true copy of that document or part unless the contrary is shown.
(3) Nothing in any of the following:
(a) section 13 of the Powers of Criminal Courts Act 1973 (under which a conviction leading to probation or discharge is to be disregarded except as mentioned in that section);
(b) section 392 of the Criminal Procedure (Scotland) Act 1975 (which makes similar provisions in respect of convictions on indictment in Scotland); and
(c) section 8 of the Probation Act (Northern Ireland) 1950 (which corresponds to section 13 of the Powers of Criminal Courts Act 1973) or any legislation which is in force in Northern Ireland for the time being and corresponds to that section,
shall affect the operation of section 74 above; and for the purposes of that section any order made by a court of summary jurisdiction in Scotland under section 182 or section 183 of the said Act of 1975 shall be treated as a conviction.
(4) Nothing in section 74 above shall be construed as rendering admissible in any proceedings evidence of any conviction other than a subsisting one.

EVIDENCE IN CRIMINAL PROCEEDINGS – GENERAL: CONFESSIONS

76. Confessions.

(1) In any proceedings a confession made by an accused person may be given in evidence against him in so far as it is relevant to any matter in issue in the proceedings and is not excluded by the court in pursuance of this section.
(2) If, in any proceedings where the prosecution proposes to give in evidence a confession made by an accused person, it is represented to the court that the confession was or may have been obtained:
(a) by oppression of the person who made it; or
(b) in consequence of anything said or done which was likely, in the circumstances existing at the time, to render unreliable any confession which might be made by him in consequence thereof,

the court shall not allow the confession to be given in evidence against him except in so far as the prosecution proves to the court beyond reasonable doubt that the confession (notwithstanding that it may be true) was not obtained as aforesaid.

(3) In any proceedings where the prosecution proposes to give in evidence a confession made by an accused person, the court may of its own motion require the prosecution, as a condition of allowing it to do so, to prove that the confession was not obtained as mentioned in subsection (2) above.

(4) The fact that a confession is wholly or partly excluded in pursuance of this section shall not affect the admissibility in evidence:

 (*a*) of any facts discovered as a result of the confession; or

 (*b*) where the confession is relevant as showing that the accused speaks, writes or expresses himself in a particular way, of so much of the confession as is necessary to show that he does so.

(5) Evidence that a fact to which this subsection applies was discovered as a result of a statement made by an accused person shall not be admissible unless evidence of how it was discovered is given by him or on his behalf.

(6) Subsection (5) above applies:

 (*a*) to any fact discovered as a result of a confession which is wholly excluded in pursuance of this section; and

 (*b*) to any fact discovered as a result of a confession which is partly so excluded, if the fact is discovered as a result of the excluded part of the confession.

(7) Nothing in Part VII of this Act shall prejudice the admissibility of a confession made by an accused person.

(8) In this section 'oppression' includes torture, inhuman or degrading treatment, and the use or threat of violence (whether or not amounting to torture).

77. Confessions by mentally handicapped persons.

(1) Without prejudice to the general duty of the court at a trial on indictment to direct the jury on any matter on which it appears to the court appropriate to do so, where at such a trial:

 (*a*) the case against the accused depends wholly or substantially on a confession by him; and

 (*b*) the court is satisfied.

   (i) that he is mentally handicapped; and

   (ii) that the confession was not made in the presence of an independent person,

the court shall warn the jury that there is special need for caution before convicting the accused in reliance on the confession, and shall explain that the need arises because of the circumstances mentioned in paragraphs (a) and (b) above.

(2) In any case where at the summary trial of a person for an offence it appears to the court that a warning under subsection (1) above would be required if the trial were on indictment, the court shall treat the case as one in which there is a special need for caution before convicting the accused on his confession.

(3) In this section:

 'independent person' does not include a police officer or a person employed for, or engaged on, police purposes;

 'mentally handicapped', in relation to a person, means that he is in a state of arrested or incomplete development of mind which includes significant impairment of intelligence and social functioning; and

 'police purposes' has the meaning assigned to it by section 64 of the Police Act 1964.

EVIDENCE IN CRIMINAL PROCEEDINGS – GENERAL: MISCELLANEOUS

78. Exclusion of unfair evidence.

(1) In any proceedings the court may refuse to allow evidence on which the prosecution proposes to rely to be given if it appears to the court that, having regard to all

the circumstances, including the circumstances in which the evidence was obtained, the admission of the evidence would have such an adverse effect on the fairness of the proceedings that the court ought not to be admit it.

(2) Nothing in this section shall prejudice any rule of law requiring a court to exclude evidence.

CRIMINAL JUSTICE BILL 1987

DOCUMENTARY EVIDENCE IN CRIMINAL PROCEEDINGS

21. First-hand hearsay
(1) Subject –
    (*a*) to subsection (2) below; and
    (*b*) to section 69 of the Police and Criminal Evidence Act 1984 (evidence from computer records),
a statement made by a person in a document shall be admissible in criminal proceedings as evidence of any fact of which direct oral evidence by him would be admissible.

(2) Subsection (1) above does not render admissible a confession made by an accused person that would not be admissible under section 76 of the Police and Criminal Evidence Act 1984.

22. Business etc documents
(1) Subject –
    (*a*) to subsection (3) below; and
    (*b*) to section 69 of the Police and Criminal Evidence Act 1984,
a statement in a document shall be admissible in criminal proceedings as evidence of any fact of which direct oral evidence would be admissible, if the following conditions are satisfied –
    (i) the document was created or received by a person in the course of a trade, business, profession or other occupation, or as the holder of a paid or unpaid office; and
    (ii) the information contained in the document was supplied by a person (whether or not the maker of the statement) who had, or may reasonably be supposed to have had personal knowledge of the matters dealt with.

(2) Subsection (1) above applies whether the information contained in the document was supplied directly or indirectly but, if it was supplied indirectly, only if each person through whom it was supplied received it –
    (*a*) in the course of trade, business, profession or other occupation; or
    (*b*) as the holder of a paid or unpaid office.

(3) Subsection (1) above does not render admissible a confession made by an accused person that would not be admissible under section 76 of the Police and Criminal Evidence Act 1984.

23. Principles to be followed by court
(1) If, having regard to all the circumstances –
    (*a*) the Crown Court –
        (i) on a trial on indictment;

    (ii) on an appeal from a magistrates' court; or

    (iii) on the hearing of an application under section 6 of the Criminal Justice Act 1987 (applications for dismissal of charges of fraud transferred from magistrates' court to Crown Court; or

  (*b*) the criminal division of the Court of Appeal; or

  (*c*) a magistrates' court on a trial of an information,

is of the opinion that in the interests of justice a statement which is admissible by virtue of section 21 or 22 above nevertheless ought not to be admitted, it may direct that the statement shall not be admitted.

(2) Without prejudice to the generality of subsection (1) above, it shall be the duty of the court to have regard –

  (*a*) to the nature and source of the document containing the statement and to whether or not, having regard to its nature and source and to any other circumstances that appear to the court to be relevant, it is likely that the document is authentic;

  (*b*) to the extent to which the statement appears to supply evidence which would otherwise not be readily available;

  (*c*) to the relevance of the evidence that it appears to supply to any issue which is likely to have to be determined in the proceedings; and

  (*d*) to any risk, having regard in particular to whether it is likely to be possible to controvert the statement if the person making it does not attend to give oral evidence in the proceedings, that its admission or exclusion will result in unfairness to the accused or, if there is more than one, to any of them.

24. Statements in documents that appear to have been prepared for purposes of criminal proceedings or investigations

Where a statement which is admissible in criminal proceedings by virtue of section 21 or 22 above appears to the court to have been prepared, otherwise than under section 27, 28 or 29 below, for the purposes –

  (*a*) of pending or contemplated criminal proceedings; or

  (*b*) of a criminal investigation,

the statement shall not be given in evidence in any criminal proceedings without the leave of the court, and the court shall not give leave unless it is of the opinion that the statement ought to be admitted in the interests of justice; and in considering whether its admission would be in the interests of justice, it shall be the duty of the court to have regard –

    (i) to the contents of the statement;

    (ii) to any risk, having regard in particular to whether it is likely to be possible to controvert the statement if the person making it does not attend to give oral evidence in the proceedings, that its admission or exclusion will result in unfairness to the accused or, if there is more than one, to any of them; and

    (iii) to any other circumstances that appear to the court to be relevant.

POLICE AND CRIMINAL EVIDENCE ACT 1984
CODES OF PRACTICE

(A) CODE OF PRACTICE FOR THE EXERCISE BY POLICE OFFICERS OF STATUTORY POWERS OF STOP AND SEARCH (a)

1. General (b).

1.1 This code of practice must be readily available at all police stations for consultation by police officers, detained persons and members of the public.

1.2 The Notes for Guidance included are not provisions of this code, but are guidance to police officers and others about its application and interpretation. Provisions in the Annexes to the code are provisions of this code.

1.3 This code governs the exercise by police officers of statutory powers to search a person without first arresting him or to search a vehicle without making an arrest. The main stop and search powers in existence at the time when this code was prepared are set out in Annex A but that list should not be regarded as definitive.

1.4 This code does *not* apply to the following powers of stop and search:
   (i) Aviation Security Act 1982, s 27(2):
   (ii) Police and Criminal Evidence Act 1984, s 6(1) (which relates specifically to powers of constables employed by statutory undertakers on the premises of the statutory undertakers).

1.5 The exercise of the powers to which this code applies requires reasonable grounds for suspicion that articles of a particular kind are being carried. Annex B provides guidance about this.

1.6 Nothing in this code affects the ability of an officer to speak to or question a person in the course of his duties without detaining him or exercising any element of compulsion.

(a) This Code of Practice is issued under ss 66 and 67 of the Police and Criminal Evidence Act 1984: it is admissible thereunder in evidence and account may be taken by the court of any relevant provision.

(b) The Notes for Guidance for this section state:

1A It is important to ensure that powers of stop and search are used responsibly and sparingly and only where reasonable grounds for suspicion genuinely exist. Over use of the powers is as likely to be harmful to police effort in the long term as misuse; both can lead to mistrust of the police among sections of the community. It is also particularly important to ensure that any person searched is treated courteously and considerately if police action is not to be resented.

---

2. Action before a search is carried out (a).

2.1 Where an officer has the reasonable grounds for suspicion necessary to exercise a power of stop and search he may detain the person concerned for the purposes of and with a view to searching him. There is no power to stop or detain a person against his will in order to find grounds for a search.

2.2 Before carrying out a search the officer may question the person about his behaviour or his presence in circumstances which gave rise to the suspicion, since he may have a satisfactory explanation which will make a search unnecessary. If, as a result of any questioning preparatory to a search or other circumstances which come to the attention of the officer, there cease to be reasonable grounds for suspecting that an article is being carried of a kind for which there is a power of stop and search, no search may take place.

2.3 The reasonable grounds for suspicion which are necessary for the exercise of the initial power to detain may be confirmed or eliminated as a result of the questioning of a person detained for the purposes of a search (or such questioning may reveal reasonable grounds to suspect the possession of a different kind of unlawful article from that originally suspected); but the reasonable grounds for suspicion without which any search or detention for the purposes of a search is unlawful cannot be retrospectively provided by such questioning during his detention or by his refusal to answer any question put to him.

2.4 Before any search of a detained person or attended vehicle takes place the officer must give the person to be searched or in charge of the vehicle the following information:
   (i)   his name and the name of the police station to which he is attached;
   (ii) the object of the search; and
   (iii) his grounds for undertaking it.

2.5 If the officer is not in uniform he must show his warrant card.

2.6 Unless it appears to the officer that it will not be practicable to make a record of the search he must also inform the person to be searched (or the owner or person in charge of a vehicle that is to be searched, as the case may be) that he is entitled to a copy of the record of the search if he asks for it within a year. If the person wishes to have a copy and is not given one on the spot, he should be advised to which police station he should apply.

2.7 If the person to be searched, or in charge of a vehicle to be searched, does not understand what is being said, the officer must take reasonable steps to bring the information in paragraphs 2.4 to 2.6 to his attention. If the person has someone with him then the officer must establish whether that person can interpret.

(**a**) The Notes for Guidance for this section state –

2A In some circumstances preparatory questioning may be unnecessary, but in general a brief conversation or exchange will be desirable as a means of avoiding unsuccessful searches. Where a person is lawfully detained for the purpose of a search but no search in the event takes place, the detention will not thereby have been rendered unlawful.

---

3. Conduct of the search (a).

3.1 Every reasonable effort must be made to reduce to the minimum the embarrassment that a person being searched may experience.

3.2 Although force may only be used as a last resort, reasonable force may be used if necessary to conduct a search or to detain a person or vehicle for the purposes of a search. A compulsory search may be made only if it has been established that the person is unwilling to co-operate (eg by opening a bag).

3.3 The length of time for which a person or vehicle may be detained will depend on the circumstances, but must in all circumstances be reasonable and not extend beyond the time taken for the search. The thoroughness and extent of a search must depend on what is suspected of being carried, and by whom. If the suspicion relates to a particular article for example an offensive weapon, which is seen to be slipped into a person's pocket then, in the absence of other grounds for suspicion or an opportunity for the article to be moved elsewhere, the search must be confined to that pocket. In the case of a small article which can readily be concealed, such as a drug, and which might be concealed anywhere on the person, a more extensive search may be necessary. (**a**)

3.4 The search must be conducted at the place where the person or vehicle was first detained or nearby.

3.5 Searches in public must be restricted to superficial examination of outer clothing. There is no power to require a person to remove any clothing in public other than an outer coat, jacket or gloves. Where on reasonable grounds it is considered necessary to conduct a more thorough search, eg by requiring someone to take off a T-shirt or headgear, this should be done out of public view (eg in a police van or a nearby police station if there is one). Any search involving the removal of more than an outer coat, jacket, gloves, headgear or footwear may only be made by an officer of the same sex as the person searched and may not be made in the presence of anyone of the opposite sex. (**a**)

(**a**) The Notes for Guidance for this section state –

3A A search in the street itself should be regarded as being in public for the purposes of paragraph 3.5 above, even though it may be empty at the time a search begins. Although there is no power to require a person to do so, there is nothing to prevent an officer from asking a person voluntarily to remove more than an outer coat, jacket or gloves in public.

3B As a search of a person in public should be a superficial examination of outer clothing, such searches should normally be capable of completion within one minute or so.

---

4. Action after a search is carried out (a).

a) General

4.1 An officer who has carried out a search must make a written record. In some cases this may not be possible such as in situations involving public disorder occurring in seaside areas during Bank Holiday weekends or the search of football supporters entering or leaving a ground. (**a**)

4.2 The record must be completed as soon as practicable – on the spot unless circumstances (eg other immediate duties or very inclement weather) make this impracticable.

4.3 The record must be made on the form provided for this purpose (the national search record).

4.4 In order to complete the search record the officer should normally seek the name, address and date of birth of the person searched, but under the search procedures there is no obligation on a person to provide these details and no power to detain him if he is unwilling to do so.

4.5 The following information can always and must be included in the record of a search even if the person does not wish to identify himself or give his date of birth:

    (i)   the name of the person searched, or (if he withholds it) a description of him;
    (ii)   where the person searched is white, Afro-Caribbean or Asian, a note to that effect;
    (iii)   when a vehicle is searched, a description of it;
    (iv)   the object of the search;
    (v)   the grounds for making it;
    (vi)   the date and time it was made;
    (vii)   the place where it was made;
    (viii) its result;
    (ix)   a note of any injury or damage to property resulting from it;
    (x)   the identity of the officer making it. (**a**)

4.6 A record is required for each person and each vehicle searched. If, for example, a person is in a vehicle and both are searched, two records must be completed.

4.7 The record of the grounds for making a search must, briefly but informatively, explain the reason for suspecting the person concerned, whether by reference to his behaviour or other circumstances.

b) Unattended vehicles

4.8 After searching an unattended vehicle, or anything in it or on it, an officer must leave a notice in it (or on it, if things in or on it have been searched without opening it) recording the fact that it has been searched.

4.9 The notice should include the name of the police station to which the officer concerned is attached and state where a copy of the record of the search may be obtained and where any application for compensation should be directed.

4.10 The vehicle must if practicable be left secure.

(**a**) The Notes for Guidance for this section state –

4A Nothing in this code affects the routine searching of persons entering sports grounds or other premises with their consent, or as a condition of entry.

4B Where a search is conducted by more than one officer the identity of all officers engaged in the search must be recorded on the search record.

[Annex A has been omitted]

ANNEX B   REASONABLE GROUNDS FOR SUSPICION

1. Reasonable suspicion does not require *certainty* that an unlawful article is being carried; nor does the officer concerned have to be satisfied of this beyond reasonable doubt. Reasonable suspicion, in contrast to *mere* suspicion must be founded on fact. There must be some concrete basis for the officer's suspicion, related to the individual person concerned, which can be considered and evaluated by an objective third person. Mere suspicion, in contrast, is a hunch or instict which cannot be explained or justified to an objective observer. An officer who has such a hunch or instinct may well be justified in continuing to keep the person under observation or speak to him, but additional grounds which bring up mere suspicion to the level of reasonable suspicion are needed before he may exercise the powers dealt with in this code.

2. Reasonable suspicion may arise from the nature of the property observed or being carried or suspected of being carried coupled with other factors including the time, the place or the suspicious behaviour of the person concerned or those with him. The decision to search must be based on all the facts which, to a careful officer, bear on the likelihood that an article of a certain kind will be found, and not only on what can be seen at the time. So an officer with prior knowledge of the behaviour of someone he sees in a certain situation, or acting on information received (such as a description of a suspected offender) may have reasonable grounds for searching him although another officer would not.

3. Reasonable suspicion cannot be supported on the basis simply of a higher than average chance that the person has committed or is committing an offence, for example because he belongs to a group within which offenders of a certain kind are relatively common, or because

of a combination of factors such as these. For example, a person's colour of itself can never be a reasonable ground for suspicion. The mere fact alone that a person is carrying a particular kind of property or is dressed in a certain way or has a certain hairstyle is likewise not of itself sufficient. Nor is the fact that a person is known to have a previous conviction for unlawful possession of an article.

4. The degree or level of suspicion required to establish the reasonable grounds justifying the exercise of powers of stop and search is no less than the degree or level of suspicion required to effect an arrest without warrant for any of the suspected offences to which these powers relate. The powers of stop and search provide an opportunity to establish the commission or otherwise of certain kinds of offences without arrest and may therefore render arrest unnecessary.

5. Paragraph 4 above is subject to the principle that where a police officer has reasonable grounds to suspect that a person is in *innocent* possession of a stolen or prohibitive article, the power of stop and search exists notwithstanding that there would be no power of arrest. However, every effort should be made to secure the voluntary production of the article before the power is resorted to.

(B) CODE OF PRACTICE FOR THE SEARCHING OF PREMISES BY POLICE OFFICERS AND THE SEIZURE OF PROPERTY FOUND BY POLICE OFFICERS ON PERSONS OR PREMISES (a)

1. General.
1.1 This code of practice must be readily available at all police stations for consultation by police officers, detained persons and members of the public.

1.2 The Notes for Guidance included are not provisions of this code, but are guidance to police officers and others about its application and interpretation.

1.3 This code applies to the following searches of premises:
  (*a*) searches of premises undertaken for the purposes of an investigation into an alleged offence with the occupier's consent other than routine scenes or crime searches and searches following the activation of burglar or fire alarms or bomb threat calls;
  (*b*) searches of premises under the powers conferred by sections 17, 18 and 32 of the Police and Criminal Evidence Act 1984;
  (*c*) searches of premises undertaken in pursuance of a search warrant issued in accordance with section 15 of or Schedule 1 to that Act.

'Premises' is a wide term which may include vessels and, in certain circumstances, vehicles.

(**a**) This Code of Practice is issued under ss 66 and 67 of the Police and Criminal Evidence Act 1984: it is admissible thereunder in evidence and account may be taken by the court of any relevant provision.

---

2. Search warrants and production orders (a).
a) Action to be taken before an application is made

2.1 Where information is received which appears to justify an application the officer concerned must take reasonable steps to check that the information is accurate, recent and has not been provided maliciously or irresponsibly. An application may not be made on the basis of information from an anonymous source where corroboration has not been sought.

2.2 The officer shall ascertain as specifically as is possible in the circumstances the nature of the articles concerned and their location.

2.3 The officer shall also make enquiries to establish what, if anything, is known about the likely occupier of the premises and the nature of the premises themselves; and whether they have been previously searched and if so how recently; and to obtain any other information relevant to the application.

2.4 No application for a search warrant may be made without the authority of an officer of at least the rank of inspector (or, in a case of urgency where no officer of this rank is readily available, the senior officer on duty). No application for a production order or warrant under Schedule 1 to the Police and Criminal Evidence Act 1984 may be made without the authority of an officer of at least the rank of superintendent.

2.5 Except in a case of urgency, if there is reason to believe that a search might have an adverse effect on relations between the police and the community then the local police community liaison officer shall be consulted before it takes place.

b) Making an application
2.6 An application for a search warrant must be supported by an information in writing, stating:
  (i)   the enactment under which the application is made;
  (ii) as specifically as is reasonably practicable the premises to be searched and the object of the search; and
  (iii) the grounds on which the application is made (including, where the purpose of the proposed search is to find evidence of an alleged offence, an indication of how the evidence relates to the investigation).
2.7 An application for a search warrant under paragraph 12(a) of Schedule 1 to the Police and Criminal Evidence Act 1984 shall also where appropriate indicate why it is believed that service of notice of an application for a production order may seriously prejudice the investigation.
2.8 If an application is refused, no further application may be made for a warrant to search those premises unless supported by additional grounds.

(a) The Notes for Guidance for this section state –
2A The identity of an informant need not be disclosed when making an application, but the officer concerned should be prepared to deal with any questions the magistrate or judge may have about the accuracy of previous information provided by that source or other related matters.

---

3. Entry without warrant.

a) Making an arrest etc
3.1 The conditions under which an officer may enter and search premises without warrant are as set out in section 17 of the Police and Criminal Evidence Act 1984.

b) Search after arrest of premises in which arrest takes place
3.2 The powers of an officer to search premises in which he has arrested a person are as set out in section 32 of the Police and Criminal Evidence Act 1984.

c) Search after arrest of premises of arrested person
3.3 The powers of an officer to search premises occupied or controlled by a person who has been arrested for an arrestable offence are as set out in section 18 of the Police and Criminal Evidence Act 1984. The record of the search required by Section 18(7) of the Act shall be made in the custody record, where there is one.

4. Search with consent (a).
4.1 Subject to paragraph 4.3 below, if it is proposed to search premises with the consent of a person entitled to grant entry to the premises the consent must be given in writing. (a)
4.2 Before seeking consent the officer in charge shall state the purpose of the proposed search and inform the person concerned that he is not obliged to consent and that anything seized may be produced in evidence. If, at the time, the person is not suspected of an offence the officer shall tell him so when stating the purpose of the search.
4.3 It is unnecessary to seek consent under paragraph 4.1 and 4.2 above where in the circumstances this would cause disproportionate inconvenience to the person concerned. (a)

(a) The Notes for Guidance for this section state –
4A In the case of a lodging house or similar accommodation a search should not be made on the basis solely of the landlord's consent unless the tenant is unavailable and the matter is urgent.
4B Where it is intended to search premises under authority of a warrant or a power of entry and search without warrant, and cooperation of the occupier of the premises is obtained in

accordance with paragraph 5.4 below, there is no additional requirement to obtain written consent as at paragraph 4.1 above.

4C Paragraph 4.3 is intended in particular to apply, for example, to circumstances where police have arrested someone in the night after a pursuit and it is necessary to make a brief check of gardens along the route of the pursuit to see whether stolen or incriminating articles have been discarded.

---

5. Searching of premises: general considerations (a).

a) Time of searches

5.1 Searches made under warrant must be made within one month from the date of issue of the warrant.

5.2 Searches must be made at a reasonable hour unless this might frustrate the purpose of the search. (a)

5.3 A warrant authorises an entry on one occasion only.

b) Entry other than with consent

5.4 The officer in charge shall first attempt to communicate with the occupier or any other person entitled to grant access to the premises by explaining the authority under which he seeks entry to the premises and ask the occupier to allow him to do so, unless:

   (i)   the premises to be searched are known to be unoccupied;

   (ii) the occupier and any other person entitled to grant access are known to be absent; or

   (iii) there are reasonable grounds for believing that to alert the occupier or any other person entitled to grant access to attempting to communicate with him would frustrate the object of the search or endanger the officers concerned or other persons.

5.5 Where the premises are occupied the officer shall identify himself and, if not in uniform, show his warrant card; and state the purpose of the search and the grounds for undertaking it, before a search begins.

5.6 Reasonable force may be used if necessary to enter premises if the officer in charge is satisfied that the premises are those specified in any warrant or other written authority and where:

   (i)   the occupier or any other person entitled to grant access has refused a request to allow entry to his premises;

   (ii) it is impossible to communicate with the occupier or any other person entitled to grant access; or

   (iii) any of the provisions of sub-paragraphs 5.4(i) to (iii) apply.

5.7 Where the search is to be made under warrant the occupier shall, if present, be given a copy of it. If he is not present the copy shall be left in a prominent place on the premises. The warrant itself shall be endorsed to show this has been done.

c) Conduct of searches

5.8 Premises may be searched only to the extent necessary to achieve the object of the search, having regard to the size and nature of whatever is sought. A search under warrant may not continue under the authority of that warrant once all the things specified in it have been found, or the officer in charge is satisfied that they are not on the premises.

5.9 Searches must be conducted with due consideration for the property and privacy of the occupier of the premises searched, and with no more disturbance than necessary. Reasonable force may be used only where this is necessary because the co-operation of the occupier cannot be obtained or is insufficient for the purpose.

5.10 If the occupier wishes to ask a friend, neighbour or other person to witness the search, then he must be allowed to do so, unless the officer in charge has reasonable grounds for believing that this would seriously hinder the investigation. A search need not be delayed for this purpose unreasonably.

d) Leaving premises

5.11 If premises have been entered by force the officer in charge shall, before leaving them, satisfy himself that they are secure either by arranging for the occupier or his agent to be present or by any other appropriate means.

e) Search under Schedule 1 to the Police and Criminal Evidence Act 1984

5.12 An officer of the rank of inspector or above shall take charge of and be present at any search made under a warrant issued under this Schedule. He is responsible for ensuring that the search is conducted with discretion and in such a manner as to cause the least possible disruption to any business or other activities carried on in the premises.

5.13 After satisfying himself that material may not be taken from the premises without his knowledge, the officer in charge of the search shall ask for the documents or other records concerned to be produced. He may also, if he considers it to be necessary, ask to see the index to files held on the premises, if there is one; and the officers conducting the search may inspect any files which, according to the index, appear to contain any of the material sought. A more extensive search of the premises may be made only if the person responsible for them refuses to produce the material sought, or to allow access to the index; if it appears that the index is inaccurate or incomplete; or if for any other reason the officer in charge has reasonable grounds for believing that such a search is necessary in order to find the material sought. (a)

(a) The Notes for Guidance for this section state –

5A In determining at what time to make a search the officer in charge should have regard, among other considerations, to the times of day at which the occupier of the premises is likely to be present, and should not search at a time when he, or any other person on the premises, is likely to be asleep unless not doing so is likely to frustrate the purposes of the search.

5B In asking for documents to be produced in accordance with paragraphs 5.13 above, officers should direct the request to a person in authority and with responsibilty for the documents.

5C If the wrong premises are searched by mistake, everything possible should be done at the earliest opportunity to allay any sense of grievance. In appropriate cases assistance should be given to obtain compensation.

---

6. Seizure and retention of property (a).

a) Seizure

6.1 Subject to paragraph 6.2 below, an officer who is searching any premises under any statutory power or with the consent of the occupier may seize:

  (*a*) anything covered by a warrant; and
  (*b*) anything which he has reasonable grounds for believing is evidence of an offence or has been obtained in consequence of the commission of an offence.

Items under (*b*) may only be seized where this is necessary to prevent their concealment, alteration, loss, damage or destruction.

6.2 No item may be seized which is subject to legal privilege (as defined in section 10 of the Police and Criminal Evidence Act 1984).

6.3 An officer who decides that it is not appropriate to seize property because of an explanation given by the person holding it, but who has reasonable grounds for believing that it has been obtained in consequence of the commission of an offence by some person, shall inform the holder of his suspicions and shall explain that, if he disposes of the property, he may be liable to civil or criminal proceedings.

6.4 An officer may photograph or copy, or have photographed or copied, any document or other article which he has power to seize in accordance with paragraph 6.1 above.

6.5 Where an officer considers that a computer may contain information that could be used in evidence, he may require the information to be produced in a form that can be taken away and in which it is visible and legible.

b) Retention

6.6 Subject to paragraph 6.7 below anything which has been seized in accordance with the above provisions may be retained only for as long as is necessary in the circumstances. It may be retained, among other purposes:

  (i)   for use as evidence at a trial for an offence;
  (ii) for forensic examination or for other investigation in connection with an offence; or
  (iii) where there are reasonable grounds for believing that it has been stolen or obtained by the commission of an offence, in order to establish its lawful owner.

6.7 Property shall not be retained in accordance with sub-paragraphs 6.6(i) and (ii) (i e for use as evidence or for the purposes of investigation) if a photograph or copy would suffice for these purposes.

c) Rights of owners etc
6.8 If property is retained the person who had custody or control of it immediately prior to its seizure must on request, be provided, with a list or description of the property within a reasonable time.
6.9 He or his representative must be allowed supervised access to the property to examine it or have it photographed or copied, or must be provided with a photograph or copy, in either case within a reasonable time or any request and at his own expense, unless the officer in charge of an investigation has reasonable grounds for believing that this would prejudice the investigation of an offence or any criminal proceedings. In this case a record of the grounds must be made.

(**a**) The Notes for Guidance for this section state –
6A Any person claiming property seized by the police may apply to a magistrates' court under the Police (Property) Act 1897 for its possession, and should, where appropriate, be advised of this procedure.

---

7. Action to be taken after searches.
7.1 Where premises have been searched in circumstances to which this code applies, other than in the circumstances covered by paragraph 4.3 above, the officer in charge of the search shall, on arrival at a police station, make or have made a record of the search. The record shall include:
(i)   the address of the premises searched;
(ii)   the date, time and duration of the search;
(iii)   the authority under which the search was made. Where the search was made in the exercise of a statutory power to search premises without warrant, the record shall include the power under which the search was made; and where the search was made under warrant, or with written consent, a copy of the warrant or consent shall be appended to the record or kept in a place identified in the record;
(iv)   the names of the officers who conducted the search;
(v)   the names of any persons on the premises if they are known;
(vi)   either a list of any articles seized or a note of where such a list is kept and, if not covered by a warrant, the reason for their seizure;
(vii)   where force was used and, if so, the reason why it was used;
(viii) details of any damage caused during the search, and the circumstances in which it was caused.
7.2 Where premises have been searched under warrant, the warrant shall be endorsed to show:
(i)   whether any articles specified in the warrant were found;
(ii)   whether any other articles were seized;
(iii)   the date and time at which it was executed;
(iv)   the names of the officers who executed it; and
(v)   whether a copy was handed to the occupier or left on the premises and if so where on them.
7.3 Any warrant which has been executed or which has not been executed within one month of its issue shall be returned, if it was issued by a justice of the peace, to the clerk to the justices for the petty sessions area concerned or, if issued by a judge, to the appropriate officer of the court from which he issued it.

8. Search registers.
8.1 A search register shall be maintained at each sub-divisional police station. All records which are required to be made by this code shall be made, copied, or referred to in the register.

(C) CODE OF PRACTICE FOR THE DETENTION, TREATMENT AND QUESTIONING OF PERSONS BY POLICE OFFICERS (a)

1. General (b).

1.1 All persons in custody must be dealt with expeditiously, and released as soon as the need for detention has ceased to apply.

1.2 This code of practice must be readily available at all police stations for consultation by police officers, detained persons and members of the public.

1.3 The Notes for Guidance included are not provisions of this code, but are guidance to police officers and others about its application and interpretation. Provisions in the Annexes to this code are provisions of this code.

1.4 If an officer has any suspicion, or is told in good faith, that a person of any age may be mentally ill or mentally handicapped, or mentally incapable of understanding the significance of questions put to him or his replies, then that person shall be treated as mentally ill or mentally handicapped person for the purposes of this code.

1.5 If any one appears to be under the age of 17 then he shall be treated as a juvenile for the purposes of this code in the absence of clear evidence to show that he is older.

1.6 If a person appears to be blind or seriously visually handicapped, deaf, unable to read or unable to communicate orally with the officer dealing with him at the time, he should be treated as such for the purposes of this code in the absence of clear evidence to the contrary.

1.7 In this code 'the appropriate adult' (c) means:
  (a) in the case of a juvenile:
    (i) his parent or guardian (or, if he is in care, the care authority or organisation);
    (ii) a social worker; or
    (iii) failing either of the above, another responsible adult who is not a police officer or employed by the police.
  (b) in the case of a person who is mentally ill or mentally handicapped:
    (i) a relative, guardian or other person responsible for his care or custody;
    (ii) someone who has experience of dealing with mentally ill or mentally handicapped persons but is not a police officer or employed by the police; or
    (iii) failing either of the above, some other responsible adult who is not a police officer or employed by the police.

1.8 Whenever this code requires a person to be given certain information he does not have to be given it if he is incapable at the time of understanding what is said to him or is violent or likely to become violent or is in urgent need of medical attention, but he must be given it as soon as practicable.

1.9 Any reference to a custody officer in this code includes an officer who is performing the functions of a custody officer.

1.10 In its application to persons who are in custody at police stations this code applies whether or not they have been arrested for an offence except section 16 which applies solely to persons in police detention.

(a) This Code of Practice is issued under ss 66 and 67 of the Police and Criminal Evidence Act 1984: it is admissible thereunder in evidence and account may be taken by the court of any relevant provision.

(b) The Notes for Guidance for this section state –

1A Although certain sections of this code (eg section 9 – Treatment of detained persons) apply specifically to persons in custody at police stations, those there voluntarily to assist with an investigation should be treated with no less consideration (eg offered refreshments at appropriate times) and enjoy an absolute right to obtain legal advice or communicate with anyone outside the police station.

1B This code does not affect the principle that all citizens have a duty to help police officers to prevent crime and discover offenders. This is a civic rather than a legal duty; but when a police officer is trying to discover whether, or by whom, an offence has been committed he is entitled to question any person from whom he thinks useful information can be obtained, subject to the restrictions imposed by this code. A person's declaration that he is unwilling to reply does not alter this entitlement.

1C In the case of persons who are mentally ill or mentally handicapped, it may in certain circumstances be more satisfactory for all concerned if the appropriate adult is someone who has experience or training in their care rather than a relative lacking such qualifications. But if the person himself prefers a relative to a better qualified stranger his wishes should if practicable be respected.

(**c**) See Note for Guidance 1C above.

---

2. Custody records (a).

2.1 A separate custody record must be opened as soon as practicable for each person who is brought to a police station under arrest or is arrested at the police station having attended there voluntarily. All information which has to be recorded under this code must be recorded as soon as practicable, in the custody record unless otherwise specified.

2.2 In the case of any action requiring the authority of an officer of a specified rank, his name and rank must be noted in the custody record.

2.3 The custody officer is responsible for the accuracy and completeness of the custody record and for ensuring that the record or a copy of the record accompanies a detained person if he is transferred to another police station. The record shall show the time of and reason for transfer and the time a person is released from detention.

2.4 When a person leaves police detention he or his legal representative shall be supplied on request with a custody record as soon as practicable. This entitlement lasts for 12 months after his release. (**a**)

2.5 All entries in custody and written interview records must be timed and signed by the maker.

2.6 Any refusal by a person to sign either a custody or an interview record when asked to do so in accordance with the provisions of this code must itself be recorded.

(**a**) The Notes for Guidance for this section state –

2A The person who has been detained, the appropriate adult, or legal representative who gives reasonable notice of a request to inspect the original custody record after the person has left police detention, should be allowed to do so.

---

3. Initial action (a).

a) Detained persons: normal procedure

3.1 When a person is brought to a police station under arrest or is arrested at the police station having attended there voluntarily the custody officer must inform him of the following rights and of the fact that they need not be exercised immediately:

  (i)   the right to have someone informed of his arrest in accordance with section 5 below;
  (ii) the right to consult a solicitor in accordance with section 6 below; and
  (iii) the right to consult this and the other codes of practice. (**b**)

3.2 The custody officer must also give the person a written notice setting out the above three rights, the right to a copy of the custody record in accordance with paragraph 2.4 above and the caution in the terms prescribed in section 10 below. The custody officer shall ask the person to sign the custody record to acknowledge receipt of this notice (**c**).

3.3 If the custody officer authorises a person's detention he must inform him of the grounds as soon as practicable and in any case before that person is then questioned about any offence.

3.4 The person shall be asked to sign on the custody record to signify whether or not he wants legal advice at this point.

b) Detained persons: special groups

3.5 If the person does not understand English or appears to be deaf and the custody officer cannot communicate with him then the custody officer must as soon as practicable call an interpreter, and ask him to provide the information required above.

3.6 If the person is a juvenile, is mentally handicapped or is suffering from mental illness then the custody officer must as soon as practicable inform the appropriate adult of the grounds for his detention and his whereabouts and ask the adult to come to the police station to see the person. If the appropriate adult is already at the police station when information is given to the person as required in paragraphs 3.1 to 3.3 above then the information must be given to the detained person in his presence. If the appropriate adult is not at the police station when the information is given then the information must be given to the detailed person again in the presence of the appropriate adult once that person arrives.

3.7 If the person is blind or seriously visually handicapped or is unable to read, the custody officer should ensure that his solicitor, relative, the appropriate adult or some other person likely to take an interest in him is available to help in checking any documentation. Where this code requires written consent or signification, then the person who is assisting may be asked to sign instead if the detained person so wishes. (**d**)

3.8 In the case of a juvenile who is known to be subject to a supervision order, reasonable steps must also be taken to notify the person supervising him.

c) Persons attending a police station voluntarily

3.9 Any person attending a police station voluntarily for the purpose of assisting with an investigation may leave at will unless placed under arrest. If it is decided that he would not be allowed to do so then he must be informed at once that he is under arrest and brought before the custody officer. If he is not placed under arrest but is cautioned in accordance with section 10 below, the officer who gives the caution must at the same time inform him that he is not under arrest, that he is not obliged to remain at the police station but that if he remains at the police station he may obtain legal advice if he wishes. (**e**)

d) Documentation

3.10 The grounds for a person's detention shall be recorded, in his presence if practicable.

3.11 Action taken under paragraphs 3.5 to 3.8 shall be recorded.

(**a**) The Notes for Guidance for this section state –

3A If the juvenile is in the care of a local authority or voluntary organisation but is living with his parents or other adults responsible for his welfare then, although there is no legal obligation on the police to inform them, they as well as the authority or organisation should normally be contacted unless suspected of involvement in the offence concerned. Even if a juvenile in care is not living with his parents, consideration should be given to informing them as well.

3B Section 7 of this code contains special additional provisions for Commonwealth citizens and foreign nationals.

3C Most Local Authority Social Services Departments can supply a list of interpreters who have the necessary skills and experience to interpret for the deaf at police interviews.

3D The right to consult the codes of practice under paragraph 3.1 above does not entitle the person concerned to delay unreasonably necessary investigative or administrative action while he does so.

3E When the custody officer gives the person a copy of the notice referred to in paragraph 3.2, he should also give him a copy of a notice explaining the arrangements for obtaining legal advice.

3F Blind or seriously visually handicapped persons may be unwilling to sign police documents. The alternative of their representative signing on their behalf seeks to protect the interests of both police and suspects.

3G If a person who is attending a police station voluntarily (in accordance with paragraph 3.9) asks about his entitlement to legal advice, he should be given a copy of a notice explaining the arrangements for obtaining legal advice.

(**b**) See Note for Guidance 3D above.

(**c**) See Note for Guidance 3E above.

(**d**) See Note for Guidance 3F above.

(**e**) See Note for Guidance 3G above.

---

4. Detained person's property (a).

a) Action

4.1 The custody officer is responsible for:

(*a*) ascertaining:

   (i) what property a detained person has with him when he comes to the police station (whether on arrest, redetention on answering to bail, commitment to prison custody on the order or sentence of a court, on lodgement at the police station with a view to his production in court from such custody, or on arrival at a police station on transfer from detention at another station or from hospital);

   (ii) what property he might have acquired for an unlawful or harmful purpose while in custody.

(*b*) the safekeeping of any property which is taken from him and which remains at the police station.

To these ends the custody officer may search him or authorise his being searched to the extent that he considers necessary (provided that a search of intimate parts of the body or involving the removal of more than outer clothing may only be made in accordance with Annex A to this code). A search may only be carried out by an officer of the same sex as the person searched. (**b**)

4.2 A detained person may retain clothing and personal effects at his own risk unless the custody officer considers that he may use them to cause harm to himself or others, interfere with evidence, damage property or effect an escape or they are needed as evidence. In this event the custody officer can withhold such articles as he considers necessary. If he does so he must tell the person why.

4.3 Personal effects are those items which a person may lawfully need to use or refer to while in detention but do not include cash and other items of value.

b) Documentation

4.4 The custody officer is responsible for recording all property brought to the police station that a detained person had with him or had taken from him on arrest. The detained person shall be allowed to check and sign the record of property as correct.

4.5 If a detained person is not allowed to keep any article of clothing or personal effects the reason must be recorded.

(**a**) The Notes for Guidance for this section state –

4A Paragraph 4.1 is not to be taken as requiring each detained person to be searched. Where for example a person is to be detained for only a short period and is not to be placed in a cell, the custody officer may at his discretion decide not to search the person. In such a case the custody record will be endorsed 'not searched', paragraph 4.4 will not apply, and the person will be invited to sign the entry. Where the person detained refuses to sign, the custody officer will be obliged to ascertain what property he has on him in accordance with paragraph 4.1.

4B Paragraph 4.4 does not require the custody officer to record on the custody record, property in the possession of the person on arrest, if by virtue of its nature, quantity or size, it is not practicable to remove it to the police station.

4C Paragraph 4.1 above is not to be taken as requiring that items of clothing worn by the person be recorded unless withheld by the custody officer in accordance with paragraph 4.2.

(**b**) See Note for Guidance 4A above.

---

5. Right not to be held incommunicado (a).

a) Action

5.1 Any person to whom paragraphs 2.1 and 3.9 apply may on request have one person known to him or who is likely to take an interest in his welfare informed at public expense as soon as practicable of his whereabouts. If the person cannot be contacted the person who has made the request may choose up to two alternatives. If they too cannot be contacted the custody officer has discretion to allow further attempts until the information has been conveyed. (**b**)

5.2 The exercise of the above right in respect of each of the persons nominated may be delayed only in accordance with Annex B to this code.

5.3 The above right may be exercised on each occasion that a persons is taken to another police station.

5.4 The person may receive visits at the custody officer's discretion. (**c**)

5.5 Where an enquiry as to the whereabouts of the person is made by a friend, relative or person with an interest in his welfare, this information shall be given, if he agrees and if Annex B does not apply. (**d**)

5.6 The person shall be supplied on request with writing materials. Any letter or other message shall be sent as soon as practicable unless Annex B applies.

5.7 He may also speak on the telephone for a reasonable time to one person unless Annex B applies. (**e**)

5.8 Before any letter or message is sent, or telephone call made, the person shall be informed that what he says in any letter, call or message (other than in the case of a communication to a solicitor) may be read or listened to as appropriate and may be given in evidence. A telephone call may be terminated if it is being abused. The costs can be at public expense at the discretion of the custody officer.

b) Documentation

5.9 A record must be kept of:
(*a*) any request made under this section and the action taken on it;
(*b*) any letters or messages sent, calls made or visits received; and
(*c*) any refusal on the part of a person to have information about himself or his whereabouts given to an outside enquirer.

(**a**) The Notes for Guidance for this section state –

5A An interpreter may make a telephone call or write a letter on a person's behalf.

5B In the exercise of his discretion the custody officer should allow visits where possible in the light of the availability of sufficient manpower to supervise a visit and any possible hindrance to the investigation.

5C If the person does not know of anyone to contact for advice or support or cannot contact a friend or relative, the custody officer should bear in mind any local voluntary bodies or other organisations who might be able to offer help in such cases. But if it is specifically legal advice that is wanted, then paragraph 6.1 below will apply.

5D In some circumstances it may not be appropriate to use the telephone to disclose information under paragraphs 5.1 and 5.5 above.

5E The telephone call at paragraph 5.7 is in addition to any communication under paragraphs 5.1 and 6.1.

(**b**) See Notes for Guidance 5C and 5D above.

(**c**) See Note for Guidance 5B above.

(**d**) See Note for Guidance 5D above.

(**e**) See Note for Guidance 5E above.

---

6. Right to legal advice (a).

a) Action

6.1 Subject to paragraph 6.2, any person may at any time consult and communicate privately, whether in person, in writing or on the telephone, with a solicitor. (**b**)

6.2 The exercise of the above right may be delayed only in accordance with Annex B to this code.

6.3 A person who asks for legal advice may not be interviewed or continue to be interviewed until he has received it unless:
(*a*) Annex B applies; or
(*b*) an officer of the rank of superintendent or above has reasonable grounds to believe that:
  (i) delay will involve an immediate risk of harm to persons or serious loss of or damage to property (**c**); or
  (ii) where a solicitor, including a duty solicitor, has been contracted and has agreed to attend, awaiting his arrival would cause unreasonable delay to the processes of investigation (**c**); or
(*c*) the solicitor nominated by the person, or selected by him from a list;
  (i) cannot be contacted;
  (ii) has previously indicated that he does not wish to be contacted; or
  (iii) having been contacted, has declined to attend;
  and the person has been advised of the Duty Solicitor Scheme (where one is in operation) but has declined to ask for the duty solicitor, or the duty solicitor is unavailable; or
(*d*) the person has given his agreement in writing or on tape that the interview (c) may be started at once.

6.4 Where sub-paragraph 6.3(*b*)(i) applies, once sufficient information to avert the risk has been obtained, questioning must cease until the person has received legal advice or sub-paragraphs 6.3(*a*), (*b*)(ii), (*c*) or (*d*) apply.

6.5 Where a person has been permitted to consult a solicitor and the solicitor is available at the time the interview begins or is in progress, he must be allowed to have his solicitor present while he is interviewed.

6.6 The solicitor may only be required to leave the interview if his conduct is such that the investigating officer is unable properly to put questions to the suspect. (**d**)

6.7 If the investigating officer considers that a solicitor is acting in such a way, he will stop the interview and consult an officer not below the rank of superintendent, if one is readily available, and otherwise an officer not below the rank of inspector who is not connected with the investigation. After speaking to the solicitor the officer who has been consulted will decide whether or not the interview should continue in the presence of that solicitor. If he decides that it should not, the suspect will be given the opportunity to consult another solicitor before the interview continues and that solicitor will be given an opportunity to be present at the interview.

6.8 The removal of a solicitor from an interview is a serious step and if it occurs, the officer of superintendent rank or above who took the decision will consider whether the incident should be reported to The Law Society. If the decision to remove the solicitor has been taken by an officer below the rank of superintendent, the facts must be reported to an officer of superintendent rank or above who will similarly consider whether a report to The Law Society would be appropriate.

6.9 In this code 'solicitor' means a solicitor qualified to practice in accordance with the Solicitors Act 1974. If a solicitor wishes to send a clerk or legal executive to provide advice on his behalf, then the clerk or legal executive shall be admitted to the police station for this purpose unless an officer of the rank of inspector or above considers that such a visit will hinder the investigation of crime and directs otherwise. Once admitted to the police station, the provisions of paragraphs 6.3 to 6.7 apply.

6.10 If the inspector refuses access to the clerk or legal executive or a decision is taken that such a person should not be permitted to remain at an interview, he must forthwith notify a solicitor on whose behalf the clerk or legal executive was to have acted or was acting, and give him an opportunity of making alternative arrangements.

b) Documentation

6.11 Any request for legal advice and the action taken on it shall be recorded.

6.12 If a person has asked for legal advice and an interview is commenced in the absence of a solicitor or his representative (or the solicitor or his representative has been required to leave an interview) a record shall be made in the interview record.

(**a**) The Notes for Guidance for this section state –

6A In considering whether paragraph 6.3(*b*)(i) and (ii) applies, the officer should where practicable ask the solicitor for an estimate of the time that he is likely to take in coming to the station, and relate this information to the time for which detention is permitted, the time of day (i e whether the period of rest required by paragraph 12.2 is imminent) and the requirements of other investigations in progress. If it appears that it will be necessary to begin an interview before the solicitor's arrival he should be given an indication of how long police would be able to wait before paragraph 6.3(*b*)(i) and (ii) applies so that he has an opportunity to make arrangements for legal advice to be provided by someone else.

6B A person who asks for legal advice should be given an opportunity to consult a specific solicitor (for example his own solicitor or one known to him) or the duty solicitor where a Duty Solicitor Scheme is in operation. If these attempts to secure legal advice are unsuccessful, the custody officer has discretion to allow further attempts until a solicitor has been contacted who agrees to provide legal advice. If advice is not available by these means, or he does not wish to consult the duty solicitor, the person should be given an opportunity to choose a solicitor from a list of those willing to provide legal advice. If this solicitor is unavailable, he may choose up to two alternatives.

6C Procedures undertaken under section 8 of the Road Traffic Act 1972 do not constitute interviewing for the purposes of this code.

6D In considering whether paragraph 6.6 applies, a solicitor is not guilty of misconduct if he seeks to challenge an improper question to his client or the manner in which it is put or he wishes to give his client further legal advice, and should not be required to leave an interview unless his interference with its conduct clearly goes beyond this.

6E In a case where an officer takes the decision to exclude a solicitor, he must be in a position to satisfy the court that the decision was properly made. In order to do this he may need to witness what is happening himself.

(**b**) See Note for Guidance 6B above.

(**c**) See Notes for Guidance 6A and 6B above.

(**d**) See Note for Guidance 6C above.

7. Citizens of independent Commonwealth Countries or foreign nationals (a).

a) Action
7.1 A citizen of an independent Commonwealth country or a national of a foreign country (including the Republic of Ireland) may communicate at any time with his High Commission, Embassy or Consulate.
7.2 If a citizen of an independent Commonwealth country has been detained for more than 24 hours he must be asked if he wishes the police to inform his High Commission of his whereabouts and the grounds for his detention. If so the custody officer is responsible for ensuring that the High Commission is informed by telephone.
7.3 If a national of a foreign country with which a Consular Convention is in force is detained, the appropriate consulate shall be informed as soon as practicable, subject to paragraph 7.6 below.
7.4 Any other foreign national who is detained must be informed as soon as practicable of his right to communicate with his consul if he so wishes. He must also be informed that the police will notify his consul of his arrest if he wishes.
7.5 Consular officers may visit one of their nationals who is in police detention to talk to him and, if required, to arrange for legal advice. Such visits shall take place out of the hearing of a police officer.
7.6 Notwithstanding the provisions of consular conventions, where the person is a political refugee (whether for reasons of race, nationality, political opinion or religion) or is seeking political asylum, a consular officer shall not be informed of the arrest of one of his nationals or given access to or information about him except at the person's express request.

b) Documentation
7.7 A record shall be made when a person is informed of his rights under this section and of any communications with a High Commission, Embassy or Consulate.

(a) The Notes for Guidance for this section state –
7A The exercise of the rights in this section may not be interfered with even though Annex B applies.
7B A list of countries with which a Consular Convention is in force is set out in the Home Office Consolidated Circular to the Police on Crime and Kindred Matters.

---

8. Conditions of detention (a).

a) Action
8.1 So far as is practicable, not more than one person shall be detained in each cell.
8.2 Cells in use must be adequately heated, cleaned and ventilated. They must be adequately lit, subject to such dimming as is compatible with safety and security to allow persons detained overnight to sleep. No addition restraints should be used within a locked cell unless absolutely necessary, and then only approved handcuffs.
8.3 Blankets, mattresses, pillows and other bedding supplied should be of a reasonable standard and in a clean and sanitary condition. (b)
8.4 Access to toilet and washing facilities must be provided.
8.5 If it is necessary to remove a person's clothes for the purposes of investigation, for hygiene or health reasons or for cleaning, replacement clothing of a reasonable standard of comfort and cleanliness shall be provided. A person may not be interviewed unless adequate clothing has been offered to him.
8.6 At least two light meals and one main meal shall be offered in any period of 24 hours. Whenever necessary, advice shall be sought from the police surgeon on medical or dietary matters. As far as practicable, meals provided shall offer a varied diet and meet any specific dietary needs or religious beliefs that the person may have; he may also have meals supplied by his family or friends at his or their own expense. (b)
8.7 Brief outdoor exercise shall be offered daily if practicable.
8.8 A juvenile shall not be placed in a police cell unless no other secure accommodation is available and the custody officer considers that it is not practicable to supervise him if he is not placed in a cell. He may not be placed in a cell with a detained adult.
8.9 Reasonable force may be used if necessary for the following purposes:

    (i) to secure compliance with reasonable instructions, including instructions given in pursuance of the provisions of a code of practice; or

    (ii) to prevent escape, injury, damage to property or the destruction of evidence.

8.10 Persons detained should be visited every hour, and those who are drunk every half hour. (**c**)

b) Documentation

8.11 A record must be kept of replacement clothing and meals offered.

8.12 If a juvenile is placed in a cell, the reason must be recorded.

(**a**) The Notes for Guidance for this section state –

8A Whenever possible juveniles and other persons at risk should be visited more regularly.

8B The provisions in paragraphs 8.3 and 8.6 respectively regarding bedding and a varied diet are of particular importance in the case of a person detained under the Prevention of Terrorism (Temporary Provisions) Act 1984. This is because such a person may well remain in police custody for some time.

(**b**) See Note for Guidance 8B above.

(**c**) See Note for Guidance 8C above.

------

9. Treatment of detained persons (a).

a) General

9.1 If a complaint is made by or on behalf of a detained person about his treatment since his arrest, or it comes to the notice of any officer that he may have been treated improperly, a report must be made as soon as practicable to an officer of the rank of inspector or above who is not connected with the investigation. If the matter concerns a possible assault or the possibility of the unnecessary or unreasonable use of force then the police surgeon must also be called as soon as practicable.

b) Medical treatment

9.2 The custody officer must immediately call the police surgeon (**b**) (or, in urgent cases, send the person to hospital or call the nearest available medical practitioner) if a person brought to a police station or already detained there:

    (*a*) appears to be suffering from physical or mental illness; or

    (*b*) is injured; or

    (*c*) does not show signs of sensibility and awareness or fails to respond normally to questions or conversation (other than through drunkenness alone); or

    (*d*) otherwise appears to need medical attention.

This applies even if the person makes no request for medical attention and whether or not he has recently had medical treatment elsewhere (unless brought to the police station direct from hospital).

9.3 If it appears to the custody officer, or he is told, that a person brought to the police station under arrest may be suffering from an infectious disease of any significance he must take steps to isolate the person and his property until he has obtained medical directions as to where the person should be taken, whether fumigation should take place and what precautions should be taken by officers who have been or will be in contact with him.

9.4 If a detained person requests a medical examination the police must be called as soon as practicable. He may in addition be examined by a medical practitioner of his own choice at his own expense.

9.5 If a person is required to take or apply any medication in compliance with medical directions, the custody officer is responsible for its sake keeping and for ensuring that he is given the opportunity to take or apply it at the appropriate times. No police officer may administer controlled drugs subject to the Misuse of Drugs Act 1971 for this purpose. A person may administer such drugs to himself only under the personal supervision of the police surgeon.

9.6 If a detained person has in his possession or claims to need medication relating to a heart condition, diabetes, epilepsy or a condition of comparable potential seriousness then, even though paragraph 9.2 may not apply, the advice of the police surgeon must be obtained.

c) Documentation

9.7 A record must be made of any arrangements made for an examination by a police surgeon under paragraph 9.1 above and of any complaint reported under that paragraph together with any relevant remarks by the custody officer.

9.8 A record must be kept of any request for a medical examination under paragraph 9.4 of the arrangements for any examination made, and of any medical directions to the police.

9.9 Subject to the requirements of Section 4 above the custody record shall include not only a record of all medication that a detained person has in his possession on arrival at the police station but also a note of any such medication he claims he needs but does not have with him.

(a) The Notes for Guidance for this section state –

9A The need to call a police surgeon need not apply to minor ailments.

9B It is important to remember that a person who appears to be drunk or behaving abnormally may be suffering from illness or the effect of drugs or may have sustained injury (particularly head injury) which is not apparent, and that someone needing or addicted to certain drugs may experience harmful effects within a short time of being deprived of their supply. Police should therefore always call the police surgeon when in any doubt, and act with all due speed.

9C If a medical practitioner does not record his clinical findings in the custody record, the record must show where they are recorded.

9D All officers dealing with detained persons are of course under a duty to observe not only the above provisions but also those set out in the Police Discipline Code.

(b) See Note for Guidance 9A above.

---

10. Cautions (a).

a) When a caution must be given

10.1 A person whom there are grounds to suspect of an offence must be cautioned before any questions about it (or further questions if it is his answers to previous questions that provide grounds for suspicion) are put to him for the purpose of obtaining evidence which may be given to a court in a prosecution. He therefore need not be cautioned if questions are put for other purposes, for example, to establish his identity, his ownership of or responsibility for any vehicle or the need to search him in the exercise of powers of stop and search.

10.2 When a person who is not under arrest is initially cautioned before or during an interview at a police station or other premises he must at the same time be told that he is not under arrest, is not obliged to remain with the officer but that if he does, may obtain free legal advice if he wishes.

10.3 A person must be cautioned upon arrest for an offence unless:

    (*a*) it is impracticable to do so by reason of his condition or behaviour at the time; or

    (*b*) he has already been cautioned immediately prior to arrest in accordance with paragraph 10.1 above.

b) Action: general

10.4 The caution shall be in the following terms:

    'You do not have to say anything unless you wish to do so, but what you say may be given in evidence.'

Minor deviations do not constitute a breach of this requirement provided that the sense of the caution is preserved. (a)

10.5 When there is a break in questioning under caution the interviewing officer must ensure that the person being questioned is aware that he remains under caution. If there is any doubt the caution should be given again in full when the interview resumes. (a)

c) Documentation

10.6 A record shall be made when a caution is given under this section, either in the officer's pocket book or in the interview record as appropriate.

(a) The Notes for Guidance for this section state –

10A In considering whether or not to caution again after a break, the officer should bear in mind that he may have to satisfy a court that the person understood that he was still under caution when the interview resumed.

10B It is not necessary to give or repeat a caution when informing a person who is not under arrest that he may be prosecuted for an offence.

10C If it appears that a person does not understand what the caution means, the officer who has given it should go on to explain it in his own words.

10D In case anyone who is given a caution is unclear about its significance the officer concerned should explain that the caution is given in pursuance of the general principle of English law that a person need not answer any questions or provide any information which might tend to incriminate him, and that no adverse inferences from this silence may be drawn at any trial that takes place. The person should not, however, be left with a false impression that non-cooperation will have no effect on his immediate treatment as, for example, his refusal to provide his name and address when charged with an offence may render him liable to detention.

---

11. Interviews: general

a) Action

11.1 No police officer may try to obtain answers to questions or to elicit a statement by the use of oppression, or shall indicate, except in answer to a direct question, what action will be taken on the part of the police if the person being interviewed answers questions, makes a statement or refuses to do either. If the person asks the officer directly what action will be taken in the event of his answering questions, making a statement or refusing to do either, then the officer may inform the person what action the police propose to take in that event provided that that action is itself proper and warranted.

11.2 As soon as a police officer who is making enquiries of any person about an offence believes that a prosecution should be brought against him and that there is sufficient evidence for it to succeed, he shall without delay cease to question him.

b) Interview records

11.3 (*a*) An accurate record must be made of each interview with a person suspected of an offence, whether or not the interview takes place at a police station.

    (*b*) If the interview takes place in the police station or other premises:
      (i) the record must state the place of the interview, the time it begins and ends, the time the record is made (if different), any breaks in the interview and the names of all those present; and must be made on the forms provided for this purpose or in the officer's pocket book or in accordance with the code of practice for the tape recording of police interviews with suspects;
      (ii) the record must be made during the course of the interview, unless in the investigating officer's view this would not be practicable or would interfere with the conduct of the interview, and must constitute either a verbatim record of what has been said or, failing this, an account of the interview which adequately and accurately summarises it.

11.4 If an interview record is not made during the course of the interview it must be made as soon as practicable after its completion.

11.5 Written interview records must be timed and signed by the maker.

11.6 If an interview record is not completed in the course of the interview the reason must be recorded in the officer's pocket book.

11.7 Any refusal by a person to sign an interview record when asked to do so in accordance with the provisions of this code must itself be recorded.

---

12. Interviews in police stations (a).

a) Action

12.1 If a police officer wishes to interview, or conduct enquiries which require the presence of a detained person the custody officer is responsible for deciding whether to deliver him into his custody.

12.2 In any period of 24 hours a detained person must be allowed a continuous period of at least 8 hours for rest, free from questioning, travel or any interruption arising out of the investigation concerned. This period should normally be at night. The period of rest may not be interrupted or delayed unless there are reasonable grounds for believing that it would:

    (i)   involve a risk of harm to persons or serious loss of or damage to property; or
    (ii) delay unnecessarily the person's release from custody; or
    (iii) otherwise prejudice the outcome of the investigation.
If a person is arrested at a police station after going there voluntarily, the period of 24 hours runs from the time of arrival at the police station and not the time of his arrest.

12.3 A detained person may not be supplied with intoxicating liquor except on medical directions. No person who is unfit through drink or drugs (**a**) to the extent that he is unable to appreciate the significance of questions put to him and his answers may be questioned about an alleged offence in that condition except in accordance with Annex C.

12.4 As far as practical interviews shall take place in interview rooms, which must be adequately heated, lit and ventilated.

12.5 Persons being questioned or making statements shall not be required to stand.

12.6 Before the commencement of an interview each interviewing officer shall identify himself and any other officers present by name and rank to the person being interviewed.

12.7 Breaks from interviewing shall be made at recognised meal times. Short breaks for refreshment shall also be provided at intervals of approximately two hours, subject to the interviewing officer's discretion to delay a break if there are reasonable grounds for believing that it would:
    (i)   involve a risk of harm to persons or serious loss of or damage to property; or
    (ii) delay unnecessarily the person's release from custody; or
    (iii) otherwise prejudice the outcome of the investigation.

12.8 If in the course of the interview a complaint is made by the person being questioned or on his behalf concerning the provisions of this code then the interviewing officer shall:
    (i)   record it in the interview record; and
    (ii) inform the custody officer, who is then responsible for dealing with it in accordance with
        section 9 of this code.

b) Documentation

12.9 A record must be made of the times at which a detained person is not in the custody of the custody officer, and why; and of the reason for any refusal to deliver him out of that custody.

12.10 A record must be made of an intoxicating liquor supplied to a detained person, in accordance with paragraph 12.3 above.

12.11 Any decision to delay a break in an interview must be recorded, with grounds, in the interview record.

12.12 Where the person interviewed is in the police station at the time that a written record of the interview is made, he shall be given the opportunity to read it and to sign it as correct or to indicate the respects in which he considers it inaccurate, but no person shall be kept in custody for this sole purpose. If the interview is tape recorded the arrangements set out in the relevant code of practice apply. (**a**)

12.13 All written statements made at police stations under caution shall be written on the forms provided for the purpose.

12.14 All written statements made under caution shall be taken in accordance with Annex D to this code.

12.15 Where the appropriate adult or another third party is present in an interview and is still in the police station at the time that a written record of the interview is made he shall be asked to read it (or any written statement taken down by a police officer) and sign it as correct or to indicate the respects in which he considers it inaccurate. If the person refuses to read or sign the record as accurate or to indicate the respects in which he considers it inaccurate the senior officer present shall record on the record itself, in the presence of the person concerned, what has happened. If the interview is tape recorded the arrangements set out in the relevant code of practice apply.

(**a**) The Notes for Guidance for this section state –

12A The purpose of any interview is to obtain from the person concerned his explanation of the facts, and not necessarily to obtain an admission.

12B If the interview has been contemporaneously recorded and the record signed by the person interviewed in accordance with paragraph 12.12 above, or has been tape recorded, it is normally unnecessary to ask for a written statement. Statements under caution should normally be taken in these circumstances only at the person's express wish. An officer may, however, ask him whether or not he wants to make such a statement.

12C The police surgeon can give advice about whether or not a person is fit to be interviewed in accordance with paragraph 12.3 above.

---

13. Persons at risk: juveniles, and those who are mentally ill or mentally handicapped (a).

13.1 A juvenile or a person who is mentally handicapped, whether suspected or not, must not be interviewed or asked to provide or sign a written statement in the absence of the appropriate adult unless Annex C applies. If he is cautioned in accordance with section 10 above in the absence of the appropriate adult the caution must be repeated in the adult's presence (unless the interview has by then already finished).

13.1 If, having been informed of the right to legal advice under paragraph 3.6 above, the appropriate adult considers that legal advice should be taken, then the provisions of section 6 of this code apply.

13.3 Juveniles may only be interviewed at their place of education in exceptional circumstances and then only where the principal or his nominee agrees and is present.

(a) The Notes for Guidance for this section state –

13A Where the parents or guardians of a person at risk are themselves suspected of involvement in the offence concerned, or are the victims of it, it may be desirable for the appropriate adult to be some other person.

13B It is important to bear in mind that, although juveniles or persons who are mentally ill or mentally handicapped are often capable of providing reliable evidence, they may, without knowing or wishing to do so, be particularly prone in certain circumstances to provide information which is unreliable, misleading or self-incriminating. Special care should therefore always be exercised in questioning such a person, and the appropriate adult involved if there is any doubt about a person's age, mental state or capacity. Because of the risk of unreliable evidence it is also important to obtain corroboration of any facts admitted whenever possible.

13C The appropriate adult should be informed that he is not expected to act simply as an observer. The purposes of his presence are, first, to advise the person being questioned and to observe whether or not the interview is being conducted properly and fairly; and, secondly, to facilitate communication with the person being interviewed.

13D A juvenile should not be arrested at his place of education unless this is unavoidable. In this case the principal or his nominee must be informed.

---

14. Interpreters.

a) Foreign languages (**a**)

14.1 Unless Annex C applies, a person must not be interviewed in the absence of a person capable of acting as interpreter if:

(*a*) he has difficulty in understanding English;

(*b*) the interviewing officer cannot himself speak the person's own language; and

(*c*) the person wishes an interpreter to be present.

14.2 The interviewing officer shall ensure that the interpreter makes a note of the interview at the time in the language of the person being interviewed for use in the event of his being called to give evidence, and certifies its accuracy. The person shall be given an opportunity to read it or have it read to him and sign it as correct or to indicate the respects in which he considers it inaccurate. If the interview is tape recorded the arrangements set out in the relevant code of practice apply.

14.3 In the case of a person making a statement in a language other than English:

(*a*) the interpreter shall take down the statement in the language in which it is made;

(*b*) the person making the statement shall be invited to sign it; and

(*c*) an official English translation shall be made in due course.

b) The deaf

14.4 If a person is deaf or there is doubt about his hearing ability he must not be interviewed in the absence of an interpreter unless he agrees in writing to be interviewed without one or Annex C applies. (Information on obtaining the services of a suitably qualified interpreter for the deaf is given in Note for Guidance 3C (**a**)).

14.5 The interviewing officer shall ensure that the interpreter makes a note of the interview at the time for use in the event of his being called to give evidence and certifies its accuracy. The person shall be given an opportunity to read it and sign it as correct or to indicate the respects of which he considers it inaccurate.

c) Additional rules for detained persons

14.6 All reasonable attempts should be made to make clear to the detained person that interpreters will be provided at public expense.

14.7 Where paragraph 6.1 applies and the person concerned cannot communicate with the solicitor, whether because of language or hearing difficulties, an interpreter must be called. The interpreter may not be a police officer when interpretation is needed for the purposes of obtaining a legal advice. In all other cases a police officer may only interpret if he first obtains the detained person's (or the appropriate adult's) agreement in writing or if the interview is tape recorded in accordance with the relevant code of practice.

14.8 When a person who has difficulty in understanding English is charged with an offence, and the custody officer cannot speak the person's language, arrangements must also be made for an interpreter to explain as soon as practicable the offence concerned and any other information given by the custody officer.

d) Documentation

14.9 Action taken to call an interpreter under this section and any agreement to be interviewed in the absence of an interpreter must be recorded.

(a) The Notes for Guidance for this section state –

14A If the interpreter is needed as a prosecution witness at the person's trial, a second interpreter must act as the court interpreter.

---

15. Questioning: special restrictions (a).

15.1 If a person has been arrested by one police force on behalf of another and the lawful period of detention in respect of that offence has not yet been commenced in accordance with section 41 of the Police and Criminal Evidence Act 1984 no questions may be put to him about the offence while he is in transit between the forces except in order to clarify any voluntary statement made by him.

15.2 If a person is in police detention at a hospital (a) he may not be questioned without the agreement of a responsible doctor.

(a) The Notes for Guidance for this section state –

15A If questioning takes place at a hospital under paragraph 15.2 (or on the way to or from a hospital) the period concerned counts towards the total period of detention permitted.

---

16. Reviews and extensions of detention (a).

a) Action

16.1 The review officer is responsible under section 40 of the Police and Criminal Evidence Act 1984 for determining whether or not a person's detention continues to be necessary. In reaching a decision he shall provide an opportunity to the detained person himself to make representations (unless he is unfit to do so because of his condition or behaviour) and to his solicitor or the appropriate adult if available at the time. Other persons having an interest in the person's welfare may make representations at the review officer's discretion.

16.2 The same persons may make representations to the officer determining whether further detention should be authorised under section 42 of the Act.

b) Documentation

16.3 The grounds for and extent of any delay in conducting a review shall be recorded.

16.4 Any written representations shall be retained.

16.5 A record shall be made as soon as practicable of the outcome of each review and application for a warrant of further detention or its extension.

(a) The Notes for Guidance for this section state –

16A An application for a warrant of further detention or its extension should be made between

10 am and 9 pm, and if possible during normal court hours. It will not be practicable to arrange for a court to sit specially outside the hours of 10 am to 9 pm. If it appears possible that a special sitting may be needed (either at a weekend, Bank/Public Holiday or on a weekday outside normal court hours but between 10 am and 9 pm) then the clerk to the justices should be given notice and informed of this possibility, while the court is sitting if possible.

16B If in the circumstances the only practicable way of conducting a review is over the telephone then this is permissible, provided that the requirements of section 40 of the Police and Criminal Evidence Act 1984 are observed.

---

17. Charging of detained persons (a).

a) Action

17.1 When an officer considers that there is sufficient evidence to prosecute a detained person he should without delay bring him before the custody officer who shall then be responsible for considering whether or not he should be charged. Any resulting action should be taken in the presence of the appropriate adult if the person is a juvenile or mentally ill or mentally handicapped.

17.2 When a detained person is charged with or informed that he may be prosecuted for an offence he shall be cautioned in the terms of paragraph 10.4 above.

17.3 At the time a person is charged he shall be given a written notice showing particulars of the offence with which he is charged and including the name of the officer in the case, his police station and the reference number for the case. So far as possible the particulars of the charge shall be stated in simple terms, but they shall also show the precise offence in law with which he is charged. The notice shall begin with the following words:

'You are charged with the offence(s) shown below. You do not have to say anything unless you wish to do so, but what you say may be given in evidence'.

If the person is a juvenile or is mentally handicapped the notice shall be given to the appropriate adult.

17.4 If at any time after a person has been charged with or informed he may be prosecuted for an offence a police officer wishes to bring to the notice of that person any written statement made by another person or the content of an interview with another person, he shall hand to that person a true copy of any such written statement or bring to his attention the content of the interview record, but shall say or do nothing to invite any reply or comment save to caution him in the terms of paragraph 10.4 above. If the person cannot read then the officer may read it to him. If the person is a juvenile or mentally ill or mentally handicapped the copy shall also be given, or the interview record brought to the attention or, the appropriate adult.

17.5 Questions relating to an offence may not be put to a person after he has been charged with that offence, or informed that he may be prosecuted for it, unless they are necessary for the purpose of preventing or minimising harm or loss to some other person or to the public or for clearing up an ambiguity in a previous answer or statement, or where it is in the interests of justice that the person should have put to him and have an opportunity to comment on information concerning the offence which has come to light since he was charged or informed that he might be prosecuted. Before any such questions are put he shall be cautioned in the terms of paragraph 10.4 above.

17.6 Where a juvenile is charged with an offence and the custody officer authorises his continuing detention he must try to make arrangements for the juvenile to be taken into the care of a local authority to be detained pending appearance in court unless he certifies that it is impracticable to do so in accordance with s 38(6) of the Police and Criminal Evidence Act 1984. (a)

b) Documentation

17.7 A record shall be made of anything a detained person says when charged.

17.8 Any questions put after charge and answers given relating to the offence shall be contemporaneously recorded in full on the forms provided and the record signed by that person or, if he refuses, by the interviewing officer and any third parties present. If the questions are tape recorded the arrangements set out in the relevant code of practice apply.

17.9 If it is not practicable to make arrangements for the transfer of a juvenile into local authority care in accordance with paragraph 17.6 above the custody officer must record the reasons and make out a certificate to be produced before the court together with the juvenile.

(a) The Notes for Guidance for this section state –

17A Neither a juvenile's unruliness nor the nature of the offence with which he is charged provides grounds for the custody officer to retain him in police custody rather than seek to arrange for his transfer to the care of the local authority.

ANNEX A [4.1]

INTIMATE AND STRIP SEARCHES

a) Action
1. Body orifices may be searched only if an officer of the rank of superintendent or above has reasonable grounds for believing:
   (*a*) that an article which could cause physical injury to a detained person or others at the police station has been concealed; or
   (*b*) that the person has concealed a Class A drug which he intended to supply to another or to export; and
   (*c*) that in either case an intimate search is the only practicable means of removing it.
The reasons why an intimate search is considered necessary shall be explained to the person before the search takes place.
2. An intimate search may only be carried out by a registered medical practitioner, State Registered Nurse, or State Enrolled Nurse, unless an officer of at least the rank of superintendent considers that this is not practicable and the search is to take place under sub-paragraph 1(*a*) above.
3. An intimate search under sub-paragraph 1(*a*) above may take place only at a hospital, surgery, other medical premises or police station. A search under sub-paragraph 1(*b*) may take place only at a hospital, surgery or other medical premises.
4. An intimate search at a police station of a juvenile or a mentally ill or mentally handicapped person may take place only in the presence of the appropriate adult of the same sex. In the case of a juvenile, the search may take place in the absence of the appropriate adult only if the juvenile signifies in the presence of the appropriate adult that he prefers the search to be done in his absence and the appropriate adult agrees.
5. A strip search (that is a search involving the removal of more than outer clothing) may take place only if the custody officer considers it to be necessary to remove an article which the detained person would not be allowed to keep.
6. Where an intimate search under sub-paragraph 1(*a*) above or a strip search is carried out by a police officer, the officer must be of the same sex as the person searched. No person of the opposite sex who is not a medical practitioner or nurse shall be present, nor shall anyone whose presence is unnecessary.

b) Documentation
7. In the case of an intimate search the custody officer shall as soon as practicable record which parts of the person's body were searched, who carried out the search, who was present, the reasons for the search and its result.
8. In the case of a strip search he shall record the reasons for the search and its result.
9. If an intimate search is carried out by a police officer, the reason why it is impracticable for a suitably qualified person to conduct it must be recorded.

ANNEX B

DELAY IN NOTIFYING ARREST OR ALLOWING ACCESS TO LEGAL ADVICE (**a**)

A) *Persons detained under the Police and Criminal Evidence Act 1984*

a) Action
1. The rights set out in section 5 or 6 of the code (**b**) (or both) may be delayed if the person is in police detention (**c**) in connection with a serious arrestable offence, has not yet been charged with an offence and an officer of the rank of superintendent or above has reasonable grounds for believing that the exercise of each right:
   (i) will lead to interference with or harm to evidence connected with a serious arrestable offence or interference with or physical harm to other persons; or
   (ii) will lead to the alerting of other persons suspected of having committed such an offence but not yet arrested for it; or
   (iii) will hinder the recovery of property obtained in consequence of the commission of such an offence.

2. Access to a solicitor may not be delayed on the grounds that he might advise the person not to answer any questions or that the solicitor was initially asked to attend the police station by someone else, provided that the person himself then wishes to see the solicitor.

3. These rights may be delayed only for as long as is necessary and, subject to paragraph 6 below, in no case beyond 36 hours after the relevant time as defined in section 41 of the Police and Criminal Evidence Act 1984. If the above grounds cease to apply within this time, the person must as soon as practicable be asked if he wishes to exercise either right and action must be taken in accordance with the relevant section of the code.

4. A detained person must be permitted to consult a solicitor for a reasonable time before any court hearing.

b) Documentation
5. The grounds for action under this Annex shall be recorded and the person informed of them as soon as practicable.

B. *Persons detained under the Prevention of Terrorism (Temporary Provisions) Act 1984*

a) Action
6. The rights set out in sections 5 or 6 of this code (or both) may be delayed if paragraph 1 above applies or if an officer of the rank of superintendent or above has reasonable grounds for believing that the exercise of either right:
   (*a*) will lead to interference with the gathering of information about the commission, preparation or instigation of acts of terrorism; or
   (*b*) by alerting any person, will make it more difficult to prevent an act of terrorism or to secure the apprehension, prosecution or conviction of any person in connection with the commission, preparation or instigation of an act of terrorism.

7. Paragraph 3 above applies except that the delay permitted is 48 and not 36 hours. The custody officer must remind any such person who has been detained for 48 hours of his right to consult a solicitor and ask him whether he wishes to exercise it.

b) Documentation
8. Paragraph 5 above applies.
9. Any reply given by a person under paragraph 7 above must be recorded and the person asked to endorse the record.

(**a**) The Notes for Guidance for this section state –
B1 Even if Annex B applies in the case of a juvenile, or a person who is mentally ill or mentally handicapped, action to inform the appropriate adult must nevertheless be taken in accordance with paragraph 3.6 of the code.
B2 In the case of Commonwealth citizens and foreign nationals, see Note 7A.
(**b**) The primary rights are contained in the Police and Criminal Evidence Act 1984, ss 56 and 58.
(**c**) 'Police detention' is defined in s 118(2) of the Police and Criminal Evidence Act 1984.

ANNEX C

URGENT INTERVIEWS (**a**)
1. If, and only if, an officer of the rank of superintendent or above considers that delay will involve an immediate risk of harm to persons or serious loss of or serious damage to property.
   (*a*) a person heavily under the influence of drink or drugs may be interviewed in that state; or
   (*b*) an arrested juvenile or a person who is mentally ill or mentally handicapped may be interviewed in the absence of the appropriate adult; or
   (*c*) a person who has difficulty in understanding English or who has a hearing disability may be interviewed in the absence of an interpreter.

2. Questioning in these circumstances may not continue once sufficient information to avert the immediate risk has been obtained.

3. A record shall be made of the grounds for any decision to interview a person under paragraph 1 above.

(a) The Notes for Guidance for this section state –

C1 The special groups referred to in Annex C are all particularly vulnerable. The provisions of the Annex, which override safeguards designed to protect them and to minimise the risk of interviews producing unreliable evidence, should be applied only in exceptional cases of need.

ANNEX D

WRITTEN STATEMENTS UNDER CAUTION [12.14]

a) Written by a person under caution

1. A person shall always be invited to write down himself what he wants to say.

2. Where the person wishes to write it himself, he shall be asked to write out and sign before writing what he wants to say, the following:

'I make this statement of my own free will. I understand that I need not say anything unless I wish to do so and that what I say may be given in evidence'.

3. Any person writing his own statement shall be allowed to do so without any prompting except that a police officer may indicate to him which matters are material or question any ambiguity in the statement.

b) Written by a police officer

4. If a person says that he would like someone to write it for him, a police officer shall write the statement, but, before starting, he must ask him to sign, or make his mark, to the following:

'I, ..., wish to make a statement. I want someone to write down what I say. I understand that I need not say anything unless I wish to do so and that what I say may be given in evidence.'

5. Where a police officer writes the statement, he must take down the exact words spoken by the person making it and he must not edit or paraphrase it. Any questions that are necessary (eg to make it more intelligible) and the answers given must be recorded contemporaneously on the statement form.

6. When the writing of a statement by a police officer is finished the person making it shall be asked to read it and to make any corrections, alterations or additions he wishes. When he has finished reading it he shall be asked to write and sign or make his mark on the following certificate at the end of the statement:

'I have read the above statement, and I have been able to correct, alter or add anything I wish. This statement is true. I have made it of my own free will.'

7. If the person making the statement cannot read, or refuses to read it, or to write the above mentioned certificate at the end of it or to sign it, the senior police officer present shall read it over to him and ask him whether he would like to correct, alter or add anything and to put his signature or make his mark at the end. The police officer shall then certify on the statement itself what has occurred.

ANNEX E

SUMMARY OF PROVISIONS RELATING TO MENTALLY ILL AND MENTALLY HANDICAPPED PERSONS (a)

1. If an officer has any suspicion or is told in good faith that a person of any age, whether or not in custody, may be mentally ill or mentally handicapped, or cannot understand the significance of questions put to him or his replies, then he shall be treated as a mentally ill or mentally handicapped person. [para 1.4]

2. In the case of a person who is mentally ill or mentally handicapped, 'The appropriate adult' means:

(*a*) a relative guardian or some other person responsible for his care or custody;

(*b*) someone who has experience of dealing with mentally ill or mentally handicapped persons but is not a police officer or employed by the police; or (*c*) failing either of the above, some other responsible adult who is not a police officer or employed by the police. [para 1.7b]

3. If the custody officer authorises the detention of a person who is mentally handicapped or is suffering from mental illness he must as soon as practicable inform the appropriate adult of the grounds for the person's detention and his whereabouts, and ask the adult to come to the police station to see the person. If the appropriate adult is already at the police station when information is given as required in paragraphs 3.1 to 3.3 the information must be given to the detained person in his presence. If the appropriate adult is not at the police station when the information is given then the information must be given to the detained person again in the presence of the appropriate adult once that person arrives. [para 3.6]

4. If a person brought to a police station appears to be suffering from mental illness, or is incoherent other than through drunkenness alone, or if a detained person subsequently appears to be mentally ill, the custody officer must immediately call the police surgeon or, in urgent cases send the person to hospital or call the nearest available medical practitioner. [para 9.2]

5. A mentally ill or mentally handicapped person must not be interviewed or asked to provide or sign a written statement in the absence of the appropriate adult unless an officer of the rank of superintendent or above considers that delay will involve an immediate risk of harm to persons or serious loss of or serious damage to property. Questioning in these circumstances may not continue in the absence of the appropriate adult once sufficient information to avert the risk has been obtained. A record shall be made of the grounds for any decision to begin an interview in these circumstances [para 13.1 and Annex C]

6. If the appropriate adult, having been informed of the right to legal advice, considers that legal advice should be taken, the provisions of section 6 of the code apply as if the mentally ill or mentally handicapped person had requested access to legal advice. [para 13.2]

7. If the detention of a mentally ill or mentally handicapped person is reviewed by a review officer or a superintendent, the appropriate adult must, if available at the time, be given an opportunity to make representations to the officer about the need for continuing detention. [paras 16.1 and 16.2]

8. If the custody officer charges a mentally ill or mentally handicapped person with an offence or takes such othe action as is appropriate when there is sufficient evidence for a prosecution this must be done in the presence of the appropriate adult. The written notice embodyng any charge must be given to the appropriate adult. [paras 17.1 to 17.3]

9. An intimate search of a mentally ill or mentally handicapped person may take place only in the presence of the appropriate adult of the same sex. [Annex A, paragraph 4]

(**a**) The Notes for Guidance for this section state –

E1 It is important to bear in mind that although persons who are mentally ill or mentally handicapped are often capable of providing reliable evidence, they may, without knowing or wishing to do so, be particularly prone in certain circumstances to provide information which is unreliable, misleading or self-incriminating. Special care should therefore always be exercised in questioning such a person, and the appropriate adult involved if there is any doubt about a person's mental state or capacity. Because of the risk of unreliable evidence, it is important to obtain corroboration of any facts admitted wherever possible. [Note 13B]

E2 Because of the risks referred to in Note E1, which the presence of the appropriate adult is intended to minimise, officers of superintendent rank or above should exercise their discretion to authorise the commencement of an interview in the adult's absence only in exceptional cases, where it is necessary to avert an immediate risk of serious harm. [Annex C, sub-paragraph 1(*b*) and Note C1]

E3 The appropriate adult should be informed that he is not expected to act simply as an observer. The purposes of his presence are, first, to advise the person being interviewed and to observe whether or not the interview is being conducted properly and fairly; and, secondly, to facilitate communication with the person being interviewed. [Note 13C]

E4 In the case of persons who are mentally ill or mentally handicapped, it may in certain circumstances be more satisfactory for all concerned if the appropriate adult is someone who has experience or training in their care rather than a relative lacking such qualifications. But if the person himself prefers a relative to a better qualified stranger his wishes if practicable should be respected. [Note 1C]

(D) CODE OF PRACTICE FOR THE IDENTIFICATION OF PERSONS BY POLICE OFFICERS (a)

1. General (b)

1.1 This code of practice must be readily available at all police stations for consultation by police officers, detained persons and members of the public.

1.2 The Notes for Guidance included are not provisions of this code, but are guidance to police officers and others about its application and interpretation. Provisions in the Annexes to the code are provisions of this code.

1.3 If an officer has any suspicion, or is told in good faith, that a person of any age may be mentally ill or mentally handicapped, or mentally incapable of understanding the significance of questions put to him or his replies, then that person shall be treated as a mentally ill or mentally handicapped person for the purposes of this code.

1.4 If anyone appears to be under the age of 17 then he shall be treated as a juvenile for the purposes of this code in the absence of clear evidence to show that he is older.

1.5 In this code 'the appropriate adult' means:
   (a) in the case of a juvenile:
      (i)   his parent or guardian (or, if he is in care, the care authority or organisation);
      (ii) a social worker; or
      (iii) failing either of the above, another responsible adult who is not a police officer or employed by the police.
   (b) in the case of a person who is mentally ill or mentally handicapped:
      (i)   a relative, guardian or some other person responsible for his care or custody;
      (ii) someone who has experience of dealing with mentally ill or mentally handicapped persons but is not a police officer or employed by the police; or
      (iii) failing either of the above, some other responsible adult who is not a police officer or employed by the police.

1.6 Any reference to a custody officer in this code includes an officer who is performing the functions of a custody officer. Any reference to a solicitor in this code includes a clerk or legal executive in Annex C, paragraph 7.

1.7 Where a record is made under this code of any action requiring the authority of an officer of specified rank, his name and rank must be included in the record.

1.8 All records must be timed and signed by the maker.

1.9 In the case of a detained person records are to be made in his custody record unless otherwise specified.

1.10 In the case of any procedure requiring a suspect's consent, the consent of a person who is mentally ill or mentally handicapped is only valid if given in the presence of the appropriate adult; and in the case of a juvenile the consent of his parent or guardian is required as well as his own (unless he is under 14, in which case the consent (b) of his parent or guardian is sufficient in its own right).

1.11 In the case of any procedure requiring information to be given to a suspect, it must be given in the presence of the appropriate adult if the suspect is mentally ill, mentally handicapped or a juvenile. If the suspect is deaf or there is doubt about his hearing ability or ability to understand English, and the officer cannot himself speak the person's language the information must be given through an interpreter.

1.12 Any procedure involving the participation of a person (whether as a suspect or witness) who is mentally ill, mentally handicapped, or a juvenile must take place in the presence of the appropriate adult; but the adult must not be allowed to prompt any identification of a suspect by a witness.

1.13 Nothing in this code affects any procedure under:
   (i)   sections 5 to 12 of the Road Traffic Act 1972, as amended;
   (ii) paragraph 18 of Schedule 2 to the Immigration Act 1971; or
   (iii) paragraph 5 of Schedule 3 to the Prevention of Terrorism (Temporary Provisions) Act 1984.

1.14 In this code references to photographs include optical disc computer printouts.

(a) This Code of Practice is issued under ss 66 and 67 of the Police and Criminal Evidence Act 1984: it is admissible thereunder in evidence and account may be taken by the court of any relevant provision.

(**b**) The Notes for Guidance for this section state –
1A For the purposes of paragraph 1.10 above consent may be given, in the case of a juvenile in the care of a local authority or voluntary organisation, by that authority or organisation.

---

2. Identification by witness.

a) Suspect at the police station – the decision as to the method of identification
2.1 In a case which involves disputed identification evidence a parade must be held if the suspect asks for one and it is practicable to hold one. A parade may also be held if the officer in charge of the investigation considers that it would be useful.
2.2 Arrangements for the parade and its conduct shall be the responsibility of an officer in uniform not below the rank of inspector who is not involved with the investigation ('the identification officer'). No officer involved with the investigation of the case against the suspect may take any part in the arrangements for or the conduct of the parade.
2.3 A parade need not be held if the identification officer considers that, whether by reason of the unusual appearance of the suspect or for some other reason, it would not be practicable to assemble sufficient people who resembled him to make a parade fair.
2.4 If a suspect refuses or, having agreed, fails to attend an identification parade or the holding of a parade is impracticable, arrangements must if practicable be made to allow the witness an opportunity of seeing him in a group of people. Such a group identification may also be arranged if the officer in charge of the investigation considers, whether because of fear on the part of the witness or for some other reason, that it is in the circumstances more satisfactory than a parade.
2.5 If neither a parade nor a group identification procedure is arranged, the suspect may be confronted by the witness. Such a confrontation does not require the suspect's consent, but may not take place unless neither a parade nor a group identification is practicable, whether because the suspect has withheld his consent to them or his co-operation or for some other reason.
2.6 A witness must not be shown photographs or photofit, identikit or similar pictures for identification purposes if there is a suspect already available to be asked to stand on a parade or participate in a group identification.

b) Notice to suspect
2.7 Before (a) a parade takes place or (b) a group identification is arranged, the identification officer shall explain to the suspect:
  (i)   the purpose of the parade or group identification;
  (ii) the procedure for holding it (including his right to have a solicitor or friend present):
  (iii) where appropriate the special arrangements for juveniles;
  (iv) where appropriate the special arrangements for mentally ill and mentally handicapped persons;
  (v)   the fact that he does not have to take part in either procedure and, if it is proposed to hold a group identification, his entitlement to a parade if this can practicably be arranged; and
  (vi) the fact that, if he does not consent to take part in a parade or other group identification, he may be confronted by a witness and his refusal may be given in evidence in any subsequent trial, where a witness might be given an opportunity of identifying him in court.
2.8 This information must also be contained in a written notice which must be handed to the suspect. The identification officer shall give the suspect a reasonable opportunity to read the notice, after which he shall be asked to sign a second copy of the notice to indicate whether or not he is willing to attend the parade or participate in the group identification. The signed copy shall be retained by the identification officer.

c) Conduct of a parade or other identification
2.9 Any parade or other group identification must be carried out in accordance with Annex A.

d) Confrontation by a witness
2.10 Any confrontation must be carried out in accordance with Annex B.

e) Street identification
2.11 A police officer may take a witness to a particular neighbourhood or place to observe the persons there to see whether he can identify the person whom he said he saw on the relevant

occasion. Care should be taken however not to direct the witness's attention to any individual. Where the suspect is at a police station, the provision of paragraphs 2.1 to 2.10 must apply.

f) Showing of photographs etc
2.12 If photographs or photofit, identikit or similar pictures are shown to a witness for identification purposes this must be done in accordance with Annex C.

g) Documentation
2.13 The identification officer will make a record of the parade or group identification on the forms provided.
2.14 If the identification officer considers that it is not practicable to hold a parade he shall tell the suspect why and record the reason.
2.14 A record shall be made of a person's refusal to take part in a parade or other group identification.

3. Identification by fingerprints (a).

a) Action
3.1 A person's fingerprints may be taken only with his consent or if paragraph 3.2 applies. If he is at a police station consent must be in writing. In either case the person must be informed of the reason before they are taken and that they will be destroyed if paragraph 3.4 applies. He must be told that he may witness their destruction if he asks to do so within one month of being cleared or informed that he will not be prosecuted.
3.2 Powers to take fingerprints without consent from any person over the age of ten years are provided by section 61 of the Police and Criminal Evidence Act 1984. Reasonable force may be used if necessary.
3.3 Section 27 of the Police and Criminal Evidence Act 1984 describes the circumstances in which a constable may require a person convicted of a recordable offence (a) to attend at a police station in order that his fingerprints may be taken.
3.4 The fingerprints of a person and all copies of them taken in that case must be destroyed if:
    (*a*) he is prosecuted for the offence and cleared; or
    (*b*) he is not prosecuted (unless he admits the offence and is cautioned for it).
An opportunity of witnessing the destruction must be given to him if he wishes and if, in accordance with paragraph 3.1, he applies within one month of being cleared or informed that he will not be prosecuted.
3.5 References to fingerprints include palm prints.

b) Documentation
3.6 A record must be made as soon as possible of the reason for taking a person's fingerprints without consent and of their destruction. If force is used a record shall be made of the circumstances and those present.

(a) The Notes for Guidance for this section state –
3A References to recordable offences in this code relate to those offences for which convictions are recorded in national police records (see s 27(4) of the Police and Criminal Evidence Act 1984).

---

4. Identification by photographs.

a) Action
4.1 The photograph of a person who has been arrested may be taken at a police station only with his written consent or if paragraph 4.2 applies. In either case he must be informed of the reason for taking it and that the photograph will be destroyed if paragraph 4.4 applies. He must be told that he may witness the destruction of the photograph if he asks to do so within one month of being cleared or informed that he will not be prosecuted.
4.2 The photograph of a person who has been arrested may be taken without consent if:
    (i)   he is arrested at the same time as other persons, or at a time when it is likely that other persons will be arrested, and a photograph is necessary to establish who was arrested, at what time and at what place; or

(ii) he has been charged with or reported for a recordable offence and has not yet been released or brought before a court [See Note 3A]; or

(iii) he is convicted of such an offence and his photograph is not already on record as a result of (i) or (ii). There is no power of arrest to take a photograph in pursuance of this provision which applies only where the person is in custody as a result of the exercise of another power (eg arrest for fingerprinting under s 27 of the Police and Criminal Evidence Act 1984).

4.3 Force may not be used to take a photograph.

4.4 Where a person's photograph has been taken in accordance with this section, the photograph, negatives and all copies taken in that particular case must be destroyed if:

(*a*) he is prosecuted for the offence concerned and cleared; or

(*b*) he is not prosecuted (unless he admits the offence and is cautioned for it).

An opportunity of witnessing the destruction must be given to him if he so requests provided in accordance with paragraph 4.1, he applies within one month of being cleared or informed that he will not be prosecuted.

b) Documentation

4.5 A record must be made as soon as possible of the reason for taking a person's photograph under this section without consent and of the destruction of any photographs.

5. Identification by body samples, swabs and impressions (a).

a) Action

5.1 Dental impressions and intimate samples (**b**) may be taken from a person in police detention only:

(i) with his written consent;

(ii) if an officer of the rank of superintendent or above considers that the offence concerned is a serious arrestable offence; and

(iii) there are reasonable grounds for suspecting that such an impression, sample or swab will tend to confirm or disprove the suspect's involvement in it.

Before the impression, sample or swab is taken the person must be informed on the grounds on which the required authority has been given, including the nature of the suspected offence.

5.2 Before a person is asked to provide an intimate sample or swab he must be warned that a refusal may be treated, in any proceedings against him, as corroborating relevant prosecution evidence. (**a**)

5.3 Except for samples of urine or saliva, the above samples and swabs may be taken only by a registered medical or dental practitioner as appropriate.

5.4 A non-intimate sample (**b**), as defined in paragraph 5.11 or a body impression other than fingerprints, may be taken from a detained suspect only with his written consent or if paragraph 5.5 below applies. Even if he consents, an officer of the rank of inspector or above must have reasonable grounds for believing that such a sample or impression will tend to confirm or disprove the suspect's involvement in a particular offence.

5.5 A non-intimate sample (**b**) or a body impression may be taken without consent if the offence in connection with which the suspect is detained is a serious arrestable offence and an officer of the rank of superintendent or above has reasonable grounds for believing that the sample or impression will tend to confirm or disprove his involvement in it.

5.6 The suspect must be informed, before the sample or impression is taken, of the grounds on which the relevant authority has been given, including the nature of the suspected offence, and that the sample or impression will be destroyed if paragraph 5.8 applies.

5.7 Where paragraph 5.5 applies reasonable force may be used if necessary to take non-intimate samples and body impressions.

5.8 Where a sample or impression has been taken in accordance with this section, it and all copies of it taken in that particular case must be destroyed:

(*a*) if he is prosecuted for the offence concerned and cleared; or

(*b*) if he is not prosecuted (unless he admits the offence and is cautioned for it).

b) Documentation

5.9 A record must be made as soon as practicable of the reason for taking a sample or impression and of its destruction. If force is used a record shall be made of the circumstances and those present. Consent to the taking of a sample or impression must be recorded in writing.

5.10 A record must be made of the giving of a warning required by paragraph 5.2 above.

c) General

5.11 The following terms are defined in section 65 of the Police and Criminal Evidence Act 1984 as follows:

(*a*) 'intimate sample' (**b**) means a sample of blood, semen or any other tissue fluid, urine, saliva or pubic hair or a swab taken from a person's body orifice;

(*b*) 'non-intimate sample' (**b**) means:

(i)   a sample of hair other than pubic hair;

(ii) a sample taken from nail or from under a nail;

(iii) a swab taken from any part of a person's body other than a body orifice;

(iv) a footprint or a similar impression of any part of a person's body other than a part of his hand.

5.12 Where clothing needs to be removed in circumstances likely to cause embarrassment to the person, no person of the opposite sex, who is not a medical practitioner or nurse, shall be present, nor shall anyone whose presence is unnecessary.

(**a**) The Notes for Guidance for this section state –

5A In warning a person who refuses to provide an intimate sample or swab in accordance with paragraph 5.2, the following form of words may be helpful –

'You do not have to [provide this sample] [allow this swab to be taken], but I must warn you that if you do not do so, a court may treat such a refusal as supporting any relevant evidence against you.'

(**b**) Sections 62 and 63 of the Police and Criminal Evidence Act 1984 deal with samples.

ANNEX A

IDENTIFICATION PARADES AND GROUP IDENTIFICATIONS [2.9]

a) General

1. A suspect must be given a reasonable opportunity to have a solicitor or friend present, and the identification officer shall ask him to indicate on a second copy of the notice to suspect whether or not he so wishes.

2. A parade may take place either in a normal room or in one equipped with a screen permitting witnesses to see members of the parade without being seen. The procedures for the composition and conduct of the parade are the same in both cases, subject to paragraph 7 below (except that a parade involving a screen may take place only when the suspect's solicitor, friend or appropriate adult is present or the parade is recorded on video).

b) Parades involving prison inmates

3. If an inmate is required for identification, and there are no security problems about his leaving the establishment, he may be asked to participate in a parade. (Group identification, however, may not be arranged other than in the establishment or inside a police station.)

4. A parade made be held in a Prison Department establishment, but shall be conducted as far as practicable under normal parade rules. Members of the public shall make up the parade unless there are serious security or control objections to their admission to the establishment. In such cases, or if a group identification is arranged within the establishment, other inmates may participate.

c) Conduct of a parade

5. Immediately before the parade, the identification officer must remind the suspect of the procedures governing its conduct and caution him in the terms of paragraph 10.4 of the code of practice for the detention, treatment and questioning of persons by police officers.

6. All unauthorised persons must be strictly excluded from the place where the parade is held.

7. Once the parade has been formed, everything afterwards in respect of it shall take place in the presence and hearing of the suspect and of any interpreter, solicitor, friend or appropriate adult who is present (unless the parade involves a screen, in which case everything said to or by any witness at the place where the parade is held must be said in the hearing and presence of the suspect's solicitor, friend or appropriate adult or be recorded on video).

8. The parade shall consist of at least eight persons (in addition to the suspect) who so far as possible resemble the suspect in age, height, general appearance and position in life. One

suspect only shall be included in a parade unless there are two suspects of roughly similar appearance in which case they may be paraded together with at least twelve other persons. In no circumstances shall more than two suspects be included in one parade and where there are separate parades they shall be made up of different persons.

9. Where all members of a similar group are possible suspects, separate parades shall be held for each member of the group unless there are two suspects of similar appearance when they may appear on the same parade with at least twelve other members of the group who are not suspects. Where police in uniform form an identification parade, any numerals or other identifying badge shall be concealed.

10. When the suspect is brought to the place where the parade is to be held, he shall be asked by the identification officer whether he has any objection to the arrangements for the parade or to any of the other participants in it. The suspect may obtain advice from his solicitor or friend, if present, before the parade proceeds. Where practicable, steps shall be taken to remove the grounds for objection. Where it is not practicable to do so, the officer shall explain to the suspect why his objections cannot be met.

11. The suspect may select his own position in the line. Where there is more than one witness, the identification officer must tell the suspect, after each witness has left the room, that he can if he wishes change position in the line. Each position in the line must be clearly numbered, whether by means of a numeral laid on the floor in front of each parade member or by other means.

12. The identification officer is responsible for ensuring that, before they attend the parade, witnesses are not able to:
   (i)   communicate with each other about the case or overhear a witness who has already seen the parade;
   (ii) see any member of the parade;
   (iii) on that occasion see or be reminded of any photograph or description of the suspect or be given any other indication of his identity; or
   (iv) see the suspect either before (or after) the parade.

13. The officer conducting a witness to a parade must not discuss with him the composition of the parade, and in particular he must not disclose whether a previous witness has made any identification.

14. Witnesses shall be brought in one at a time. Immediately before the witness inspects the parade, the identification officer shall tell him that the person he saw may or may not be on the parade and if he cannot make a positive identification he should say so. The officer shall then ask him to walk along the parade at least twice, taking as much care and time as he wishes. When he has done so the officer shall ask him whether the person he saw in person on an earlier relevant occasion is on the parade.

15. The witness should make an identification by indicating the number of the person concerned.

16. If the witness makes an identification after the parade has ended the suspect and, if present, his solicitor, interpreter, or friend shall be informed. Where this occurs, consideration should be given to allowing the witness a second opportunity to identify the suspect.

17. If a witness wishes to hear any parade member speak, adopt any specified posture or see him move, the identification officer shall first ask whether he can identify any persons on the parade on the basis of appearance only. When the request is to hear members of the parade speak, the witness shall be reminded that the participants in the parade have been chosen on the basis of physical appearance only. Members of the parade may then be asked to comply with the witness's request to hear them speak, to see them move or to adopt any specified posture.

18. When the last witness has left, the suspect shall be asked by the identification officer whether he wishes to make any comments on the conduct of the parade.

d) Conduct of a group identification
19. The arrangements for a group identification are the sole responsibility of the identification officer and must as far as practicable satisfy the requirements of (*c*) above.

e) Documentation
20. If a parade is held without a solicitor or a friend of the suspect being present a colour photograph of the parade shall be taken unless any of the parade members objects. A copy of the photograph shall be supplied on request to the suspect or his solicitor within a reasonable time.

21. Where a photograph is taken in accordance with paragraph 20, at the conclusion of the proceedings the negative will be destroyed.

22. If the identification officer asks any person to leave a parade because he is interfering with its conduct the circumstances shall be recorded.

23. A record must be made of all those present at a parade or group identification whose names are known to the police.

24. If prison inmates make up a parade the circumstances must be recorded.

25. A record of the conduct of any parade or group identification must be made on the forms provided.

ANNEX B

CONFRONTATION BY A WITNESS [2.5 and 2.10]

1. The identification officer is responsible for the conduct of any confrontation of a suspect by a witness.

2. The suspect shall be confronted independently by each witness, who shall be asked 'Is this the person?' Confrontation must take place in the presence of the suspect's solicitor, interpreter or friend, where he has one, unless this would cause unreasonable delay.

3. Confrontation may take place either in a normal room or one equipped with a screen permitting a witness to see the suspect without being seen. In both cases the procedures are the same except that a room equipped with a screen may be used only when the suspect's solicitor, friend or appropriate adult is present or the confrontation is recorded on video.

ANNEX C

SHOWING OF PHOTOGRAPHS [2.12]

a) Action

1. An officer of the rank of sergeant or above shall be responsible for supervising and directing the showing of photographs. The actual showing may be done by a constable.

2. Only one witness shall be shown photographs at any one time. He shall be given as much privacy as practicable and shall not be allowed to communicate with or overhear any other witness in the case.

3. The witness shall be shown not less than twelve photographs at a time. These photographs shall either be in an album or loose photographs mounted in a frame and shall, as far as possible, all be of a similar type. If the photographs include that of a person suspected by the police of the offence concerned by the police, the other photographs shall resemble the suspect as closely as possible.

4. When the witness is shown the photographs, he shall be told that the photographs of the person he saw may or may not be amongst them. He shall not be prompted or guided in any way but shall be left to make any selection without help.

5. If a witness makes a positive identification from photographs, then, unless the person identified is otherwise eliminated from enquiries, other witnesses shall not be shown photographs. But both they and the witness who has made the identification shall be asked to attend an identification parade or group identification if practicable unless there is no dispute about the identification of the suspect.

6. Where the use of a photofit, identikit or similar picture has led to there being a suspect available who can be asked to appear on a parade, or participate in a group identification the picture shall not be shown to other potential witnesses.

7. Where a witness attending an identification parade has previously been shown photographs or photofit, identikit or similar pictures then the suspect and his solicitor must be informed of this fact before any committal proceedings or summary trial.

8. Any photographs used shall be retained for production in court if necessary, whether or not an identification is made.

b) Documentation

9. Whether or not an identification is made, a record shall be kept of the showing of photographs and of any comment made by the witness.

Road traffic penalties

ROAD TRAFFIC PENALTIES

Note: Level 1 – £50
      Level 2 – £100
      Level 3 – £400
      Level 4 – £1,000
      Level 5 – £2,000

[Note: this table reproduces in part Sch 4 of the Road Traffic Act 1972; column 7 indicates the Magistrates' Association's suggested penalties]

1 Provision creating Offence	2 General Nature of Offence	3 Mode of Prosecution	4 Punishment	5 Disqualification	6 Endorsement and penalty points	7 Magistrates' Assoc. suggested penalties (1985)
1	Causing death by reckless driving.	On indictment.	5 years.	Obligatory.	Obligatory.	
2	Reckless driving.	(a) Summarily.	6 months or the prescribed sum.	(a) Obligatory, if committed within 3 years after a previous conviction of an offence under section 1 or 2. (b) Discretionary if committed otherwise than as mentioned in paragraph (a) above.	Obligatory. (10)	£300 and consider disqualification.
		(b) On indictment.	2 years or a fine or both.			

1 Provision creating Offence	2 General Nature of Offence	3 Mode of Prosecution	4 Punishment	5 Disqualification	6 Endorsement and penalty points	7 Magistrates' Assoc. suggested penalties (1985)
3	Careless, and inconsiderate, driving.	Summarily.	Level 4.	Discretionary.	Obligatory. (2–5)	£60, but consider degree of carelessness.
5(1)	Driving or attempting to drive when unfit to drive through drink or drugs.	Summarily.	6 months or level 5 or both.	Obligatory.	Obligatory. (4)	£200, disqualify (see Note A).
5(2)	Being in charge of a motor vehicle when unfit to drive through drink or drugs.	Summarily.	3 months or level 4 or both.	Discretionary.	Obligatory. (10)	£100.
6(1)(a)	Driving or attempting to drive with excess alcohol in breath, blood or urine.	Summarily.	6 months or level 5 or both.	Obligatory.	Obligatory. (4)	£200, disqualify (see Note A).
6(1)(b)	Being in charge of a motor vehicle with excess alcohol.	Summarily.	3 months or level 4 or both.	Discretionary.	Obligatory. (10)	£100.
7(4)	Failing to provide a specimen of breath for a breath test.	Summarily.	Level 3.	Discretionary.	Obligatory. (4)	£50.
8(1)	Failing to provide a specimen for analysis or laboratory test.	Summarily.	(a) Where the specimen was required to ascertain ability to	(a) Obligatory in case as mentioned in paragraph (a) of column 4.	Obligatory. (4)	£200, disqualify 18 months.

			drive or proportion of alcohol at the time offender was driving or attempting to drive, six months or level 5 on the standard scale or both. (b) In any other case, 3 months or level 4 or both.	(b) Discretionary in any other case.		
22	Failing to comply with traffic directions.	Summarily.	Level 3.	Discretionary, if committed in respect of a motor vehicle by a failure to comply with a direction of a constable or an indication given by a sign specified for the purposes of this paragraph in regulations made by the Secretary of State for Transport.	Obligatory, if committed as described in the entry in column 5 relating to offence. (3)	£40.
25(4)	Failing to stop after accident and give particulars or report accident.	Summarily.	Level 5.	Discretionary.	Obligatory. *Stop* (5–9) *Report* (4–9)	£125 £125 } should disqualify if both offences.

1 Provision creating Offence	2 General Nature of Offence	3 Mode of Prosecution	4 Punishment	5 Disqualification	6 Endorsement and penalty points	7 Magistrates' Assoc. suggested penalties (1985)
40(5)	Contravention of construction and use regulations.	Summarily.	Level 5 in the case of an offence of using, or causing or permitting the use of, a goods vehicle or a vehicle adapted to carry more than eight passengers, (*a*) so as to cause, or to be likely to cause, danger by the condition of the vehicle or its parts or accessories, the number of passengers carried by it, or the weight, distribution, packing or adjustment of its load; or (*b*) in breach of a construction and use requirement as to brakes, steering-gear, tyres or any	Discretionary if committed as described causing or permitting the use of, any motor vehicle or trailer: (*a*) as described in paragraph (*a*) in the entry in column 4 relating to this offence; or (*b*) in breach of a construction and use requirement as to brakes, steering-gear, or tyres; except where the offender proves that he did not know and had no reasonable cause to suspect that the facts of the case were such that the offence would be committed.	Obligatory if committed by using, or in the entry in column 5 relating to this offence, but subject to the exception there mentioned. (3)	*Brakes* £50 driver. £125 HGV owner. *Steering* £50 driver. £125 HGV owner. *Insecure load* £200 HGV driver. £400 HGV owner. *Tyres* £50 driver. £125 HGV owner per tyre. *Goods vehicles – dangerous use* £60 driver. £200 HGV owner. *Other cases* £15 driver. £40 HGV owner. In all cases consider degree of responsibility of owner and driver.

44(1)	Using, etc., vehicle without required test certificate being in force.	Summarily.	description of weight; (c) for any purpose for which it is so unsuitable as to cause or be likely to cause danger; level 5 in the case of an offence in carrying on a goods vehicle a load which by reason of its insecurity or position is likely to cause danger; level 4 in any other case.		£20.
84(1)	Driving without a licence.	Summarily.	Level 3.	Discretionary, if the offence is committed by driving a motor vehicle in a case where either no licence authorising the driving of that vehicle could have been granted to the offender or, if a pro-	Obligatory, if committed as described in the entry in column 5 relating to this offence. (2)	£75 if endorseable.

1 Provision creating Offence	2 General Nature of Offence	3 Mode of Prosecution	4 Punishment	5 Disqualification	6 Endorsement and penalty points	7 Magistrates' Assoc. suggested penalties (1985)
				visional (but no other) licence to drive it could have been granted to him, the driving would not have complied with the conditions thereof.		
99(*b*)	Driving while disqualified.	(*a*) Summarily. (*b*) On indictment (may be abolished).	6 months or the prescribed sum [£1,000] or both. 12 months or a fine or both.	Discretionary.	Obligatory. (6) (Under age case 2 points).	Consider custodial penalty. (Under age case £50).
101(4) (including application by 103(4))	Failing to produce licence to court for endorsement on conviction of offence involving obligatory endorsement or on committal for sentence, etc., for offence involving obligatory or discretionary disqualification when no interim disqualification ordered.	Summarily.	Level 3.	—	—	—

143	Using motor vehicle while uninsured or unsecured against third-party risks.	Summarily.	Level 4.	Discretionary.	Obligatory. (4–8)	£125 (see Note B).
159	Failing to stop vehicle when required by constable.	Summarily.	Level 3.	—	—	—
166(1)	Failure by driver, in case of accident involving injury to another, to produce evidence of insurance or security or to report accident.	Summarily.	Level 3.	—	—	—

Note A Driving with excess alcohol (80mg blood = 35μg breath = 107mg urine): disqualification recommended by Magistrates' Association is 12 months basic, *but*
18 months if over 150mg blood (ie 66μg breath, 200mg urine)
2 years if over 200mg blood (ie 88μg breath, 267mg urine)
3 years if over 250mg blood (ie 110μg breath, 333mg urine).

Note B In cases of driving without insurance the Magistrates' Association point out that regard should be had to whether the offence was deliberate or inadvertant; if deliberate the offender should normally be disqualified or receive 7–8 penalty points.

Index

Absolute discharge
  order, court's power to make, 252
  young person in trouble, 265
Accused
  costs awarded against, 206–207
Admission
  Crown Court, trial at, 142–143
Adult
  non-custodial sentence. *See* SENTENCE AND
    SENTENCING
Alibi
  defence, trial at Crown Court, 146
  warning, committal proceedings, 102–103
Ammunition
  search warrant, police powers as to, 60
Appeal
  bail, refusal of,
    Crown Court, to, 195–196
    High Court, to, 196
  Crown Court, from,
    application for leave, 178–179
    Attorney General, reference by,
      179–180
    case stated, by way of, 180
    conviction, against, 175–177
    costs, on, 178
    example of case, 180–181
    legal aid contributions, on, 178
    procedure, 179
    Secretary of State, reference by,
      179–180
    sentence, against, 177–178
    specimen application, 182–185
  magistrates' court, from,
    bail, refusal of, 195–196
    Crown Court, to,
      conviction, against, 163–164
      equivocal plea, after, 165
      sentence, against, 165–166
    High Court, to,
      bail, refusal of, 196
      judicial review, for,
        certiorari, order of, 166–168
        ex parte stage, 169
        generally, 166
        inter partes stage, 169–170

Appeal – *continued*
  magistrates' court, from – *continued*
    High Court, to – *continued*
      judicial review, for – *continued*
        mandamus, order of, 167, 168
        prohibition, order of, 168–169
        stages of, 169–170
      point of law, on,
        drawing up statement, 171
        generally, 170–171
        hearing, 171, 174
        specimen application, 172–173
        statement of case, application to
          magistrates for, 171
        transmission of case, 171
Arraignment
  Crown Court, trial at, 124
Arrest
  general conditions, 53
  handcuffs, use of, 51
  juvenile, of, 84
  legal aid awarded on, 207
  news of, notification to friend or relative,
    67
  physical restraint, 51
  police, powers of, 53–55
  private person, by, 52, 54
  search after, 58–59
  specimen case, 3–8
  symbolic restraint, 51
  unlawful detention, 51
  warrant,
    bail, 187–188
    magistrate, issued by, 51–52
    without, 52–54
  when occuring, 51
Arrestable offence
  arrest without warrant, 52
  meaning, 52
  search warrant, issue of, 60
  serious, suspect's rights in case of, 67
Attachment of earnings order
  fine, failure to pay, 251
Attendance centre
  young person in trouble committed to,
    264–265

Attorney General
Court of Appeal, reference to, 179–180
Autrefois acquit
Crown Court, trial at, 126–128
Autrefois convict
Crown Court, trial at, 126–128

Bail
appeal,
Crown Court, to, 195–196
High Court, to, 196
committal, at, 196–197
Crown Court, at,
appeal from, on, 198
generally, 197
meaning, 187
police,
person arrested on warrant, 188
person arrested without warrant,
187–188
remand hearing, at,
conditions, power to impose, 192
further offence, likelihood of defendant
committing, 191–192
objections to, 189–191
offender, power to remand, 188–189
police witness, likelihood of defandant
interfering with, 191
procedure, 192–193
specimen forms, 194, 199–203
subsequent applications, 193, 195
sureties for, 187
Bind-over
court's power to order, 247–248
young person in trouble, 265
Breach of peace
arrest without warrant, 52
Brief to counsel
specimen case, 11–25
Burglary
stop and search in connection with, 55

Care order
care proceedings, 263
charge and control condition, 263–264
community homes, 263
criminal proceedings, 263
foster-homes, 263
Care proceedings
generally, 160–161
order resulting from, 263–264
stages of, 161
Caution
juvenile, proceedings involving, 162
voluntary statement under, 73
Certiorari
order of, application to High Court,
166–168
Charge
attendance at court following, means of
achieving, 81–82
committal proceedings, 102–103

Child
police station, at. *See* POLICE
written statement from, committal
proceedings, 101
Co-defendant
plea, evidence of, 134–135
Committal proceedings
alibi warning, 102–103
appropriate Crown Court, assignment to,
105–106
bail at, 196–197
charge, 102
defence,
case, 103
submission by, 101–102, 103
old-style, 100–104
procedure, 107–108
prosecution case,
child, written statement from, 101
generally, 100
oral evidence, 100
sick person, written statement from,
101
written evidence, 101
rationale, 99–100
reporting, 103–104
serious fraud cases, 109
short form, 104–105
specimen case, 8–10
summary offenc, 97
types of, 100, 107
voluntary bill of indictment, 109–110
witness orders, 106–107
Committal warrant
fine, failure to pay, 251
Community service order
breach of, 249
fine, failure to pay, 251
further offences, 249
nature of, 249
power to make, 248–249
Compensation order
court's power to make, 252–254
young person in trouble, 265
Computer records
admissibility as evidence, 140
Conditional discharge
order of, 247–248
young person in trouble, 265
Confession
admissibility of, 75–76
Contempt
Crown Court, of, 150–151
Controlled drugs. *See* DRUGS
Conviction
appeal against,
Crown Court, from, 175–177
Crown Court, to, 163–164
Costs
accused, award against, 206–207
appeal on, 178
civil proceedings, 205
criminal proceedings, 205

Costs – *continued*
defendant's order,
Court of Appeal, 205
Crown Court, 205
generally, 205–206
House of Lords, 205
magistrates' court, 205
private prosecutor, of, 206
See also LEGAL AID
Counsel
brief to, specimen case, 11–25
Court of Appeal
appeal from Crown Court. *See* APPEAL
Attorney General, reference by, 179–180
costs, 205
legal aid, 207
Secretary of State, reference by, 179–180
Crime. *See* INVESTIGATION OF CRIME
Criminal bankruptcy
Crown Court, powers of, 256
Criminal damage case
magistrates' court, jurisdiction of, 96
Criminal procedures, rules of
bail. *See* BAIL
committal proceedings. *See* COMMITTAL
PROCEEDINGS
costs. *See* COSTS
crime, investigation of. *See* INVESTIGATION
OF CRIME
Crown Court. *See* CROWN COURT
legal aid. *See* LEGAL AID
magistrates' court. *See* MAGISTRATES' COURT
police station, at. *See* POLICE
Criminal proceedings
care order resulting from, 263
juvenile, involving,
cautioning, 162
generally, 161
procedural safeguards, 162
qualified informants, 162
Cross-examination
Crown Court, trial at, 135–136
Crown Court
admissions, 142–143
appeal. *See* APPEAL
arraignment, 124
assignment of work, 105–106, 111
autrefois acquit, 126–128
autrefois convict, 126–128
bail,
appeal from, 198
generally, 197
refusal of, appeal, against, 195–196
classes of judges, 105
computer records, 140
conditionally bound witnesses, 138
contempt of court, 150–151
costs, 205
course of trial, 132 *et seq.*
creation of, 111
criminal bankruptcy, powers with regard
to, 256
cross-examination, 135–136

Crown Court – *continued*
defence,
alibi, 146
case for, 144–146
submission, 143–144
defendant,
attendance of, 113
co-defendant's plea, 134–135
different, separate trial of, 119–121
remaining silent, 128–129
duplicity rule, 121–123
evidence,
co-defendant's plea, 134–135
documentary, 138–140
objections to, 140–142
police, 136–138
prosecution, 133–134
examination in chief, 135
fitness to plead, 129
indictment,
contents, 113
date, particulars of, 115
duplicity rule, 121–123
joint enterprise, 115
meaning, 113
ownership, particulars of, 116
place, particulars of, 115
specimen, 114
joinder and severance,
different charges, separate trial of, 116–118
different defendants, separate trial of,
119–121
generally, 116
jury, 129–132
legal aid, 207
opening speech, 132–133
plea of guilty, 124–126
practice directions, 123
prosecution evidence, 133–134
re-examination, 136
sentencing,
imprisonment, 235
jurisdiction, 221–223
summary of procedure, 228–229
serious fraud cases, 123–124
speeches, 147–148
summing-up, 147–148
verdict,
finality of, 150
generally, 148–149
guilty of lesser offence, of, 149
majority, 149
special, 149–150
Custody
mentally ill offender, treatment of,
268–269
officer, duties of, 65–67
record,
commencement of, 66
specimen, 20–21, 68–69
suspect's rights while in, 67–71
time limits, 97
youth, 261–262

Date
indictment, particulars on, 115
Deception
obtaining property by, stop and search in connection with, 55
Defence
advance information to, 153–154
alibi, 146
committal proceedings,
case, 103
submission, 101–102, 103
Crown Court, trial at,
case, 144–146
submission, 143–144
Defendant
character and record, process of sentencing, 225
costs order, 205–206
Crown Court, trial at. *See* CROWN COURT
evidence, proof of, specimen case, 18
magistrates' court, absence from, 155
reform of, as purpose of sentence, 228
Deferred sentence
power of, 251–252
Deportation
court, powers of, 255–256
Detention
police, by. *See* POLICE
young person in trouble, of. *See* JUVENILE
Detention centre
young person in trouble committed to, 262–263
Deterrence
sentence, as purpose of, 228
Disqualification
driving, from, 255, 265
road traffic case. *See* ROAD TRAFFIC CASE
Documents
evidence, trial at Crown Court, 138–140
legal privilege, subject to, 62
search warrant, special rules applicable to, 62
Driving
disqualification from, 255, 265
See also ROAD TRAFFIC CASE
Drugs
search warrant, police powers as to, 59
stop and search in connection with, 56
Duplicity rule
Crown Court, trial at, 121–123

Entry
private premises, of, without warrant, 53–54
search, and. *See* SEARCH
Evidence
committal proceedings,
child, written statement from, 101
oral, 100
sick person, written statement from, 101
written, 101
Crown Court, trial at,
co-defendant's plea, 134–135

Evidence – *continued*
Crown Court, trial at – *continued*
computer records, 140
documentary, 138–140
objections to, 140–142
police, 136–138
prosecution, 133–134
identification, of. *See* IDENTIFICATION
proof of, specimen case, 18–19
Examination in chief
Crown Court, trial at, 135
Explosives
search warrant, police powers as to, 60

Fines
Crown Court, in, 250
failure to pay, subsequent orders,
attachment of earnings, 251
committal warrant, 251
community service, 251
money payment supervision, 250
suspended warrant, 251
magistrates' court, in, 250
means of offender, 250
road traffic cases, 257
traffic offences, 349–350
young person in trouble, 265
Fingerprinting
police powers, 78–79
Firearms
search warrant, police powers as to, 60
Forfeiture order
court's power to make, 254–255
Fraud cases
committal proceedings, 109
Crown Court, trial at, 123–124

Guilty
lesser offence, of, verdict of, 149
plea of,
post, by, 154–155
summary trial, 154–155
See also VERDICT

Habeas corpus
application to High Court for, 83–84
release on motion for, following unlawful detention, 51
Handcuffs
physical restraint, use for, 51
High Court
appeal,. *See* APPEAL
assignment of work, 105–106
bail, appeal against refusal of, 196
habeas corpus, application for, 83–84
judicial review, application for,
certiorari, order of, 166–168
generally, 166
mandamus, order of, 167, 168
prohibition, order of, 168–169
stages of,
ex parte, 169
inter partes, 169–170

High Court – *continued*
 legal aid, 207
Hospital order
 mentally ill offender, 267–268
House of Lords
 costs, 205

Identification
 evidence of, 78
 witness, by,
  parade, 80
  photograph, 79–80
Imprisonment
 Crown Court, sentences passed by, 235
 extended sentences, 243
 length of sentence,
  actual, 237
  restrictions on, 232–233
 magistrates' courts, sentences passed by,
  235
 parole system, 236
 prison system, 233–234
 restrictions on, 231–232
 shorter sentences, need for, 237–238
 suspended sentences,
  further offence, commission of,
   239–240
  partly, 241–243
  power to suspend, 238–239
  supervision orders, 240–241
  when appropriate, 238
Impropriety
 interrogation, conduct of, 73–74
Indictment
 contents, 113
 date, particulars of, 115
 duplicity rule, 121–123
 joint enterprise, 115
 meaning, 113
 ownership, particulars of, 116
 place, particulars of, 115
 specimen, 114
 specimen case, 13
 voluntary bill of, 109–110
Informant
 qualified, proceedings involving juvenile,
  162
Information
 advance, to defence, 153–154
 drafting, 86, 88
 duplicity, rule against, 88
 hearing of, 86
 proceedings commenced by, 86, 88
 specimen, 87
Interrogation at police station. *See* POLICE
Interview
 police station, at. *See* POLICE
Investigation of crime
 arrest. *See* ARREST
 road blocks, 58
 search,
  arrest, after. *See* SEARCH
  warrant. *See* SEARCH

Investigation of crime – *continued*
 stop and search. *See* STOP AND SEARCH

Joinder
 Crown Court, trial at, 116–121
Judge
 assignment of work, 105–106
 circuit, 105, 106
 High Court, 105, 106
Judicial review. *See* HIGH COURT
Jurisdiction
 Crown Court, 111–112
 magistrates' court. *See* MAGISTRATES'
  COURT
Jury
 challenges, 131–132
 counsel, information given to, 130–131
 magistrates distinguished from, 85
 panel,
  selection from, 131
  waiting outside court, 129–130
 praying a tales, 132
 qualification for service,
  generally, 130
  persons disqualified, 130
  persons ineligible, 130
 summons to attend, 130
 swearing of, 132
Justice of peace. *See* MAGISTRATE
Juvenile
 arrest, 84
 attendance centre, 264–265
 care order, 263–264
 court proceedings,
  care proceedings, 160–161
  cautioning, 162
  criminal proceedings, 161
  procedural safeguards, 162
  qualified informants, 162
  separate court system, 159–160
 detention,
  centre, 262–263
  further, 84
  generally, 261
  initial, 84
 interrogation, 84
 minor penalties, 265
 supervision order, 264
 youth custody, 261–262

Kidnapping
 search warrant, issue of, 60

Law Society
 solicitor, role of, on, 76–77
Legal advice
 suspect, right of access to, 70, 71
Legal aid
 application for, 207–210
 contributions, appeal on, 178
 doubt about order, 208
 occasions when available, 207
 refusal of, 208

Legal aid – *continued*
  specimen forms,
    application, 211–213
    statement of means, 214–217
  Widgery Committee on, 208
  See also COSTS
Legal privilege
  documents subject to, 62

Magistrate
  appointment of, 85
  arrest warrant, issue of, 51–52
  court. *See* MAGISTRATES' COURT
  jury distinguished from, 85
  search warrant, power to issue, 60, 62
  stipendiary, 85–86
Magistrates' court
  appeal from. *See* APPEAL
  clerk, 86
  committal proceedings. *See* COMMITTAL
    PROCEEDINGS
  composition, 85–86
  costs, 205
  criminal damage cases, 96–97
  custody time limits, 97
  function, 99
  imprisonment, sentences passed by, 235
  information, proceedings commenced by
    laying, 86–88
  jurisdiction to try offence charged,
    generally, 92, 93
    offence triable either way, 93
    offence triable only on indictment, 93
    summary offence, 93
  juvenile court proceedings,
    care proceedings, 160–161
    cautioning, 162
    criminal proceedings, 161
    procedural safeguards, 162
    qualified informants, 162
    separate court system, 159–160
  legal aid, 207
  offence triable either way,
    jurisdiction to try, 93
    procedure, 93–96
  process,
    generally, 88–89
    summons, 89–90, 92
    warrant, 91, 92
  sentencing, summary of procedure,
    228–229
  summary offence,
    committal for trial of, 97
    hearing of information, 88
    jurisdiction to try, 93
  summary trial,
    advantages, 159
    decision, 158
    defence case, 157–158
    disadvantages, 159
    generally, 155
    no case, submission of, 157
    opening speech, 155–156

Magistrates' court – *continued*
  summary trial – *continued*
    proscution evidence, 156–157
  trial before,
    defence, advance information to,
      153–154
    defendant, absence of, 155
    generally, 153
    plea,
      generally, 154
      guilty, of, by post, 154–155
Mandamus
  order of, application to High Court, 167,
    168
Mentally ill offender
  hospital order, 267–268
  treatment,
    custodial sentence, during, 268–269
    probation with condition of, 268
Money payment supervision order
  fine, failure to pay, effect of, 250
Motor vehicle
  stop and search in connection with, 55
Murder
  samples, police power to take, 79
  search warrant, issue of, 60

Non-custodial sentence. *See* SENTENCE AND
  SENTENCING
Notes of interrogation
  conclusion of interview, made after, 72
  contemporaneous, 72

Obscene article
  search warrant, police powers as to, 60
Offence
  arrestable,
    arrest without warrant, 52
    meaning, 52
  sentence. *See* SENTENCE AND SENTENCING
  summary. *See* SUMMARY OFFENCE
  triable either way,
    magistrates' court, jurisdiction of, 93
    procedure, 93–96
  triable only on indictment, 93
Offender
  mentally ill. *See* MENTALLY ILL OFFENDER
  young. *See* JUVENILE
Offensive weapon
  stop and search in connection with, 56
Oppression
  interrogation, conduct of, 74–75
  meaning, 74
Order
  care, 263–264
  community service. *See* COMMUNITY
    SERVICE ORDER
  hospital, 267–268
  non-custodial sentence. *See* SENTENCE AND
    SENTENCING
  probation. *See* PROBATION

Order – *continued*
  witness,
    committal proceedings, 106–107
    conditional, 138
Ownership
  indictment, particulars on, 116

Palmprints
  police power to take, 78–79
Parade
  identification, 80
Parole system
  introduction of, 236
  local review committee, powers of,
    236
  Parole Board, powers of, 236
  revocation of licence, 236
Peace. *See* BREACH OF PEACE
Penalties. *See* FINES; SENTENCE AND
    SENTENCING
Photograph
  witness, identification by, 79–80
Place
  indictment, particulars on, 115
Plea
  co-defendant, of, evidence of, 134–135
  equivocal, appeal to Crown Court after,
    165
  fitness to plead, 129
  guilty, of, 124–126
  mitigation, in, 227
  summary trial,
    generally, 154
    guilty plea, by post, 154–155
Police
  arrest, powers of, 53–55
  bail,
    person arrested on warrant, 188
    person arrested without warrant,
      187–188
  custody officer, duties of, 65–67
  detention,
    charge, procedure following, 81–82
    continued, authorisation of, 82
    habeas corpus, application for, 83–84
    juvenile, of, 84
    legal aid awarded on, 207
    limits on, 80–84
    review of, 80–81
    warrant of, 82–84
  evidence, trial at Crown Court, 136–138
  private premises, entry without warrant,
    53–54
  report, specimen case, 22–23
  road blocks, powers with regard to, 58
  search warrant, powers with regard to,
    59–63
  station, at,
    arrival at, 65–67
    custody record,
      commencement of, 66
      specimen, 20–21, 68–69
    fingerprinting, 78–79

Police – *continued*
  station, at – *continued*
    identification,
      generally, 78
      parade, 80
      witness, by,
        identification parade, by, 80
        photograph, by, 79–80
    interrogation,
      accuracy of record, 72
      confession, inducement of, 75–76
      contemporaneous notes, 72
      impropriety in conducting, 73–74
      inadmissibility as evidence, 72, 74
      juvenile, of, 84
      notes made after interview
        concluded, 72
      oppressive conduct, 74–75
      recording of, 73
      silence, right of suspect to, 71–72
      tape recording, 72
      voluntary statement under caution,
        73
    search on arrival, 66–67
    solicitor,
      role of, 76–78
      suspect's right to consult, 67, 70–71
    suspect,
      rights of, 67, 70–71
      solicitor, right to consult, 67, 70–71
Post
  plea of guilty by, 154–155
Practice directions
  pre trial hearing, 123
Prison system
  after-care facilities, 234
  closed, 234
  local, 233
  misbehaviour, loss of remission of
    sentence for, 234
  open, 234
Private person
  arrest, powers of, 52, 54
Private premises
  entry without warrant, police right of,
    53–54
Probation
  after-care facilities, 234
  mentally ill offender, with condition of
    treatment, 268
  order,
    conditions attached, 245–246
    discharge of, 247
    enforcement of, 246–247
    power to make, 245
    variation of, 247
  social enquiry report, 24–25
Process
  securing attendance of person charged,
    88–89
  summons,
    service of, 89, 92
    specimen, 90

Process – *continued*
  warrant,
    procedure, 92
    specimen, 91
Prohibition
  order of, application to High Court,
    168–169
Prosecution
  committal proceedings,
    child, written statement from, 101
    generally, 100
    oral evidence, 100
    sick person, written statement from,
      101
    written evidence, 101
  evidence, trial at Crown Court, 133–134
  private prosecutor, costs of, 206
  sentencing, presentation of case, 223–225
Public
  court's duty to protect, 228
Public place
  search in, 57

Re-examination
  Crown Court, trial at, 136
Record
  computer, admissibility as evidence, 140
  custody,
    commencement of, 66
    specimen, 20–21, 68–69
Recorder
  assignment of work, 105, 106
Remand
  hearing, bail at,
    conditions, power to impose, 192
    further offence, likelihood of defendant
      committing, 191–192
    objections to, 189–191
    offender, power to remand, 188–189
    police witness, likelihood of defendant
      interfering with, 191
    procedure, 192–193
  specimen case, 3–8
Remedies
  stop and search, abuse of power of,
    57
Report
  committal proceedings, 103–104
  police, specimen case, 22–23
  probation service, specimen case, 24–25
Restitution order
  court's powers, 254
  young person in trouble, 265
Road blocks
  authority for, 58
  police powers, 58
Road traffic case
  disqualification,
    discretionary, 258
    obligatory, 257–258
    penalty point, 258–259
  fine, 257
  generally, 256

Road traffic case – *continued*
  penalties for main offences, courts'
    assessment of, 349–355
  penalty points, 257
**Royal Commission on Criminal
  Procedure**
  stop and search, on, 56–57

Samples
  intimate, 79
  police power to take, 79
Search
  after arrest, 58–59
  public place, in, 57
  stop and. *See* STOP AND SEARCH
  suspect, of, on arrival at police station,
    66–67
  warrant,
    abuse, avoidance of, 62–63
    arrestable offence, in connection with,
      60
    documents, special rule applicable to,
      62
    entry and search under, time for, 63
    grounds for obtaining, 59–60
    magistrate, power to issue, 60, 62
    police powers, 59–63
    specimen, 61
    urgency, action in case of, 60
Secretary of State
  Court of Appeal, reference to, 179–180
Sentence and sentencing
  appeal against,
    Crown Court, from, 177–178
    Crown Court, to, 165–166
  Crown Court,
    jurisdiction, 221–223
    summary of procedure, 228–229
  defendant's character and record, 225
  deterrence, 228
  generally, 227–228
  imprisonment. *See* IMPRISONMENT
  magistrates' court, summary of
    procedure, 228–229
  non-custodial,
    absolute discharge, 252
    ancillary orders, 252–256
    bind-over, 247–248
    community service order, 248–249
    compensation order, 252–254
    conditional discharge, 247–248
    criminal bankruptcy, 256
    deferred sentence, 251–252
    deportation, 255–256
    driving, disqualification from, 255
    fines, 250–251
    forfeiture order, 254–255
    probation, 245–247
    road traffic cases, 256–259
  other offences taken into consideration,
    225–226
  plea in mitigation, 227

Sentence and sentencing – *continued*
powers available to all courts, 230
process of, 221–230
prosecution case, presentation of,
223–225
public, court's duty to protect, 228
punishment of offender, 228
reform of offender, 228
relevant matters, 227–228
social enquiry report, 226
traffic offences, 349–355
Serious fraud cases. *See* FRAUD CASES
Severance
Crown Court, trial at, 116–121
Sexual assault
samples, police power to take, 79
Silence
defendant, of, 128–129
Social enquiry report
probation service, 24–25
sentencing, process of, 226
Solicitor
police station, role at, 76–78
suspect's right to consult, 67, 70–71
Speeches
Crown Court, trial at, 147–148
Statement
voluntary, under caution, 73
witness, specimen case, 14–17
written,
child, from, 101
sick person, from, 101
Station. *See* POLICE
Stipendiary magistrate
appointment of, 85–86
Stolen article
search warrant, police powers as to, 59
stop and search in connection with, 55
Stop and search
conditions to be satisfied, 56
grounds for, 55–56
origin of provisions, 56–57
police powers, 55–58
Summary offence
committal for trial of, 97
hearing of information, 88
magistrates' court, jurisdiction to try, 93
Summary trial. *See* MAGISTRATES' COURT
Summing-up
Crown Court, trial at, 147–148
Summons
service of, 89, 92
specimen, 90
Supervision order
money payment, 250
suspended sentence, 240–241
young person in trouble, 264
Suspect
legal advice, right of access to, 70, 71
police station, at. *See* POLICE

Suspended sentence. *See* IMPRISONMENT
Suspended warrant
fine, failure to pay, 251

Tape recording
interrogation, of, 72
Theft
search warrant, issue of, 60
stop and search in connection with, 55
Traffic case. *See* ROAD TRAFFIC CASE
Trial
committal for. *See* COMMITTAL
PROCEEDINGS
Crown Court, at. *See* CROWN COURT
magistrates' court, before. *See*
MAGISTRATES' COURT
specimen transcript, 26–47
summary. *See* MAGISTRATES' COURT

Unlawful detention
habeas corpus, release on motion for, 51
Urgency
search warrant dispensed with in case of,
60

Verdict
Crown Court, trial at,
finality of, 150
generally, 148–149
guilty of lesser offence, 149
majority, 149
special, 149–150
Voire dire
process of, 75

Warrant
arrest. *See* ARREST
committal, 251
further period of detention by police, of,
82–84
procedure, 92
search. *See* SEARCH
specimen, 91
suspended, 251
Weapon. *See* OFFENSIVE WEAPON
Widgery Committee
legal aid, on, 208
Witness
identification by,
parade, 80
photograph, 79–80
order,
committal proceedings, 106–107
conditional 138
statement, specimen case, 14–17
Wounding
samplers, police power to take, 79

Young person. *See* JUVENILE